MEDITATION
AND SELF-STUDY

Theosophy Trust Books

MEDITATION
AND SELF-STUDY

BY

RAGHAVAN IYER

COMPILED BY
THE EDITORIAL BOARD OF THEOSOPHY TRUST

THEOSOPHY TRUST BOOKS
WASHINGTON, D.C.

Meditation and Self-Study

Theosophy Trust books may be ordered through Amazon.com and other booksellers, or by visiting:

https://www.theosophytrust.org/theosophy-online-books.htm

ISBN 978-0-9793205-9-0
ISBN 0-9793205-9-3

Library of Congress Control Number 2010935649

Printed in the United States of America

Dedicated To

All Those Who Have Tried

to Learn Meditation and the

Practice of Self-Study, and Even More,

Those Who Have Tried and Failed

May This Work Help Them Succeed

KRISHNA

"He who has attained to meditation should constantly strive to stay at rest in the Supreme, remaining in solitude and seclusion, having his body and his thoughts under control, without possessions and free from hope. He should in an undefiled spot place his seat, firm, neither too high nor too low, and made of kusa grass which is covered with a skin and a cloth. There, for the self's purification he should practice meditation with his mind fixed on one point, the modifications of the thinking principle controlled and the action of the senses and organs restrained. Keeping his body, head, and neck firm and erect, with mind determined, and gaze directed to the tip of his nose without looking in any direction, with heart at peace and free from fear, the Yogee should remain, settled in the vow of a Brahmacharya, his thoughts controlled, and heart fixed on me. The devotee of controlled mind who thus always bringeth his heart to rest in the Supreme reacheth that tranquility, the supreme assimilation with me."

The Bhagavad-Gita, Ch. VI

CONTENTS

INTRODUCTION

When Professor Iyer spoke to theosophical students of either meditation or self-study, he invariably employed the phrases "deep, daily meditation" and "thorough self-examination" to emphasize the importance of these practices to the successful endeavours of spiritual aspirants. In his private discourses, meetings and conversations, and in his public lectures and writings, Prof. Iyer pointed to Patanjali's *Yoga Sutras* as the model upon which a real discipline of spiritual meditation should be based, and took great pains to separate that ancient system of meditation from all of the forms of self-hypnosis that currently pass as "meditation". In Patanjali's system, which is that of the Raja Yoga school, meditation is a distinct quotidian practice that has well-charted points of entry, a cycle or rhythm of activity, and points of exit; it is also the dominant undertone to one's life, that upon which the heart is set, the "line of life's meditation". Whether meditation is considered as a constant undercurrent carried on while engaged in the necessary duties of life, or as a distinct and daily practice undertaken at specific time, both aspects of real meditation must be nourished, strengthened, and sustained.

Likewise Prof. Iyer consistently pointed to the practice of self-study enjoined upon the brotherhood of Pythagoras and expressed in his *Golden Verses*: "Do not let sleep close your tired eyes until you have three times gone over the events of the day. 'What did I do wrong? What did I accomplish? What did I fail to do that I should have done?' Starting from the beginning, go through to the end. Then, reproach yourself for the things you did wrong, and take pleasure in the good things you did."

In his article, *Pythagoras and His School*, Prof. Iyer notes "what is said in the *Golden Verses* about proper self-examination, which is an activity very different from offering a confessional before a priest, or going to a psychiatrist and having oneself analysed, or engaging in one or another form of tedious, furtive and repressive discussion of the shadow. In the Pythagorean teaching, the shadow cannot understand itself. The shadow is void of the very possibility of self-knowledge. Real understanding can come solely through the light of self-awareness which is inherent in every human being." The heart of the matter is this: we must learn to conduct a patient and thorough examination of the lower, personal self by the light of the Higher Self, accompanied by an affirmation of one's fundamental identity with one's true Self, the Self of All, and a simultaneous negation of any false identification with the personal and transitory self. Such an activity could become a daily discipline that makes the quest for self-definition and authentic self-actualization possible.

The purpose of this book is to bring together in a convenient and coherent form the many HERMES articles written by Prof. Iyer that dealt with this subject. In truth, meditation and self-study represent two sides of one human activity, something analogous to the operation of the systolic and diastolic movements of the human heart. The one is the centrifugal movement of consciousness expanding to Universals beyond the limits of Self; the other is the centripetal movement focusing with laser-like precision upon the particulars within the limits of Self. They represent roughly the sub-principles of *Buddhi* and *Manas* acting within the incarnated Manasic principle; for the spiritual aspirant they should – in time - become as natural as breathing in and breathing out. These two aspects of the inbreathing and outbreathing within the neophyte's consciousness are dealt with in the three treatises of *The Voice of the Silence,* as well as in Prof. Iyer's seminal article, *Meditation and Self-Study*:

> We might begin to wonder whether perhaps there is a golden chord that connects the golden sphere of a man of meditation and the complex intermediary realms in which he must, by pain and anguish and awakening, by knitting together minute golden moments rescued from a great deal of froth and self-deception, come to know himself. If there were not a fundamental connection between meditation and self-study, something of the uniquely precious wisdom in this great text would be lost to us. When we begin to realize this in our lives, we come to appreciate that, while we may not be in a position to make judgments about teachers and schools

in a vast and largely unrecorded history or in our own time, nonetheless we do know that there is something profoundly important in stressing both meditation and self-study, in bringing the two together. We must reconcile what looked like a pair of opposites and get beyond despair to something else which allows an existential and dynamic balance between meditation and self-study.

Alas, most of us find this existential balance to be elusive, as there are many obstacles to such a natural and easy relationship to meditation and self-study, obstacles that have been self-created and reinforced over many lifetimes of misdirected thought and attempts to short-circuit what is unavoidable in the spiritual path: the careful and painstaking unwinding of the coils of self-induced delusions. These obstacles are detailed in the *Yoga Sutras* with surprising brevity and familiarity, suggesting to the perceptive reader that the author had so thoroughly studied and mastered the subject that he is able to reduce the issues to their fewest essential elements. Early in the First Book (*Samadhi Pada*, verses 30-32), Patanjali gives the diagnosis of the hindrances and the prescription for their removal:

> 30. The hindrances which cause mental distractions are disease, dullness, doubt, heedlessness, indolence, addiction to sense-objects, distorted perception, failure to find a footing and instability in any state.
>
> 31. These distractions are accompanied by sorrow, depression, bodily restlessness and spasmodic breathing.
>
> 32. To check these, there should be constant practice of one truth or principle (*eka-tattva*).

Patanjali also notes the antidote to self-induced mental pollution, that one's mind "becomes purified through the practice of friendliness, compassion, gladness and indifference respectively towards happiness, sorrow, virtue and vice." (V. 33) It may be at this point that the practitioner gains his/her first intimation that in this Path, "to whatever place one would go, that place one's own self becomes". (*Dnyanesvari*, quoted in *The Voice of the Silence*.)

The obstacles noted above are not to be taken lightly or ignored, as they are the product of spiritual negligence in this and previous lifetimes, and, by law, must produce the same result in future lives. They are not easily overcome. These obstacles produce the condition – familiar to everyone who has honestly attempted meditation and self-study – of the interior consciousness appearing to oneself like a void, a dark and lightless place, where the interior space seems to be utterly empty of light, life and hope. But as we discover by perseverance and consulting the experiences of those who have gone before, in this endeavor, we must create our own light. In *The Gayatri Invocation*, Prof. Iyer points to the root cause of the major obstacles to this endeavor: ignorance combined with inertia (*tamas*), which, when conjoined together, produce a "stony and indifferent heart" and a "repeated persistence in a restricted view of the world". It may seem strange, but some individuals contract to the point where they actually enjoy "the dingy, the cloudy, the chaotic and the claustrophobic." This self-torture produces a condition in which the tormented soul cannot attach meaning to the common language of the most simple acts of decency and kindness, and because of their pollution, cannot believe they are capable of resonating to a sense of the sacred. They may be able to use sacred language in stringing together sentences that produce the illusion of intimate knowledge, but such acts only result in an empty analytical familiarity and routinized repetitions. Their heart light is nearly extinguished, and the electric fire of wisdom finds no tinder in the ashes in their hearts. Such is the sad result of lives of misuse of the sacred Teachings.

Persistence in dullness, heedlessness, and distorted perception will also cause additional obstacles for the future, as Prof. Iyer notes in his article, *The Six Dharshanas*.

> "A thorough training in logic is required not only in all philosophical reasoning, exposition and disputation, but it is also needed by those who seek to stress mastery of *praxis* over a lifetime and thereby become spiritual exemplars. This at once conveys the enormous strength of an immemorial tradition as well as the pitiable deficiencies of most professors and pundits, let alone the self-styled so-called exoteric *gurus* of the contemporary East. Neither thaumaturgic wonders nor mass hypnosis can compensate for mental muddles and shallow thinking; indeed, they become insuperable obstacles

to even a good measure of gnosis and noetic theurgy, let alone authentic enlightenment and self-mastery."

However, the most common obstacles to the moderating influence of the *yamas* and *niyamas* – the restraints and observances - of the Yoga discipline outlined by Patanjali are the negative and self-destructive thoughts that swarm round humankind like unwelcome flies: thoughts of impure acts; the desire to do harm to others because of a perceived wrong or injustice; self-indulgence, self-deception and self-assertion. Providing a home to such thoughts creates an atmosphere that can only result in the defeat of one's spiritual resolves and commitments. Rather than give in to these energies, the wise aspirant should treat with great respect the advice offered in the article *Sadhana Pada*:

> Instead of suppressing such scattered thoughts or wallowing in hideous self-pity, one must firmly and deliberately insert into the mind their potent opposites – love for hate, tenderness for temerity, sweetness for spite, virile confidence for the devilry of self-doubt, authentic self-conquest for compulsive self-indulgence. Thus what begins as a shrewd defence against deleterious thoughts becomes a deft substitution of one kind of thought for another and results in sublimation, the skilful transformation of the tonality and texture of consciousness. Strict and consistent measures are needed to deal with subversive thoughts, not in order to repress them or to hide guilt for having them, but only because they induce depression and self-loathing, with predictable and pathetic consequences. Facing unworthy thoughts firmly, and thereby exorcising them, is to free oneself from their nefarious spell.

In much the same way that the delights of the *sattva guna* can become a distraction or obstacle in the way of the yogin, Prof. Iyer shows, in the article *Vibhuti Pada*, how shifts in the activity of the *gunas* in one's perceptions can produce an entirely different sort of obstacle, one that is difficult to identify as such because it is so welcome and attractive:

> "Since any significant refocussing of the mind produces dazzling insights and diverse phenomena, Patanjali conveyed their range and scope. For *yoga* they are not important in themselves because the goal is *kaivalya*, liberation, but they are vitally important as aids or obstacles on the way to achieving

the goal. Patanjali could not dismiss or overlook them, since they are real enough and inescapable, and so he delineated them clearly, knowing fully that all such arcane information can be abused. One who willingly uses such knowledge to stray off the arduous path to emancipation brings misery upon himself. One who would use this knowledge wisely needs to understand the many ways one can be misled into wasting the abundant resources accessible to the *yogin*. Profound alterations in states of consciousness through *sanyama* can bring about awakened powers called *siddhis*, attainments, many of which may seem to be supernatural and supernormal to the average person. They are, however, neither miraculous nor supernatural, since they suspend, circumvent or violate no laws. Rather, they merely indicate the immense powers of controlled consciousness within the perspective of great Nature, powers that are largely latent, untapped and dormant in most human beings. They are suggestive parameters of the operation of the vast scope and potency of consciousness in diverse arenas of *prakriti*."

Finally, any viable conception of perfectibility requires a continuous and attentive care for the imperfections in the lunar vestures and what we so mistakenly call ' I '. These imperfections may be transmuted if a vigilant individual generates fresh patterns of thought or feeling, which can then do their magical work. Prof. Iyer was noted for oft expressing his unshakable faith that for every incarnate human being, it is always possible to change the polarity and quality of the life-atoms in the lower vestures by attracting new sets of elementals with greater degrees of porosity than those we have attracted by our negative and ultimately self-destructive patterns of thought. This is a creative and courageous task, and it can be carried out only if one faces the facts about oneself. In the path of self-purification, we must always be willing to face up to and settle our karmic accounts. We must always be willing to look honestly where we stand in relation to the ideal of the perfected human being and to the moment of death. We must learn to see through and beyond entire realms of appearances and so take a moral stand based on well thought out and rational ethical principles. Their deeper meanings and deft applications must be located within the sacred sphere of one's duty.

The goal of meditative purification is to strengthen the spiritual will and garner continuous inspiration in the daily performance of duty such that one's commitment to the discipline becomes irrevocable and indefatigable. After a point, as Prof. Iyer notes in *The Mahamudra of Voidness* and *The Descent of Manas*, rather than see encounters with the spiritual as an unwelcome intrusion upon one's precious "personal time", the aspirant will come to look forward to them, and one's mind will naturally turn to sacred themes. The benefit of this mental discipline is a simplicity of stance that takes nothing for granted, but rather finds joy in the profound privilege of contemplating and reaffirming the fundamental principles of the spiritual life. No longer prone to the errors of futile speculation, and having forsaken attempts to reconcile the irreconcilable by adapting the spiritual sciences to material conceptions, the joyous aspirant will honour the basic rules of their self-chosen discipline by sharpening their Buddhic discernment through practice, staying within the forward current, and gaining true self-respect. They will come to see that the mere thought of falling away from the discipline through attaching blame upon the external world rapidly destroys that which they hold most sacred, the foundation of discipleship.

Metaphysically, there is no other more fundamental reason to engage in self-purification than the "duty one owes oneself as a trustee of Nature and a servant of mankind. If one grasps the idea of monadic evolution metaphysically, and not merely statistically or speculatively, it is evident that there are myriad daily opportunities for engaging in sacrificial acts of service to others." It is the exalted privilege of a *Manasa* - a self-conscious human being - to be able to serve all life-atoms through the concentrated power of compassionate thought. To a true spiritual seeker, a *sadhaka*, who thinks in this archetypal mode, the sole reason for skillfully performing any act in life is to render gentle and gracious service to others, to human beings as well as to all the life-atoms that one encounters and interacts with in every circumstance of life.

Prof. Iyer frequently made the observation that every authentic spiritual tradition insisted upon the purification and cleansing of the heart as a precondition and constant companion of real spiritual meditation. Before the mind can be mastered, he insisted, the heart must be cleansed of its impurities - those distorted, complex and awkward elements in one's feeling nature, the hideous deformities of one's feeling nature - which can only be perceived as such because of the soul's awareness of its intrinsic beauty and purity. "Like a craftsman with the highest standard of excellence, the soul surveys its self-evolved vestures with an objective and critical eye."

Self-purification must encompass purification of one's motive and steadfastness in relation to our deepest integrity, honesty, and fidelity of commitment. Eventually, this arduous task produces *Bodhichitta*, the seed of Enlightenment, where we can "rejoice in the inner purification that has taken place. Even one's perspective changes in regard to what is truly helpful to the immortal soul and what is harmful. Once one touches the current of this supreme detachment and begins to enter the light of the void through efforts at *dhyana*, one may begin to make one's own honest and yet heroic, courageous and cheerful way towards gaining greater continuity, control and proficiency in meditation. Blending the mind and heart, one may enter the way that leads to the *dhyana* haven."

> The *Dhyana* gate is like an alabaster vase, white and transparent; within there burns a steady golden fire, the flame of *Prajna* that radiates from *Atma*.
>
> Thou art that vase.
>
> *The Voice of the Silence*

Editor, Theosophy Trust
August 11, 2010

(The articles in this book and many others by Prof. Iyer can also be found separately in the Lead Articles section of Theosophytrust.org at https://www.theosophytrust.org/RNI-article)

THE YOGA SUTRA

This is the royal knowledge, the royal mystery, the most excellent purifier, clearly comprehensible, not opposed to sacred law, easy to perform, and inexhaustible.

Sri Krishna

A careful study of Patanjali's priceless aphorisms on *Raja Yoga* is immensely valuable to all who wish to learn the discipline of true meditation while at the same time discerning the sharp contrast between the psycho-spiritual and the psycho-physical systems of yogic training. Metaphysics and ethics are linked through psychology. A therapeutic program of self-study, undertaken with discrimination and detachment, is integral to the progressive realization of knowledge of spiritual law and a calm reliance upon the moral order. The subtle externalizations implicit in the separative and pseudo-autonomous portraits of human nature, found in all psycho-physical systems of self-development, are incompatible with gnostic metaphysics of the highest spiritual sort and subvert the ethical ideal of compassionate direction of all one's emanations. 'The divine discipline' involves a grasp of correspondences between the universal and the particular, the macrocosm and the microcosm in man, and requires a noetic fusion of the psychological and spiritual. Patanjali could assist us in this art of self-study and in the science of mind control, but to make full use of his teaching, we must not lose sight of the dual metaphysical and ethical basis of his aphorisms.

Spiritual growth may be regarded as a gradual deepening of perception and strengthening of will. As personal beings, bound by desire to the material limitations of the phenomenal world of sense-objects, our perceptions are crude and our volition is perverted. It is the limited perception of life, the inability to sense conscious or even

1

individual existence outside of form or beyond the material plane, that constitutes real death. "Real life is in the spiritual consciousness of that life, in a conscious existence in Spirit, not Matter." Meditation is needed to free ourselves from the limitations imposed by our fleeting sensory perceptions and by our false sense of identity and personal volition. The point of departure of Patanjali's text is the diffusive, fragmented, ephemeral, limiting nature of our everyday consciousness, i.e., our mental awareness of objects and subjects and of our own natures. Spiritual consciousness is, by contrast, concentrated, deliberate, unifying, liberating and permanent. This is not merely an initial contrast but one that persists even as we ascend through higher levels of awareness, planes of perception and states of will-activity. The aphorisms have meanings and implications that recur with a heightened significance as we proceed with meditation and self-study.

Perception and will are bound up with two forces – noetic (from *nous*) and psychic (from *psyche*), derived from *Buddhi* and *Prana* (moral perception and vital energy) – and the possibility of the former using the latter. We can attach a minimal, everyday sense to the notion of moral power, acting on the will of man. This moral power and energy in man can be consciously cultivated by individuals and by groups and applied courageously to the quest. We must always distinguish between what is salutary and what is pleasant, between *sreyas* and *preyas*, to achieve a harmony between thought, word and deed, so that life becomes a fulfilled oath, a constant vow or *vrita*, a perpetual pilgrimage, a continual sacrifice. The votary of truth is not a muddled idealist but a man who meditates before getting into action. He does not take refuge in theoretical speculation but remains steadfast in contemplation while constantly trying to endow his whole life of conscious activity with a pervading sanctity of *pavitra*. It is only by personal steadfastness, by holding on to his vow that a man may be useful to others to an exceptional degree. It is impossible to live as a *sadhaka* in the midst of society if one's entire life is not a fulfilled oath.

The metaphysical basis of Patanjali's text is laid down in a few aphorisms in each of the four parts of the *sutra*. Book I, the *Samadhi pada*, points to a fundamental truth which must be grasped even before we embark on meditation and self-study:

> The state of abstract meditation may be attained by profound devotedness toward the Supreme Spirit considered in its comprehensible manifestation as *Ishwara*.
>
> *Ishwara* is a spirit, untouched by troubles, works, fruits of works, or desires.
>
> In *Ishwara* becomes infinite that omniscience which in man exists but as a germ.
>
> *Ishwara* is the preceptor of all, even of the earliest of created beings, for He is not limited by time.
>
> Book I: 23-26

Beyond the phenomenal universe lies pure spirit, known in its comprehensive manifestation as *Ishwara*, unmodified by material form or phenomenal change, untouched by sorrow-producing sensations or by particular precipitations, by causal connections and external conditions, or the stimuli of impulses and desires. The germ of omniscience – the knowledge of this unmodified reality – exists in man and becomes infinite in *Ishwara*. Man can move from the atomic to the infinite through mental awareness and change of consciousness if he grasps and applies the truth of the distinction between his ever modified mind and his status as a soul, a spectator without a spectacle.

> At the time of concentration the soul abides in the state of a spectator without a spectacle.
>
> The student whose mind is thus steadied obtains a mastery which extends from the Atomic to the Infinite.
>
> That meditation which has a subtle object in view ends with the indissoluble element called primordial matter.
>
> Book I: 3, 40, 45

These aphorisms point to the metaphysical realization possible to every monadic consciousness, and also indicate a relationship to primordial matter, the indissoluble element that exists in the very constitution of the manifested universe. Lest a false impression of these states should arise and contribute to moral indifference, Patanjali declares:

> Although the Universe in its objective state has ceased to be, in respect to that man who has attained to the perfection of spiritual cultivation, it has not ceased in respect to all others, because it is common to others besides him.

> Book II: 22

Book II of the aphorisms, the *Sadhana pada*, is concerned with the practical means of establishing concentration. Ignorance or *avidya* is identified as the cause of the variety of mental afflictions and is defined in its metaphysical sense:

> Ignorance is the notion that the non-eternal, the impure, the evil, and that which is not soul are, severally, eternal, pure, good and soul.

> Book II: 5

The culmination of ignorance, inhibiting self-awareness, is the natural tendency to material manifestation and the self-reproductive power of externalization:

> The tenacious wish for existence upon earth is inherent in all sentient beings, and continues through all incarnations, because it has self-reproductive power. It is felt as well by the wise as the unwise.

> Book II: 9

We must see this power for what it is, but our valuations alter if we recognize, as in aphorism 28, that the entire universe, visible and invisible, compounded of the purity of the unmodified *Ishwara* (reflected in primordial matter), the activity and the withdrawal involved in manifestation, the material elements and organs of action, that all exist for the soul's experience and emancipation.

Aphorism 20 of Book II defines the soul as the Perceiver, vision pure and simple, unmodified, which looks directly upon ideas. Hence the possibility of omniscience set forth in Book III:

> By concentrating his mind upon the true nature of the soul as being entirely distinct from any experiences, and disconnected from all material things, and dissociated from the understanding, a knowledge of the true nature of the soul itself arises in the ascetic.

> From the particular kind of concentration last described, there arises in the ascetic, and remains with him at all times, a knowledge concerning all things, whether they be those apprehended through the organs of the body or otherwise presented to his contemplation.

> In the ascetic who has acquired the accurate discriminative knowledge of the truth and of the nature of the soul, there arises a knowledge of all existences in their essential natures and a mastery over them.

> Book III: 36, 37, 50

Aphorisms 23 to 26 of Book II show why man is bound and why he can free himself, why he is actually ignorant and potentially omniscient – the soul is conjoined with the organ of thought and thus with nature. The conjuncture is caused by ignorance, but the quitting of bondage to matter is possible through perfect discriminative knowledge.

Aphorism 9 of Book III, the *Vibhuti pada* concerning yogic attainments, shows that while the modifications of mind produce a train of self-reproductive thought, so too another train of self-reproductive thought arises when the mind is engrossed solely with the truth.

> There are two trains of self-reproductive thought, the first of which results from the mind being modified and shifted by the object or subject contemplated; the second, when it is passing from that

modification and is becoming engaged only with the truth itself; at
the moment when the first is subdued and the mind is just becoming
intent, it is concerned in both of those two trains of self-reproductive
thought, and this state is technically called *Nirodha*.

Book III: 9

The cycle of cosmic involvement is ideation, manifestation and
retention of transcendence. For the individual the cycle is reversed –
impure involvement or false ideation, disengagement and self-subsisting
universal self-awareness. Once attained, this could be followed by a
new cycle in which the individual creates in the manner of spirit – by
ideation, constructive manifestation (through the power of projection)
and retention of transcendence. This divine and human prerogative is
enshrined in the doctrine of *Jnana Yagna*, the practice of *Buddhi Yoga*, and
the spiritual powers of *Kriyashakti* and *Icchashakti*.

These involve a grasp of Karma (Book III, 23), *sattwa* or the property
of luminousness (Book III, 21), *udana* or vital energy (Book III, 40), and
the five classes of properties in the manifested universe (Book III, 45).
Thus we can gain the knowledge that saves us from involuntary rebirth
(Book III, 55) and the condition of emancipation or Isolation of the Soul
(Book III, 56). Book IV says more about the perfections (Book IV, 1), the
transformation of nature (Book IV, 2), the mental deposits left by Karma
(Book IV, 8), the three qualities of objects (Book IV, 13), our awareness of
time (Book IV, 32), and the re-absorption of the qualities (Book IV, 33).

All this is abstruse, a statement of principles and possibilities. How
are we to make this knowledge accessible? By drawing the ethical
corollaries of the metaphysical truths given. The mind cannot be
withdrawn from its repeated modifications to the unmodified state of
the soul without constant practice – *abhyasa*. To do this we require a
firm position, growth in dispassion to displace the power of *tanha* and
the desire for externalization through attachment and repulsion, and a
knowledge of the soul as distinct from all else.

This exercise is a firm position observed out of regard for the
end in view, and perseveringly adhered to for a long time without

intermission.

Dispassion is the having overcome one's desires.

Dispassion, carried to the utmost, is indifference regarding all else than soul, and this indifference arises from a knowledge of soul as distinguished from all else.

Book I: 14-16

The obstacles to concentration are set out in Book I, 30 – sickness, languor, doubt, carelessness, laziness, addiction to sense-objects, erroneous perception, failure to attain to abstraction, instability in any state when attained. To prevent these, according to aphorisms 32 and 39 of Book I, any one truth which one appreciates should be dwelt upon until the mind is steadied. Further, the mind must be purified through the practice of benevolence, tenderness, complacency, disregard for objects of happiness, grief, virtue and vice. Hence the enormous importance of detachment and resignation and forbearance, the essential and universal duties, and special religious observances or ascetic rules.

Forbearance consists in not killing, veracity, not stealing, continence, and not coveting.

These, without respect to rank, place, time, or compact, are the universal great duties.

Religious Observances are purification of both mind and body, contentment, austerity, inaudible mutterings, and persevering devotion to the Supreme Soul.

Book II: 30-32

These 'Religious Observances' or *niyamas* are especially relevant to all who wish to pursue the path of spiritual growth, but they must be developed on the firm basis of constant practice of the universal great duties, the *mahavritam*. One of the oldest meanings of *vrita*, as found in the *Rig Veda*, is "divine will or command." The order (*Rta*) observable in nature was considered to be the consequence of the *vrita* of the gods, and it could be reflected in human society through the deliberate and vigilant performance of *Dharma*. The instinctual behaviour of the lower kingdoms and the motions of natural objects have a rhythm and a reliability that men must consciously emulate if they are to become conscious embodiments of the divine power that pervades the universe. Any conscious or unconscious infringement of the divine order is to be expiated by imposing on oneself some sort of self-denial. Such a resort to *vrita* was supposed to purify the performer and elevate him spiritually. The observance of vows is even more necessary for the aspirant to a life of complete renunciation or for a seeker after mystical attainment as in the *Yoga Sutra*. Dispassion must accompany the discrimination sought through the special religious observances. Then meditation will become meaningful and fruitful. The task is arduous, but every effort brings strength and joy.

Hermes, August 1976
Raghavan Iyer

JNANA YAJNA

For the good man 'tis most glorious and good and profitable to happiness of life, aye, and most excellently fit, to do sacrifice and be ever in communion with heaven through prayer and offerings and all manner of worship.

Plato, The Athenian Stranger

During the primeval dawn of human evolution, the whole of humanity was suffused with a spontaneous devotion to *Gurus* and Preceptors. Simultaneously, all found no pain but a pure pleasure in the performance of the daily duties of life, revealing an intimate connection between devotion and duty. The conception of such a humanity differs totally from our own. It is like a Golden Age far removed from our time, because for many centuries we have engendered, with extraordinary violence and pertinacity, the falsehood of a separate identity for each human being, supposedly gestated at birth and terminated at death. People tend not to think about death and live as if they have a kind of invulnerability. But they blunder through without any knowledge of who they are, and find themselves oppressed by a sense of inward confusion, which only allows them to speak and think in terms of comparison and contrast. They are driven by their dwarfed conceptions of success and failure and are trapped in differentiated consciousness based on unending comparison and contrast. At the same time, this consciousness assumes an apparent stability not intrinsic to it, but involving a shutting out of the archetypal moments of birth and death. In time, this means forgetfulness, an indifference to the primary facts that apply to all humanity – that there is a great continuity to the human pilgrimage, that death is followed by rebirth, that this is true not only for particular souls but also that there is a continuous passage from generation to generation. The whole process is so vast that the moment we try to limit it, in terms of crude conceptions of duty or obligation, we also feel that any personal devotion we show is gratuitous. Captivated by personal differentiated consciousness, we live under the sway of the specious idea that the universe is for one's own private benefit and that each one is favouring the world, favouring other human beings, by an egocentric stance, by supererogatory acts, and that if one is devoted one has set up some kind of claim upon the object of devotion.

All of this thinking is distorted, inverted, and perverted, bound up with the descent of consciousness into matter. At a certain point of material density and fragmentation of consciousness, the pale reflection of the unmanifest light of the Immortal Triad assumes a false centrality. This would be like a shift from the self-luminous centre of a circle to a lit-up region which only seems luminous by contrast with the shadow around. The latter is the spurious ego, the limited personal consciousness. Given this condition, every human being can, at one level, understand that there is something very beautiful and elevating, something extremely authentic, in poetic accounts of a Golden Age of primordial humanity, when human beings moved naturally and related to each other beautifully. They were spontaneously held together by an effortless sense of moral and spiritual solidarity with the whole of nature, with those before and those yet to come, and above all, with their great Teachers. Though we can resonate with such an Age, we also know that if we have to ask questions about it, we already presuppose that it is estranged from us.

What good, then, can come of talking about devotion for a person who has become totally convinced that he has no capacity for any feeling, any devotion for anyone else? Who is that person? A cerebral machine, chatting away, insecure, confused yet making judgments? Is that the whole of that person? But if he has assumed this is all he or anyone else is, how can talking about devotion make a difference? Suppose such a person were told that there are great beings like Krishna and the Buddha, hosts of hierophants who are seated in meditation and constantly engaged in ideation upon universal good, who have so vast a perspective of endless time, boundless space and ceaseless motion, that they can see the rises and falls of civilizations and epochs in perspective. Suppose he were told that they can see the antics of human beings in much smaller spans of time and space with unwavering compassion, and also that they can see the root illusion. These beings are involved in universal welfare and uplifting the whole of humanity. Any human being who can vibrate in mind, heart and self to the tune of the great universal impulse of these mighty beings, may serve as a focal point through whom some mitigation of human misery and some elevation of consciousness is possible.

To the sick, as in the time of Jesus, the idea of a super-healthy human being does not speak. Similarly, how can a person completely incapable of ordinary feelings grasp the idea of such noble beings? Unconsciously that person has been ceaselessly worshipping at the altar of the material self – and not even doing a very good job at it, not even being constant in devotion to his own personal self – inattentive, afraid, fickle, confused. With the lunar shadow as his only focus, how can such a person comprehend the light of the Spiritual Sun? How can such a person grasp the perspective of *Mahatmas*? But then, even if the person cannot comprehend those beyond him, can he still apprehend something that is at once universal and archetypal, which is found throughout the animal kingdom in the love and protection shown by animals for the young, which is found in the human kingdom between mothers and children? Even with all the corruption of modern modes and relationships, we still find this pulse of decency, warmth and kindness, a dauntless trust that is in the human heart. Surely a person should be able to reawaken that which now has been buried and obscured but which was once strong and secure.

This is the point at which a person can benefit from the teaching of *Jnana Yajna* – Wisdom-sacrifice. Lord Krishna came at a time when he knew that humanity could not go back and restore its child-state without any effort. But on the other hand, he also knew that human beings were going to be enormously vulnerable to self-righteous merchants of the moral language who narrow and limit conceptions of duty and morality by institutionalizing them, and thereby bind human beings through fear to mere externalities of conduct. Therefore an alternative had to be shown. Being magnificently generous, Krishna speaks at the widest cosmic level of how the *Logos* functions out of only a small portion of itself and yet remains totally uninvolved. It is like the boundless ocean on the surface of which there are many ships, and in which there are many aquatic creatures, though the depths of that boundless ocean remain still. The whole world may be seen from the standpoint of the *Logos*, which is essentially incapable of incarnating and manifesting within the limitations of differentiated matter. The *Logos* can only overbrood. This overbrooding is joyous, producing myriad kaleidoscopic reflections within which various creatures get caught. Krishna gives the great standpoint, the divine perspective, which is all sacrifice. That is the critical relationship between the unmanifest and the manifest, because if the unmanifest can never be fully manifested, how can the manifest ever be linked to the unmanifest? There is always in everything that is manifest, behind the form, behind the facade, a deathless core of the very same nature and of the very same essence as that which is unmanifest. Where a human being can, by the power of thought, bring this to the centre of individual consciousness, it is possible to consecrate. It is possible to act as if each day corresponds to the Day of an entire universe, or to a lifetime. It is possible to act in each relationship as if it were a supreme expression of the very highest relationships between teacher and pupil or mother and child. It is possible to act in a small space as if there is the possibility of an architecture and rearrangement which can have analogues to the grand arrangements of solar systems and galaxies.

This is the great gift of creative, constructive imagination without illusion. What makes it Wisdom-sacrifice is that one trains personal consciousness – the chattering mind, the divided and wandering heart, the restless hands – one centres all of these energies around a single pivotal idea, having no expectations. If an ordinary human being had no expectations whatsoever, the person would die simply because typically a person lives on the basis of some confused and vague expectations in regard to tomorrow, next year and the future. Deny a human being all expectations, all claims and personal consciousness usually will collapse. Of course this cannot be done from the outside. The shock would be too great. But human beings can administer the medicine to themselves progressively and gradually. Merely look at the years already lived and see how many expectations have been built up. Either you dare not look back at them and how they were falsified – which means there is a cowardliness, a lie in your very soul – or you have replaced them so fast by other expectations that you are caught in a web of externalizing expectations. To initiate a breakthrough you can earnestly think, "Supposing I have only one day more to live; supposing everything that I have is taken away from me; supposing I can rely on nothing and expect nothing. What would be the meaning of joy, the dignity of grief?"

At that point, if a person thinks of Sri Krishna, of the unthanked *Mahatmas* and Adepts, and thinks of them not as distant from the human scene but as the ever-present causal force behind the shadow play of history, then he finds an incredible strength in that thought, a strength in consciousness but without a solidification of the object of consciousness. One can act with a freedom that is ultimately rooted in total actionlessness, like the supreme light of the *Atman* which is in eternal motion but which is not involved in what we call motion, refracted by differentiated matter. At the same time, one can live as if each act is supremely important, sublimely sacred. The person who really comes to think this out trains himself in this mode of thinking, feeling, breathing, acting and living and can in time gain a new lightness and economy, a fresh conception of real necessity, but above all a fundamental conception of identity – merely as one of manifold unseen and unknown instruments of the one *Logos*.

This is the great teaching of *Jnana Yajna* which, stated in this way, looks difficult, but is at the same time at some level accessible to each. It is a teaching so sacred that it is veiled in the *Gita* – hidden when it is given in the fourth chapter and again at the very end of the eighteenth chapter. It is a teaching which, if fully grasped, is the gateway to freedom and will enable one to become karmaless, to avoid becoming caught through the mind in the intertwining chains of karma. Clearly, karmalessness was not possible for early humanity, but it had all the ingredients of the quality which must belong to the mature person of the present when adopting the standpoint of those pioneers of the future who act self-consciously with a universal perspective and without residue, without becoming involved in the externalities or, as Gaudapada taught, without leaving any footprints.

The difficulty of this can be appreciated when we recall that in the fourth chapter of the *Gita* Krishna says that there are some who sacrifice the in-breathing and the out-breathing, while others chant the texts, and still others actually surrender themselves. All these sacrifices arise out of action. They arise out of the non-self and retain the illusion of an agent. In every one of these sacrifices we can distinguish archetypally five elements. There is that which is the oblation offered in sacrifice. There is the fire into which it is offered. There is the instrument – a ladle or whatever – with the help of which the offering is placed in the fire. Then there is the agent, the 'I,' the person who says, "I am performing the sacrifice." There is the object of the sacrifice. All of these exist at one level in a universe of differentiated matter, constituted of innumerable beings that are ever at work and interacting in ceaseless motion. There is the interplay of subject and object, the deceptive contrast between light and shadow. There are separate objects and a background. All of this is *maya*, the projective yet veiling power of the *Logos*, of the *Ishwara*, of Krishna.

A human being does not have to project or be taken in by the veiling. It is possible for him to stand apart from roles, from sounds and sights, and to see through and beyond the seeming separation of objects. To take a simple example, we have artificial light, and by it we see and focus. We see many colours, a room, separate people. If we turn all the lights off, some people will be uncomfortable. Suddenly we no more see objects, selves, colours, contrasts, but we can then experience the breathing and pulsation of human beings. Paradoxically, we would have a greater sense of what it is to be human when all lights are turned off, when we can sense the collective breath of so many human beings, than when in an illuminated room we see faces, contrasts, colours, and all the *differentia* of the external plane.

This is true of every archetypal mode of sacrifice rooted in action. It is mayavic. Wisdom-sacrifice begins with the recognition that all of these are mere epiphenomena, only appearances cast upon the one *Brahman*, the ever-expansive, immeasurable force, essence, spirit, primordial matter – call it what you will because no distinctions apply at that level. That boundless existence, *Brahman*, the Supreme Spirit, is the offering; *Brahman* is the fire; *Brahman* is the mode of making the offering; *Brahman* is each of us and the person making the offering; *Brahman* is the object of the sacrifice. If *Brahman* is all these, why become focused upon specific *differentia*?

We all have experience of this when we witness a noble piece of music performed by a superb orchestra, or when we watch a moving play with the most highly synchronized and dedicated actors. As Shakespeare said, "The play's the thing." There is a sense of something beyond all the details, the incidents, the scenery and the individual actors. There is an intricate interplay that points beyond itself. But we try to reconstruct – and that often happens, alas, because it is one of the futile tendencies of human beings – instead of keeping very quiet and assimilating a deep experience in music or in drama. We are tempted to share it with someone else, and in the telling, we distort, fragment and emphasize contrasts. When one gets to the extreme condition of those congenital critics who are compelled to do this habitually, a sad destruction takes place. The person who does this propagates a distortion. His life is truly "a tale told by an idiot, full of sound and fury, signifying nothing." How much did such a human being add to the sum-total of good when he breathed his last? What difference did his life make to other human lives, to the relief of human pain, to the liberation of human minds, to the enlightenment of human hearts?

We have to recover the sense of the transcendental, unmanifest One. We have to reach again and again to that which is above the head, that which is without any parts or attributes, that light which can never be mirrored except in *Buddhi*, the only part of a human being that is capable of mirroring *Atman*. *Buddhi* is usually wholly latent, but if *Buddhi* mirrors *Atman* there is an infallible result, a decisiveness and assurance which nothing else can give. *Nischaya* is the word in Sanskrit, meaning 'without any shadow.' When a person, in the depths of meditation, out of the very finest ineffable feeling, touches that pure vessel of the *Atman* in the inmost brain, a perfect mirror of the colourless omnipresent light, there arises an assurance and certainty which is constant and can never be destroyed. Equally, it can never be shared or verbalized though it becomes the constant, central fact of life. This is irreversible. Even though a person has made many mistakes over many years – wasted words, harsh sounds, violent speech, empty words – even though a great deal of karma has been generated, all of which will have to be rendered in full account in future lives, nevertheless, if one truly touches the inmost core of the soundless sound and achieves that supreme sense of decisiveness, clarity, confidence, and calm, then it is possible to negate and counteract a lot of the karma produced in the past.

Wisdom-sacrifice is the mode of creative speech in silence, meditating upon the soundless sound, where there is no attachment, no involvement, and one does not participate in lesser emanations. The Pythagorean Monad, like the human triad, emanates out of the total darkness, initiating a universe, and withdraws forever after into the darkness. Human beings can initiate in that spirit, can come out of the vast silence of contemplation to begin something and let a whole series follow while withdrawing totally. They thus exemplify the archetypal stance of the *Bodhisattvas*. The very fact that we can think about such ideas, understand and appreciate them, means there is that in us which, though fearful of death, is willing to cooperate now with the consciousness which after death will witness the separation of the principles, and take stock of a lifetime to prepare itself for the karma of the future. It is possible to cooperate in waking life with that perception which, in deep sleep, represents an unbroken, undivided consciousness. Then there is no limitation of space, time or energy in one's perspective and understanding of humanity and the universal good, and one can insert oneself into the whole.

Anyone who can, as a result of deep meditation, start with small beginnings and try to utter a word to help or heal another human being, or who can stay in a period of silence for the sake of some larger purpose of benefit to humanity, can come to know what it is to initiate. To gain the power of the Initiator, one must both specialize and concentrate magnetism and be attentive enough to apply a thought with such controlled precision and perfect timing to the needs of another human being, that one can make a permanent change for the good in that person's life. In the light of Wisdom-sacrifice, *Jnana Yajna*, good and bad are merely relative appellations from the standpoint of differentiated consciousness in time and space. We grow over a lifetime in making finer and finer discriminations because the cruder relativities with which we live prevent us from understanding a great deal of human life. If this is true of the world around us, it is also true of ourselves.

This has been put in the form of a story about the three *gunas* – *sattva*, *rajas* and *tamas* – all of whom are compared to impostors who accost a man in the jungle. We are told that *tamas* is the one who assaults the victim for the immediate purpose of robbery, *rajas* is the one who binds him up for the purpose of making the proper kill, and *sattva* is the one who releases the person, can take him to the edge of the forest but cannot go any further. *Sattva* is afraid of what is outside the forest. He is also a thief, but his theft is through goodness. It is an attempted theft of that illimitable light of the spirit which can never be captured or translated into attributes.

A person must see all his limitations and weaknesses as shadows of certain qualities which are the painstaking results of karmic good works in previous lives, but which still are bonds, because they become ways in which one defines oneself. *Sattva* involves one as a personal self in imagining that one is better than others, in imagining that one is separate from the beast and the most wretched. It also is fundamentally unable to rise to the level of the compassion of Krishna, who can see in all the same diffused light throughout the great masquerade of *maya*, but who also perceives the many degrees of enslavement to the masquerade which can only be overcome during a long period of time. He says to Arjuna that though Arjuna is grieving for all these people, they are better off gone. They cannot in their present incarnation emancipate themselves from their lifelong qualities, but they can in the future. In an unlimited universe there is hope for all, but in any limited period of time everybody cannot progress equally or to the same extent. To understand this is common sense. It is part of the mathematics of the universe. But to use that understanding with wisdom and compassion means we must not become excited about beginnings and endings or about when and where such and such happened to whom. We must not be caught up in all of this because this is the very framework that binds, especially when it is cloaked in one's better qualities. The light of the *prajnagarbha* – the *Atman* beyond and above all the *gunas* and qualities – is a wisdom that is essentially unmanifest and is the perpetual motion which is pure motionless self-existence.

We need to say to the personal conditioned self, "Even though you are incapable of appreciating the grandeur of the cosmic sacrifice, I, that Self which knows that you are incapable, take you and throw you into the cosmic fire." Now this can be treated ironically but it is also profoundly sacred. It is what H.P. Blavatsky termed 'will-prayer.' At any given time we do not know what more we are capable of tomorrow, but there is no reason for us, equally, to exaggerate the facts as they are. Even more important than either our changing perspective of tomorrow's possibilities or our present view of today's actualities, is our need to see beyond ourselves altogether. We must lift ourselves from the egotism of the shadow to the egoity of that which looks towards the light and which at some point is absorbed in its selfless expansive wonderment at the one supreme, single light of spirit. If this is what we are required to do, we have got to give up any sense of identity. It is more difficult to give up a sense of identity when it is bound up with good qualities, with our spiritual assets and whatever we have worked towards for so long. All of these have got to go. One has to train oneself to be established in a state of mind with no expectations. Without expectations we are less liable to distort and obscure what is going on, because what is going on manifests on many levels. What is going on involves *maya*. Though this *maya* veils and we add to *maya* by projecting and fantasizing, it is also possible to use *maya* to reveal what is relevant and what is at the very core.

This therapeutic art involves training, and it cannot come if one is either blinded by the film of one's own goodness or the nightmare of one's own badness. One must see a whole universe of myriads of selves and monads, and the saga of humanity as a vast, essentially untold and unfinished story. At any given moment what is unmanifest is most important and what people are feeling deep down is more important than what they say. What they are unable to think in the language that they use, and which somehow negates their thoughts even if it only makes them tired and go to sleep, still comes closer to the ground of being as the field of abstract potential. Coming to see it as a living realm of awareness is to function on the truly causal plane. We may thus come closer to those beings who initiate potent and beneficent causes upon the human scene. We might even make that difference to the soul of another human being which may not show for many future lives, but which could eventually be crucial.

We do not know all the arithmetic – how it all adds up, how it interconnects – but we prevent ourselves from knowing a great deal that we could know by imposing expectations, by over-analysis, but above all by a false dramatization of our personal egos. If we can let go of all of these, and if we can look beyond and behind the shadow play of personal selves, we can see in the divine dark the mighty manifestation of the great hosts represented by Krishna, the *Logos*, the *Christos*. We can see this in ourselves, even if the only way we can see it in ourselves is by making it a point. Before we can make it a point, we have to reduce our composite astral form to a cipher. We have to void the very language and categories of the personal self. An ancient scripture teaches that any feeling of like or dislike reinforces, expands, aggravates that shadow. Pandit Bhavani Shankar suggests that when one enters the spiritual path and reaches the *karana sharira*, one reads therein the archetypal origins of like and dislike. They are much more difficult to understand than their materialized manifestations. Attraction towards existence and aversion from non-existence bind the individuality itself. Their personal reflection is a pseudo-attraction and a pseudo-repulsion that maximizes the elemental interaction of the shadow. This has to be cut at the root. One has to go beyond 'history' to see all events as participating in a common medium, all beginnings and endings as existing merely in the region of form. One has to gain that unbroken consciousness which does not participate in succession, in simultaneity, in contrast or comparison. One of the necessary steps to get to this stage is to see beyond the deceptive contrasts of good and evil as pictured by the personal self. One must become so humble before universal welfare that one can only say one does not know what is the supreme criterion of the sum-total of human good, of the optimal use of everything.

This perspective is radically different from our ordinary way of looking at the world, where we have elaborated our childhood fears and traumas and created notions of success and failure which have bound us. We must get away from this altogether, voiding it in our consciousness. In the beginning you have to reach, even if you cannot go beyond, that point where in the very act of reaching you render obeisance – in the words of the *Gita*, a long prostration – devoted service to those *Mahatmas* who embody par excellence the *yajna* of Jnana Yoga. If you do the best you can, and lose yourself in the adoration of those who do so much more, a sort of healing takes place. There is a progressive dissolution of the personal self and a gradual atrophy or dying out of *ahankara*, the ' I -making' faculty.

It will take time for this process to work itself out fully, because every now and again you will be tempted, like a miser counting his coins, to count your blessings in terms of some plausible story of your progress over a period of seven years, over a lifetime, over the remaining length of time until the moment of death, linking this up to some notion of before and after. The moment you start to dwell on such thoughts, you have short-circuited the process. You have restored egotistic concern. Therefore, you will have to make the voiding of self a whole way of living that applies to everything. Initially you can apply it to one thing, two things, more things. If you can link it up to the most elementary necessities of life like waking up, going to sleep, eating and bathing – if you can link it up to these archetypal activities whereby you are discharging debts on the lower planes of consciousness – and you can do this with an awareness of the cosmic host – then in time you can make a decisive difference. In due course you can actually create out of the very ashes of your former sense of being, from a germ and an embryonic seed, a new vesture or *rupa*, a supple astral form saturated with the sacrificial energy of steadfast devotion. Its tropism will naturally help it to turn towards the holy *Hiranyagarbha*, the golden vesture of Krishna and Buddha. *Mahatmas* are continually engaged in giving a forward impulse to human evolution, without any attachments to the relativities and partialities of the perceptions of beings bound upon the great wheel of change.

Wisdom-sacrifice begins where one is, but its end is beyond one's capacity to reckon or conceive. It resembles Jacob's ladder. It is the *Ahavaniya* of the *Vedas*, the great sacrificial ladder. It is like fire which must arise for each as a spark at some point, but which can become a leaping flame bursting the boundaries of all our maps of manifested existence. Hence it is called the fire of knowledge, the sovereign purifier. There is something about fire that is non-discriminatory. It is involved in a relentless process of purgation. Self-conscious participation in the cosmic fire of universal sacrifice is the great privilege offered in an initiatory mode by Krishna to Arjuna, and to all those disciples who could use the sacred teaching for the sake of adding to the sum of universal good.

Hermes, January 1977

MEDITATION AND SELF-STUDY

Atmanam atmana pasya

Meditation and self-study are of immeasurable importance to every single person. They concern the longest journey of the soul, the divine discontent in human life. The quest for true meditation and the yearning for real self-knowledge are as old as thinking man. Today, more than ever before in recorded history, there is a widespread hunger for teaching and instruction concerning meditation and concentration. Some seek even more, longing for a way of life irradiated by the inward peace and joyous strength of contemplation. Ours is an age of acute, almost obsessive, self-consciousness. Everyone is oppressed by the ego-games endemic to contemporary culture, the thought-forms and speech habits, the paranoid, loveless and competitive modes seemingly required merely to keep body and soul together. We are tempted to think that there is some inescapable necessity to assert ourselves to survive, to protect ourselves from being exploited, engulfed or drowned. At the same time, we look in many directions, to ancient and modern as well as to new-fangled schools of psychological health, hoping to enhance our capacity for self-analysis, mental clarification, and minimum control over our personal lives.

The hunger for authentic knowledge and reliable techniques of meditation, and the poignant concern for self-definition, are paramount needs of our time. They are more fundamental, more lasting and more bewildering than all other clamorous claims. But they appear to move in opposite directions. The impulse toward meditation seems to be towards opting out of the world – the world of illusion – or at least the decaying structure of any society. It suggests liberation, an escape from the great wheel of birth and death and the whole life-process. It involves the desire for an equivalent to the conventional concepts of heaven. Images of eternal, nirvanic and absolute self-transcendence are often analogous to the perpetual and perfect release which men desperately seek and fail to find on the physical plane of the lower *eros*. On the other hand, the entire concern for self-analysis and self-understanding is bound up with the need to improve our relation to our fellow men, our capacity for survival, the abject dependence on acceptance and love. It is so much directed to a re-entry into the world that self-study and meditation seem to represent poles that fly off in opposite directions. And in both cases there are more teachers than disciples. There are so many schools, so many sects, such a vast range of panaceas that there is something absurd and also deeply sad about the ferment on the threshold of the 1975 cycle.

If we think for a moment of another age, a distant time in which men sought for supreme wisdom concerning the immortality of the Self and the ultimate joys of contemplation, we may discern that there were men and women who gave their whole lives to a sustained and desperate search. They consecrated everything they had for the sake of finding some answer by which they could live, and from which they could gain a more fundamental insight, a more permanent solution, not only for themselves, but also in relation to the intense human predicament, the malaise of mankind. Today we certainly do not find anything comparable to the exacting demands and the aristocratic sense in which many are called, few persist, fewer are chosen, and very few succeed. There is a tantalizing statistic in the *Bhagavad Gita* suggesting that one man in a million succeeds in the quest for immortality. When we think of that exalted perspective upon the journey, in an age where there is an almost universal concern, and if we consider it in impersonal terms, for the sake of all and not only for ourselves, we are bound to feel deeply puzzled. Something is going wrong. Yet there must be a legitimacy in what is happening. How can one understand this? Where can one find the true wisdom and teaching? Where are the real teachers? Where are those authentic men of meditation who can by their compassion consecrate the whole endeavour, showing not only discrimination in the choice of deserving disciples, but also a supreme justice befitting the total need of the world as a whole? The more we ask questions of this kind, the more we must retreat, if we are honest, into a cleansing confession of absolute ignorance.

We do not know whether there is in the world any knowledge, of which there are external signs that are absolutely certain, in relation to a sovereign method. The conditions, the requirements and the object of the quest are obscure to us. Viewing the immense need of our age, we are uncertain whether there is anything that could adequately serve the diverse needs of vast numbers of varied kinds of human agony, sickness and pain. We might think we are in the Dark Ages, that the Wise Men have gone, and that there is no longer access to the highest conception of wisdom in relation to meditation or self-knowledge. This answer would come naturally to a humble and honest man in the context of the immemorial tradition of the East. In the West one might be inclined either to argue that having no way of knowing whether the whole thing is a distraction, it is better not to look in any direction, or, to see our plight in terms of the messianic religious traditions of the Piscean Age.

Thus there is a restless intensity to the search for a technique or formula, which is not merely a surefire method of meditation or of self-study, but which is in fact a panacea for salvation. Those who are not only concerned for themselves, but share a sense of awareness of the common needs of men, think less in terms of a mere panacea than of a mandate for universal salvation. They seek what is not only supremely valid, decisive and certain, but what could also be made available to all and is capable of ready use by human beings as they are – with all their fallibilities, limitations and imperfections – whether as apprentices and beginners, or merely for the sake of avoiding the slide into self-destruction. They are looking for what can in fact be widely marketed and made available. Put in another language, the idea of a mandate for salvation becomes more understandable, and can be lent a certain minimal dignity. It is as if one says that one wants, for any ordinary person in the street, not the knowledge he needs for him to become a saint or a sage, or a man of meditation perfected in self-knowledge, but simply the knowledge that would enable him to have what he cannot find in any pill or potion, and cannot get from any physician or psychiatrist.

It is the knowledge that will help him to balance his life and to gain, in a chaotic time, enough calm and sufficient continuity of will-energy, to be able to survive without succumbing to the constant threat and danger of disintegration, ever looming large like a nightmare. What is needed is the ability to avoid the dreadful decline along an inclined slope tending towards an awful abyss of annihilation and nothingness. On that inclined slope are steps that are very painful and readily recognisable, not only by oneself but by each other. They represent the weakening of the will and the progressive inability to reinforce the will, especially amidst the breakdown of all those collectivised goals of societies and men in terms of which one was once able to generate a kind of extraordinary will-energy. In our Promethean or Faustian culture individuals simply do not have the will-energy required for the most minimal notions of survival. When we put the subject in this agonizing contemporary context, and not in a classical context seemingly removed from our time, we are entitled to ask whether there is any Theosophical text on meditation and self-study worthy of scrutiny and deeply relevant in one's life, which is in principle capable of universalization and could have the widest relevance to our contemporary condition.

Here one may turn to the meticulous and enigmatic wisdom of that immensely compassionate and extraordinary human being whom we know as Helena Petrovna Blavatsky. She chose, though only at the very end of her life, to give to the world and yet dedicate to the few, a translation from unknown Tibetan sources of stanzas, still chanted in monasteries and sanctuaries of initiation, which she called *The Voice of the Silence*. This beautiful book was blessed in her time by the man whose karmic privilege it was to assume the custodianship of all the orders and schools in Tibet, the Dalai Lama of her day. Early in this century it was published in a Peking edition that had a preface from the Panchen Lama. It is a book that has been blessed by the visible representatives of the authentic tradition of Tibet. For those who have read the book and compared it to the *Bhagavad Gita,* and to the classical Indian texts on meditation and the Self, either going back to Patanjali or Shankaracharya or coming down to modern representatives of the old tradition – to those who have done this at even some elementary level, it is clear that the book is extremely difficult but also that it is an invitation and a challenge.

There are those who have actually taken very seriously, on trust, the words of H.P. Blavatsky on the very first page of the book – "Chosen Fragments from the Book of the Golden Precepts, for the Daily Use of Lanoos." Only wishing to become a *lanoo* or a disciple, they aspire to a discipline that is divine but which must be practised every single day. Those who are simple enough, like God's fools, to have this kind of response to the book, and who use it, soon find themselves in the position of asking whether they really understand what is being taught and whether these instructions are living and relevant realities in their lives. No doubt there may be moods in which the text may seem to be empty words, but over a period does it honestly make a difference to one's consciousness, one's daily life, one's capacity for calm self-control and growth in self-knowledge? When a person applies these tests to himself, all that can be said in advance is that people who have so used the book have found it of sufficient help to them to become immeasurably grateful to those responsible for giving the world this version of an old and traditional discipline, which we associate with the Theosophical Movement. Indeed, there must surely be a few for whom the book ultimately ceases to be a book, and for whom the very pathway of ascent through portals becomes a supreme reality in their lives. For them the problem becomes not one of questioning this reality, but one of relating it to the so-called realities of the world in which we live. How do we live this life, not in some secluded and protected spot on earth, but here and now? In crowded cities, among lowly human beings, everything seems to drown and crowd out the message of this book. Anyone who wishes may consider meditation and self-study in the context of the teaching in *The Voice of the Silence*. It seems only appropriate that Theosophical students should avail themselves of the privilege of doing this, not only for their own increasing benefit, but also out of a genuine wish to share with those who may not have had the opportunity to give themselves a chance to use this teaching and this book. Minimally, one could say that this would be no worse than anything else they could think of. But each one must decide on his own.

If we do approach the subject in this context, we might ask how this book, even what one knows of it, helps to link up the contemporary agony with the supreme flights of meditation of the classical past. Astonishingly, both are in the book – at the beginning and at the end. Early in the book we are told about the immense tragedy of the human condition – "Behold the Hosts of Souls. Watch how they hover o'er the stormy sea of human life, and how, exhausted, bleeding, broken-winged, they drop one after other on the swelling waves. Tossed by the fierce winds, chased by the gale, they drift into the eddies and disappear within the first great vortex." The crisis of identity, the psychological terror, the desperate struggle for survival and for a minimum meaning to be attached to one's life – these are all around us. At best we can only imagine the boundless compassion of beings so much greater than ourselves who are capable of comprehending the enormity of the anguish. At the same time, the book tells us what the ideal man of meditation would be like. It gives us a moving and compelling picture, a vibrant image of the man of meditation. It shows how he is mightier than the gods, that he is so strong that he "holdeth life and death in his strong hand." His mind, "like a becalmed and boundless ocean, spreadeth out in shoreless space. So great is the emergence of such a Being, at any time or place hidden in the obscurity of the secret history of mankind, that it is known and recorded and receives a symphonic celebration in all the kingdoms of nature. The whole of nature "thrills with joyous awe and feels subdued."

The text evokes in us memories of a forgotten past, of mythic conceptions, of golden ages that are gone, when men, like children, sat in an atmosphere of trust and peace, with abundant leisure, under the shade of trees. While some came for shelter, some to fall asleep, some to sit and learn, and some to sit and chat about everything ranging from the most metaphysical to the most practical, still others came for the sake of the existential embodiment of the discipline of a life of contemplation. Images of this kind come into our minds, while at the same time we perhaps see that there is a continuity within the agony of mankind throughout history. There is a deeper anguish, a divine discontent at the very core of the human condition, which is as old as man and which is as strikingly pertinent as all the accounts of the needs of our age. Somewhere there is a connection between the tremendous consummation of the Supreme Master of meditation and light – he who has become one with the universe, who has become a living mirror of the glory of the garment of God, of the universe as a whole, of the Self of all creatures – somewhere there is a connection between that Being, if he is a part of the family of man, and all those who are on the verge of disintegration.

There is in every single human being the embryo of this ideal man of meditation, and we can at least imagine what it would be like for such a being to be present somewhere in our midst, if not in ourselves. We also can recognize that we have our own share in the desperate demand for psychological survival. In this way we restore an integrity to our own quest and are somewhat deserving of that illumination which will take hold in our consciousness in relation to the great and priceless teaching. We might begin to wonder whether perhaps there is a golden chord that connects the golden sphere of a man of meditation and the complex intermediary realms in which he must, by pain and anguish and awakening, by knitting together minute golden moments rescued from a great deal of froth and self-deception, come to know himself. If there were not a fundamental connection between meditation and self-study, something of the uniquely precious wisdom in this great text would be lost to us. When we begin to realize this in our lives, we come to appreciate that, while we may not be in a position to make judgments about teachers and schools in a vast and largely unrecorded history or in our own time, nonetheless we do know that there is something profoundly important in stressing both meditation and self-study, in bringing the two together. We must reconcile what looked like a pair of opposites and get beyond despair to something else which allows an existential and dynamic balance between meditation and self-study. This is the quality of compassion. It is in the heart of every human being in his response to human pain, and brings him truly into the fellowship of those Beings of Boundless Compassion.

A man is a Buddha before he seeks to become a Buddha. He is a Buddha potentially. The Buddha at one time must have had a desire to become a Buddha, to understand human pain. The Buddha vow is holy because it is a vow taken on behalf of all. There is in everyone the capacity to want something for the sake of all, and also honestly to want it for oneself. In this there is an authentic mirroring, in every human heart, of the highest, the holiest and the most pregnant of beginnings of the quest. There are many beginnings, many failures, and many seeming endings. The quest itself, since it applies to all beings and not only to any one man, is beginningless and endless. It is universal, since any individual quest in this direction becomes at some point merged into the collective quest. Put in poetical form, or recognized in the simplest feelings, there is something metaphysically important and philosophically fundamental to the connection between meditation or self-transcendence, and the kind of self-study which makes true self-actualization possible. There is a way in which a man can both be out of this world and in this world, can forget himself and yet be more truly himself. These paradoxes of language are difficult to explain at one level and yet we all know them to be the paradoxes of our very lives. In our moments of greatest loneliness we suddenly find a surprising capacity to come closer to beings far removed from us, men of different races and alienated groups in pain. Then we come to feel a brotherhood that is so profound that it could never be secured in any other way. These are part of the everyday experience of mankind.

Here we touch on a crucial emphasis, maintained sedulously by the *Gelukpa* tradition of Tibet, which affirms that unless you spend sufficient time in refining, studying and purifying your motive, in using compassion as fuel to generate the energy needed to take off and land, you should not begin to rush into meditation. It is a slow school, but it greets the aspirant in the name of all. It scorns powers and the notion of one man becoming a superman in isolation from the quest of other men. Making no promises or claims, it does not insult our intelligence by promising us something to be attained without effort.

Are we not old enough in history to be somewhat apprehensive of schools that promise too much and too soon, when we know that this does not work in any sphere of life? Would we go to some local, loud-talking musician who tells us that he could make us as good as Casals in a week? Would we even take him seriously? We might go to him out of fun or sympathy or curiosity. Why in the most sacred of all realms should we be misled? Is it because of our impatience, our feeling of unworthiness, an advance fear of failure? These questions throw us back upon ourselves. In raising them, in probing our own standpoint at the original moment of the beginning of the quest, we make discoveries about ourselves. They are very profound and important, as they may sum up for us a great deal of the past. They would also be crucial in the future where we may come to sense the supreme relevance all along the way, when it is hard and rough, of what Merlin said to Arthur: "Go back to the original moment." If one could understand the fullness of what is anticipated in that original moment of our quest, one could trace the whole curve of our growth that is likely to emerge, with its ups and downs. Yet it cannot tell all as long as there are unknown depths of potentiality and free will in a human being.

A statement in *The Morning of the Magicians* suggests that as long as men want something for nothing, money without work, knowledge without study, power without knowledge, virtue without some form of asceticism, so long will a thousand pseudo-initiatory societies flourish, imitating the truly secret language of the 'technicians of the sacred.' There must be some reason why the integrity of the quest requires that no false flattery be made to the weaker side in every man. *The Voice of the Silence* tells us early on: "Give up thy life, if thou would'st live." That side of you which is afraid, which wants to be cajoled and flattered and promised, which would like an insurance policy, must go, must die. It is only in that dying that you will discover yourself. We all limit ourselves. We engage in a collective act of daily self-denigration of mankind. We impose, in addition to our tangible problems, imaginary and insurmountable difficulties owing to our dogmatic insistence on the finality of our limitations.

The Wisdom-Religion is transmitted so as to restore in the human being, and collectively in the world, the reality of the perfectibility of man, the assurance that men are gods, that any man is capable of reaching the apex, and that the difference between a Buddha or a Christ and any one of us is a difference of degree and not of kind. At the same time it shows that the slaying of the dragon, the putting of the demon under the foot, the command of the sovereign will of the Adept, "Get thee behind me, Satan," are heroic deeds every one of us could accomplish. Potential gods could also become kings. Every man could be a king in his own republic, but he can only become a king and eventually a god if he first experiences the thrill of affirming what it is to be a man – man *qua* man, one who partakes of the glory, the potentiality, the promise and the excellence of human nature, one who shares points of contact with the mightiest man of meditation. He must understand what the power of his thought can do, and discern a connection between the imagination of children and the disciplined imagination of perfected teachers.

With this exalted view of the individual embodiment of the collective potentialities of man, a person can say, "I'm proud to be a man and man enough to give myself a minimum of dignity. I'm willing to be tried, to be tough, to go through a discipline. I'm willing to become a disciple, and dissipate that portion of myself which is pretentious, but which is also my problem and my burden – like the donkey the man carries on his back in the Japanese fable – instead of making it an ever-lengthening shadow by walking away from the sun. I can make that shadow shrink by walking towards the sun, the *Logos* reflected in the great teachers, which is real and in me and every single living being." This is a great affirmation. To make it is profoundly important. It is to affirm in this day and age that it is meaningful for a man to give up lesser pretensions and engage in what may look like presumption, but is really an assertion in his life that he can appreciate the prerogative of what it is to be a *manushya*, a man, a self-conscious being. That is a great step on the path of progressive steps in meditation and self-study.

So far all that has been said is about beginnings, but this really is an arena where the first step seems to be the most difficult. Also, it is a matter of how you define the first step. An analogy may be made here with our experience in the engineering of flying machines. The designs were there; the diagrams were there; the equations were there; the knowledge of what is involved in maintaining a jet engine at high altitudes was there. The tough part was the take-off and landing problem. We now know more widely, in an age when people turn in desperation to a variety of drugs, that it is very difficult to have control over entry into the higher states of consciousness in a manner that will assure a smooth re-entry into ordinary life. It is because of the take-off and landing problem that we need both to be very clear about our beginnings and also to see the whole quest as a re-sharpening of the integrity of the beginning, in relation to meditation and self-study.

In the *Gelukpa* schools one would be told to spend a lot of time expanding compassion but also meditating on meditation. What is one going to meditate on? Meditate on meditation itself. Meditate on men of meditation. In other words, the more you try to meditate, the more you realize that meditation is elusive. But this is an insight that protects you from self-deception. Ultimately, the entire universe is an embodiment of collective mind. Meditation in its fullness is that creative power of the Platonic Demiurge, of the Hindu Visvakarman, of the *Logos* of the Gnostics, which could initiate a whole world. That initiation or inauguration of a world is a representation of the mighty power of meditation. You can become, says *The Voice of the Silence*, one with the power of All-Thought, but you cannot do so until you have expelled every particular thought from your mind-soul. Here is the philosophical and cosmic basis of meditation in its fullness. All meditations can only be stepping stones towards a larger meditation. What will give us a gauge of the quality, strength and meaningfulness of our power to meditate, and of our particular meditations, is our ability to harvest in the realm of self-knowledge that which can be tested in our knowledge and understanding of all other selves. To put this in another way, if to love one person unconditionally is so difficult for us, how extraordinarily remote from us seems to be the conception of those beings who can unconditionally love all living beings. We cannot do it even with one. Now someone might say, "No, but I can do it with one or a few sufficiently to understand in principle what it would be like to do it for all." Someone else might say, "Oh, when I look at my life I find that I don't know what it is fully to love any one, but I do know that somewhere in my loneliness and pain I feel the closeness of anonymous faces, a silent bond of brotherhood between myself and many others.

There are different ways by which we could see in ourselves the embryo of that boundless love and compassion which is the fruit of self-knowledge at its height, where a man becomes self-consciously a universal embodiment of the *Logos*, having no sense of identity except in the very act of mirroring universal light. There must be a tremendous integrity to a teaching and discipline which says that every step counts, that every failure can be used, and that the ashes of your failures will be useful in regrafting and rejuvenating what is like a frail tree that has to be replanted again and again. But the tree one is planting is the tree of immortality. One is trying to bring down into the lesser vehicles of the more differentiated planes of matter the glorious vesture of immortality, which showed more clearly when one was a baby, which one saluted in the first cry of birth, and of which one becomes somewhat aware at the moment of death.

There is a hint at the moments of birth and death, something like an intimation of the hidden glory of man, but during life one is not so awake. This becomes a problem of memory and forgetfulness. The chain of decline is started. It was classically stated in the second chapter of the *Gita*: "He who attendeth to the inclinations of the senses, in them hath a concern; from this concern is created passion, from passion anger, from anger is produced delusion, from delusion a loss of the memory, from the loss of memory loss of discrimination, and from loss of discrimination loss of all!" Every man is fragmenting himself, spending himself, limiting himself, finitizing himself, localizing himself, to such a degree, with such an intensity and irregularity, and such a frenetic, feverish restlessness, that he is consuming himself. Physiologically we know that we cannot beat the clocktime processes of the changes in the physical body. Therefore we cannot expect to find the elixir of immortality on the physical plane. But we all know that by attending to the very process of growth and change, and by awareness of what happens to us in sickness, that we do have some control and can make a difference by our very attitude and acceptance of the process. If you are very ill, by worrying about it you are going to make yourself worse, but there are people who are really quite ill, who by acceptance have gained something of the aroma of well-being.

These are everyday facts having analogues and roots in a causal realm of ideation and creative imagination which gives shape and form to the subtle vehicle, through which a transmission could take place of the immortal, indestructible and inexhaustible light of the *Logos* which is in every man and came into the world with every child. It is the radiance of Shekinah, the *nur* of Allah, the light of St. John. It is a light that looks like darkness and is not to be mistaken for those things that have a glamour on the sensory plane. To bring it down or make it transmit through the causal realm and become a living *tejas* or light-energy issuing forth from the fingers and all the windows and apertures of the human body is, of course, asking for a great deal. But what one is asking is meaningful, and we have got to try to understand.

It is so important in this quest to keep asking questions, both about apprenticeship in meditation and the repeated attempts and failures at gaining self-knowledge, that this in itself brings about a great discovery.

There is a critical factor or determining role that may be assigned to what *The Voice of the Silence* calls the principle of sifting. "'Great Sifter' is the name of the 'Heart Doctrine.'" The ratio between meaning and experience, which in Plato's definition of insight is the learning capacity of the human soul, is that which enables one man to learn from one experience what another man will not learn in a lifetime. We see this all around us. We often see ourselves repeating the same mistakes and at other points we are relieved that we finally learnt something sufficiently well. That is the x-factor, the mystery of each human being, the capacity to be a learner when it is tough, to say, "I don't want to kid myself." In this way a man builds a raised platform of confidence that is authentic and stable because the man at the height of the quest is a man of such supreme confidence that it is no longer personal. It is the confidence of the universe, and he embodies it. He becomes a conscious agent of the collective and creative will in the universe. What this means in another sense is spontaneous forgetfulness of self. He is so assured that he doesn't have to claim anything. He can forget name and form. He can totally afford not to think of the small self, the little 'me,' because he has accepted and inherited, come to embody, renounce and enjoy, the entirety of a universe of infinite possibilities. He acquires the psychological capacity to maintain a meaningful relationship between a universe of ontological plenty, analogous to a realm of illimitable light where giving does not deplete, and a universe of scarcity, a region of finite matter where there are hard choices to be made and where to move in one direction is to negate another, to take one thing is to give up something else, and to use time or energy in one way is to deny their use in other ways. Not to see the latter is to be a fool. Not to see the former is to deny oneself the opportunity to enjoy and actualize the potentiality and plenty of the universe in every man.

Instead of being depressed that we cannot really do more than meditate in small ways and that we are liable again and again to get into the cuckoo cloud of fantasy which we have to give up, we must say, "I will persist." What is important in meditation is continuity of consciousness. All attempts at meditation are merely fumbling attempts at building a line of life's meditation. A being who does this fully, like the Buddha, could say when asked whether he was a man or a god,

"I am awake." To be fully awake is difficult. We are partly awake and partly asleep. One only fully meditates when one is fully awake and one cannot be fully awake except in relation to the One which is hidden, the supreme reality which has no form, which will never show its face, and yet which can include all faces and assume all forms. One is fully awake only when one can know proportionality, and accurately assign relative reality to everything. One must be able to say, "Yes, that's true. I can understand Eichmann. I know there is that in me which can be the embryo of a Hitler. I also know there is that in me which makes me feel close to Christ." A man can then expand his conception of the Self, so that nothing outside annoys or attracts him of which he cannot see in himself exact and genuine analogues. He can also say, "Somewhere I understand, at the very root of my nature, what it would be like to visualize the Golden Age where all men are consciously and continually bathing in the noon-day glory of the Divine." As Paul Hazard said: "As long as there are children, there will be a Golden Age." All of us can attempt to make mental images of the Golden Age, and to do so is deeply therapeutic, individually and collectively.

The *Gelukpa* tradition, which seems so demanding, has points of contact for all of us with our daily lives. One could say that to meditate is to remove hindrances to continuity of consciousness caused by the modifications of the mind. We do have to go on doing this again and again. You do it much better when you sit down to it and prepare for it properly, but above all you do it best when you meditate on universal good, as Plato taught. When you sit down to meditate on universal good – which you cannot conceptualize and which includes and transcends all conceptions of welfare and particular goods – you can free yourself from a great deal of tension. But you cannot stay there very long without the danger of falling asleep, of becoming passive, of fantasizing. You have to pull out at the right time. You do not want to dilly-daily, least of all to be anxious and settle for imitations. You want the real thing even if for a moment. The more you do this, the more it becomes like breathing. You do not have control over breathing, but fortunately most of the time your breathing can take care of itself.

What about mental breathing? That is where discipline is needed in regard to meditation. You can do something about the disordered, unregulated mental breathing, the way in which you receive the world of objects and in which you forget that awareness which you do have of the One that is hidden. Unless you can regulate this mental breathing, you cannot authentically laugh at and look at the absurdities and weaknesses of your lower self and make it genuinely meaningful for you to say, "I am more than you think. I am more than anyone else understands. And so is everyone else." Not only that, but this can be extended. One can be convinced in one's darkest hour, like men in concentration camps, that there is something profoundly precious to one's own individual sense of being human. One can be proud of what one somewhere knows one has to give to the world, which can be an authentic gift to the whole of mankind. When one can legitimately be proud of that, and increase the content of that knowledge, it ceases to be a feeling. Then one is not afraid of anything in oneself. Then one can understand and rejoice in the statement in the *Light on the Path*:". . . no man is your enemy: no man is your friend. All alike are your teachers."

Life is a school. There is an eternal learning and at any given time you alone can determine how much improved you are as a learner. One comes to see that while the whole of life is a teacher of concentration, that the whole of life also makes it difficult for you to retain the power needed to become continuous in your consciousness. This means that you are both immortal and mortal. To recover immortality while you are aware that you are mortal is not easy. You can do it at one level in one way at one time. You can feel it at some other time in a certain mood. To really do it, however, you have to know it in the classical sense defined by Plotinus – by reason, by experience, and by illumination, independently and by each. You have only half-knowledge otherwise. Knowing it mentally is not enough, though it is important. Knowing it in terms of a peak experience, though very grand, is not adequate to the demands of life. That we may fail to know independently by an appeal to illumination, reason and experience is to say that we know nothing. Yet, what we seek potentially includes all knowledge. These are paradoxes which become realities, truths about consciousness, because consciousness knows no limitations. The power of identification, the power of projection, the power of making yourself, of self-analyzing reflection or *svasamvedana*, is immense. You can play roles and if you can play every role, you can also play the role of the Christ. You can play the role of the Buddha. But you cannot begin to understand what this means unless you can also recognize what it is to play the role of a Hitler, and furthermore, what it means to be the *Kutastha,* he who plays no role whatsoever.

There is an integrity to this quest which is coeval with the whole of life. No one can reduce it to a technique. It is a very beautiful teaching. There never could be enough time, nor could there be any meaningfulness in assuming that anyone could ever fully tell anyone else what is involved. In the end each has to plunge into the stream. Every attempt at meditation within the context of universal meditation, and every attempt at self-knowledge within the context of the fullest concept of self-knowledge, is a meaningful stepping-stone. It can be carried forward in a ceaseless process of alchemy. Once we decide not to settle for the easier way out, once we taste the joy of the toughness of the Path, then we also find it is fun. It is enjoyable. One can truly say that he even enjoys knowing his failures. Then one may fall into another trap. One may too much enjoy being aware, but if one does, life will correct. We will suddenly look' and find that we are ready to plunge into the abyss again.

All of these are representations of what in reality is a process of building, out of the repeated dyings of our vehicles, that fabric of stable, subtle, radiant matter which can be inhabited by ceaseless ideation and universal contemplation, so that one can be a man of meditation who can live as and for every other being. You are a *Bodhisattva.* You can become a Buddha. It is not possible for any of us to say this to ourselves except in the context of some genuine understanding. Otherwise it is false. Hence, of course, we need teachers. The best Teachers give us the confidence that we have access, each uniquely but within ourselves, to that triadic sanctuary within, which becomes the gateway to the cosmic triad. We can then say, as did the ancient Aryans, *Atmanam Atmana pasya*: – "See the universal self through your own immortal self." The issue is one of reaffirmation but it is a reaffirmation we can receive only from those who, as they affirm it, can make us believe. Of this we could never be judges, because we would never know whether the problem was in us or in them. But if we are sufficiently in earnest we will know, even though we will make mistakes. We will say, "This is real. This not only speaks to me; this speaks within me. I am hearing a voice which is the voice of my own Self." When this becomes real for a man, then indeed he is blessed. He enters that kind of initiation and reaches that threshold beyond which the quest will be extremely challenging, but from which he cannot fall back.

There is such a point. To reach that point is possible. This is the great priceless boon of learning the truth about meditation and the Self that all the great texts give, which was for long periods of time used as the basis of a discipline in secret sanctuaries of initiation, and which we have in *The Voice of the Silence*, the voice of *Brahma Vach*. It is possible for any person to make the wisdom of this book a living power in his life. Then he does not have to be wasting energy and time as to what he thinks of someone else, because that no longer matters, since there is no longer any 'someone else.' He has become the One. The seeker has become the object of his quest. There is no gap between himself as a knower and the known and the knowledge. The three are in one. They are all in one at the beginning, but unconsciously to him. Self-consciously they become one again. Until he reaches that point, or until he makes a proper beginning, let him not waste time running around in circles, expending energy, asking all those kinds of questions which are really the questions of the man who is never going to climb mountains, who is never going to swim, who is never going to walk. The lame cannot be made to walk unless they want to walk upon this path. The sick cannot be healed unless they wish to be healed. Therefore we are profoundly grateful to all those Teachers of *Gupta Vidya* who once again gave us the knowledge and the assurance, the faith and the conviction, that we are the Path, that we can heal ourselves, and that we can become what we may now think is impossible. We can become that, not for our own sake, but for the sake of all and thereby become guides and exemplars to those who need our help.Toronto

October 9, 1971
Hermes, March 1976

THE DAIMON

Great Zeus, Father of men, you would deliver them all from the
evils that oppress them, if you would show them what is the Daimon
of whom they make use.

Pythagoras

In the ancient world the term 'genius' essentially meant the tutelary spirit, the *daimon*, of every person. The philosophic conviction that each human being is guarded by his or her own spiritual genius was strongly held in Roman times. In the literature of the Renaissance, we encounter the phrase 'evil genius', reflecting the growing awareness that there is a sort of specialization and concentration, a peculiar intensity that marks the perversity, cunning and cynical defiance of the person who has become his or her own conspicuous enemy. For example, a self-tormented individual may often start with a good intention and at some level wish to convey generosity out of a sincere spirit. Yet whenever such a person seeks to express his or her feeling in language or gesture, it is so twisted and truncated that it is a deformed shadow of the original intent. There is an appalling awkwardness, a tragic distortion; something compulsive intervenes. This sad state of affairs is connected with the tortuous inversions of *kama manas*, the rationalizing mind enslaved by nebulous desires. With the complex mutations and disillusionments of self-consciousness, the term 'genius', originally applied to every individual's tutelary spirit, is pejoratively restricted to the evil embodiment of the soul of concentrated cunning. In contemporary society, a shrunken notion of genius has emerged from the egalitarian concern to categorize beings in terms of some limiting and standardized concept of intelligence. Individuals with exceptional intellectual ability or creative skill in any sphere – whether in music or mathematics or whatever – cannot be readily accounted for under the conventional rules or in routinized ways. Since these anomalies cannot be ascribed to the typical educational process and established modes of training, such persons stand apart as inexplicable phenomena or fortuitous freaks. Applied only to seeming exceptions, the word 'genius' simply signifies the refusal to think more about them, for lack of any instructive explanation that pertains to human potential.

The classical conception of *daimonion ti*, as Plato suggested, internalizes the influences external to the spirit and objectifies its inner demands, thus maintaining a dynamic balance between man and god. The belief in *daimones* as mediating spirits between gods and men was customary in ancient Athens and sacrosanct in Vedic India. Socrates regarded the intervention of the *daimon* – what Gandhi called his 'inner voice', which sometimes spoke to him and remained silent at other times to his deep despair – not so much as a command laid down on the human spirit by an external power as "an absolute law of the spirit itself", to quote Hegel's terms for the sacred task of the Delphic oracle. To make this interior voice wholly subjective is to destroy its spiritual character and distort the position claimed by Socrates and Gandhi. For a few pre-Socratic writers and for some Indian mystics, the *daimon* or devata was no more than the genius or overbrooding spirit unique to each person. If we adopt a facile rationalist attitude and take the *daimon* merely as an inflated metaphor for a familiar psychological process, thus denying it all transcendence and regarding it simply as a pathological oddity, a hallucination or a paranoid or hysterical symptom, we are, in fact, denying that it is an instrument of any meaningful communication and leaving Gandhi and Socrates, and many of the great mystics, enclosed in themselves, in a sort of autarchy, a pathetic state of self-deception. Even if we wish to deny the objective reality of the mystic's experience, which is strictly no easier than to affirm it, it is both unnecessary and presumptuous to deny categorically its subjective validity, or the veracity and testimony of the mystics.

Theosophically, there is a meticulous precision to the proper use of the word 'genius'. An essay by H.P. Blavatsky on the subject of genius stresses a significant distinction between *manas* and *Buddhi*. *Buddhi*, or divine discernment, is the centrifugal principle of expansive sympathy together with an exalted feeling for the fitness of things, for archetypal justice and for architectonic proportion. On the other hand, *manas* is the cool capacity for total concentration, bringing together to one centre the potential power of thought and the active energy of ideation, which in itself is unrestricted, unconditional and boundless. In individuals completely ruled by *Buddhi*, understood as the pure and potent diffusion of the universal Logoic light of the *Atman*, *manas* is a translucent mirror for the untrammelled manifestation of *Atma-Buddhi*. Such individuals are gods – luminous beings who literally are not involved in the shadowy world of manifestation through identification with the lower principles. They are, so to speak, standing above and behind their visible selves and are aloof from the mayavic masquerade in limited space and clock-time. Their consciousness is one with That, which is utterly unmanifest, while simultaneously they have a vigilant and discerning awareness of the patterns and possibilities in chains of causes and consequences inherent in the shadow-play in which their radiant personalities are apparently manifest. They are exemplars of godlike freedom. Creative genius, with its intermittent sparks, may be shown by those in whom the divine Triad is not fully activated and in total control, but who are moving significantly in that direction. When higher *manas*, the self-reproductive power of unconditioned consciousness or of pure, formless ideation, is able to subordinate memory patterns, references to the past, and the illusion of time broken up into little bits, then the individual is functioning as a *Manushya* – Man thinking. Such beings may be truly termed 'geniuses', not if they merely function in this way intermittently or sporadically, but if they can do so consciously and continuously. They maintain complete control and pellucid awareness of the pleasing illusions brought to them by sense impressions and thrown up by those internal images of external impressions which are edited memory traces. They are amusedly aware of all these but are not at all bound up in them. They pass through earthly settings and scenarios without experiencing any compulsive self-involvement.

A spiritual genius is a magnanimous person able to function at all times in terms of a pure individuality that has no involvement, either through attachment or repulsion, in the myriad pairs of opposites and the many vicissitudes of change in the world. In such enlightened individuals the lower *manas*, the more specialized reflecting intelligence which participates in the concepts, categories and languages shared among human beings, is an obedient and precise instrument of the higher *manas*. A genius knows the archetypal logic of the relation between the unknowable, the unmanifest and the manifest. At the same time he could use elementary deductive logic with one part of his intelligence, observe the rules of inference, weigh in his mind the relative worth of the premises, but he would do all this with a detached lightness and timely effectiveness. He knows that it is a gross and shadowy representation, a kind of monkey trick in relation to the archetypal logic of the universe, which most people simply cannot grasp owing to their preoccupation with externalities. The spiritual genius is a thinking being who is without any adherence to past, present or future or any allegiance to name and form. He is wholly free from any inward mental involvement in the illusions of those who cling to exaggerated and emaciated tokens of reality. At the same time he can see these in perspective, without aversion or alienation, and he can participate compassionately with others in the temporal duties of mundane existence. Such a person is markedly different from what is conventionally seen as genius.

No disproportionate development in any one direction can be explained except as a throwback to skills secured in previous incarnations. Although one may suddenly be able to tap such abilities, they have no intrinsic moral significance and no internal relationship to higher consciousness. Higher Manasic or spiritual genius is ever involved in the morality of all things, requiring continual reference to motivation and thought. A person in whom the *daimon* shines forth is aware of every thought as it arises, and of everything implicit in its translation into a series of acts. He is always able to see the difference between primary and secondary orders of causation. When most people, whether in relation to a war or a crisis in personal or collective life, are talking moralistically, they are merely being intensely emotional and wondering whom to blame. They are not functioning as fully thinking beings. Others, who are partially capable of true thought, may still be caught up in externalities, trying to explain events in terms of the linear sequence of past trends. A higher Manasic being will see at the very core of this vast complexity a single and central illusion inherent in a false conception of the changing relationship between the actor, his mental framework, and other beings. Seeing that, he would know that all the rest is bound to follow.

Higher Manasic genius is vitally aware of the necessities of things, while simultaneously seeing all these necessities as relative realities. They are even somewhat absurd in relation to the supreme oneness of all beings, which is behind and beyond manifestation. Consciously rooted in his constant awareness of his immortal individuality as a spirit-soul, he lives in eternity and is not ensnared by the illusions of time. One cannot reach this lofty condition merely by rushing in one direction. One may move towards it partly, but whether one moves towards it by stages or embodies it fully in all contexts, it works in every direction because it partakes of unconditional energy. There can be no hit-and-miss development along this path. Memories from previous lives could play a part in this, because one cannot fully be a genius in one way at a certain time and not at another time in a different context. Fundamentally, to be moving towards genius is for something to be happening to oneself that is omnidirectional. It connotes the ability to look at a vast collection of beings and simultaneously see in relation to any of them that which represents their own possibility of transcendence of their own relative illusions. At the same time, the *daimon* allows one to maintain an equal distance from every one of a multitude of relative illusions. At first, one may only be able to do this at a certain level, and cannot move from this plane suddenly to the height of genius. Even to reflect upon the myriad-minded conception of spiritual genius, the descent of the *daimon*, would be helpful because one could begin to use it as an authentic spiritual and occult intelligence test. It might also be called an illusion test, where one sees one's own life, makeup, and reactions in terms of the exaggerations, falsities and absurdities, as well as the partialities, that are involved in one's moral responses, emotional reactions and so-called intellectuality.

When one can break up all of these and see them for what they are, one is making a beginning in the direction of spiritual genius. This may be done by taking the opaque, brittle, blurred and confused nature that one thinks is one's exclusive and only self and which we are afraid we dare not face, and confronting it with the luminous portrait of the lustrous man of spiritual genius, the true exemplar of moral excellence, mental brilliance and intuitive insight.

It is only when human beings can deliberately think away from limiting conceptions of energy, and a purely physicalist view of breathing and infusing, that they can begin to understand what was involved in the original meaning of the term 'spiritual'. Owing to the concretization of concepts that has taken place over a long time, it is more helpful to see the word 'spiritual' in terms of its equivalent in Sanskrit, the language of the gods. The spirit is *Atman*. The word *Atman* in its etymology refers to eternal motion. Spirit is that which is eternally in movement and yet is never caught in any form nor ever expressed in any set of conditions. It may also aid in resuscitating one's conception of spirit to make a mental image, such as is sometimes evoked when one looks at the soft, mellow light over the ocean after a rain. If one looks at the ocean and sees the soft and supple light, one can gain subtle intimations of how what is showing is suggestive of something which is not being shown. This is like the mystical allusions to the bright light of the sun hidden within the dark depths. Such thoughts and images evoke an awareness that what we are seeing is like a partial yet perceptible intimation of that which can never be manifest to the mind which is modified by the *sensorium*.

Perpetual motion has very little relationship even to the finest and most abstract concepts in contemporary science, or to the subtlest conception of light-energy that one can possibly bring to mind. It is even subtler than that, and it can enable us to imagine better what is involved in the term 'spiritual'. We could think in terms of the night of non-manifestation where there are no universes, no solar systems, nothing in existence, and see that there is a tremendous rhythmic activity, in an undifferentiated medium of matter, of potential ideation which a *Rishi* once compared to the pulsations in the very depths of the vast unconscious ocean. Behind and beyond all the surface movements – the ebb and flow of tides, the ripples or the patterns in formation – one must try to imagine what the depths of the ocean are like, not merely at a distance out from oneself, but also at a distance downwards from the surface. We can imagine an ineffable stillness and peace which is accompanied by the most rhythmic pulsations and imperceptible movements. Then we are coming closer to understanding the conception of a boundless and changeless ocean of spiritual light, which has nothing to do with forms as we know them, with sounds as we hear them, with thoughts as we think them, with any concept of identity of existence as we normally experience it, obscuring the light and the voice of the *daimon*.

If one wants to make functionally meaningful the ancient classifications of human principles, it is necessary to keep moving, by a continual negation through a series of increasingly accurate approximations, to what is implicit in words like *Atman, Buddhi, manas,* or in a term like 'spiritual'. In the end one must move far away from any definable conceptions of infinity and eternity, which have a certain relativistic shadow cast upon them by all our narrower categories of space and time. The same applies even more in regard to motion and causality. One has to keep moving by trying to make an image, continuing to contemplate, to hold the mind upon an abstract idea which is unbounded. When one comes closer to it, renounce it and start all over again until one really makes void the sense of the self as the container of consciousness, which comes in one's way quite apart from what is inherited and what is shared in language. This can only be done in solitude and by closer communion with the *daimon*. When a person has made the effort alone, he will come to know that he has truly done it if he can also do it silently in the presence of others. It is necessarily something that has to be attempted again and again in a variety of conditions. In all of them one is experiencing an awareness of the unconditional, not of the unconditional merely as a negative contrast to particularized conditions, but as the realm of creative potentiality in terms of which all conditions are but incomplete representations. A profound and fundamental re-inversion of standpoint is needed to commence the ascent through the conditioned circles of necessity, onwards towards reunion with the spiritual *daimon* that was in the beginning, and to rebecome self-consciously the presiding spiritual genius of one's own evolution as an integral unit indissolubly united with the universe of nature and humanity.

Hermes, December 1977

KNOWLEDGE AND NEGLIGENCE

*Fix thy Soul's gate upon the Star whose ray thou art, the flaming
Star that shines within the lightless depths of ever-being, the boundless
fields of the Unknown.*

The Voice of the Silence

Every human being is endowed with a mind which is a focussing
mirror for concentrated thought and cognition. Every being in the seven
kingdoms of nature is sentient at some level of intrinsic and potential
intelligence and apperception. Human beings, as self-conscious monads,
are capable of deliberate reflection, of making every item in the external
world an object of intense thought, and also pondering upon themselves
in relation to other selves. If all beings participate in an expanding
universe of mind, in degrees of awareness which are heightened by the
plastic power of self-consciousness, what is the basis of the ubiquitous
distinction between knower and known, subject and object? If there is to
be an intelligible universe of multiple manifestation arising from a single
source but only partly related to it, there must also be an array of minds
capable of focussing the light of universal awareness in varying degrees
in relation to fields of cognition that are partly governed by the porosity
of material vestures – the physical body, the astral form, the subtler veils
that belong to every being and which are more distinctly differentiated
at the human level. Consciousness in a world of heterogeneous objects
differentiated through a variety of vestures must necessarily involve the
ever-changing contrast between the knower and the known. It takes a
long series of meditations to discern the unmodified unity behind the
multiplicity of objects. To understand this ethically is even more difficult.
It means using the persistent distinction between subject and object as
the foothold for recovering a sense of unity in the realm of relativities
and contrasts.

Ethically, the thinking individual encounters the need to put oneself
into the position of another person, who is both an active knower and

a moral agent. Given the initial difficulty of apprehending the contrast of subject and object, how can one comprehend the mystical teaching of Shankaracharya which seems to suggest that the knower is an illusion? If the knower is an illusion, what sense is to be made of knowing? If a person sees the illusion of separateness, what meaning may be assigned to percepts, concepts and the very act of cognition? Such questions merely start the protracted process of enquiry into the knower, the known and knowing. A person who has passed through a preliminary period of earnest questioning may reach a point where he or she may meditate upon the ancient teaching concerning the *Atman* and the *Atmajnani*. The *Atman*, the one source of all light, life and energy, is itself the pristine reflection of the attributeless reality of the Divine Ground, *Brahman*. The *Atman* is the light in every atom and the *Logos* overbrooding every human being. It is the fully incarnated deity in the *Atmajnani*, the self-governed Sage, the initiator into *Atmavidya*, the wisdom of the *Atman*.

How can the ordinary human being make use of a recondite teaching about what seems far beyond everyday experience and ordinary modes of thinking? The kernel of Shankaracharya's teaching is that in reality there is no above and beyond, there is no near and far. *Atmavidya* is itself dimensionless like the *Atman*. The *Atman* is without axes in either physical or conceptual space. The *Atman* is omnipresent, homogeneous and impenetrable. If the light of the *Atman* is hidden in the heart of every human being, its radiance is reflected in all human longings. One must love the *Atman* if one hopes to focus upon the light of the *Atman* and if one aspires to unite completely with the *Atman*. True meditation is self-sustaining to some degree. For the Sage it is utterly uninterrupted at all times because he is ever established in that exalted state of meditation. He merely assumes a mayavic form for the sake of serving a self-chosen mission of mercy in the sphere of cyclic time. If every human being daily comes closer to the *Atman* in deep sleep, everyone is essentially capable of that Atmic awareness which transcends the polarity of known and unknown, knower and knowing. Human beings live ostensibly in a world of fugitive time, fragmented space and differentiated objects. Time is differentiated in terms of seconds and minutes, days and months, for the sake of availing oneself of cyclic rhythms and linear succession. Space is differentiated by place and relationship, and this helps one to locate oneself and one's role in a world of shifting boundaries and continuous reconstruction.

How can one make use of a metaphysical teaching that is typically realized only in a few moments of dreamless sleep every night? The only way this can become continually relevant is by a conscious exercise of contemplation. We need to enter repeatedly into that state of consciousness which transcends the polarities and pairs of opposites, the fluctuating contrasts of light and shade. Since this is far from easy, the opportunity must be taken to do something in this direction on a regular basis, to concentrate the mind on a central truth, to see it from the standpoint of one's own immediate needs but also to grasp it philosophically and impersonally. To look at an idea independently of one's personal standpoint requires effort; to see it from the standpoint of many other people is even more difficult. Nonetheless, it is vital to sustain the effort, to increase continuity by recognizing and overcoming discontinuities. So as long as there is discontinuity in consciousness, the mind will be captive to the sharp distinction between the knower and the known and knowing, will reinforce rather than transcend the sense of separateness. Self-correction is the basis of science and philosophy, but such correction is usually confined to the level of perception or awareness at which the error is identified and the subsequent correction is applied.

Through daily meditation one has a firm basis for self-study, for scrutinizing one's sets of thoughts, behaviour patterns and modes of cognition in terms of discontinuity and continuity. If one is truly trying to maintain continuity, then one is most concerned to examine why one loses it. By persisting in self-study on a regular basis, one may come to see clearly the causes of recurring patterns of deviation, forgetfulness and irresponsibility. At some point of intensive enquiry, one isolates the root causes of sporadic effort, shallow resolve and diffused desire. Shankaracharya teaches that the chief cause of bondage is captivity to a false identity which has no basis in reality but is merely like a photograph one mistakes for oneself. The true Self cannot be known until one can consciously live in and through other beings. Every person does this to a limited extent. Otherwise, there would be no possibility of communication, no extension of empathy, no growth in understanding. Yet human beings are not sufficiently motivated to strengthen the innate capacity for transcendence of the false self. Scattering of consciousness arises through mistaken identification with the *persona*, with name and form, likes and dislikes, borrowed opinions and ill-digested insights, with everything that is like excess luggage which cannot be carried by the immortal soul at the moment of death when the lower vestures are discarded. For the immortal soul – the *Atman* in its pristine ray – there is no illusion of separateness, no tension through duality, no captivity to the conceptualization of particulars.

> The *Atman* dwells within, free from attachment and beyond all action. A man must separate this *Atman* from every object of experience, as a stalk of grass is separated from its enveloping sheath. Then he must dissolve into the *Atman* all those appearances which make up the world of name and form. He is indeed a free soul who can remain thus absorbed in the *Atman* alone.

The persistent asking of the question "Who am I?" raises a person beyond the boundaries of the personality. The lower mind is typically trapped in the realm of external differentiation, of comparison and contrast. It is fragmented through the fleeting succession of states of consciousness which produces the illusion of time. It is delusively dependent through its polarization between past and future, regrets and anticipations, fears and fantasies. Through deep meditation it is indeed possible to silence the lower mind and initiate a state of true calm. It is essential to release the serene awareness of the higher mind, which is inherently capable of abstraction, universalization and thinking through particulars (*dianoia*). By repeated and regular efforts in meditation and self-scrutiny, one could correct the more glaring discontinuities. One might make it a daily practice to prepare before sleep by reflecting upon the *Anahata*, the deathless vibration in the secret heart, the ceaseless pulsation of the *AUM*. This could be fused with a true feeling of compassion for all beings, as evoked by *The Voice of the Silence* in its poignant lament:

> Alas, alas, that all men should possess *Alaya*, be one with the Great Soul, and that possessing it, *Alaya* should so little avail them! Behold how like the moon, reflected in the tranquil waves, *Alaya* is reflected by the small and by the great, is mirrored in the tiniest atoms, yet fails to reach the heart of all. Alas, that so few men should profit by the gift, the priceless boon of learning truth, the right perception of existing things, the knowledge of the non-existent!

All rays of light emanate from a single source. Once one has abstracted from habitual identification with a name and a form and assumed the mental posture of an individual ray of light, one may experience the effulgence of the *Atman*. Self-knowledge will spontaneously arise through active contemplation, which will be food for the soul. If one found that despite proper preparation at night, one still woke up with no lucid recollection in the mind, intense self-questioning is needed. Who is the 'I' that entered *sushupti* and what is the 'I' that cannot remember? One has to make daily experiments with truth. All of this is valuable and valid as a process of knowing, though it is only the partial awareness of a partly self-conscious being of dim reflections of a deeper realm. Nothing learnt is ever lost by the immortal soul. It is important to see the painful process of progressive knowing as constructive and continuous. It is helpful to lose the thraldom and tension of effort by devotedly meditating upon the invisible form of the *Guru*, the *Atmajnani* in whom the knower, knowing and the known are all one. This is uplifting because it elevates one's level of consciousness to meditate on the Self as incarnated in a fully self-conscious Sage, who is outside time and yet in contact with the temporal, who is beyond visible space yet omnipresent, and always accessible on subtler planes of manifestation.

One is only partly awake when asking questions about the true Self; one is more awake when one actively meditates and even more awake when one ardently seeks the Knower of the *Atman*. The *Atmajnani* is in a steady state of *Turiya*, continuous spiritual wakefulness. Total wakefulness is only possible on the plane of the *Atman*, wherein no distinctions made by the mind have any meaning. It is a pure, primordial state of consciousness which is incommunicable. It can neither be described nor characterized but it is approached to some extent when emptying out, when negating and questioning. It is the miniature light in the eyes of every human being. To kindle the small spark of light into the blazing fire of divine wisdom is the task of many lifetimes. The *yogin* is fully consumed, says Shankaracharya, in the fire of true knowledge. The important thing for each and every person is to make an honest effort to keep moving towards an ideal state of inward freedom. One must grasp all available opportunities for greater knowing, for deeper self-knowledge, profounder knowledge of the Self and pure selflessness.

The feeling of responsibility is the first step towards selflessness. All spiritual Teachers promulgate what everyone already knows at some level – that everything adds up, that nothing is lost, that no one can evade anything. The homilies and proverbs of all traditions only point to the accumulated wisdom of humanity. The half-asleep individual has lost the key and does not know how to use the heritage of universal truth. Great Teachers descend amidst humanity so that a second birth is possible for the disciples who are ready. This profound awakening of spiritual consciousness takes place among many at critical thresholds in human evolution. The karma of the whole of humanity for the duration of an epoch is nobly assumed by one of the Brotherhood of Sages, who comes into the world and becomes responsible for the progress of humanity during a cycle of awakening. The *Bodhisattva* elevates the idea of responsibility to its greatest height. What does it mean to be responsible for an age and to be responsible for the whole of humanity? This is an awesome and staggering conception. How can it be even sensed by those who refuse to recognize their errors and the future consequences to be faced?

In general, an awareness of individual responsibility is the mark of a *Manasa*, a thinking being and moral agent. Though one cannot put everything right in this life and all the people one has affected are no longer around or alive, still some things can be rectified right now. It is possible to clean up one's copybook significantly without any clues to the complex mathematics of the cosmos. It is a waste of energy to fret and fume over the past, which is already part of our present make-up. Every cell of one's being carries the imprint of every thought, feeling, emotion, word and deed that one emanated in this life. At least, one can be responsible in relation to what one can see. At the present point of history the sense of responsibility has been enormously heightened for the whole of humanity. Never before have there been so many millions of human beings in search of divine wisdom, the science of self-regeneration. *The Voice of the Silence* instructs the disciple: "Look not behind or thou art lost." It is an exercise in futility to look behind because what has receded will recur. Instead of idle regret, it is possible to use the gospel of gratitude to transmute every precipitation of Karma into an avenue for fundamental growth through courageous self-correction.

Gratitude is no longer a threatening term, even in the United States. Many people everywhere respond to the beauty of reverence as it is truly innate to the human soul. Miseducation may foster mental presumption but it cannot extinguish the immortal spark of devotion. In all human beings there are natural feelings and intuitions which can be awakened and quickened. It would indeed be wrong to think that purely by penitence one could wipe out the consequences of past irresponsibility. This is a costly failure to understand the law of ethical causation. If one already has wronged others wilfully or thoughtlessly, feelings of remorse or empathy cannot erase past debts. This untenable doctrine of moral evasion did much harm over two thousand years. It was a travesty of true religion, an arbitrary breach of natural harmony. The irresponsible dogma of vicarious atonement traduced the exalted ethical teaching of Jesus. He taught that the Divine is not mocked: *as ye sow, so shall ye reap.* This is a central tenet in the teachings of all Initiates, and the erosion of the idea of responsibility is everywhere the consequence of priestcraft and ceremonialism. There are myriad ways in which people run away from the mature acceptance of full responsibility for past misdeeds. The Aquarian sees that true responsibility begins in the realm of thought and must include every thought. Surely one can appreciate the profound integrity of the teaching that every thought connects each human being with every other. The intuitive recognition of universal interdependence and of human solidarity is the basis of an ever-expanding conception of moral responsibility, renewed and refined through successive lives of earthly probation by a galaxy of immortal souls in a vast pilgrimage of self-discovery reaching towards universal self-consciousness.

It is helpful to make a start by recognizing that to become more selfless, one must become more responsible. This is a critical clue for daily self-study. When embarked upon self-therapy, the moment one even begins to blame anyone else, one should see that one is going wrong. The moment one looks for excuses one is off course. The moment one is compulsively peering around or seems too tired to face the truth, one is vainly running away from the Self, from the Wheel of *Dharma*, from the *Atman* and the *Atmajnanis*. One may crouch and kneel and beg for forgiveness, but the Law can exempt nothing and no one. *Atmajnanis* work in harmony with the *Atman*, and the *Atman* is Karma. Sages dare not still the movement of Karma. The disciple under trial should fundamentally rethink all relationships – to Teachers, to companions, to dependents and to oneself. One will need far more than a few crumbs of self-knowledge garnered carelessly, while holding onto a convenient self-image. One needs a stronger current through a deeper meditation upon the *Atman* and the *Agathon*, the central source of universal good. This will arouse increased wakefulness so that one can recognize seemingly remote connections between causes and consequences. One can come alive as a human being, a moral agent, an immortal soul, as a person who is truly trying to do the best without settling for a smug and shadowy sense of responsibility. One is willing and ready to assume the fullness of responsibility that constitutes the dignity and divinity of being human in a universe ruled by rigid justice. Thus one can strengthen one's clear perception, in others and in oneself, of those graces which are universal among human beings, which are conveyed through authentic gestures of gratitude, reverence and renunciation. Some people have dim memories of other times when they sought to cut corners in ways that might apparently make sense if there is only one life, but which make no sense whatsoever if there are successive incarnations and if every event has a hidden lesson which must be mastered.

To grasp the rudiments of the Philosophy of Perfectibility and to learn the axioms of the Science of Spirituality, one must deepen the sense of the sacred through some daily exemplification of the Religion of Responsibility. Shankara taught that negligence, the inversion of responsibility, is death. Negligence in breathing results in physical death; negligence of the mind leads to atrophy of the power to think. Negligence of the conscience culminates in moral blindness and negligence of the soul obscures intuition and inhibits the creative will. The immortal soul cannot make sufficient use of its instruments to fulfil its purposes on earth. Since negligence works at all levels and is ruinous to oneself, what is the deeper negligence of which Shankaracharya speaks? In terms of the mathematics of the soul, a feeble or a distorted use of opportunities for growth blocks future possibilities over lives. This is the worst kind of negligence. If one has the priceless gift of access to the waters of life-giving wisdom and neglects one's opportunity, one will be propelled backwards in ways that become irreversible. If one comes into the presence of a life-giving source of wisdom, one is hardly expected to be perfect, and one is certainly not immune from mistakes and misconceptions, let alone trials and tribulations. Teachers may even recommend strong medicine at certain times to enable the weak to observe minimums. Any human being who comes any closer to a life-giving source of wisdom must either go up or go down. As Gandhi saw, human nature is such that it must always either soar or sink. What determines this is negligence in relation to what one knows in some measure. This spiritual teaching of Shankara necessarily means that one must make a much better use of the future time available on earth, which will determine, at the moment of death, the outcome of succeeding lives. Each one is already carrying the burden of former lives, especially the last three, and to some extent can explain one's present patterns in terms of entrenched tendencies. If these are so tenacious, it is because they were not begun recently but were fostered through recurring rationalizations, excuses and reinforcement.

One has therefore to cut to the very core of one's *psyche*, and this will need courage and care. That does not mean one should brood over one's shadow, or exaggerate one's personal self. The more one broods, the worse it will get, and the more one talks about it, the more it will lengthen. This is such a potent teaching that anybody who continued in this way even after knowing better would be much worse off. One must always exercise the privilege of speech with care, and never be negligent in the use of sound. Invoking the words of divine wisdom on behalf of the shadowy *persona* can lead to corruption of consciousness and astral pollution. Past negligence and misuse can be carefully corrected by present observation of compulsive patterns and neglected needs of the soul. There is hope because the immortal soul can always take control of its sluggish vestures, but this cannot be done overnight if there has been a solidification in the vestures through long-standing neglect of meditation and self-study. Be more deliberate, thoughtful and detached; then one will be more relaxed. Let go. Do not try to do everything all at once, but daily do something constructive. Find a balance that is appropriate, and it is wise to aim higher than one's weaknesses would suggest, while also making due allowance for the resistance offered by deeply lodged tendencies. Find out what works as a stimulus to growth and how one's golden moments may be renewed and fused into an active force for good.

Making a sincere start can release the spiritual will, the calm assurance that one is honest, one's perception is clear and one's mind is unclouded. The mists of illusion are dispelled precisely because one has seen through a glass darkly. There is no need to claim that when one sees clearly, one sees everything. Having found that one can see as clearly as possible what it is essential to do, then relax the tension of striving. The *Atman* is without any strain and is felt by the power of calmness. The *Atman* is pure joy, pellucid truth and self-sustaining strength. The pristine quality of pure love is the pathway to self-knowledge. These cannot be aroused at once but they are all latent in oneself. Though the mind has been blunted by negligence in meditation, it still has considerable elasticity and unrecognized resilience. One may discern in the heart the resonance of the *Atman*, even though the heart might have been obscured and wounded by perverted emotions and distorted feelings. Like a wounded soldier, one can still summon the unseen resources of the spirit.

There is a hidden current of continuity that preserves humanity. This is much deeper and more mysterious than the mere instinct of physical survival. The profounder the continuity, the greater the universality. One may learn as much as one can in relation to as much as one knows, in relation to as much as one can use with as much courage and strength as one can summon. With the *Atman* there is nothing to run away from, nothing to run away to. The *Atman* is everywhere. Though its light is ever available, it can only be reached by raising one's consciousness to the universality of the empyrean. When one is seemingly on one's own, one is mostly if unconsciously in contact with the lower forces in nature. When one ardently seeks divine wisdom and meditates upon the *Atmajnani*, one comes into the radius of an invisible fellowship of disciples on the Path of disinterested service to Humanity.

All growth really depends upon the extent of repeated self-correction in all one's patterns of use, misuse, non-use and abuse. The fundamental negligence of which Shankaracharya speaks consists in forgetting the Self in the realm of the non-Self. This is consistently mistaking the non-Self for the Self. The spiritual Teacher is not addressing the lower mind, but is reaching to the silent inner Self. One must see beyond the visible, and what is thought to be invisible is only so in relation to the visible. If selfhood is seen as a series of veils, the more earnestly one unties the mental knots that result in recurring negligence and repeated forgetfulness, the more easily one will unravel the finer threads of subtler causes. As spiritual wakefulness increases, there will be a distinct replenishment through calmness, contentment and cheerfulness. The *Atman* knows no differentiation or death. Like a vast waveless expanse of water, it is eternally free and indivisible. It is pure consciousness and the Witness of all experiences. Its intrinsic nature is joy, it is beyond form and action, it is the changeless Knower of all that is changeable. It is infinite, impartite and inexhaustible.

Let there be no negligence in your devotion. Negligence in the practice of recollection is death – this has been declared by the seer Sanat Kumara.

For a spiritual seeker, there is no greater evil than negligence in recollection. From it arises delusion. From delusion arises egoism. From egoism comes bondage and from bondage misery.

Through negligence in recollection, a man is distracted from awareness of his divine nature. He who is thus distracted falls – and the fallen always come to ruin. It is very hard for them to rise again....

Control speech by mental effort; control the mind by the faculty of discrimination; control this faculty by the individual will, merge individuality in the infinite absolute *Atman* and reach supreme peace.

Hermes, January 1979

MIRRORING THE MACROCOSM

In the first place revere the Immortal Gods as they are established and ordained by the Law.

Reverence the Oath. In the next place revere the Heroes who are full of goodness and light.

Honour likewise the Terrestrial Daimons by rendering them the worship lawfully due to them.

Honour likewise thy father and thy mother, and thy nearest relations.

Of all the rest of mankind, make him thy friend who distinguishes himself by his virtue. Always give ear to his mild exhortations, and take example from his virtuous and useful actions. Refrain, as far as you can, from spurning thy friend for a slight fault, for power surrounds necessity.

Never set thy hand to the work, till thou hast first prayed the Gods to accomplish what thou art going to begin.

When thou hast made this habit familiar to thee, thou wilt know the constitution of the Immortal Gods and of men; even how far the different Beings extend, and what contains and binds them together.

Thou shalt likewise know, in accord with Cosmic Order, that the nature of this Universe is in all things alike, so that thou shalt not hope what thou oughtest not to hope; and nothing in this world shall be hid from thee..

The Golden Verses of Pythagoras

Spanning the centuries and continents, from the myths of hoary antiquity to the cogitations of modern man, certain primeval ideas and intuitions may be dimly discerned. These underlie the views held among different civilizations regarding hierarchies of beings and levels of evolution, the laws of nature and the central harmony of the cosmos, and human obligations which are rooted in a recognition of moral responsibility and are realized in a variety of relationships. There have been numerous theories concerning the citizen's political and social obligations; there have been innumerable formulations of the norms of individual excellence and collective progress. These provide the philosophical and ethical foundations of culture and society.

In our century man has to re-learn the ancient, archetypal truth that he is a microcosm, a world in himself, the mirror of an invisible universe that is around and beyond him. An educated person who does not recognize the value of reverence for Nature, for Nature's laws and for one's fellow men, cannot be regarded as a cultured individual. Intuitive thinkers of our time, like Dr. Albert Schweitzer, have realized that the collapse of civilizations came about in the past when men and women had lost their reverence for life, their sense of joy in adventure, their spirit of wonder and humility.

> Reverence for life which I apply to my own existence, and reverence for life which keeps me in a temper of devotion to other existence than mine, interpenetrate each other.

The nature of this interpenetration cannot be fully grasped unless we regard man, as did Pythagoras and Pico della Mirandola, as "the measure of all things". Man is the centre of a series of concentric circles, of little worlds extending from the 'here and now' to the infinite expanse of Space and Time. Man is a microcosm in many senses and in different dimensions of his complete individuality. His family is a small macrocosm, the range and heritage and hereditary character of which he reflects in his own being. Each day in his life is like a miniature aeon during which he emanates and absorbs fresh currents of thought and energy. As a citizen, man reproduces the attitudes and characteristics of his neighbourhood, his locality, his village or city, his province and his country. As a member of present-day humanity and of the contemporary world, man embodies the trends and forces that constitute the matrix of this great macrocosm. Man's life in a particular personality reveals the spirit of the age to which he belongs.

This manifold microcosmic nature of man gives rise to the complex of interactions between local and global, ephemeral and enduring cultures. A truly and fully cultured man is able to absorb the beneficial currents that flow from all directions and at all times; he perceives the beauty of the great macrocosm within the boundaries of the small; he enjoys the grandeur of lasting realities amidst the flux of fleeting illusions and shadows. He takes the whole universe for his province, regards the world as a city, considers humanity as his family. Like Goethe's Faust, he apostrophizes the passing moment: "Stay! How wonderful thou art!" In appreciating art, music and literature he compares the unfamiliar with the familiar and proceeds from the known to the unknown, showing an awareness, however slight, of the patterns and rhythms of Nature, the cosmic dance of the elements, the changing positions of the stars, the strange music of the spheres, the mighty magic of *prakriti* (matter). Recognizing that in every speck in space and in every form of matter is to be found the motion of invisible intelligences, of *devas* (gods) and *devatas* (nature spirits), he pays honour first to the Immortal Gods of whom Pythagoras spoke, of whom Plotinus wrote in his fifth *Ennead*:

> For them all things are transparent, and there is nothing dark or impenetrable, but everyone is manifest to everyone internally, and all things are manifest; for light is manifest to light. For everyone has all things in himself and sees all things in another; so that all things are everywhere and all is all and each is all, and the glory is infinite. Each of them is great, since the small also is great. In heaven the sun is all the stars, and again each and all are the sun. One thing in each is prominent above the rest; for it also shows forth all. There a pure movement reigns; but that which produces the movement, not being a stranger to it, does not trouble it. Rest is also perfect there, because no principle of agitation mingles with it.

Reverencing those cosmic intelligences which we call Gods of Wisdom, we are able to see the Order that "hath established Their Choirs". We can attempt to mirror on earth that Divine Harmony or *Rta* and its action or Karma by reordering our social institutions in terms of *Dharma*, the Law of Duty, the Religion of Works, and *Swaraj*, the Rule of the One Self. In the memorable words of the sixth Book of The Republic of Plato:

> ... are not those who are verily and indeed wanting in the knowledge of the true being of each thing, and who have in their souls no clear

pattern, and are unable as with a painter's eye to look at the absolute truth and to that original to repair, and having perfect vision of the other world to order the laws about beauty, goodness, justice in this, if not already ordered, and to guard and preserve the order of them – are not such persons, I ask, simply blind?

For he, Adeimantus, whose mind is fixed upon true being, has surely no time to look down upon the affairs of earth, or to be filled with malice and envy, contending against men; his eye is ever directed towards things fixed and immutable, which he sees neither injuring nor injured by one another, but all in order moving according to reason; these he imitates, and to these he will, as far as he can, conform himself. Can a man help imitating that with which he holds reverential converse?

This is a magnificent ideal, difficult to conceive, apparently impossible to achieve. In continuing to strive to draw nearer to this glorious goal, we are inspired by those "Heroes full of goodness and light" and the "Terrestrial *Daimons*" to whom, according to Pythagoras, we must pay "the worship lawfully due to them". Every person should endeavour to enter into inmost communion with the hero-souls of all lands and eras who still live, especially in their own immortal works. As Plutarch says, in his life of Aratus:

But surely a man in whom, to use Pindar's words, 'the noble spirit naturally displays itself as inherited from sires', and who, like those, patterns his life after the fairest examples in his family line – for such men it will be good fortune to be reminded of their noblest progenitors, ever and anon hearing the story of them, or telling it themselves. For it is not that they lack noble qualities of their own and make their reputation dependent on their praises of others, nay rather, they associate their own careers with the careers of their great ancestors, whom they hail both as founders of their line and as directors of their lives. . . . For it is the lover of himself, and not the lover of goodness, who thinks himself always superior to others.

It is necessary to celebrate not only the lives of the "Heroes full of goodness and light" but also the thoughts and writings of the "Terrestrial *Daimons*" of our age and of the past. Plutarch wrote both the Lives and the Morals, the former setting forth to us, from an ideal point of view, what the ancient world had accomplished in the world of action, and the other, in like manner, what it had aimed at and accomplished in the world of thought. Even in the Lives, Plutarch is far more the moralist than the historian. A study of the archetypal ideas underlying human culture and the offering of homage to gods, adepts and geniuses are not ends in themselves but ways in which we can make of ourselves men and women of culture, of enlightenment and grace. Self-culture is in itself not the final goal, but only the means by which we can become the servants and custodians of the ideals that inspire and sustain the whole world.

Pythagoras offered the distilled wisdom of the ancients when he said:

Above all things, respect thyself.

Never do anything which thou dost not understand; but learn all thou oughtest to know, and by that means thou wilt lead a very pleasant life.

Examine all things well, leaving thyself always to be guided and directed by the understanding that comes from above, and that ought to hold the reins.

Integrity, uprightness and self-respect – these are the very roots of real culture. Intelligent, deliberative action and an awareness of the norms of goodness and beauty (of what the Greeks called *arete*) – these constitute the fragrance or aroma of culture, the "sweetness and light" of which Matthew Arnold wrote. The joy of silent contemplation and the repose of a lofty, well-controlled mind – these are the fruits of culture, the harvest of prolonged cultivation. Cultural development, whether individual or collective, is a continuing process, a creative activity, an exciting pursuit. As Plotinus counsels in his very first *Ennead*:

Withdraw into yourself and look. And if you do not find yourself beautiful as yet, do as does the creator of a statue that is to be made beautiful; he cuts away here, he smooths there, he makes this line lighter, this other purer, until he has shown a beautiful face upon his statue. So do you also; cut away all that is excessive, straighten all that is crooked, bring light to all that is shadowed, labour to make all glow with beauty; and do not cease chiselling your statue until there shall shine out on you the godlike splendour of virtue, until you shall see the final goodness surely established in the stainless shrine.

Great and enduring changes in the world in which we live cannot come through the efforts of partisan politicians unless they are inspired and directed by the wider vision of seers, poets and artists. The concept and goal of a united world community have been foreshadowed by a long line of creative writers, especially poets, from the earliest eras. In our own epoch, several leading writers have shown a lively sense of their social responsibilities. In his fine Presidential Address in 1953 to the Amsterdam Congress of the International P.E.N., Mr. Charles Morgan appealed to the writers assembled

> ... not to take peace for granted but to live each hour of it fully and without fear. Above all let us not allow the name of peace to be taken in vain and perverted to the uses of terror. If its sands are running out, so are the sands of our lives. That is not a reason to allow our faith to disintegrate or our pens to tremble in our hands.

Admittedly, writers, like sensitive seismographs, are peculiarly responsive to the prevalent horrors and imminent terrors of our time. But the very immensity of the dangers that loom before us and the time ahead, according to Mr. Charles Morgan, should be a means of grace":

> It deprives materialism of its profit and tyranny of its power. It is a reason to love and to be at peace. It is an amnesty to all the imprisonments of the mind; it empties out all the philosophies of disintegration.

It would be a betrayal of their mission if writers refused to rise above the predicament of mankind and offer a message of comfort and courage. Mr. Lewis Mumford fully appreciated this point in his In the Name of Sanity. In the chapter entitled "Mirrors of Violence", he declared:

> If our civilization is not to produce greater holocausts, our writers will have to become something more than merely mirrors of its

violence and disintegration; they, through their own efforts, will have to regain the initiative for the human person and the forces of life, chaining up the demons we have allowed to run loose, and releasing the angels and ministers of grace we have shamefacedly – and shamefully – incarcerated. For the writer is still a maker, a creator, not merely a recorder of fact, but above all an interpreter of possibilities. His intuitions of the future may still give body to a better world and help start our civilization on a fresh cycle of adventure and effort. The writer of our time must find within himself the wholeness that is now lacking in his society. He must be capable of interpreting life in all its dimensions, particularly in the dimensions the last century has neglected; restoring reason to the irrational, purpose to the defeatists and drifters, value to the nihilists, hope to those sinking in despair.

~

Inquire of the earth, the air, and the water, of the secrets they hold for you. The development of your inner senses will enable you to do this.

Inquire of the holy ones of the earth of the secrets they hold for you. The conquering of the desires of the outer senses will give you the right to do this.

Inquire of the inmost, the one, of its final secret which it holds for you through the ages.

Light on the Path

Hermes, March 1979

ASCENT AND DESCENT

*Not even the light which comes down nearest to the earth from
the sun is mixed with anything, nor does it admit dirt and defilement,
hut remains wholly pure and without stain and free from external
influences among all existing things.*

Emperor Julian

The logic of a pregenetic unity to the cosmos requires that we adopt some principle of real or apparent division of aspects, entities and qualities in existence. Metaphysically, this principle is found in the concept of a triad of divine aspects. Arithmetically, the number 1 gives the notion of number, 2 the idea of duplication, and 3 the concept of elaboration, that is, permutation and combination. Geometrically, the point and the line can generate a triangle, the simplest enclosure of space in a plane. But the idea of rotation – in this case, the rotation of an isosceles triangle about an axis from the apex through the centre of its base – produces the cone or vortex, the origin of three-dimensional space. Ontologically, the triad implies an inner side (called Spirit by A.E.), an outer side (the material medium of spirit) and a dynamic principle which draws the two together. Theosophically, this third element is sometimes called *Fohat*, the active aspect of spirit from the standpoint of matter, and the energetic aspect of matter from the standpoint of spirit. If effects can never be completely alienated from their causes, the unity present at the advent of existence will be found at every level of its unfoldment, and *a fortiori* the triad is implicit in everything from a universe to a grain of sand.

The spiritual alchemy of the Renaissance was rooted in the premise that every base metal was essentially gold *ab ovo* made gross by the infusion of a chaotic, derivative, aqueous element – metalline organization obscuring gold's archetypal structure. Transmutation is the process of purifying the base metal of the aqueous element until only the natural gold remains. Alchemists knew well that aurifaction is shadowed by aurifiction, the production of a metallic substance which assumes some of the external characteristics of gold, usually by mixing minute quantities of gold with lesser metals. Along with transmutation, decisive tests for genuineness of results were performed. Moral aurifiction will be exposed on the psychic plane by its fascination with images and on the plane of action by the projection of appearances. Both may contain a golden residuum in a crude alloy, but unless the tests for gold are known, one will as likely seize upon the lesser as the true metal. The concept of transmutation (along with a constellation of interrelated and supporting ideas) can apply *mutatis mutandis* to the cosmos, the psychic nature of man and the path to illumination. Spiritual alchemy enunciates the view that there is a correspondence between physical and spiritual nature, and a continuous interaction between them.

A.E. perceived the purest spiritual nature within and throughout the grossest material nature. To the extent that a particular permutation of the two natures imposes itself, under law and circumstance, upon our consciousness it becomes real to us. Similarly, the degree of will we apply to a particular level of the interrelated aspects of the Unknowable determines the clarity of appearance which that level must assume. The *psyche*, as a complex of thought, will and feeling, changes under these internal and external impulses, and each psychic state is strictly correlated with some level of substance. If the senses are instruments of the power of perception, then there are senses for different levels of being and consciousness that can be experienced. The mystic path is the conscious and willing activation of subtler senses so that the *psyche* may become fully aware of what it always implicitly reflects.

> In that mysterious journeying from time to eternity, where the soul moves on to ever higher planes of its own being, there must be many transformations of the *psyche*. Something I think goes with it from this world to that other. 'The gods feed upon men.' Something comes back with it from Heaven to Earth. 'The gods nourish us.

> AE, *Song and Its Fountains*

The ascent and descent of the *psyche* is the illumination of the soul at different levels and interstices. The *psyche* aspires; the *nous* inspires.

> As our aspiration is, so is our inspiration. The higher nature takes our fragmentary knowledge, thought, experience, and our aspiration, which is sacrifice, and it is transfigured, made whole and returned to us. What is earth-born is lifted up and perfected, shot through and through with the light of that higher world where the *psyche* nigh to its divine root imagines the perfection or truth in all things. Much must be lost of that transcendental lucidity and beauty of the heavenly consciousness when the *psyche* sinks through murky clouds of desire back to the body again. But something returns.

The transient ascents of the *psyche* are not ephemeral events, for the illumination of the *psyche* works a change in its nature. True rapprochement of the *psyche* with the divine root clarifies its obscuration so that it reflects the higher light more adequately. "Our inspiration will be as our aspiration."

A.E.'s convictions sprang from his own experience and a steadfast concern to make use of the analogies and correspondences which flooded into his awareness. Ordinary waking thought is insufficient to provide the existential and experimental basis for understanding the process of consciousness.

> Intuition, feeling, thought are too swift in their coming and going, too elusive for a decisive argument over their nature. Though they may shake us by what they import, though what they in an instant hint at may be sacred to us, their coming and going are too swift for precise thought about themselves. In normal thought the fusion between inner and outer is so swift that it deceives the most attentive sense into the idea of unity, and we come to believe that there is no other creator of thought than the thinker who resides in the brain, who is with us from moment to moment, and we do not know what rays from how many quarters of the heavens are focussed on the burning point of consciousness.

> Unaware of the elemental denizens pervading waking consciousness, much less the specific effects of collective and individual patterns of thought upon ourselves, we cannot discern their nature. In

the subjective dream state, however, we make discoveries.

> In dream there is a dramatic sundering of the *psyche*. One part of us is seer and another is creator. The seer of dream is unconscious of creation. He looks on the forms which appear as he might look on a crowd drawn together by impulses not of his creation. He does not think all this when he dreams, but, when he wakens and remembers, he knows that the creator of dream had a magical power transcending anything which he could do in his waking state. It can project crowds of figures, set them in motion, make them to move with perfect naturalness, and wear the fitting expression for the deeds they do. Yet in the waking state of the dreamer, let him be given canvas, paints and brushes, and he might boggle as a child would over the drawing of a figure. The creator in dream is swift inconceivably. What seems a long dream to the seer of dream often takes place in an instant, and may be caused by sound or touch which wakens him. Transformations, too, take place in dream which suggest a genius to which psychic substance is instantly malleable.

The *psyche*, when released through withdrawal from the constraints of concrete matter, operates upon a subtle material medium commensurate with itself. Psychic substance readily takes the impress of intellect and the *psyche* witnesses instant presentments and elaborations. The seer is unaware of doing anything, and therefore one suspects a superior intelligent force operating in this medium.

> The seer in dreams is apart from the creator. It is not unreasonable to surmise an intellectual creator able to work magically upon psychic substance. Sometimes, indeed, at the apex of dream I have almost surprised the creator of it peering in upon me as if it desired by these miracles to allure me to discovery of itself. In the exploration of dream we acquire some knowledge of the working of the *psyche*. And at times in the making of poetry I have been able to discover the true creator of the poem withdrawn far within from the waking consciousness. The poem seemed like an oracle delivered to the waking self from some dweller or genie in the innermost..

A.E. knew from his Theosophical studies that at least seven kinds of dreams could be distinguished, and that the dreams he frequently experienced intimated a higher awareness than he found readily accessible.

> Whence come vision and high imagination? I think they come from a centre of consciousness behind the sphere of dream. Here I pass from experience to rely on intuition and the wisdom of others. It is to the seers who wrote the *Upanishads* I turn for illumination. They speak of four states of soul – waking, dreaming, deep sleep and spirit waking – the last a state in which the spirit is unsleeping in its ecstasy of infinite vision.

The last state – *Turiya* – is outside the order of the other three, and is that in which Spirit is at once seer and creator, and where seeing is the activity of shedding the light that is the *prima materia* of creation. Since all four states are implicit at every level of consciousness, the perceptive mystery of creation is present in every dream. When the *psyche* is unobscured by preconception and fascination, it is illuminated and hence becomes the seer – a condition more readily recognized in the dream state than in either waking consciousness or deep and traceless sleep. The seer in the *psyche* cannot see the creator precisely because it is that creator itself. Since its activity is less pellucid than pure spirit, it is the channel of both seership and creation. Poetry can emerge from states of varying illumination because this light of conscious awareness is also the sound of understanding. *The Voice of the Silence* addresses one who has become a master of *Samadhi* – the state of faultless vision – in terms of light and sound.

> And now, Lanoo, thou art the doer and the witness, the radiator and the radiation, Light in the Sound, and the Sound in the Light.

When this sovereign state of consciousness free from all change and interruption is reached, the text declares:

> Behold! thou hast become the Light, thou hast become the Sound, thou art thy Master and thy God. Thou art THYSELF the object of thy search: the VOICE unbroken, that resounds throughout eternities, exempt from change, from sin exempt, the Seven Sounds in one, *The Voice of the Silence*.

A.E. never claimed to achieve in consciousness such irreversible and transcendent heights. But he touched chords in the *psyche* which evoked deep spiritual resonances and gave meaning to the Upanishadic teaching.

> But for a moment I understood what power might be in sound or incantation. It made me understand a little those mystics who speak of travelling up a Jacob's Ladder of Sound to the *Logos*, the fountain of all melody. I found later if meditation on the Spirit is prolonged and profound enough we enter on a state where our being is musical, not a music heard without but felt within as if the soul itself had become music, or had drawn nigh to the ray of the *Logos*, the Master Singer, and was for that instant part of its multitudinous song.

Like Socrates, who taught the way to beauty itself by recounting the words of Diotima, A.E. took sufficient steps on the Path of Infinite Promise to be able to affirm it with confidence.

> I am a far exile from that great glory, and can but peer through a dusky transparency to a greater light than the light of day. That greater light shines behind and through the *psyche*. It is the light of spirit which transcends the *psyche* as the *psyche* in its own world transcends the terrestrial ego. The *psyche* has a dual nature, for in part it is earth-bound, and in part it clings to the ancient spirit.... While I could comprehend a little about the nature of the *psyche*, I could not apprehend at all the spirit which transcends the soul, for, as the seers said of it, it is eternal, invisible and universal. Yet because it is universal we are haunted by it in every motion of mind. It is at the end of every way. It is present in sunlight.

A.E.'s meditations were all intent on the discovery of the nature of soul and spirit, and his own poetic singing constituted an array of oracles from the *psyche* – partial, eclipsed by external trappings of phrase and circumstance, and bound by limited vision.

> Yet they themselves may pay reverence to the voices of conscience or of intuition which also are oracles out of undiscovered depths in their own being, and intuition and conscience may utter themselves in song as well as m fugitive illuminations of mind, heart or will.

The consciousness of the seer, when controlled and focussed by a profound philosophical and psychological framework, could import glimpses of pure and undiffused light from loftier realms.

> Just as the needle-point of a nerve in the eye is sensitive to light from the whole of the heavens spread above us, so at moments we feel that all knowledge is within us. But we have not yet evolved mind to be the perfect instrument to mirror universal mind as the eye mirrors infinitudes of light and darkness. But out of that centre in us through which all the threads of the universe are drawn there may come at times flashes of supernature.

Within the aurifiction of his varied visions and dreams, A.E. perceived the possibilities of the aurifaction of true seership and touched that great work within the laboratory of his own endeavours. Even more important than the content of his visions is his method for achieving an elusive transforming awareness.

> I do not think we shall ever come to truth otherwise than by such gropings in the cave of the soul, when with shut eyes we are in a dim illuminated darkness, and seek through transient transparencies to peer into the profundities of being.

AE, Song and Its Fountains

Hermes, October 1979

THE GAYATRI INVOCATION

ॐ भूर्भुवः स्वः
तत्सवितुर्वरेण्यं
भर्गो देवस्य धीमहि
धियो योनःप्रचोदयात्

Aum bhur bhuvah svah
tatsaviturvarenyam bhargo devasya dhimahi
dhiyo yo nah prachodayat. Om.

AUM. In all three worlds – terrestrial, astral,
and celestial – may we meditate upon the splendour
of that Divine Sun who illuminates all. May its golden
light nourish our understanding and guide us on our
journey to its sacred seat. OM.

It is a very ancient and sacred teaching that the *Gayatri*, corresponding to *Vach*, consecrating the Light of the *Logos* in Sound, should only be invoked on behalf of universal welfare. In general, all those who have any attraction to spiritual ideas must cleanse their hearts and strengthen those feelings in them that are truly universal and limitless, even though they may not know in advance what limitless love is. They must be willing to move towards unconditional and boundless love. They must refuse to consolidate partial loves and blinding hates and especially those shadows of love which contribute to human sorrow and deception. In affirming true love they must show spiritual courage and kindle the light of daring in the heart. The more one attempts this, the more one can keep moving. There is no way in which one could really grow without repeatedly assisting in the disintegration of a limited equilibrium which worked at one time. Either one does it, or it will be done to one. If it is done from outside, it may happen slowly, but when it comes, one may collapse. Whereas, if one does it consciously, refusing to consolidate even the finest traits or the glittering *simulacra* of virtue, if one is willing again and again to take stock and rebuild one's self-conception, the more one will have a chance of bringing closer the inmost urges that are in line with the highly potent spiritual invocation of the *Gayatri mantram*, and of negating the familiar and latent elements of conditionality in one's nature.

In many old cultures wisdom is often shown in cooperating with the seasons of nature and the cycles of time. Individuals may make some sort of inward affirmation of benevolence towards all that lives. If one simply enjoys the thought of being a friend to every living being, one could make discoveries about oneself and about the correction of habits, and then one can take stock like a craftsman. One can discern certain patterns and link them up to causes that are recognizable in certain mental states and thought-patterns. One may then counteract them, but in the process of doing this, one must recognize that it cannot be accomplished all at once. At the surface level people do not self-consciously mature in the manner in which everything in nature grows, giving time sufficient scope to do its own healing magic. Therefore impatience arises with impetuosity as the stimulus, resulting in inertia and defeatism. This is the loud assertion of mortality, and even those who have heard the sacred teaching of immortality may still bring to it something of the intensity and the frenetic nature of mortality. This is implicit in the human condition, the translation downwards from the higher to the lower, from the immortal to the mortal, from Duration to the language of Time. One has to penetrate these categories and see that in the indivisible hidden moment there is a mirroring of boundless Duration, that within the invisible atom there is boundless Space. This is the metaphysical basis of the *Gayatri* invocation to the Spiritual Sun. To be able to use this daily and especially in reference to human relationships, in reference to all one's obligations, in reference to one's *dharmas* and *karmas*, requires great wisdom.

One must truly feel compassion for that in all human beings which represents inertia, stultification, coldness, disintegration and death. The major obstacles to growth, producing a stony and indifferent heart, are ignorance combined with inertia – *tamas* – leading to a repeated persistence in a restricted view of the world. One of the asymmetrical characteristics of the universe is that individuals can expand without limit, but personalities cannot contract without limit. One may contract to a point where one might even enjoy contraction, where one becomes habituated to the dingy, the cloudy, the chaotic and the claustrophobic. This is the sense in which many people, habituated to self-torture and self-torment, find that they cannot attach meaning to any language, and cannot give credibility to themselves with reference to the sacred. They may know the noblest teachings, but they bring to them a facile sort of analytical familiarity and a stale routine in their response. A point comes when they become cold, when the psychic fire has burnt itself out and the cool waters of wisdom wash over dead ashes.

This has analogies with what goes on in the astronomer's universe. When a planet goes sufficiently far away from the sun – and there is a decisive difference between the parabolic movement of some bodies and the elliptical movement of others – it cannot keep pace at a certain level of intense, rapid, whirling motion around the powerful, incandescent centre. Then a point is reached when one of these bodies in its slow movement is expelled, going further and further away from the solar centre. It becomes cold because it enters into a state which must eventually culminate in a kind of disintegration or death, a tragic fulfilment of Nature's laws. There is an analogy between what takes place in reference to matter in the galaxies and what takes place within the solar system of the human form. The *Atman* is like the sun (in the *Gayatri mantram*) and all the other principles are like planets or comets in relation to it. It is possible that a person, though familiar at some level with a sacred teaching, especially the idea of immortality, may be constantly translating downwards in terms of what is dark and sombre. The person may after a point experience something comparable to an extreme coldness, an amazing lack of any spiritual vitality. Sometimes this can combine with an extraordinary versatility in acting out roles in the world, an atavistic skill in mimetics.

The origin of this may be sought in one of two ways. Either in another life the person, having made considerable spiritual progress, may have been stymied and halted because of some deep-seated fear, pride or selfishness, and therefore there was a damage to the astral form which must reoccur in life after life until it is met by commensurate compassion, self-conquest and self-modification. But the person does not know this, though somewhere deep down he or she senses it. Or

– and this is the general cause – it is the result of the gravity effect exercised by the sum-total of human weaknesses, stagnation and inertia upon anyone who, by the Light of the *Logos*, by the power of thought and the purity of sacred speech, tries, in the words of Jesus, to "Come out from among them and be ye separate." This is not easy. It is precisely when one tries to stand apart, as Arjuna found in the first chapter of the *Bhagavad Gita*, that one becomes acutely self-righteous because the weak can work through the virtues of the strong. One of the greatest causes, metaphysically, for the collective brake that eventually must work at individual levels as well, is self-righteousness. This is why the ancient teaching is, "Do not fancy you can stand aside from the bad man or the foolish man. They are yourself, though in a less degree than your friend or your master.... Therefore, remember that the soiled garment you shrink from today may have been yours yesterday, may be yours tomorrow." One cannot feel any different, any better than any being that is alive. Out of the very harshness of judgement or the ignorant attempt to separate oneself from even a Hitler, one will actually draw to oneself shadows of spiritual pride. To invoke the *Gayatri mantram* is truly to bid farewell to all self-righteousness. Self-righteousness is the illusory source of self-preservation – or what looks like it in the short run – but which in the long run is a barrier that sunders one from the whole of life.

The Voice of the Silence says, "Give up thy life, if thou would'st live." All the great Teachers have spoken in terms of eternal life versus what is thought to be life but which is really selfishness. One either lives in the immortal individuality that focusses the life of the universal or within the prison-house of the *persona*. A fundamental choice is involved in the *Gayatri* invocation and this is very much connected with the evolutionary processes of Nature. Physiologically, life is a losing race against death; every moment everyone is dying. Why, then, is there life in the physical body? Why is there homeostasis? Why is there resistance to the ocean of life and to all the forces of disintegration? This has to do with the power of cohesion, which involves the mind and its wakefulness. It involves the heart and its rhythms. But it also involves the spiritual will, an act of faith in one's purposefulness and in the meaningfulness of one's existence, in one's relevance to the human condition. To be able to find meaning and relevance from the largest standpoint, as in the *Gayatri mantram*, is from the beginning and also daily to say good-bye to ordinary conceptions of terrestrial life.

No doubt a person who intones the *Gayatri mantram* will participate in the world, will go through the duties of life, will enter into relationships that involve sharing the concerns of others with all their limitations. In this very process a pilgrim may lose the thread and become forgetful, rather like a visitor to Plato's cave, unable to penetrate through the cacophony of sounds in the dark den where the shadows have acquired exaggerated significance, unable to stand apart from the false language of success and failure, honour and dishonour, of human beings who entertain worldly perspectives. This is precisely the risk that is taken by every pilgrim who consciously incarnates for a high and holy purpose. At the same time, one must recognize that in the process of incarnation one is going to forget. In that sense, as Plato taught, the whole of life is involved with the basic problem of remembering and forgetting. How much one forgets depends upon what one cares for and chooses to remember. What one remembers at a deep level must be instructive to the levels at which one may forget. Human beings need a variety of aids, such as writing down what is true and good and beautiful, what is enduring and unconditional. Connecting ideas with events in nature, with the rhythms and cycles of day and night, of sleeping and waking, with the various seven-year cycles in life as well as the seven-day week, one may begin to discover analogies and correspondences. It is as if one is constantly cooperating with the eternal memory of Nature (enshrined in the Spiritual Sun) and always overcoming, amidst the inevitable forgetfulness, the danger of forgetting what is important. Hence the daily invocation of the *Gayatri*.

Wise disciples periodically renew the vow that they first took, continually summoning the golden moment of original awakening. If one thinks of the truest, most beautiful moment in one's life, when something was so real that one's whole being responded, it can be summoned repeatedly by the power of thought if one is not falsely convinced that it belongs to the past. Past and present have nothing to do with that which gives reality in consciousness to an idea. The individual must endow it with a sense of reality through the energy of meditation.

Human beings become prisoners of the process of change and forget that the very capacity to endow reality springs from the timeless Self in man, and its pristine light of divine wisdom. The archetypal example of this may be found in the life of the Buddha. Even so great a being as Gautama Buddha knew before he took birth that to incarnate means to participate in the ignorance, pain and delusion of the world. It is also to risk much. It is said that the Buddha, having attained enlightenment and pondering the *Bodhisattva* path, looked upon the world and thought, "All human beings are like lotuses in a pond. There are those human beings, alas, very many, who, even if I remain in the world to show them the way to enlightenment, to the Spiritual Sun, will not listen. They are mired in *maya* and so much enjoy it that they are like lotuses still caught in the wet earth at the bottom of the pond, unable to rise to the light of the sun. There are human beings who are already like lotuses that have moved to the surface of the waters, opening out to the light of the sun, and who do not need me because they are able to bloom on their own. Why, then, do I have to remain in a body? For the sake of those, whoever they be, who are struggling in *maya* but wish and will to reach upwards. They need the assurance that they can do it. And for these I shall remain." Thus the *AUM* is enacted in word and deed.

It is indeed possible to preserve an extraordinary, cool, wise, detached, discriminating and beautifully proportioned sense of purpose to one's life. The point of this compelling myth about the Buddha is that when, as Gautama, he goes through all his trials before his supreme enlightenment, when he encounters *Mahamaya*, the great tempter Mara, one of the temptations is – and it is also one of the temptations of Christ – the charge that his work will be irrelevant, that he will not succeed. Such pre-vision puts one on the plane which is above success and failure, enabling one to grasp the central logic of an incarnation. The *Bodhisattva* vow is voluntary, but because it is recorded in time, it can only do so much and no more to mitigate the sum of human misery. If there is a sufficiently long period of evolution and a sufficient number of souls, as well as many hazards and repeated failures over many lives, something like this must be true. Therefore, the wish of the *Bodhisattva* to come to the world is merely to make some small difference to the earthly scene. But what is small relative to numbers may be very great when seen in terms of time. The potent impulse released by a Buddha or a Christ twenty-five hundred or two thousand years ago is alive today and will reverberate thousands of years from now. It has a vertical dimension as well as lateral influence. It is a vibration that can be repeatedly picked up, and if it is picked up by some individuals here and there who are totally seized with it and transform themselves, then they in turn become very powerful magnets for other souls to do the same, all tapping the supreme source of strength, the Spiritual Sun.

So mysterious, then, are the currents of Karma that much of what is called living is only on the surface of existence. It is perceived in terms of years and months and days, but this has application not even to the astral but to the physical form most of the time. It does not reveal the immortal saga of the soul, its immemorial pilgrimage through space and time, linked up to myriads of souls. One's conception of life must become so different, so universal, that in relation to that larger life one can consecrate a lesser life, but not the other way around. To become ensnared in the small, in ones's micro-conception of living, is to deny oneself an openness to a larger concept of life. One can test this every day and night. Negate each day and intone the *Gayatri mantram* before going to sleep. Repeat it as many times as one can, clearly and silently, and see if one can wake up with the *mantram* as one's first thought. Do this again and again through the week to see if one really can carry the vibration through deep sleep. To be able to do this is to know what it means to overcome the barriers between lives, the illusion of *devachan*, the debris of *kama loka*, to cut through the *Mahamaya*. To be unable to do it simply means that there is a great deal in oneself that is disconnected between the highest and the lowest. Instead of wallowing in a state of despair or panic, one should persist.

The *Gayatri* invocation is an infallible means to self-transcendence. Sometimes one cannot use it as well as at other times, but even if it is not the first thought on waking, one can keep reminders for oneself. It is eventually possible to train the memory cells in every single part of each vesture, all of which have their own mode of registration, enlisting them all in the service of one's highest motivation rooted in a universal plane of creative ideation. If one partakes of daily meditation, experiencing a sense of Duration, then one can repeatedly transcend the boundaries of time and its compression into secondary causes and effects. One can let go every psychic preoccupation with external relations in visible space, and develop a deeper, noetic sense of what it is to live inwardly. Daily, replenished by the cool stream of insight that flows from the Spiritual Sun, one may actualize the *Gayatri mantram* with a deep resolve that will endure without wavering, releasing a mighty current of unacknowledged but incalculable benefit for the entire human family and indeed for all living beings.

Feeling, while going about, that he is a wave of the ocean of Self: while sitting, that he is a bead strung on the thread of universal consciousness: while perceiving objects of sense, that he is realizing himself by perceiving the Self: and, while sleeping, that he is drowned in the ocean of bliss; – he who, inwardly constant, spends his whole life thus is, among all men, the real seeker of liberation.

All this world, consisting of name and form, is only the particular manifestation (*vyashti*) of the universal Substance (*viraj*); it moves and knows all objects by virtue of the primal life (*mukhya-prana*) that inspires it. This Self like the sun, is neither the doer nor the enjoyer. Thus, directly realizing, does he that is full of knowledge and realization live his life, through incessant contemplation of the Supreme Self.

Just as the one sun, independent of other objects, yet, by virtue of reflection in several waters, becomes many and has the same stability or motion as the medium reflecting it; so does the Supreme Self seem to be affected by properties by virtue of its reflection of all beings, high and low, but, when clearly realized, shines unaffected by those properties.

The Supreme Self has three aspects, namely, the full, the self and the not-self, the first being the unconditioned Self, the second being that which is conditioned by the consciousness, and the third being a mere reflection, in the same way as space has three aspects in respect of water, namely, that which is inside and outside of the water, that which is conterminous with water, and that which is reflected therein. When the conditioned self is merged in the unconditioned, then the condition together with its consequences vanishes altogether.

Shankaracharya

Hermes, December 1979

THE DESCENT OF MANAS

Lead the life necessary for the acquisition of such knowledge and powers, and Wisdom will come to you naturally. Whenever you are able to attune your consciousness to any of the seven chords of 'Universal Consciousness,' those chords that run along the sounding-board of Kosmos, vibrating from one Eternity to another; when you have studied thoroughly 'the music of the Spheres,' then only will you become quite free to share your knowledge with those with whom it is safe to do so. Meanwhile be prudent.... Do not attempt to unveil the secret of being and non-being to those unable to see the hidden meaning of Apollo's HEPTACHORD – the lyre of the radiant god, in each of the seven strings of which dwelleth the Spirit, Soul and Astral body of the Kosmos, whose shell only has now fallen into the hands of Modern Science... Let rather the planetary chains and other super- and sub-cosmic mysteries remain a dreamland for those who can neither see, nor yet believe that others can.

The Secret Doctrine, i 167

The complex teachings concerning states and planes of consciousness, invisible globes and chains of worlds, and the evolutionary pilgrimage of monads, may be grasped through meditation upon the fundamental axiom that Law and Deity are one. It is also necessary to notice the septenary principle in terms of which the *Logos* emanates everything in manifested Nature. It must be seen at the outset that there is an essential difference between the three highest planes – belonging to the Archetypal Universe – and the four lower planes of the world of formation. The latter, along with everything that exists as a manifesting entity, comprises the various sevenfold chains of globes. Further, since virtually all human beings primarily function by using five senses appropriate only to the most material of those globes, their terrestrial eyes betray them into a needlessly narrow and restricted view of Nature and what is 'natural'. Seeing illusory forms, sharp contrasts and seeming divergences at the grossest level, the unwary experience an intense feeling of separateness and a false sense of confinement in their vestures and relationships. Given this sad predicament, a mental bridge must be consciously extended from the lower planes to the metaphysical verities which are shrouded in invisible Nature, the heavens above, and even beyond. Outside metaphysics, neither occult philosophy nor spiritual progress are possible. Only when the seed ideas of the *Gupta Vidya* are vivified through meditation and nourished by praxis can they serve as the hidden roots of an expansive consciousness delicately attuned to the deeper purposes of soul-evolution, the music of the spheres and the heartbeat of the human race.

The marriage of meditation and duty gives birth to the *Bodhisattva* ideal of renunciation through service. This is the sacred and archetypal meaning of *dhyana*, *Dharma* and *karuna*, which are all magically fused in *bodhichitta*, the jewel in the lotus, God in Man as in the cosmos. Originally anchored in the notion of "that which holds", *Dharma* is the self-sustaining factor in Nature through which self-conscious beings in a world of change are able to support themselves in the realm of action by a sublime idea common to a variety of simple tasks, and relevant to humane relationships of every sort. When the power and potency of *Dharma* are invoked through voluntary sacrifices and sacred pledges, through self-chosen obligations and consequent trials, duty becomes a self-validating principle shining by its own light, independent of anything outside it. Those alone who are unequivocally committed to *Dharma*, and who have passed through preliminary initiations, can profit from the secret teachings proffered to them. Each and every sincere aspirant on the path of duty can truly hope to discover the guiding light and sovereign talisman of selfless service. But, as a Master has intimated, if the disciple would perceive even the dim silhouette of one of the 'planets' on the higher planes, he has to first throw off the thin clouds of astral matter that stand between him and the next plane. Krishna in the *Bhagavad Gita* stressed the critical shift from a sense of duty supported by social structures to a self-consecrated conception of *Dharma*, whereby human beings are continually defining themselves and shedding the light of self-conscious thought within the radius of their obligations to others and to themselves.

Virtually all the practical difficulties encountered in the daily performance of duty – such as trivialization, routinization and staleness – may be traced to the force of habit and the hypnosis of automatism on the astral plane. Whenever one is passive, one is far from spiritually awake, and hardly functioning from a universal standpoint in the local habitations of particulars. But, if through joyous meditation one secures an elevated basis for one's emanations into the world, then one's words and actions directed toward other beings reflect a reverence for them as immortal souls. One can also help to enhance the latent self-consciousness in all the life-atoms of the seven kingdoms of Nature. Such capacities are not superogatory gifts in rare human beings at this stage in evolution, but rather basic obligations for all. Since the commencement of the Fourth Round all the lower kingdoms of Nature have vitally depended upon man for their continued development and collective evolution. The summoning of elementals into potent and creative combinations is the theurgic task of human benevolence, noetic deliberation and calm continuity of spiritual purpose. Individuals who come to understand this process will discover an ease and lightness in the pilgrimage of life that seem paradoxical to others who are burdened by a dour sense of duty. Sadly, those who are already weighted down by their own muddled misconceptions often aggravate this burden through compulsive speech, complaining about kindred souls and against life itself. Occultism begins when one ceases from all complaints, tortuous games and cowardly delay, and instead silently resolves to come to terms with the manifold karma of an incarnation. Rather than infecting and polluting the elementals of one's astral photosphere by excessive statements of intention, idle speculation and resentment of supposedly external duties, one must embrace the initially painful recognition that duty is inherent to one's status as a human being. Even a week of wise and cool reflection upon the *Dharma* of being human and potentially divine can lighten a lifetime, but those who do not even make this effort will never understand the point. On the contrary, they strangely seem to enjoy wallowing in guilt and self-pity, and thus, as they chew the cud of their ill-digested ideas and stew in the acid juices of their bitterness, they further weaken the fragile connection between the overbrooding Triad and the manifesting quaternary. Whereas, as soon as one takes a firm stand upon what is truly human, and through deep thought and meditation cuts to the core of essential self-respect and inescapable responsibility to the whole of life, one can create a passage in that aspect of *Manas* which is conjoined to the lower principles, through which the light of *Buddhi* can illumine the field of duty. Thus *Kurukshetra* becomes *Dharmakshetra*.

The criterion of whatever is genuinely Buddhic is that it is effortlessly self-sustaining. *Buddhi*, as a human principle, correlates with exalted planes of consciousness and ethereal globes of the earth chain, which are impermeable to the discontinuities of thought and feeling that inhibit terrestrial cerebration and emotion. The sense of separation and fragmentation engendered on the lowest plane weakens the will and dulls the mind by rendering the electrical connection with the immortal Triad fitful and inconstant. Spiritual will is generated by and works through seminal ideas. The more one allows the mind to soak in the sublimely abstract, until this is more real than anything else, the more one is able in a Promethean way to direct the flow of consciousness through concentrated thought. Such meditative purification strengthens the spiritual will and provides continuous inspiration in the daily performance of duty. When one becomes familiar with its cleansing effects, one will look forward to every encounter with the spiritual, and even in brief spells of leisure one's mind will naturally turn to sacred themes. Those who freely benefit from this mental discipline are truly fortunate in their simplicity of stance. Without taking anything for granted, they cherish the profound privilege of contemplating and reaffirming the fundamental principles of spiritual life. They are thereby protected against the errors of futile speculation, and against complex attempts to reconcile the irreconcilable by adapting the spiritual sciences to material conceptions. By honouring the basic rules and sharpening discernment through practice, they stay within the forward current and gain true self-respect. They recognize that the mere thought of falling away from it, through foisting blame upon the external world, rapidly destroys the sacred foundation of discipleship. Men and women, in general, may not be able all at once to live purely by the power of thought and ideation. But if even a small number of people make an honest effort to do so, lending beauty and significance to their days in the knowledge that others are doing the same, a strong magnetic field may be generated whereby weaker brethren would be held up, whilst those who build strength would not be brought down by the weakest links in the chain. Everyone could be pulled up together; there would be a proper balancing because different people experience the different cycles of moods at different times. If their minds and hearts are focussed upon the collective effort, if they feel part of and have inserted themselves into a larger whole reflecting the will and the wisdom of *Shambala*, the mighty Brotherhood of *Bodhisattvas*, then they will move in dulcet harmony with the Demiurgic Mind of the cosmos. They will taste the rapture of self-conscious participation in the Divine Motion of noumenal reality, the awesome Dance of Shiva as well as the playful sport of Krishna and the *gopis*.

To a *sadhaka* or seeker who thinks in this archetypal mode, the sole reason for skilfully performing any act in life is to render gentle and gracious service to others, to human beings as well as to life-atoms. There is, for example, no other metaphysically sound reason to clean and care for one's physical body than the duty one owes oneself as a trustee of Nature and a servant of mankind. If one grasps the idea of monadic evolution metaphysically, and not merely statistically or speculatively, it will be evident that there are myriad opportunities daily for engaging in sacrificial acts of service to others. It is the exalted privilege of a self-conscious monad to be able to serve all life-atoms through the concentrated power of compassionate thought. The humanity of the future will readily associate its healing exposure to the mellow light of the early morning sun, or its cool enjoyment of pellucid water, with a vivid awareness of invisible beings that are magically fused in a divine dance. Bringing Buddhic perception to creative acts, they will balance the antipodes of human nature, suffusing the most ordinary and simple tasks with the exhilarating fragrance of veiled serenity. Once a person becomes adept in this art of service, the whole of life becomes a song of ceaseless and silent sacrifice, the true 'music of the spheres' intimating the mystery of Apollo's lyre. A point is soon reached at which one can scarcely believe that one could waste a single hour brooding over the shadowy self, though one will recognize that this is precisely what one did in life after life of ignorance, even in the presence of the Divine Wisdom and its loving exemplars. Then one will appreciate what the wise have always taught, that anyone who misuses, let alone flouts and betrays, a great opportunity, will not in any future life be able to come into a close relationship with any Spiritual Teacher. Where such laws are involved, nothing happens merely for the first time; whenever the karma of groups of people sharing abnormal tendencies brings them together in order to work them off, these tendencies will be made to look normal. The souls concerned may, when they are brought together, actually convert their condition into a general theory of the world, thus reinforcing and absolutizing their abject ignorance. Then, for those who toil for the restoration of the rhythms that are natural to the human heart, there is what a Master called "uphill work and swimming *in adversum flumen*". He asked, "Why should the West... learn...from the East...that which can never meet the requirements of the special tastes of the aesthetics?" He then spoke of "the formidable difficulties encountered by us in every attempt we make to explain our metaphysics to the Western mind". Stressing the intimate connection between occult philosophy and true metaphysics, H.P. Blavatsky conceded:

> It is like trying to explain the aspirations and affections, the love and the hatred, the most private and sacred workings in the soul and mind of the living man, by an anatomical description of the chest and brain of his dead body.

The Secret Doctrine, i 169-170

The arcane teachings of the sevenfold nature of the earth and Man are not offered for the sake of those who would "nail every shadow to the wall". Nor are they intended to be reconciled with the conceptions of a modern science which cannot acknowledge any matter except that which falls under the purview of the corporeal senses. The esoteric teaching regarding septenary chains is intended for those who are dedicated to the sacrificial awakening of spiritual intuition in the service of all, and those who are prepared to make Buddhic application of Divine Wisdom in daily life.

For example, it is the enigmatic teaching of *The Secret Doctrine* that the moon which is seen by the physical eye is a corpse, and that this moon, together with all the physical planets, is visible in this way only because it belongs to a particular plane of perception. But if each visible world is part of a chain and there are six invisible globes which are involved in the causal forces associated with each planet, it is important especially to understand the relation between the moon and the earth. This is analogous to the relationship between the astral when it is saturated by *kama* and that aspect of the astral which is ensouled by *prana*, or life-energy. We often notice that a mentally healthy individual is full of life and therefore very cheerful and generous, reaching out to others, due to this natural energy within the astral-physical body, the energy of *prana*. But there is also that aspect of the astral which is affected by lunar forces, by obsessional thoughts, and yet is constantly fluctuating like the visible moon. What is going on within the human being is causally connected with the relations between the different invisible aspects of the visible planets. The moon, as the ancients knew, is much older than the earth, being but the visible remnant of an entire chain of globes that was the parent of the earth chain. And therefore even though what we see as the visible moon does not look, certainly unlike the sun, to be a parent of the earth, nonetheless what we see is the representative of the corpse, the *kama rupa* of an entire lunar chain of globes, the higher principles of which have long since passed into the earth chain. Beings on earth have astral forms because these vestures are themselves the progeny of the lesser *pitris*, the lunar ancestors. As the lunar chain was dying out in its last Round, it sent all its energy and 'principles' into a neutral centre of latent force, a *laya* centre, thereby informing a new nucleus of undifferentiated substance and calling it to active life. The lunar ancestors are also connected with the ancestral germ that was transmitted over an immense period of time and makes even physical conception possible. Metaphysically, everything physical is actually astral, so the process of conception has its roots in aspects of astral form, matter and substance which go back to the lunar *pitris*. Therefore there is a direct sense in which terrestrial humans are able to function as sevenfold beings only because of this inheritance, which is a mixed blessing.

Because many human beings have identified with their physical bodies despite the fact that they are self-conscious beings, they have forgotten both their divine inheritance and their myriad debts, even on the physical plane, to those who went before. While some older cultures may have been preoccupied with ancestor worship, modern societies are almost blind to what they owe to the lunar *pitris*. If they were true to this inheritance, they would have a greater grasp of the right use of all the senses, because these would all be recognized as vital powers, the reflections of divine potencies upon the astral plane. This would bring a sense of the sacred to the use of sight, hearing, taste, smell and touch. Instead, there is constant abuse of all the sense-perceptions and therefore there is a sense in which people are vampirizing the lunar *pitris*, living upon them without acknowledgement, misusing the energies derived from them. This neglect of duty entails a costly vulnerability to the *kama rupa* of the moon which goes through its own cyclical changes, appearing on the physical plane as the waxing and waning of the physical moon in its mutual relations with the sun and earth. Behind this visible process lies a whole set of disintegrating tendencies which were discarded as unusable from an earlier period of evolution, but which exercise a powerful negative effect upon those vulnerable to them through the misuse of their own energies.

Such people are recognizable by their appalling lack of natural gratitude. The idea that all life is an expression of gratitude through service and duty, which is entirely natural to solar beings, seems strange to them because it brings back bad memories of base ingratitude in other lives. Familiar with gratitude merely as a passing emotion, they can hardly resonate to Pliny's teaching that the whole earth is a kind nurse and mother to mankind, and its elements are not at all inimical to mortals. Their moral and spiritual deficiency goes back to the lost continent of Atlantis, wherein they were engrossed in utilizing spiritual knowledge for the sake of self-aggrandisement. As a result, there was enormous damage to the Third Eye, which then closed. Therefore they now experience a technical difficulty in being intuitive, as well as in conserving, consolidating or controlling astral tendencies. Owing to their alienation from their spiritual heritage through the astral damage they have done to themselves, they tend to concoct theories which purport to disprove the possibility or use of any metaphysical intuition at all in the human race. Meanwhile, they remain subject to the affinities they have formed with classes of elementals, shells and elementaries, and hence to the sullen state of depressed consciousness that is their inescapable karma. What they must learn, and what their karma affords them the opportunity to learn, is that they exist solely for the sake of reaching out to something larger than themselves. If through the initially painful recognition of their own awesome responsibility and austere duty they learn this lesson, it will work to the long-term good of the soul. But if they indulge and engage in this perverse and cyclical state of mind, they are only prolonging the karma that goes back to other lives.

Individuals must one day come to see that in a universe of Law all human qualities are connected with cosmic sources and forces. Nothing is accidental. A person cannot be a silent worshipper of the Spiritual Sun and cannot constantly think of it without always being full of optimism and benevolence. On the other hand, one cannot be caught in the meshes of cynicism and pessimism without having connected oneself to the dark side of the moon through *adharma* and the persistent misuse of powers. In *Kali Yuga* there are many such souls, and though they desperately need help, and do not know how to help themselves, they try to lay down the conditions of life for all. Harming and even destroying each other in their ignorance, they use up human bodies, and in extreme cases through annihilation there is a compassionate release of the immortal Triad altogether from the astral form so that another cycle of incarnations may be initiated by the Triad. The soulless shell that is left behind is dominated by the perverse energies of the tortuous mind, and only dissipates after it goes through a terrible torment. Long before this extreme condition, there are warnings and whispers by the divine Triad, and if these last chances are taken promptly, there can be a gradual restoration. If they are not taken they may be given again, though each time the signals will be fainter. But if they are repeatedly flouted, doom is inevitable. Seen in this light, much that goes on in human life in the name of rationalizations and ideologies, much that is repeated again and again as a form of inefficient self-hypnosis, amounts to nothing but a pathetic and soul-destroying denial of the meaning and justice of life. If people persist in this despite abundant evidence to the contrary, they are only rendering irreversible their own passage down the lunar path of self-destruction. In the presence of the solar light everything is rapidly intensified. If one receives and becomes a sacrificial user of the life-giving current of the wisdom, at whatever level, this is sane. Every authentic effort counts. It is not so important to take a constant inventory of where one comes out; what is vital is the refusal to give up on the effort and the steadfast will to maintain a strong line of courageous conviction, inserting oneself into a larger and larger perspective. If one does not do this, one will accentuate the opposite tendencies. Such is the nature of light. In the presence of light-energy the dark will necessarily be activated, and all the ghouls and vampires, all the nefarious elements connected with doomed sorcerers, will deposit themselves in the astral corpus, the *linga sharira*. Truly, it is for the sake of all souls that such occult teachings as the correspondences of human principles and planetary globes are given out, not for the amusement of dilettantes or the derision of scoffers.

'Gratification of curiosity is the end of knowledge for some men,' was said by Bacon, who was as right in postulating this truism, as those who were familiar with it before him were right in hedging off WISDOM from Knowledge, and tracing limits to that which is to be given out at one time... Remember:

..... knowledge dwells
In heads replete with thoughts of other men,
Wisdom in minds attentive to their own . . .

The Secret Doctrine, i 165

The mind that is able to absorb Divine Wisdom is itself an inherently pure substance which can reflect the light of Spirit. But when it is continually used in association with the voracious sense-organs of an astral form chained to a physical body, in order to feed the appetites, the desires, the fancies and the tyrannical will of the boisterous elements that make up the *persona*, the mind gravitates downwards. This may be called the lunar activity of the mind, whereas when the mind draws upwards to the Spirit, it is solar. When the mind ascends towards the Spiritual Sun, becoming itself a great luminous globe close to the causal realm, this is the mysterious sacrifice of *Manas*. Also, because *Manas* has come down one plane there is acute awareness and imperious intelligence in the fickle world of materiality. Hence there is a solemn responsibility for all thoughts and sensory consciousness in a world of contrast, differentiation and moral choice. Because of the descent of *Manas* down one plane, all life is ethical, therapeutic and probationary, from the impartial standpoint of the immortal soul. The test of being truly human is to see everything as involving ethical issues. The moment one starts to see all life as fraught with extremely complex choices which invoke the highest and profoundest morality that is concerned with soul-evolution, linking consciousness with motive and the welfare of every single soul in its pilgrimage, one discovers an exalted concept of ethical sensitivity, far superior to the ersatz notions of right and wrong in conventional morals. At best, these *dicta* embody worldly wisdom based on the past, and are only able to support social expediency and, occasionally, certain good habits. True morality involves the direction, either upward or downward, that is given to every single life-atom. Its enormous scope encompasses the vast sweep of the Root Races of humanity, which "commence with the Ethereal and end with the spiritual on the double line of physical and moral evolution – from the beginning of the terrestrial round to its close." The moral task of the immortal soul summons it in a great sacrifice, for it takes the daunting risk of descent into a restricting vesture of clay. Its awareness is lent in the direction of differentiation and disunity, the direction of potential death through discord, doubt and despair. This materialization of the spiritual energies belonging to mind takes place macrocosmically and microcosmically, involving both the principles of sevenfold man and the globes of the planetary chain."...it is a case of descent into matter, the adjustment – in both the mystic and physical senses – of the two, and their interblending for the great coming 'struggle of life' that awaits both entities."

Dynamically, only the *Atman* and *Buddhi* are of the spiritual plane because they have an eternally self-sustaining light-energy. The *Atman* is in perpetual motion and *Buddhi* is the diffused but indestructible light of the *Atman*. *Atman* and *Buddhi* do not typically incarnate in human beings. If they did, human beings would be gods. But before human beings can become gods, they must become heroes. For them to become heroes they must enter the thought-sphere of *Manas* and elevate it towards higher altitudes. This is what the Buddha meant by dictating terms to the mind, made captive through craving to the world-illusion. In this paradigmatically human arena most testing takes place on a plane that is invisible to the *persona*. As a result, people without a sense of morality rooted in *Manas* suppose that they are not being tested, or that they can get away with mental dishonesty and sanctimonious hypocrisy. But if, as in Edward Bellamy's strange story, all human beings were endowed with telepathy, there would be a quick ending to furtiveness and religiosity since all particularized thoughts would be instantly known to all. No doubt there would be deeper secrets locked up in *Atma-Buddhi* – but there would be a much purer mode of communication because a great deal of the humbug masquerading behind the mask of self-righteousness would be transparent. There would be no room for deceptive facades and moral evasion. This is only a pale anticipation of the state of consciousness of civilizations yet far in the future, in the Fifth and the Sixth Rounds, when the state of consciousness would be so exalted, that beings enigmatically referred to as Sixth Rounders like the Buddha or Shankara, or Fifth Rounders like Plato and Confucius, would represent the average of those future humanities. The entry of such beings into the Fourth Round, like raindrops that presage the monsoon, must remain mysterious. Such beings speak in terms of experience concerning invisible realities, using language to intimate and evoke latent perceptions in human beings who, even in the Fourth Round, have not taken full advantage of the Fifth Race, which is archetypally characterized by pure thought. Rationality and reason in the best sense constantly look for universality and effortlessly practise the Golden Rule, never expecting of another what one dare not expect of oneself, always putting oneself to the test and eschewing all negative judgement of others. By these criteria, many human beings have fallen below the potential of the fifth sub-race of the Fifth Root Race of the Fourth Round, and behind even the powers of thought of its first sub-race. This abnormally retarded condition is quite independent of *Kali Yuga*, and goes back to the fourth sub-race as well as to the Fourth Root Race. It is a strong persistent shadow which again and again obscures a variety of individuals. An individual may make progress in three lives upon the Path and may have the good fortune to be in the presence of Teachers and co-disciples whose consciousness is naturally magnanimous, and who naturally represent the graces of the Golden Age. But the fourth time around this individual could be pursued by the dweller on the threshold, by the conglomeration of all the terrible tendencies which had not been worked out and which go back to an earlier incarnation. When it comes, it has to be faced, and the light of Spirit must be heroically reaffirmed in the midst of the worldly maelstrom.

Manasic or ethical evolution rests on a fundamental distinction between what is self-sustaining, enduring and indestructible in the spiritual realm, and what is changing, evanescent and discontinuous in the material realm. Because of the downward movement of thought from the spiritual plane into the material plane and upward back to the spiritual plane, there is a constant possibility of the crass materializing of the spiritual, the effete etherealizing of the material. When a human being wakes up to the practical and profound alchemical implications of the metaphysical teaching that every moment one has the opportunity either to choose ethereal and refined conceptions or the opposite, then the doctrine of the seven globes comes alive. One can take even the most worldly material events and lend them beauty, significance and meaning from the standpoint of the immortal soul through the power of Manasic consecration. For the noetic mind it is natural even to take the most trivial subject and to give it a deeper meaning, whereas the mind caught in the blind toils of *kama* can take even sacred themes and constantly concretize them. Those who understand what is really at stake and who begin to reflect upon etherealization versus concretization could then look at their feelings, their thoughts, and particularly their words, to find out how much they are raising consciousness and how often they are lowering it. The tone of voice becomes important; the light in the eyes becomes relevant; one's first thought on waking and one's last thought before speaking become valuable tests. When the spiritual life becomes real in these ways, life itself is transformed, enriched, elevated, even beatified.

H.P. Blavatsky urges, as do the *Mahatmas*, that people become aware of these tendencies. Again and again the Masters of the East have written with great pain about the difficulty of teaching spiritual wisdom to a materialistic age because of the constant danger of over-categorization, over-definition and concretization, which are real dangers that affect what happens to the Teachings. While some of this is due to materialization of terms, obscuring the meanings behind the veil of words, the real problem is in consciousness, not language. The difference in the end is between Wisdom and knowledge, between the Sun and the planets, between the *Atman* and the other principles. Without the Soul Science, *Gupta Vidya*, the Secret Wisdom, the *Atma-Vidya*, true Spiritual and Divine Wisdom, all the other facets of occult knowledge will be useless. They will merely become mechanical activities, mixed up with psychic fantasy. Although they may increase the operation of instinctual behaviour, and be often mistaken for the spiritual, they will have little to do with the spiritual, least of all with fully self-conscious spiritual impulses.

> Without the help of *Atma-Vidya*, the other three remain no better than surface sciences, geometrical magnitudes having length and breadth, but no thickness. They are like the soul, limbs, and mind

of a sleeping man: capable of mechanical motions, of chaotic dreams and even sleep-walking, of producing visible effects, but stimulated by instinctual not intellectual causes, least of all by fully conscious spiritual impulses.

The Secret Doctrine, i 169

The great danger is that if one is caught up in the exoteric form of the esoteric teaching, through lack of meditation, inattention to duty, and insufficient assimilation of the ideal of sacrifice rooted in metaphysical understanding, one will merely activate a lunar astral form and generate the *kama rupa* of a disciple. In other words, everything will become merely the mimetics of mechanical motions. On the other hand, if one is truly in search of the immortal soul, viewing spiritual realities and seminal ideas as one's true invisible companions, then one will be constantly probing into the hidden depths of one's own nature in silence with calmness, serenity, contentment and cheerfulness. One will deepen and strengthen whatever elements of these qualities one can already find within, always putting the onus upon oneself, and never on the side of others or on the side of discontent, psychic noise and petulant complaint. The sovereign responsibility and golden opportunity in the use of this teaching are great because if it is applied in earnest each day, it will infallibly deepen all one's perceptions. Seeing beyond the outer surface of terrestrial life to the inmost depths of every other human soul, one will truly become a friend and a helper of the entire human race.

Hermes, October 1980

ATMA VIDYA

Just as milliards of bright sparks dance on the waters of an ocean above which one and the same moon is shining, so our evanescent personalities – the illusive envelopes of the immortal MONAD-EGO – twinkle and dance on the waves of Maya. They last and appear, as the thousands of sparks produced by the moon-beams, only so long as the Queen of the Night radiates her lustre on the running waters of life: the period of a Manvantara; and then they disappear, the beams – symbols of our eternal Spiritual Egos – alone surviving, re-merged in, and being, as they were before, one with the Mother-Source.

The Secret Doctrine, i 237

Late in the nineteenth century the *Maha Chohan* spoke of the great dual principles, right and wrong, good and evil, liberty and despotism, pain and pleasure, egotism and altruism. Pointing to the degraded moral condition of the world and particularly of its so-called civilized races, he declared that this sad plight is *prima facie* evidence of religious and philosophic bankruptcy. The intervening century, with its virtually unrelieved record of bloodshed and cruelty, should have clearly demonstrated that the dark forces of superstition – disguised as nationalism, ideology and racism – and materialism, with its sterile promise of technocratic utopias, obscure the pathway to adequate explanations and effective solutions to fundamental problems. Insoluble though these may appear, and although the world may seem to be locked in its "mad career towards the unknown", especially to those who are dazed and numbed by the spectacle, this is a time of immense opportunities for courageous individuals who aspire to constitute themselves as creative pioneers of the civilization of the future. As in the classic Tale of Two Cities, it is the best of times and the worst of times. For each person today the critical difference turns upon whether one chooses the standpoint of *Shamballa* or that of *Myalba*. Either one learns to trace the eternal beam of the spiritual Ego back to its invisible seat in the Atmic Sun, and thereby perceives the sacred and sacrificial purpose of personal existence – twinkling and dancing on the running waters of life – or one is swept away in the stormy sea of human life. Whilst every perceptive person must develop the Manasic determination and Buddhic insight to attain reunion with the Divine Monad, all souls must fully insert themselves into the mighty currents of cosmic and human evolution.

Over five thousand years ago, Krishna gave the profound and potent teaching that all the pairs of opposites are relative to each other. From the standpoint of abstract and absolute Unity, the entire world is seen as an interplay and interpenetration of various grades and degrees of light and shadow. What is stated archetypally in the *Bhagavad Gita* in terms of light and dark is also pertinent to all the dualities of physical, psychic and mental existence. This applies not only to sensuous states of matter and correlative states of consciousness, but also to consciousness and matter on all the seven planes. Hence, one may speak of sound and silence, light and darkness, existing entirely outside the average range and sector of rates of vibration apprehended by ordinary sensation. Unfortunately, most people are far from fully using even their physical senses. Consider the human eye. It is an extraordinary instrument, a divine gift, capable of seeing objects but a few inches away and also able to view the distant stars and galaxies. This tremendous elasticity of the human power of vision intimates what the mystics speak of as spiritual vision and the spiritual eye. It is as a seer and perceiver that each human being is a truly self-conscious, Manasic being capable of infinite extension of the power of vision from the highest transcendental realms to the most concrete regions of sensuous existence. Therefore, the first step in meta-psychology, the effective transcendence of the pairs of opposites, is to cognize the immanent reality of the immortal soul, the *Atma*-Buddhic Monad.

The *psyche* is merely the projected ray of the divine Monad. As the Monad functions on a plane of space and time removed from that which is customarily apprehended by the *psyche*, the Monad is only partially incarnated. If it were not incarnated at all, human existence would be impossible. One might visualize *Atma-Buddhi-Manas* as being above one's head, with a pristine ray of light – which would be *Buddhi* – entering the head and passing through the brain, through the spinal cord and down to the feet. This would be a graphic way of representing the metaphysical truth that the human being is overbrooded from head to toe by the imperishable Monad. The Fohatic current pictured as passing into the body from above would be the radiation of *Manas*. This downward current of reflected *Manas* mingles with the mixed energy-currents flowing through the astral vesture. Just as blood circulates in the physical body, there are electric and magnetic currents flowing in the *linga sarira*. These astral currents are insipid in comparison to the intense levels of energy generated by pure Manasic ideation. *Manas* may be understood as the essential ability to separate oneself, through self-consciousness, from the hooking-points in the astral vesture. The process of regaining access to the higher energy fields of the Monad is accomplished through abstraction, withdrawal and detachment from the field of the self-cancelling pairs of opposites on the plane of the senses.

When in meditation one assumes the standpoint of the *Mahat-Atman*, the spectator without a spectacle, one shuts out the light of the illusory physical world with all its seemingly separate subjects and objects. When these recede into the darkness of the Void, one may picture a point. That point can be transformed into a triangle, analogous to the cosmic Monad, which then expands continuously and scatters triadic sparks which scintillate throughout the invisible universe. These sparks, streaming forth like rays from a single source, may be seen to be reflected in the underworld of dense matter, the dungeon or cave of terrestrial existence, wherein they seem to be like sun sparks scattered through the leaves of a tree. Between the billions upon billions of leaves of the World Tree, there are scattered myriads of sparks of brilliant light. These points of illumination are the noetic intimations to be found in every religion, philosophy and science, every civilization and culture, of the divine inheritance of humanity. Scattered throughout the great gallery of nature and scintillating in what Shakespeare called "the book and volume of my brain", they are but a partial screening and panoramic reflection of the electromagnetic activity of the cosmic brain. Great as is this central source of cosmic illumination which enormously surpasses human conception, it is still minute in comparison to the transcendental sources of noumenal light that are hidden in the Divine Darkness beyond the infinite *Kosmos*.

Given this possibility of initially apprehending the vital relationship between human existence and the infinite universe, one may begin to comprehend Universal Good (the *Agathon*) in terms of the sacrificial circulation and return of the life essence to its invisible source, continually sifting what is needed by the immortal Monad and casting off the rest for appropriate redistribution amongst the lower kingdoms of nature. Evil is that which consolidates and which refuses to acknowledge the source. In terms of the relativity of opposites, evil is that which obscures the light, whilst good is that which transmits the light. The highest good is self-luminous. Light and obscuration exist at many different levels and in a great variety of modes. For example, one might simply pass one's hand in front of a candle, blocking its light. Or one might observe an eclipse of the sun or of the moon. During an eclipse, as astronomers know, nothing really happens. It is only because of the relative positions of the sun, earth and moon from the standpoint of the observer that there appears to be an eclipse. It is all mayavic. The relative modes of movement of the observer and the objects create the appearance of obscuration. Similarly, an eclipse of the sun or of the moon may seem good or evil, depending upon one's perspective and point of view. H.P. Blavatsky pointed out that if the homogeneity of the one Absolute is accepted, then one must also accept in the realm of the heterogeneous that good and evil are twin offshoots of the same trunk of the Tree of Being. If one does not accept this, then one is committed to the absurdity of believing in two eternal absolutes.

> Indeed, evil is but an antagonizing blind force in nature; it is reaction, opposition, and contrast – evil for some, good for others.

> There is no *malum in se*: only the shadow of light, without which light
> could have no existence, even in our perceptions.... There would be no
> life possible (in the Mayavic sense) without Death, nor regeneration
> and reconstruction without destruction.... On the manifested planes,
> one equilibrates the other.
>
> *The Secret Doctrine*, i 413-414

For a truly fundamental understanding of good and evil, along
with all the other pairs of objective opposites, one must turn to the
quintessential distinction between the manifest and the unmanifest. This
distinction is a modern formulation of that drawn by Shankaracharya
between the Real and the unreal. Given the relationship between the
good and inward acknowledgement of the source of illumination, it
is significant that Shankaracharya, when expounding the Teaching
concerning the Real and the unreal, invokes the Upanishadic sages
and their revelation of the Path leading from death to immortality.
As Shankaracharya explicitly states, there can be no realization of the
Atman and its unity with *Brahman* apart from a reverential and grateful
recognition of predecessors and preceptors. It is only when one realizes
the true meaning of the posture of authentic humility, assumed by even
so great an Initiate as Shankaracharya in relation to the ancient *Rishis*,
that one may begin to understand the unwisdom of the modern age.
The ingratitude of latter-day Europeans towards Islamic scholars who
transmitted the teachings of the classical world, the earlier ingratitude
of Christian theologians towards the children of Israel, and the even
earlier instances of ingratitude between Greece and Egypt, between
Egypt and Chaldea, between Chaldea and India, and between Brahmins
and the Buddha, have all left a heavy burden of unacknowledged debts
which contribute to the moral bankruptcy of the modern age. The sad
consequences of this spiritual ingratitude are to be discerned in the
moral blindness of contemporary society, in the restrictiveness of its
range of vision, so that the succession of events is seen as a random
series of amoral happenings.

As long as the inward spiritual senses of man – *Buddhi* and *Manas*

– remain obscured, karma must appear mayavic in the realm of physical space and time, whilst life itself seems to be largely meaningless. Real meaning in human life can only be regained by lifting the horizon of consciousness above the level of secondary causes and effects. This can only be done by rising to the Causeless Cause, *Nada Brahman*, the Light and Sound of the *Logos* identical with the Wisdom Religion (*Brahma Vach*), even beyond the Soundless Sound. The Soundless Sound is rather like a serene ripple upon the boundless ocean of space. It is sacred because in its boundlessness it reverberates to the silent breathing of That, which is beyond all categories of space, time, causality and motion, and which transcends all incarnated conceptions of the true and the false, of good and evil, the meretricious and the plausible, the beautiful and the ugly. The arduous ascent from the manifest to the unmanifest, from the unreal to the Real, cannot take place without the aid and guidance of the *Guru*, and hence it is taught that outside the portals of Initiation the wings of ratiocinative thought must forever remain clipped. "Thus far and no further" is the story of human endeavour. Human beings live on tiny hillocks in space and time in comparison with the mighty Himalayas where Masters of Meditation reside, or with Mount Kailas, the abode of Shiva, the *Maha Yogin*. Nonetheless, there is an imperfect analogy between every tiny hill and the Himalayas , and any increment of detached calm and meditative elevation that an individual can achieve is helpful in attempting to go beyond all concretizations and constant thraldom to the pairs of opposites. Each genuine effort towards meditation undertaken in a spirit of devotion and sacrificial service can aid in the discovery of the *sanctum sanctorum* in the temple of the human form, hidden in the depths of the spiritual heart.

The complex human form represents a matrix of polarities and interconnections, all of which are subordinated to the overbrooding *Atman* which is beyond all polarity or hint of heterogeneity. Just as there is a north and south pole to the earth, there is also a north and south pole to the body. There is also a polarity of the astral vesture and, most important, a polarity of the mind (*manomaya kosha*). At one level the reflective *Manas* stands as a moon towards the sun above it, whilst at another level higher *Manas* stands as the sun in relation to lower *Manas* or the lunar mind. Good is that which is pleasing to the *Krishna-Ishwara* within. In the heart of every human being there is a ray of Krishna, programming the possibilities for that soul during incarnated existence and for its participation in all the three worlds. There is no being in any of the worlds which entirely lacks the possibility of entering into the realm of light, and not a single person can wholly avoid participation in the darkness of *moha*, delusion, of *maya*, illusion, and of *kama*, *krodha* and *lobha*, desire, anger and greed. This is represented in Buddhist iconography by elaborate *tankas* which display the vast array of archetypal and collective human faults surrounding samsaric existence. Early in the *Gita*, Krishna speaks of the omnipresent obscuring power of *rajo-gunam*, the common enemy of humanity, that which leads the best of persons to lose their firm foothold in the realm of the Divine. This progenitor of evil operates upon the mind which, as a dynamic field, may be seen to manifest a positive and negative polarity, together with a third intermediate factor. By placing *rajas* on one side and *tamas* on the other, with *sattva* in the middle, like the central column in the Kabalistic tree of life, one may picture everything below a certain plane as a continual alternation of *rajas* and *tamas*, activity and inertia. But this cannot take place without a nodal equilibrium point in between, which is called a *laya* centre, a motionless point.

If one considers a child's top spinning on the ground, there must be a motionless point where the spindle of the top touches the ground and also a motionless point at the crown of the spinning top. These two points, however, only exist because one has already assumed the reality of the spinning top, but, as Shankaracharya teaches, such reification of objective forms is merely a superimposition. Ultimately there is nothing 'going on'. There is only the mayavic appearance of the spinning top. Similarly, in the region of appearances there seems to be a great deal going on in the periodic alternations and movements of the polarities within the human principles as they revolve and rotate in and around *laya* centres in the human constitution. In contrast to this complicated and chaotic realm of events, every human being experiences in deep sleep a state of consciousness which is simply not remembered in terms of the succession of so-called events. Ordinarily, because they are so immersed in the outward flux of temporal events, human beings find it exceedingly difficult to recall or recover the state of consciousness they experienced in deep sleep, and it seems to be a blank. It is, therefore, a helpful preliminary discipline and a salutary spiritual practice to prepare oneself for sleep each night by meditation, by study of sacred texts and by directing the mind deliberately and self-consciously towards the unmanifest. Here one can test oneself by seeing whether the last thought one ponders, however briefly, before passing into sleep can be made the first thought that one entertains upon returning from sleep to wakefulness.

In this effort to reverse the polarity of the mind, changing it from involvement with concrete manifest particulars to immersion in the unmanifest universal *Atman*, the attention should not cling to the content of particular thoughts. All thoughts are relative. They are affected by the peculiar condition of one's physical and astral bodies as well as by the state and subprinciples of one's personal and higher mind. Hence it is helpful to pursue the path of negation embodied in the *mantram* 'Neti, Neti'. One can deliberately affirm that one is not the body or brain, not one's likes or dislikes, not one's friends or so-called enemies, not the various sense-perceptions, and not one's lower mind or *kama*. One should not merely say these things to oneself but actually think them, withdrawing consciousness from each successive element and voiding a series of connections with form. In a sense, this is like switching off a series of lights. Here technology mirrors what is possible in consciousness – the actual process of disengaging from the astral form through the power of self-consciousness. Through this withdrawal from the transitory connections one has apparently established with the lower principles, one can ascend through them, but this must be done calmly whilst wide awake.

One must familiarize oneself with this internal mountain climbing because otherwise one is liable to get hurt, to stumble and fall, and then it will become very difficult to pick oneself up and begin the ascent again. It is, naturally, unavoidable that over eighteen million years almost everyone has become dizzy and fallen repeatedly. This gives an important clue to the corruption of consciousness that takes place through rationalization and myriad excuses for spiritual failure. This is the fertile source of evil. The moment one rationalizes and justifies one's failings, one is spiritually stymied during that incarnation. But if one is willing to let go of pride and see things for what they are, recognizing the agencies at play, then one may take full responsibility for oneself and for the entire kingdom of elemental beings that constitute one's vestures. One must be willing to take responsibility for what happened over millions of years and also for the strong likelihood that one has taken spiritual vows in past lives. This must necessarily have great consequences for oneself, particularly if one is so privileged as to contact the Teachings of the *Mahatmas* in this life. The more deeply one thinks about this, the more clearly one will come to understand that one's life up to the present time and indeed every day that one lives is largely a re-enactment of everything that one has done over past lives.

Once one begins to initiate the process of Manasic withdrawal, one will rapidly discover that much of the cacophony and noise of the outer world is a pathetic and perverse degradation of the sacred. This lack of silence, which is equivalent to a loss of reverence for the sacred power of speech, is the result of human beings attempting to run away from their own karma. Inevitably it leads to a desecration of the earth and of nature and the arousing of hosts of angry elementals which congregate in every wasteland abandoned by human failures. Like the *djinn* of the desert that hover above the sites of buried cities, they inspire nervousness and fear in all those who pass by. The desire for revenge in the elementals is so intense because the devastation of the earth through the misuse of human powers has gone on for so long and has not been acknowledged or corrected. In response to this agitation many people develop a kind of a death-wish because their lives are devoid of meaning and they themselves have become empty vessels. Being afraid of death, whilst not knowing how to live, they end up game-playing, producing more noise and further obscuring the light of spirit. In the face of this restlessness and ennui, one must learn to preserve silence whilst coolly performing one's duty.

One must learn to set a good example by concentrating upon one's work, by exemplifying calm concentration, and by generating a true spirit of friendliness rooted in the depths of one's heart. One should render help when possible and also point out the source for further help. Through the grace of compassion one must remove the dryness and stiffness of one's own nature, but one should not become engrossed in compensatory reaching out to others which is only a mask for inadequate meditation. One must learn to restore a deeper spiritual breathing in one's mind and in one's actions. Generally in the realm of speech and conduct, "less is more" is the *mantram* that one needs to apply. "Bigger is always better" is an Atlantean mode of thought which is enraptured by excess and sheer bulk and considerations of quantity rather than quality. It is impossible to avoid the world of illusion, but one should learn to practise self-chosen ascetic disciplines lest one become a slave to the stomach, or subject to all forms of physiological, psychological, mental and spiritual indigestion, through lack of proper assimilation.

What may be seen from one side as an ascetic withdrawal from noisy and habitual involvement in the pairs of opposites on the psychological and sensory planes may be seen from the other side as learning the magical enactment of the *AUM*. The *Uttara Gita* hints that just as there is an archetypal polarity between the spiritual, immovable mind and the sensuous, movable mind, there is also a vital difference between noisy, uttered speech and the sacred and silent power of noiseless speech which invokes *Sarasvati-Vach*. The text also depicts the operation of the various vital winds or breaths passing as currents through the human form in their relation to the seven senses spoken of as priests or *hotris*. In essence, every action has sacrificial import and meaning but this can only be properly grasped when one abandons all concretized and exteriorized theories of value and adopts the cosmic perspective of universal sacrifice – *Adhiyajna*. Owing to mechanistic and instrumental theories of value, which are the bane of all institutions and societies, a false dichotomy arises between creators and consumers of value. In truth, human beings need to learn that all must equally share in universal modes of sacrifice.

Whilst individuals will vary in the roles and degrees through which they participate in sacrifice, each can strengthen his or her own sense of the sacred in every duty performed. Each must harmonize and modulate the rates of mental breathing by adjusting the ratio of the unmanifest to the manifest in everyday consciousness. At a minimum, everyone must try. This is a take-it-or-leave-it proposition with regard to the life of the sacred. The amount of progress made is much less important than the regularity and persistence of the effort. As in the Buddhist metaphor of the filling of the jar, what is most important is that drops of clean water actually fall into the jar. As one collects in one's vessel what *The Voice of the Silence* calls 'heaven's dew drops', the Real will displace the unreal and one will become prepared for the time when "night cometh and no man shall work". It is self-evident that one can only come to experience the waters of compassion through enacting the Word with the motivation of selfless love towards all, even those who are ensnared in their own failures. There must be no desire to discover some Noah's Ark of salvation for oneself but rather a willingness to use every opportunity in life to be a messenger of goodwill and a witness to the wisdom one has received freely from within. If one would not be caught in the mad rush of those who are like the gathering swine in the *New Testament*, one must understand that every golden moment of new beginnings for oneself must be self-consciously transformed into a deepened spirit of dedication to the welfare of all, *Lokasangraha*.

As one patiently perseveres in 'the divine discipline' of enacting the *AUM* in deeds, one may receive timely intimations of the vast perspective of the Army of the Voice, the Host of the *Logos*. Remaining above the plane of immanent, relative polarities, they see the essential core of everything. They are *Tattvajnanis* – those who see the essence of each of the *tattvas*. They are *Brahmajnanis* – those who see *Brahman* in every atom and being. They are *Atmajnanis* – those who see by the light of the manifested *Logos*, sometimes called *Ishwara*, and its mirroring in *Atman*, although one cannot separate the two. Terms like 'mirroring' and even 'light' can be misleading when referring to a plane of primordial matter or homogeneity wherein there is hardly any difference between subjectivity and objectivity. Having awakened the three highest centres of human consciousness, and also attuned the corresponding states to the three *arupa* planes in *Kosmos*, they have become Masters of *Atma Vidya*. Having realized the mystic bond of Being and Non-Being within the depths of their own unmanifest Self, they stand as luminous witnesses to the nobility and promise of human endeavour. Established within the circle of boundless light, they are able to perceive the metaphysical origins of human suffering and strife. H.P. Blavatsky depicts the impersonal nature of the problem:

> In human nature, evil denotes only the polarity of matter and Spirit, a struggle for life between the two manifested Principles in Space and Time, which principles are one *per se*, inasmuch as they are rooted in the Absolute. In *Kosmos*, the equilibrium must be preserved. The operations of the two contraries produce harmony, like the centripetal and centrifugal forces, which are necessary to each other – mutually inter-dependent – "in order that both should live". If one is arrested, the action of the other will become immediately self-destructive.

> *The Secret Doctrine*, i 416

The Silent Watchers, awake during periods of *pralaya*, having transcended the primal pair of *pralaya* and *manvantara*, through a process of partial descent and incarnation under karmic law participate in the vast round of human existence. With mathematical precision they are able to determine precisely which elements in human volition and consciousness are operative at any given time and the exact nature of the evolutionary task before humanity in any given period. Every human being, whether consciously or unconsciously, is performing the evolutionary task inherently necessary owing to the sevenfold constitution of man and the earth. For human beings in the Fourth Round, the aim is to become self-determining and self-conscious in relation to the evolutionary process. True self-consciousness cannot be awakened through any exterior means but only through establishing the true posture of inner devotion to the *Guru*. The *Guru* alone can kindle that inner light which can quicken in every human being the powers of higher self-consciousness. The degree of self-consciousness attained by any individual will be a product both of the intensity of devotion and the starting-point in any given life. Hence there is a vast variety of degrees of intelligence, self-determination and energy displayed by particular human beings.

The integral relation between *Guru* Yoga and *Atma Vidya*, which must be realized by the human Ego, is embodied in the Hermetic maxim that the *Guru* is Spiritual Fire.

> Unless the Ego takes refuge in the *Atman*, the ALL-SPIRIT, and merges entirely into the essence thereof, the personal Ego may goad it to the bitter end.... Uproot the plant and transfer it to a piece of soil where the sunbeam cannot reach it, and the latter will not follow it. So with the *Atman*: unless the higher Self or EGO gravitates towards its Sun – the Monad – the lower Ego, or personal Self, will have the upper hand in every case.... Metaphysically, or on the psychic and spiritual plane, it is equally true that the *Atman* alone warms the inner man; i.e., it enlightens it with the ray of divine life and alone is able to impart to the inner man, or the reincarnating Ego, its immortality.

> *The Secret Doctrine*, ii 109-110

In each succeeding Round, the degree of incarnation of the *Atman* and the corresponding degrees of human perfection and karmic responsibility increase. With the advent of the Fifth Round, human beings will be held fully responsible for their descents from sphere to sphere, and those who are unable to fulfil this responsibility will not be able to accomplish the transition from the Fourth to the Fifth Rounds. Unable to fulfil the evolutionary programme, they will not be able to incarnate in future Rounds, and their shells will be incinerated by nature. Hence in the Fourth Round great courage is needed. Without it one is going to be afraid of the abyss, but there is no reason to be afraid because every human being is of a divine degree and can cooperate with the upward movement. Those who have become perfected in Buddhic-Manasic responsibility during the Fourth Round and have become capable of universal cognition and become great in the power of sacrifice will prepare over millions of years for the descent of a still more perfect and intellectual race. Whilst the full fruition of this race lies in the far distant future, the turning-point has already been reached with regard to its karmic inception. This is due to the extremely abnormal condition of humanity produced and perpetuated by the misuse and atrophy of spiritual powers during the Fourth Round. This condition was characterized in the last century by H.P. Blavatsky:

> . . . the selfishness of the personality has so strongly infected the real inner man with its lethal virus, that the upward attraction has lost all its power on the thinking reasonable man. In sober truth, vice and wickedness are an abnormal, unnatural manifestation, at this period of our human evolution – at least they ought to be so. The fact that mankind was never more selfish and vicious than it is now, civilized nations having succeeded in making of the first an ethical characteristic, of the second an art, is an additional proof of the exceptional nature of the phenomenon.

> *The Secret Doctrine,* ii 110

The aftermath of two world wars and the slaughter of millions of people in this century have not brought humanity any closer to peace on earth and the reign of justice. Viewing humanity through the eyes of compassion and seeing the tragedy of human misery everywhere, one cannot help but notice the victims of injustice. To let them hear the Law, whilst at the same time the Law must take its course, would take something much stronger than was even imaginable in the time of the Buddha and Christ. It would need something golden and generous and divine and free, such as in the time of Krishna or as sung by Shelley, but at the same time it would need the immense preparation that comes from the silent work of all the sages and *rishis* who know that human beings could only become truly human through meditation. Thus a time will come, though not in this century, when there will be men of meditation and exemplars of compassion in every part of the globe. In order to protect and promote the interests of the humanity of the future and to wipe out the humbug of the ages, the pristine avataric descent of the Aquarian cycle has been accompanied by a tremendous acceleration in the programme of evolution. The misuse of the human form had to be halted. All over the world this is sensed, and although there are those who, as Shakespeare put it, "squeak and gibber in the streets", there is a resonant feeling of joy amongst the greater portion of humanity which recognizes what has already begun to take root.

The meaning of the sounding of the keynote of the Cycle in relation to the great globe itself can only be understood in terms of the relation of the *Logos*, of *Avalokitesvara*, to the descent of *Atman* in the human race in its entirety. In the last century Mahatma Morya gave a clue to the mystery when he said, "We have yet some *Avatars* left to us on earth." As it was in the past, it is now and it always shall be that the entire sacred tribe of Initiates serves Dakshinamurti, the Initiator of Initiates. For over eighteen million years they have been the faithful witnesses to the mysterious bond between the Ever-Living Human Banyan, the fiery Dragon of Light, Fire and Flame, and the seventh principle in the Cosmos which extends beyond all the manifested cycles of galaxies. Those who seek intimations of the meaning of the end of the old habits, modes and orders and of the auspicious birth of the new, which is the oldest of the old, should meditate deeply upon these words of Pymander:

> The Light is me, I am the *Nous* (the mind or *Manu*), I am thy God, and I am far older than the human principle which escapes from the shadow ('Darkness,' or the concealed Deity). I am the germ of thought, the resplendent Word, the Son of God. All that thus sees and hears in thee is the *Verbum* of the Master, it is the Thought (*Mahat*) which is God, the Father.
>
> *The Secret Doctrine*, i 74

Hermes, November 1981

THE INMOST SANCTUARY

The 'Master' in the Sanctuary of our souls is 'the Higher Self'
– the divine spirit whose consciousness is based upon and derived
solely (at any rate during the mortal life of the man in whom it is
captive) from the Mind, which we have agreed to call the Human
Soul (the 'Spiritual Soul' being the vehicle of the Spirit). In its turn
the former (the personal or human soul) is a compound in its highest
form, of spiritual aspirations, volitions, and divine love; and in its
lower aspect, of animal desires and terrestrial passions imparted to it
by its associations with its vehicle, the seat of all these.

H. P. Blavatsky

Restoration of the right relationship between the Master in the inmost sanctuary and the incarnated consciousness is gained only through a sacrificial process of self-purification. Obscuring and polluting tendencies nurtured in the mind through its misuse over many lives must be removed by a self-chosen and self-administered therapy. Like the Pandava brothers exiled from their kingdom through their own folly, or like the master held prisoner in his own house by those who should be his servants in the parable of Jesus, the pristine divine ray of the *Logos* in man is trapped and stripped of its sovereign place in human life unless consciously sought by the aspirant. This invocation of wisdom through the supplication of the mind to the spirit was seen by the ancient Greeks as the cultivation of *sophrosyne* – the subordination of the inferior element to the superior. It is shown in *The Voice of the Silence* as the *shila* virtue – the attunement of thought, will and feeling to the pulsation of divine harmony, *Alaya-Akasha*. The mind stands as the critical link between the divine and the animal nature. The recovery and right use of the privilege of human existence depend upon the subordination of the elements of the lower *rupa* existence to the spiritual ideation of *Arupa Manas*.

The sacrificial posture and selfless motive required for this self-purification can be readily grasped through a telling analogy. There is not a modern metropolis which does not maintain the equipment needed to neutralize the *effluvia* of human waste and thereby reduce the danger of infection to its population. Similarly, a large number of devices are available, both to cities and to individuals, for the purpose of removing sediments and impurities from drinking water, through distillation, filtration and osmosis, to make it available in a purer and fresher form. With the human mind the same principles of public health and civic responsibility would require that each individual and every society strive to purify the muddy stream of human passions which pollute those coming into contact with it. Every human being has received the crystalline waters of life in a pure and unsullied condition, and therefore everyone has the karmic responsibility for every failure to return these waters to the ocean of life in a pristine condition. Insofar as this responsibility has been neglected by individuals, under karma in successive lives they are self-condemned to immersion in the waters they themselves have poisoned. Under the laws of karma affecting the processes of reincarnation and the transmigration of life-atoms, individuals owe it to their neighbours and their descendants, as well as to themselves, to purify their mental emanations.

In practice, this implies a continuous cleansing of one's thoughts, one's words and one's actions; these in turn fundamentally depend upon the purification of the will. Unfortunately, purification of the will, which is vital to the spiritual regeneration of humanity, is itself seriously misunderstood as a consequence of the process of pollution of consciousness and magnetism. Mired in the morbid obscuration of higher consciousness, too many people suppose that a bolstering of the lower will is a means to survival. Nothing could be farther from the truth. The higher spiritual will does not itself need to be strengthened, but it may be released through the removal of obscurations and hindrances. So long as the will is activated by the individual only on behalf of passions and the illusion of the *persona*, that will is not worth having. Hence, many people have discovered that the will cannot be released on behalf of lesser purposes. This predicament is conspicuous in those diseased societies which place an inordinate emphasis upon the personal will. Will itself is a pure colourless principle which cannot be dissociated from the energy of the *Atman* released through breathing. Thus when human beings breathe benevolently, blessing others with every breath, they can release the beneficent will-energy of the *Atman*. As soon as the will is released on behalf of the personal ego, however, against other human beings, it is blunted. This inevitable paralysis of the antagonistic lower will is indeed a beneficent and therapeutic aspect of karma.

Viewed from a collective standpoint, many human beings can be seen as having been weakened because they have absorbed life-atoms from others who have misused spiritual knowledge and the potency of the higher will. Throughout the world perhaps one in ten persons has insistently used the will against other human beings in this or previous lives. This may have been for the sake of bolstering the insecure identity of the *persona* or, worse, through the misuse of spiritual knowledge connected with false meditation, indulgence in drugs and mediumistic practices. Since 1966 contemporary society has witnessed the emergence of a number of centres of pseudo-spiritual activity; now it is witnessing the inevitable psychological breakdown of many who were responsible for this moral pollution. The waves of spiritual influence initiated by the descent of Krishna offer golden opportunities to all souls, including those inverted natures self-blocked from inward growth by their own failures on the Path in previous lives. Amongst these there were some too cowardly to make a new beginning, who sought instead to compensate for their own weakness and delusion by cashing in on the currents of the New Cycle. Having forfeited timely opportunities offered through compassion, they are self-destroyed when Krishna takes a firm stand on behalf of the entire human family because they are unable to generate a genuine concern for others. Never having generated an interest in the welfare of the vast majority of mankind, they are self-condemned. Sadly, they cast a long shadow over a much larger class of weaker souls who are affected by them, no doubt through their own delusions and vulnerabilities.

Persons are sometimes drawn into dangerous orbits of misused knowledge through loose talk about such sacred subjects as *kundalini*, *kriyashakti* and the activation of the higher spiritual centres in man.

Ordinary people who enjoy a normal measure of spiritual health wisely avoid those places where they are likely to hear profane chatter. Through a natural sense of spiritual good taste they simply shun those places where self-deluded con men congregate to make a living off the gullible. Today, because the moral and spiritual requirements for participation in the humanity of the future have become more evident to many people, the market for such deceptive opportunism has begun to diminish. The America of P.T. Barnum, where it was said that a sucker is born every moment, has been replaced to a large extent by the America of Abraham Lincoln, where, as is well known, one cannot fool all the people all the time. Although many souls have to travel a great distance along the path of self-integration, they have learnt enough not to be duped by pseudo-spiritual blandishments. Just as they have learnt not to believe everything conveyed by the mass media and not to leap at every free offer or supermarket discount, they have also learnt to pass up invitations for instant development of *kundalini* and every facile promise of spiritual development that dispenses with the judicious control of the emotions and passions.

Even in the difficult area of sexuality the idea of strength through celibacy [1] has gained some currency amongst many people, young and old, who find the burden of ego-games and unequal experimentation intolerable. There is nothing wrong with the sacred act of communion and procreation, and as the ancient Jews believed, God is pleased when a man and a woman come together in true unison. Nor need this issue be obscured by pseudo-arguments concerning the Malthusian spectre of over-population. As the economist E.F. Schumacher pointed out, even if the entire population of the globe were concentrated in America, this would result in a population density no greater than that of Great Britain, a nation long noted for the spaciousness and greenery of its countryside. North America itself, over its ancient and almost entirely unwritten history, has supported many varied civilizations, some of which displayed a much greater spiritual maturity than is evidenced in its recent history. Broadly, one cannot understand the physical facts of life on earth, much less the spiritual facts of life, through a language of

---

1   Gabrielle Brown, *The New Celibacy*, McGraw-Hill (New York, 1980).

conflicting claims and counter-claims, rationalizations and compensatory illusions, or pseudo-sophisticated statistical arguments based upon a selfish and shallow view of the nature of the human psyche.

The purification and release of the will must be comprehended in terms of human individuality, and therefore must be considered in the light of the mystery of every human soul. Since this mystery encompasses an entire series of reincarnations extending over eighteen million years, it can only begin to be appreciated through careful consideration of the motley evidence offered by one's participation in varied states of consciousness in the present life. Any individual concerned to recover the spontaneity and benevolence of the spiritual will must be willing to examine courageously the manner and extent to which he or she has become the servant not of the divine Ego, but rather of the lower astral form and its attendant *incubi* and *succubi*.

> For this 'Astral' – the shadowy 'double' (in the animal as in man) is not the companion of the divine Ego but of the earthly body. It is the link between the personal SELF, the lower consciousness of *Manas* and the Body, and is the vehicle of transitory, not of immortal life. Like the shadow projected by man, it follows his movements and impulses slavishly and mechanically, and leans therefore to matter without ever ascending to Spirit.
>
> H. P. Blavatsky

Plato explains, in a myth in the *Timaeus*, that when the Demiurge was fashioning the form of man, he endowed the human body with a stomach. This was done, according to the myth, out of compassion because otherwise man, unlike the animal, would be in danger of eating continually. Not only would this be disastrous for human health, but it would needlessly preoccupy consciousness with the intake and elimination of physical food. If human consciousness is to mature fully, it cannot be preoccupied with the *persona*, with the stomach and the libido, with physical space, time and motion. Consciousness must be freed to contemplate eternal motion, boundless space and infinite duration. This liberation from the bonds of the *persona* cannot be accomplished all at once but must be attempted again and again, through persistent efforts over a lifetime of meditation.

The radical reorientation of consciousness, away from the *persona* and towards the Divine, requires ceaseless striving and unremitting patience. Such continuity cannot be sustained over a lifetime unless it can be sustained for a year or even a week. In this arena, where clean beginnings and steadiness of application are crucial, one may gain great help from the example of the good gardener, who comes again and again to tend seedlings and plants, and yet allows nature time to work its magic. In fact, people who actually do some planting can gain considerable benefit through the restoration of their contact with the earth and by gaining an organic sense of growth. They can learn that all life is sacred, including the human body, and that every form of life can and should be treated with due respect. To recover this lost sense of the inviolable integrity of nature, however, one must be able to insert oneself into the whole, gaining intimations of what it is like to be a single blade of grass in a field or a single tree in a vast forest. As a modest experiment one might go to a nursery and purchase a seed, a pot and some soil. If one asks properly, the clerk will give whatever instructions are necessary and then one can take these materials home, carefully and with respect. Then after planting the seed in the soil with humility and love, treating it not as a symbol but as life, one can set the pot firmly upright in a place prepared for it. Each day one can give to the growing plant what it requires by way of water and nourishment, but it is important to do this with an assurance and confidence that comes with humility before nature. Forgetting oneself and without anxiety, one can observe the process of organic growth. In doing this properly, one will also be sowing in oneself the seeds of a new confidence rooted not in fear, not in deceit, but rather in fearlessness and truth, the source of authentic humility.

As one spends a few moments each day noting the growth of the plant, one may see this as linked magnetically to the seed of the new astral form which one seeks to gestate within oneself out of the soil of the old astral. This old astral is chiefly composed of patterns of selective memories, which are instinctual, habitual and compulsive, as well as somewhat inefficient and so unreliable that they would be unacceptable in any court of law. Having no firm basis in either fact or truth, they are primarily externalizations based upon misconceptions and predilections directed against those to whom we owe so much. Rather than remaining captive to an appalling burden of memories and an attendant tendency to judgementalism towards parents, grandparents and ancestors – of whose trials and difficulties one knows little or nothing – one should mainly concentrate the mind upon the nurturing of the new astral form to which one is attempting to give birth. Indeed, one's motive in doing this should be to benefit all those who have come before and to whom one should be grateful. One is aiming at the attainment of an active state, where one has energy, but in which one is not bound to one's *persona* and irrational self through the forces of *kama, krodha* and *lobha* – desire, anger and greed. Speaking of the purifying and benevolent energy of the spiritual will, H.P. Blavatsky pointed to the fundamental requirements of spiritual regeneration and their connection with the discovery of one's true immortality.

> It is only when the power of the passions is dead altogether, and when they have been crushed and annihilated in the retort of an unflinching will; when not only all the lusts and longings of the flesh are dead, but also the recognition of the personal Self is killed out and the 'astral' has been reduced in consequence to a cipher, that the Union with the 'Higher Self' can take place.
>
> H. P. Blavatsky

The path of inner gestation and self-regeneration depends critically upon the recovery of the capacity to think clearly, freely and creatively. This prerogative, guaranteed to every human being by the cosmos, which never has been (and nor can it ever be) abridged by any terrestrial institution, is the sacred and sacrificial birthright of every Monadic being blessed with the fire of *Manas*. Whilst true thinking may be rare, this is not the fault of any society or government, and it is irresponsible and immature in the extreme to blame one's lack of thoughtfulness upon anything outside oneself. Thinking, in fact, has nothing to do with blame; the more one thinks, the less one will be involved with blaming altogether. As Merlin exhorted Arthur, "Think! Think! THINK!" It is extraordinary how rare true thinking is, but as soon as one does begin to think, thinking things through – *dianoia* – then one begins to concentrate and gains the ability to go back to an original moment. Those who have completed this training, true disciples who have gained effortless mastery over their astral forms at will, can instantly summon the moment of birth or of death. Herein lies the authenticity and integrity of the true spiritual Path. If ever one hears someone speak of astral travel who is unable to say what his thoughts were before the moment of birth, one should know immediately that such a person is deluded, or a dupe. It is too late to be taken in by such twaddle, much less participate in it.

One should begin by trying to think through what is essential in one's life, seeking to recover, if not one's moment of birth, then one's moment of spiritual awakening in this life. What were one's dreams as a child before seven? Was there any moment of awakening then, when one realized that one was worth more than all of one's toys and trinkets? Was there any moment of awakening between the ages of seven and fourteen, when bright possibilities of the future were glimpsed, and was there a moment around the age of puberty, when one was filled with hopes and ideals in relation to human brotherhood? Did the possibilities of human growth, beauty, fulfilment and promise fire ones's imagination? What were the secret dreams and longings for the good that one whispered to one's closest friend in school but did not mention to adults? Were there certain withdrawn and sensitive moments in one's life which one did not mention to another living soul, but rather honoured in the heart? Each person must self-consciously recover these golden moments for himself or herself because no one else can do this for another. Each person must discover the seeds of goodness within himself or herself and nurture them. If one is to take into account one's failures, mistakes and errors, then it is only fair that one should also note in one's life-ledger one's golden dreams and finest thoughts. One should learn to accentuate the positive and not become preoccupied with the negative. The best means to do this is not to speak very much about oneself to others. Be silent for awhile. Learn to talk less and think more. Then, as one takes note of the truest things in one's life, one will begin gradually to see connections within, and one will no longer be a slave to connections imposed from outside by others.

Ultimately, one's life is one's own. It does not belong to parents or friends or spouse or any other. In one's spiritual life one cannot come closer to the *Guru* until one has become worthy of the blessing, and this can only be done by voluntarily putting oneself through vows within a period of probation. During that period of probation there will be a tremendous testing brought on by no one else but oneself. By putting oneself as oil in a refinery, or as a jewel in a cleansing solvent, one chooses precisely which trials and tests are to be brought upon oneself by oneself. Through the power of one's resolve one enters upon an alchemical process of removal and burning out of impurities in one's nature. If, for example, one pronounces a sacred word like *Atman*, then one both blesses and curses oneself. One curses oneself in that the darkness will be drawn out; one blesses oneself in that the Light of the *Atman* will be shed upon one's nature. One can choose to stand in the Light of the *Atman*, but then there will be war – war between that part of oneself which loves and is one with the Light, and that part which is incompatible with the Light. It is impossible to cling to Light and darkness at the same time. One cannot worship both God and Mammon. One must choose, and even though one cannot choose all at once, each choice on behalf of the Light increases self-respect. Every time one chooses to meditate instead of cerebrate, every time one chooses to contemplate instead of chit-chat, every time one chooses to learn from other human beings instead of becoming judgemental, one gains dignity and a measure of self-respect. And unless one respects oneself, one cannot earn the respect of others. This does not mean that one should work at this anxiously and with strain. Rather, one should accept and recognize one's unimportance, seeing oneself as only one amongst billions of human beings, treating this not as an excuse but as one of the primary facts of life.

Human beings must find out for themselves individually the meaning and purpose of their life. Each human soul in incarnation has a sacred mission and goal. One must have the courage to discover what one has come to earth to do. If one has come to work for the City of Man, then one must train oneself. One must come out of Necropolis, the city of the dead. One cannot work for the City of Man whilst remaining captive to the city of the dead. One must learn compassion for the morally and mentally crippled, the blind and lame, the victims of crime and ignorance, as well as the criminals themselves. One must become a person of strong nerves capable of loving more and more people, and along with this one must become aware of what one can handle and what one cannot. Each individual is different, and it is necessary to learn something about the plastic potency of one's own astral vesture. What are its capabilities and what its limitations? There is also great meaning and value in meditating upon a vast and general promise which is the glorious goal of universal human evolution. It is good to envisage in the mind, not merely for oneself but on behalf of all, the prospect of that sacred moment far along the Path when

> ... the 'Astral' reflects only the conquered man, the still living but no more the longing selfish personality, then the brilliant *Augoeides*, the divine SELF, can vibrate in conscious harmony with both the poles of the human Entity – the man of matter purified, and the ever pure Spiritual Soul – and stand in the presence of the MASTER SELF, the *Christos* of the mystic Gnostic, blended, merged into, and one with IT forever.
>
> H. P. Blavatsky

Mahatma K. H., commenting upon the Tibetan proverb that everyone is master of his own wisdom, states that each is at liberty either to honour or degrade the slave. He then goes on to link this with the eternal process of evolving subjective matter into objective atoms. This intimates that one must, through the power of meditation upon extremely abstract and subjective thoughts, evolve new life-atoms. It is these fresh and pure life-atoms which will push out the old life-atoms of one's astral body. This is analogous to taking a purgative medicine to clean out unhealthy and unwanted residues in the body. It is even more analogous to the taking of an antibiotic, such as penicillin, which was discovered in bread mould by Sir Alexander Fleming. One must, so to speak, extract out of the fungus of one's chaotic mind a purifying idea capable of cleansing one's entire mental field. One must directly and deliberately intervene in the war between creators and the destroyers within one's astral frame. Like an antibiotic medicine derived from life itself, yet capable of destroying harmful bacteria, one's heartfelt ideals, distilled and clarified through meditation, have the power to release the purifying and benevolent energy of the spiritual will. This is only an analogy pointing to the process of mental self-purification through sacrificial meditation, which is a vital part of the sacred science of spirituality. That science is mathematically exact and precise in its laws and is therefore not possessed by human beings who are captive to the illusions of terrestrial existence. It is an arcane science which combines meta-chemistry with meta-biology, and it is rooted in a metaphysics which only becomes dynamized and activated when it is rendered into meta-psychology – that wisdom which is used and applied in daily life. When it is properly used, and this has nothing to do with mere words – though it has a great deal to do with the use of the tongue – it is extremely powerful and is equivalent to the release of the spiritual will flowing from the *Atman*.

For the neophyte, the initial step is to become a true pragmatist by putting to use the idealism which is within the soul and which is consubstantial with the plane of *Mahat*-mic ideation in the cosmos. It will then become possible to bring into the unreal world of time, which ordinary human beings mistake for reality, the fruit of meditation, the flower of contemplation and the fragrance of self-study and self-correction. When one is filled with the milk of human kindness, it will become possible to extract from the depths of one's divine nature the ambrosia of immortality. In deep sleep, when one is far from the *persona*, when the personal nature is reduced to a cipher, one may receive the gift of Krishna, a drop of the divine elixir. The personal nature will know nothing of this secret gift, and when one awakens, it matters little what the personality makes of the change. What is important is that one honour and treasure it and go forth into the day, sifting and selecting that which is of value, that which is good and true and beautiful. One should not do this strenuously, but rather with a lightness and relaxation consistent with one's own sense of unimportance in relation to the entirety of mankind.

All forms of over-exertion and strain are signs of a sense of personal self-importance and a desire for attention incompatible with spiritual maturity. Karma cannot condone an abnormal desire for attention for oneself at the expense of the human race, because Karma cannot shelter the propensity to indulge in attention to the shadowy *persona*. Therefore, one must learn and enjoy a new set of rules wherein one does not ask for more ego space than one is entitled to. But if one understands what it is to be only one amongst billions of human beings upon the earth and only one of a smaller though extensive class of beings who have come into the presence of the Avatar, then one will know how to do this. Instead of yielding to the backward tendency to impose one's personality and problems upon others, one will learn to do *tapas* in silence, so as to prepare oneself for the opportunity to serve which comes with being in the presence of other human souls.

If one would become worthy of being in the presence of Krishna, then one must begin by attempting to understand what Krishna meant when he said that he established this entire universe with but a single portion of himself and yet remains separate from it. Whatever be the percentage of that portion of himself, and that would vary with the needs of the era, his essential nature remains *Kutashtha* – He who standeth apart. The sense in which Krishna is separate from the universe is mystical and metaphysical, but one cannot hope to begin to understand this if one remains subject to the delusion that one can understand oneself by understanding Krishna. This is a typically Western misconception. One must understand oneself through understanding other human beings; when one has understood oneself through all other human beings, then one may begin to understand Krishna. Through love and devotion one can cross the barriers of the mind and the heart and the self, and prepare oneself for *Mahasmashana* – the burning of the corpse of the *persona*. There one is consumed by the fire of devotion so as to be reborn to live purely for the sake of others and not at all for oneself. Only those who have crossed that sacred threshold, difficult of approach, can participate in the conscious creation of their lower self. Very few have heard of this mystical threshold, and of these, even fewer have been able to approach it. Fewer still are those who have made a burning-ground of their hearts for the sake of the *Guru*, and thereby truly entered his service. Yet such is the great teaching and rich promise given by Krishna to his devotees, to all those heroic souls who would become willing servants of the City of Man.

Hermes, February 1982

ENLIGHTENMENT

The 'last vibration of the Seventh Eternity' was 'fore-ordained' – by no God in particular, but occurred in virtue of the eternal and changeless LAW which causes the great periods of Activity and Rest, called so graphically, and at the same time so poetically, the 'Days and Nights of Brahma.' The expansion 'from within without' of the Mother, called elsewhere the 'Waters of Space,' 'Universal Matrix,' etc., does not allude to an expansion from a small centre or focus, but, without reference to size or limitation or area, means the development of limitless subjectivity in to as limitless objectivity. 'The ever (to us) invisible and immaterial Substance present in eternity, threw its periodical shadow from its own plane into the lap of Maya.'

The Secret Doctrine, i 62-63

The transcendence of *maya*, the awakening of wisdom and the realization of immortality are three in one. Though they may be distinguished for the sake of understanding and therapeutic meditation, they are in truth but aspects of unified perfection. Like the triple hypostases of the *Atman*, they form a purely noumenal matrix hinting at the inconceivable ideal of full enlightenment. That enlightenment has no specific ground, is not a state and is no event. Tautologically, it is the realization of the Real. Philosophically, it is the consummation of *philos* in *sophia*, the two becoming one, the extinction of divisions between subject and object. Inaccessible through mere affirmation or even negation, it is the One Truth (SAT) beyond all illusion, ignorance and death. It may be approached only by following the small, old path, the path that begins and ends outside of self. One must first become the path to enter it, and then one must realize that one travels on that path "without moving".

Ultimately, there can be no true comprehension of enlightenment or of the path outside of enlightenment itself. Mortality cannot judge of immortality; *avidya* cannot conceive of *vidya*. The insubstantial self of mayavic matter cannot encompass the boundlessness of the Real. The shadow cannot comprehend the light that casts it. Whether understood in terms of the attraction and repulsion of *tanha* that constricts motivation and the will, or in terms of the delusion of the mind through dichotomies, the lesser and partial cannot comprehend the supreme and complete. Nonetheless, there is latent in every human being the precious seed of enlightenment, *bodhichitta*. Consubstantial with the highest planes of cosmic substance, it is the core of that consciousness perfected by Buddhas and *Bodhisattvas*. It is the immutable ground of immortality, inseparable from the One Life or the Rootless Root of all manifestation. To begin to understand the permanent possibility of enlightenment pervading manifested life, one must ponder the ontological status of that unmanifest wisdom, the possibility of which is envisaged by esoteric philosophy.

In the *Bhagavad Gita*, Lord Krishna tells Arjuna that there is no non-existence for that which is, and no existence for that which is not. If supreme and boundless unmanifest wisdom constitutes reality, there can be no non-existence of wisdom bound up with what are called illusion, ignorance and death. Similarly, if these three themselves are not reality, then they are nothing which can pass into non-existence with the awakening of wisdom. If unmanifest wisdom is without antecedent, it is also without residue. Typically, however, human beings conceive of enlightenment as some sort of real change –a contradiction in terms. Put crudely, they suppose either that eternal wisdom has somehow become real, or that the unreal realm of *maya* has somehow become non-existent. Too objective a mind will produce the first misconception, too subjective a turn of mind will produce the second. In either case, the theoretical and, what is the same thing, the practical possibility of enlightenment is obscured. This root imbalance or eccentricity in the soul's vestures and in human understanding is multiplied a myriad times, affecting every arena of mundane thought and action.

In order to ameliorate this condition, H.P. Blavatsky devoted considerable attention, in *The Secret Doctrine*, to the emerging phases of manifestation from the long night of *Pralaya*. Whilst these considerations are so abstract as to be of immediate interest only to the highest Adepts, they nevertheless have a direct relevance to all who seek to enter the path. If absolute abstract Space, unconditioned Consciousness and boundless

Duration are the fundamental terms in the equation of manifestation, then they must also be the ultimate factors in any adequate conception of self-reference, self-regeneration and self-realization. Through meditation upon *Mulaprakriti* and *Prakriti, Parabrahm* and *Mahat,* boundless Duration and conditioned Time, the mind can be balanced and brought into proper orientation to the problem of Self and non-self. As this inner posture is steadied by devotion, entry onto the path will come through intuition and a strengthening of the heart.

Non-self has its roots in a process which H.P. Blavatsky characterized as "the development of limitless subjectivity into as limitless objectivity". Put more symbolically, in terms of *Mulaprakriti,*

> . . . the ever (to us) invisible and immaterial Substance present in eternity, threw its periodical shadow from its own plane into the lap of *Maya.*
>
> *The Secret Doctrine,* i 62-63

Mulaprakriti is pre-cosmic Root Substance, the noumenal origin of all differentiations and types of matter –the latter term referring to the aggregate of objects of possible perception. *Mulaprakriti* is wholly noumenal and so subjective that it cannot remotely be imagined by the human mind through extrapolation from a world of phenomenal objects. Even the subtlest abstractions employed in the sciences, involving intra-atomic particles and fields, will not yield a conception of the abstractness of *Mulaprakriti.*

To be able to visualize *Mulaprakriti,* one must imagine the disappearance of all worlds, all planets and all galaxies, a dissolution so complete that no thing remains. When this negation is pushed to the fullest cosmic level, one must visualize in what may be called absolute abstract Space a primordial substratum or field. At that level of abstraction, space and substance mutually imply each other. This inconceivable degree of abstract homogeneity and limitless subjectivity is prior to all worlds and continues to be at the hidden root whilst all worlds manifest and are dissolved. Therefore, it is eternal. Having no reference to change, it is unchangeable and thus ever exists in eternity. *Mulaprakriti,* unmodified homogeneous *prima materia,* must not be confused with the objectivized conception of prime matter entertained by nineteenth century scientists, for it represents the most noumenal and primal conception of substance, beyond all objectivized universals. That it cannot be imagined is attested even by contemporary cosmology with its limited notion of beginnings and endings, or of one specific Big Bang. Other more audacious astronomers will not surrender to a belief in temporal finitude.

Once one can begin to conceive of *Mulaprakriti* as an invisible and immaterial substance present in eternity, and by definition unrelated to time, one must consider its relationship to matter in any possible system of worlds. In an objective world, even the most subtle abstract manifesting or manifested matter at the sub-atomic level is only a shadow. It is, in the words of the Commentaries, a shadow thrown from that homogeneous eternal realm into the lap of *maya*. One analogous approach is to think first of darkness and light, then of a series of reflections. But even such analogies are inadequate because they are based upon a conditioned view of space as characterized by extension, and of time as characterized by succession. Such assumptions, rooted in the illusion of a separative personal existence, cannot comprehend pure primal pre-cosmic *Mulaprakriti*. Such limiting conceptions obscure recondite questions in contemporary science about the reversibility of events. But they also obscure the Divine Darkness, which is only a metaphorical expression for this invisible and immaterial substance, that is mystically said to cast a periodical shadow. The casting of this shadow already assumes the emergence of a world of seeming objectivity divided into planes and rays. Even at the most primordial level of this assumed division into what are called the primary seven *Dhyan Chohans*, comparable to the Ah-Hi, there is the assumption of a kind of shadowy partial existence. And that shadowing continues, replicating itself a myriad times, so that on the densest possible plane of objective matter the one primal substance is shadowed by a dazzlingly complex panorama of forms, changing and interacting, scintillating in ceaseless transformation.

To gain an accurate conception of the ontological status of this boundless plane of seeming objectivity arisen from limitless subjectivity, absolute abstract Space, one must take account of the potency of ideation and intelligence in the unfolding of cosmic process. If one overlooks noetic intelligence and pursues only matter and substance, the immense realm of *prakriti*, one will derive the impression that all these forms of matter are ultimately shadowy by reference to *Mulaprakriti*, which is timeless, without immanence and involvement even in the vastest periods of time. It is beyond them; thus it has been called a veil upon the Absolute, a veil upon *Parabrahm*, almost indistinguishable from the Absolute. Just as the Absolute, if it is to be truly the Absolute, cannot enter any possible relationship with anything relative, so too *Mulaprakriti* cannot possibly be converted into anything else. It cannot possibly be related to any form of *prakriti*. This puzzling and challenging fact must be counterbalanced by similar considerations with regard to intelligence.

At the level of immaterial Root Substance, there must also be a pre-cosmic Ideation which is pure subjectivity, unconditioned, unmodified consciousness. This pure potential subjectivity is prior to any modified consciousness restricted by any object, by any relations between objects, or by any limited modes of self-reference. In gestating pure subjectivity, one comprehends that a totally negative field is ontologically prior to the act of negation. Again, one should ask what conceivable relationship there could be between this pure limitless subjectivity and the limitless realm of objective existence. In the abstruse metaphysics of the ancient Hindu schools, it is taught that the Absolute, *Parabrahm*, could be viewed as *nirguna* – attributeless. As soon as one predicates attributes of the Absolute, one has obscured the attributeless Absolute, *Nirguna Brahman*. To remain true to the pure thread of philosophic thought, one must withhold all qualifications and predications of the Absolute. One cannot even say that It was, It is or It will be.

What *Mulaprakriti* is to *prakriti* –primal Root Substance to noumenal matter –*Nirguna Brahman*, the attributeless Absolute, is to *Mahat* or cosmic mind. To gain any intuition of the profound meaning of this paradigmatic truth, one must meditate upon the early passages from the Stanzas of Dzyan, which characterize the long night of non-manifestation – *Maha Pralaya*.

> THE ETERNAL PARENT (Space), WRAPPED IN HER EVER INVISIBLE ROBES, HAD SLUMBERED ONCE AGAIN FOR SEVEN ETERNITIES.

TIME WAS NOT, FOR IT LAY ASLEEP IN THE INFINITE BOSOM OF DURATION.

UNIVERSAL MIND WAS NOT, FOR THERE WERE NO AH-HI TO CONTAIN IT.

These Stanzas attempt the virtually impossible task of characterizing an immense period of total non-manifestation, wherein matter, mind and time were not. Whilst these Stanzas have a vital significance for those at certain high levels of abstract meditation, striving after universal self-consciousness, they also have a great theoretical importance for human beings merely trying to emancipate themselves from fragmented consciousness in a world of objects.

The apprentice at meditation must begin by considering non-manifestation metaphysically. One must first conceive of the possibility, and then proceed to ponder further questions, which may be resolved through the instruction of the Stanzas. From total non-manifestation, where the Absolute is as much as during a period of manifestation, there is an anticipation of manifestation as a whole. Something analogous to this may be experienced in the early morning hours, in the passage from extreme darkness to a noumenal participation in the progressive dawn. Because embodied human beings are already subjects and objects, minds in forms, they can conceive of this process in two ways: by visualizing *Nirguna Brahman*, the attributeless Absolute, generating the possibility of universal mind, which in turn becomes *Mahat*, the cosmic mind of a particular system; or by visualizing *Mulaprakriti*, primordial pre-cosmic Substance, becoming the noumenon of matter in relation to a sphere of potential existence. We may move either from unlimited pre-cosmic Ideation or from unlimited pre-cosmic Substance through the most abstract sense of limit –limit in the most extreme degree applying to millions upon millions of years and to myriads of worlds within worlds.

The purpose of this profound meditation is to shatter the association of space with extension and of time with succession. These conceptions must be destroyed at the root, so that one may return to the deepest possible ground of pure potential universal awareness. At every point, there is, predictably, the risk that the deepening of consciousness may be arrested through identification with material forms, even the most subtle. But there is another and equally profound risk, the fundamental nature of which can be readily grasped by those who have spent some time with the Indian schools of philosophy, especially Vedanta. H.P. Blavatsky noted that:

> With some schools, *Mahat* is 'the first-born' of *Pradhana* (undifferentiated substance, or the periodical aspect of *Mulaprakriti*, the root of Nature), which (*Pradhana*) is called *Maya*, the Illusion.

The Secret Doctrine, i 62

Unlike the various Vedantin doctrines, the esoteric teachings do not hold that *Mahat* is derived from the illusory or periodic aspect of *Mulaprakriti*. As H.P. Blavatsky explained, the Wisdom-Religion holds that

> . . . while *Mulaprakriti*, the noumenon, is self-existing and without any origin –is, in short, parentless, *Anupadaka* (as one with *Brahman*) – *Prakriti*, its phenomenon, is periodical and no better than a phantasm of the former, so *Mahat*, with the Occultists, the first-born of *Gnana* (or gnosis) knowledge, wisdom or the *Logos* –is a phantasm reflected from the Absolute *Nirguna* (*Parabrahm*, the one reality, 'devoid of attributes and qualities'; see *Upanishads*); while with some Vedantins *Mahat* is a manifestation of *Prakriti*, or Matter.

The Secret Doctrine, i 62

Because these idealistic schools of thought strongly stress the need for union between the individual *Jivatman* and the *Paramatman*, one with *Parabrahm*, they also seem to suggest that the whole world is an illusion, from that philosophical standpoint which sees even the cosmic mind –*Mahat* –as only an outgrowth or outcome of *prakriti*, or matter. Yet if it is only an outgrowth of matter, it becomes totally unreal. Earlier in *The Secret Doctrine*, H.P. Blavatsky discussed a similar divergence between the views of the *Yogacharya* and *Madhyamika* schools of *Mahayana Buddhism*, concerning their understanding of the terms *Paramartha* and *Alaya*. Calling the *Yogacharyas* the great spiritualists and the *Madhyamikas* the great nihilists, she again drew a distinction between too vehement idealism and the Teachings of Theosophia or *Brahma Vach*.

If *Mahat* is prior to *prakriti*, one might be tempted to ask whether *Mahat* is prior to *Mulaprakriti*. But *Mahat* is to *Nirguna Brahman* as *prakriti* is to *Mulaprakriti*, which is *Anupadaka*. The precedence of *Mahat* to *prakriti* is the key; ideation and consciousness are prior to everything else, save the veil over *Parabrahm*. If an individual human being ardently longs to attain to universal self-consciousness, he or she must be able to reduce everything to its homogeneous essence, to see through the relative reality and unreality of the world, yet acknowledge that in the world of unreal time there is that which is consubstantial with the Absolute. In the language of Ishopanishad, it is erroneous to reject either the Transcendent or the Immanent. The Absolute is neither. One must come to sense the Transcendent in the Immanent, and, as a first step in meditation, the Immanent in the Transcendent. *Parabrahm* is neither Being nor Non-Being; IT IS BE-NESS.

To gain universal self-consciousness one has to experience the continuity of consciousness from the highest to the lowest, from the most boundless to the most limited. This is perhaps the hidden intent of Vedanta, all too often obscured by schools of idealism, which emphasize the subjective approach to metaphysics. Subjective idealists like Berkeley, phenomenalists, even German phenomenologists – all, like Vedanta, are fundamentally concerned with the distinction between Being and Becoming. All require a doctrine of *maya* which involves either saying that *maya* is a superimposition or that it is an unreal shadow. But whatever it is, it leaves intact the fundamental ground, and therefore one has to cancel everything out and go back to that fundamental ground to gain enlightenment. Unfortunately, this view could become a justification for those who want to become absorbed in the whole, negating everything, without gaining universal self-consciousness and coming back into the world with that self-consciousness intact. Yet, it is just this process which enshrines clues to the sacred mystery of incarnation, especially of the Avatar.

To convey something of the development of limitless objectivity out of limitless subjectivity, it is helpful to employ concepts like expansion and contraction. When talking at the most macrocosmic level of the unmanifest and the manifest, non-being and being, it would be better to avoid such terms. To understand the Stanzas when they speak of an expansion "from within without", it is necessary to purge the notion of expansion of any spatial reference. The entire range of mundane experience equally constrains the capacity to devise diagrams and models. For the expansion of the Stanzas is purely metaphysical and has no relation to objective space. It is best intimated by the lotus, which is phanerogamous, i.e., contains in its seed form the complete flower in miniature, just as an embryo develops into a human being. Because it is completely present in prototype, the unfoldment of the lotus is merely an elaboration of what is already present. This is the closest analogy to the unfoldment from the prototypic universal ideas in the cosmic mind into the world of many types and forms. But becoming accustomed to so lofty a conception is like acclimatizing oneself to the rarefied altitude of high mountains. Just as one must learn to breathe the thin air, while maintaining activity, so one must in meditation learn to give a sense of reality on the mental plane where there are no forms and beings but only Darkness. This cannot be done without purging all those notions that have been acquired through manifested existence in a world circumscribed by limited space and time.

Just as the cosmic lotus flowers in a space without extension, so too it flowers in a time without succession. Thus, the esoteric philosophy

> . . . divides boundless duration into unconditionally eternal and universal Time and a conditioned one (*Khandakala*). One is the abstraction or noumenon of infinite time (*Kala*); the other its phenomenon appearing periodically, as the effect of *Mahat* (the Universal Intelligence limited by Manvantaric duration).

The Secret Doctrine, i 62

These two different dimensions of time – *Kala* and *Khandakala* – stand to each other as *Parabrahm* and *Mulaprakriti* to *Mahat* and *prakriti*. It is possible to recognize that there is an unconditional, eternal and universal time that has nothing to do with clocks and chronometers. It is a time that has to do with consciousness, but not with embodied, differentiated and externalizing consciousness - When through meditation consciousness is deliberately turned inward, when it can do what Nature does when *Pralaya* comes, then it is possible to approach unconditional, eternal, universal time. But one must recognize that conditioned time is merely an effect of *Mahat* and a characteristic of *prakriti*. Boundless Duration is prior to *Mahat*, and therefore closer to *Mulaprakriti* and *Parabrahm*.

To understand this and to make it the basis of meditation, it is helpful to ponder upon the process of universal dissolution. The powerful mythic and poetic descriptions of the onset of the night of *Pralaya* in a variety of Indian texts can be made the basis of a purifying and meditative discipline. One can learn to experience within oneself the progress of universal dissolution, experiencing the destruction and absorption of the element of earth into water, the absorption of water into fire, of fire into air, and of air into ether –the rudimentary property of which is sound. Even that is dissolved into what may be called a seed of consciousness on the plane of *Mahat*, the primary property of which is *Buddhi* at the universal level. Even that must ultimately be transcended. All the elements are progressively gathered back into one element, and that is converted from a single universal field of sound through a root or germ of consciousness back into a field of pure ideation –and beyond. Hence the potency of A-U-M, merging back into the soundless OM. If one sees all manifestation as one vast golden egg of Brahma, in that luminous egg (*Hiranyagarbha*) the same process is ever taking place.

The Dawn of manifestation and the Twilight of the onset of *Pralaya* are not to be thought of as two points of sequential time separated by vast intervals. They are metaphysically fused in boundless duration as ceaseless creation – *Nitya Swarga* – and ceaseless dissolution – *Nitya Pralaya*. The individual who, through meditation upon these ideas, arouses intuition can reverse all that has happened since entering the mother's womb. Having experienced the shock of being thrown into the womb, and having progressively become involved through a series of identifications and limitations, human beings may be seen as fallen gods. Therefore, to overcome the bonds of illusion, ignorance and death, it is necessary to reverse this process, but not at the crude concretized level of those who talk of the primal scream and going back to the womb. It must be reversed cosmically, because nothing can ever be done fundamentally at the individual level unless it is understood cosmically.

This is the indispensable foundation of the Wisdom-Religion, of *Brahma Vidya*. As above, so below. As below, so above. In the below one must reach for the above; one must concern oneself with all humanity, on a metaphysical level, before any fundamental and irreversible change can be made in oneself. To understand this intuitively is to see that when one withdraws in meditation, at a steady and high level of abstraction, one is striving to experience the night of non-manifestation, where there are no worlds. To be able to do this is to empty and reabsorb all elements, dissolving everything elementally and at the level of ideation. To transcend the veils of conditioned existence whilst retaining full awareness is to realize the one primal Root Substance in boundless Duration. That is pure self-consciousness – *Atma Vidya*, one with the supreme attributeless unmanifest wisdom in *Parabrahm*.

> Say not that It is One, as there can be no second, nothing other than That. There is neither uniqueness nor commonality, neither entity nor non-entity; this secondless One is neither void nor plenum. How can I convey this supreme wisdom?

Shri Shankaracharya

Hermes, March 1983

CONTINUITY OF CONSCIOUSNESS

What does modern science know of the duration of the ages of the World, or even of the length of geological periods?

Nothing; absolutely nothing . . . . Indeed, in the Cimmerian darkness of the prehistoric ages, the explorers are lost in a labyrinth, whose great corridors are doorless, allowing no visible exit into the Archaic past. Lost in the maze of their own conflicting speculations, rejecting, as they have always done, the evidence of Eastern tradition, without any clue, or one single certain milestone to guide them, what can geologists or anthropologists do but pick up the slender thread of Ariadne.... They are 'prehistoric' to the naked eye of matter only. To the spiritual eagle eye of the seer and the prophet of every race, Ariadne's thread stretches beyond that 'historic periods without break or flaw, surely and steadily, into the very night of time; and the baud which holds it is too mighty to drop it, or even let it break.

The Secret Doctrine, ii 66-67

Ariadne's thread represents unbroken continuity of consciousness in the One Life. In relation to perception (*samvriti*) and knowledge (*prajna*), it stands for the principle of *Buddhi*, spiritual intuition, which by analogy and correspondence cuts through the maze of detail to the heart of the matter. Ariadne's thread is also the *sutratman*, the integrity of the immortal soul, the meta-psychological basis of individual awareness extending back over eighteen million years and serving as the storehouse of soul-memory (anamnesis). Through its capacity to tap *Akasha*, the universal empyrean upon which are recorded all the archetypal truths behind the mass of manifested projections, the immortal soul, by reference to its inherent wisdom, can recover the most illuminating continuity of consciousness. It can bridge apparent gaps on the physical plane – between days and nights, between seasons and years – and cross chasms between incarnations. Even more important, it can span the *pralayas*, the periods of obscuration between Races and Rounds. This timeless wisdom of the soul cannot be comprehended by the ratiocinative, rationalizing mind.

Through material evidence, sensory data and induction, it is possible to accumulate masses of information which may then be submitted to logical or methodological analysis. Thus one can infer conjectural estimates of the age of the sun and the moon, of the earth and man. But such inferences, however intriguing, shed no light upon the complex relationship between cosmic and human chronology. Even if one extends anthropological estimates of the age of man to a period of nearly twenty million years, as suggested in the late work of L.S.B. Leakey, one grasps no sense of what happened to humanity during those unchronicled years. And, seeing only fragments of the conscious life of humanity, it is nearly impossible to conceive of the humanity of the hoary past, and its vital relationship to the decisive lighting up of *Manas* eighteen million years ago at the mid-point of the Fourth Round. With regard to more antique times and previous Rounds, empirical evidence that the physical earth and physical entities in space go back hundreds of millions of years reveals no helpful connections between all these enormously ancient relics and human evolution. In short, nearly nothing that is significant or definitive can be known about the primordial origins of conscious life through a reductionist methodology relying upon sensory evidence and inference from external shells and petrified astral deposits.

Instead of expecting such an unphilosophical methodology to assist in the recovery of universal continuity of consciousness, one must adopt a radically different approach, grounded in metaphysics. Employing a dialectical methodology analogous to the ontological process it seeks to apprehend, one must begin with persistent enquiry into the profound connection between the One and the many, the *Logos* and the *Logoi*. One must meditate upon phases of progressive manifestation, coming down from the most subjective level conceivable to the most objective visible level.

This radical transformation of method requires introversion, a turning within the immortal soul. But, since external evidence is so incomplete and so inadequate to understanding millions of years of conscious life, and since at the same time it is immensely difficult to turn within, it may seem impossible to make much progress. Without seed thoughts for meditation, it may appear hopeless even to begin the enquiry. Yet, this is not true. It is merely a presumptive delusion arising from the protracted hubris of Occidental pseudo-culture, which, out of its habitual ignorance of other languages, simply has not seriously considered the calendars and chronologies of ancient Indian, Chinese and other cultures. As H.P. Blavatsky repeatedly and forcefully affirmed a century ago, one must revert to time-honoured Eastern sources even to make sense of what may be sporadically inferred from physical evidence.

Paradoxically, despite the pioneering efforts of intrepid thinkers in the latter part of the nineteenth century in philology and phonetics connected with the entire stock of Indo-European languages, there has been subsequently an enormous shrinkage of chronologies in reference to Eastern civilizations. The balance has been redressed somewhat, in reference to China, largely through the work of Joseph Needham over the past thirty years. More recently, John Kaye, in his remarkable book, *The Discovery of India*, observes that there are five times as many books on India in the London Library as on China. Many were written by nineteenth-century Englishmen who confidently explored such various topics as the early relationship between India and Mediterranean civilization, the parental connection between Sanskrit and other languages, and the suggestive similarities between the oldest forms of architecture in India and architectural forms which later became prominent in Gothic Europe and throughout the Middle East.

Whilst many of these authors were overwhelmed with admiration by what they discovered over a lifetime – if not blinded by religious orthodoxy – they nonetheless could not recognize the continuing relevance of the ancient Indian records. This block arose either because they did not have free access to them and also to accurate Brahminical explanations, or because they were obsessed by the supposed primacy of Greek civilization. Now, all of this has been exploded, and anyone with a lively sense of karma can appreciate the appropriateness of atonement for past ingratitude. When modern Europeans came in contact with the much older and essentially noble civilization of India, and found elements far more ancient than Egyptian relics, something went clearly wrong with xenophobic assumptions and even with regard to 'scholarly' dating. *The Discovery of India* invaluably demonstrates that many Europeans, even before the twentieth century, had traced the origins of major elements of Western civilization to ancient India. Despite their discomfort in proceeding to the fullest conclusions, they established the necessity of taking Eastern records seriously.

It is no wonder, then, that H.P. Blavatsky took the trouble in *The Secret Doctrine* to spell out certain details of ancient Indian and Brahminical calendars and chronologies. Before specifying exact figures, she remarked:

> The best and most complete of all such calendars, at present, as vouched for by the learned Brahmins of Southern India, is the...Tamil calendar called the '*Tirukkanda Panchanga,*' compiled, as we are told, from, and in full accordance with, secret fragments of Asuramaya's data. As Asuramaya is said to have been the greatest astronomer, so he is whispered to have also been the most powerful 'Sorcerer' of the 'WHITE ISLAND, which had become BLACK with sin,' i.e., of the islands of Atlantis.... He was an Atlantean; but he was a direct descendant of the Wise Race, the Race that never dies. Many are the legends concerning this hero, the pupil of Surya (the Sun-God) himself, as the Indian accounts allege.
>
> *The Secret Doctrine,* ii 67

According to this calendar, 1,955,884,687 years had elapsed between the beginning of evolution on Globe A of the earth chain in the First Round and the year 1887. It also located the manvantaric period of astral evolution in the sub-human kingdoms, and distinguished it from the subsequent period after the appearance of incipient 'humanity' on the earth chain. H.P. Blavatsky cited certain puzzles connected with the internal figures in this Tamil calendar, and also contrasted it with other orthodox Hindu calendars. As she explained both here and elsewhere, these riddles develop because esoteric figures cannot be revealed outside initiation. She then proceeded to present a simpler schema computed by Rao Bahadur P. Sreenivas Row, which begins with a single mortal day and extends all the way to the Age of Brahmâ. The telling significance of these figures is that they show that abundant knowledge is available, not only in the inaccessible cave libraries of the Kunlun Range, but also in calendars in common use in South India today, which could be employed as the basis of study. To understand this, one needs something more than a knowledge of mathematics: the method of analogy and correspondence.

Sanskrit and what is now called Tamil are *reliquiae* of ante-Diluvian and ante-Poseidonian languages. In them critical terms like *kalpa* and *manu* have a depth of occult symbolism which can only be grasped by taking them as generic terms applicable to the large and to the small and to many diverse levels of manifestation. This plasticity of meaning affords some protection to those who made these figures available but wanted to hold back certain clues that could, in the hands of unprepared human beings, become dangerous. At the same time, because of the generic nature of these words, one can understand by analogy and correspondence that what pertains to the vast Maha-*kalpa* also applies to the *kalpa* in the small. What applies to a hundred years of Brahmâ applies to one day of Brahmâ and also to the much smaller period of a Maha-yuga.

All of this poses a formidable challenge to the intuition and provides a great deal of food for thought and meditation. Working by analogy and correspondence with various sets of figures, myriad applications may be made not only on the vast scale of cosmic evolution, but equally on the minute scales of days, hours and minutes. For example, H.P. Blavatsky cited the views set forth by Dr. Laycock in Lancet regarding the universal applicability of septenary cycles of days and weeks to all animal life, from the ovum of an insect up to man, and affecting all their vital functions, including birth, growth, maturity, disease, decay and death.

> Dr. Laycock divides life by three great septenary periods; the first and last, each stretching over 21 years, and the central period or prime of life lasting 28 years, or four times seven. He subdivides the first into seven distinct stages, and the other two into three minor periods, and says that 'The fundamental unit of the greater periods is one week of seven days, each day being twelve hours'; and that 'single and compound multiples of this unit, determine the length of these periods by the same ratio, as multiples of the unit of twelve hours determine the lesser periods. This law hinds all periodic vital

phenomena together, and links the periods observed in the lowest annulose animals, with those of man himself, the highest of the *vertebrata*.' If Science does this, why should the latter scorn the Occult information, namely that (speaking Dr. Laycock's language) 'one week of the manvantaric (lunar) fortnight, of fourteen days (or seven *manus*), that fortnight of twelve hours in a day representing seven periods or seven races – is now passed'? This language of science fits our doctrine admirably.

The Secret Doctrine, ii 623

Anyone who tentatively explores such mysterious connections between numbers and daily life begins to touch the Ariadne's thread of the immortal soul. Exactly how this is done and what its effect will be depends upon one's motivation and the tropism of one's soul. Some, ill at ease with the shrunken categories of modern science, yet enthralled with the sky, the planets and the galaxies, may be able to discern intuitive connections which inspire them in their dreams and activate their soul-memory. Others, who tend to think philosophically and metaphysically, may find that such enquiries arouse a hunger for meditation, which in turn helps them to see the archetypal logic of these processes. At the very least, such enquiries will yield an enormous sense of freedom from all that limits the horizons of human thought, all that constrains the reach of the human imagination. Once the imagination is freed, one can make one's own discoveries, through myth and symbol, and express them, through poetry or otherwise. The core discovery strengthened by all this enquiry is a sense of kinship, not only with all humanity and all past civilization, but also with the flora and fauna of the earth, and ultimately the living cosmos in its entirety.

The recovery of continuity of consciousness and the reawakening of soul-memory are central to *The Secret Doctrine*. These cannot emerge except through devotion and gratitude, and through preparing oneself to sit at the feet of real *Gurus*. Hence, H.P. Blavatsky's repeated insistence that the West must relinquish its adolescent egotism; hence, too, her constant recurrence to the figure of the *Arhat*, the perfected man, the Adept and Initiate. Before one can recover continuity of consciousness in the *sutratman*, one must acknowledge the existence not only of soul-memory but also of perfected sages, souls free from the illusion of time and able to witness vast periods of evolution as ordinary human beings watch moments. For the Mahatma, Ariadne's thread stretches in unbroken continuity and total wakefulness beyond the manifestation of this world and into the night of *pralaya* and beyond.

The highest ideal in the Brotherhood of *Bodhisattvas* is to gain a sense of continuity with the substratum of reality that persists even when there are no worlds, but only the night of non-manifestation. By plumbing the depths of that night, even beyond the night of time, Buddhas and *Bodhisattvas* find a freedom and detachment that enables them to see worlds and aeons through an instantaneous flash of Buddhic light. What the perfected human being can do in fullness every human being can attempt, if he or she will practise the toughest of all kinds of mental asceticism – turning a deaf ear to the conventional unwisdom of the exoteric world whilst remaining constantly attentive to every source of potential learning. To release this oceanic sense of universal continuity, one should turn to the sky and the stars, to the poets and the prophets.

To trace Ariadne's thread across incarnations, much less *pralayas* affecting Races and Rounds, requires the tremendous courage that can come only through systematic meditation. This inner discipline is not merely one activity amongst others, capriciously undertaken. It is, rather, the basis for awakening the powers of discrimination of different levels of composition or aggregation, of reduction, reabsorption and dissolution. The mastery of these processes, which takes place within the subtle vestures and is centered on the *karana sharira*, has a direct relationship with the alternation of *manvantara* and *pralaya*. Broadly, the septenary Teachings of *Gupta Vidya* concerning the seven planes of matter and seven states of consciousness have a general reference to all systems within the cosmos. The Teachings also have a more specific reference to the solar system and a primary focus for humanity on this earth. Humanity, circling round the seven globes, finds itself in the Fourth Round on Globe D, the most material of the terrestrial spheres. This globe is preceded by three ethereal globes and succeeded by three globes which are also ethereal but represent a more evolved state of consciousness.

In the present fourth life-wave, occupying millions upon millions of years in its circuit through the seven globes, humanity finds itself evolving through a sevenfold series of vestures that are adapted to matter as it exists in this system. Having attained self-consciousness over eighteen million years ago, in the middle of the Third Root Race, and now belonging to the Fifth Sub-Race of the Fifth Root Race, it still must experience many periods of relative activity and rest before arriving at the close of the present Round. The most immediately relevant shift in the basis of active manifestation applicable to humanity in general is the gradual transition from the Fifth to the Sixth Sub-Races of the Fifth Root Race. Because the Law of periodicity is universal, this transition cannot take place without a pralayic dissolution of aspects of the human vestures and their subsequent remanifestation in a transformed mode. Whatever the subtle consequences of this significant change on the four lower planes, the essential locus of this transmutation is in the fifth and sixth principles of human nature – *Manas* and *Buddhi*. Hence, the meaning and magnitude of the present transformation cannot be apprehended from any standpoint bound up with the lower quaternary, but only from within the Manasic principle of self-consciousness through its meditative attunement to *Buddhi*. Otherwise, the apparent *pralaya* of contemporary civilizations, as well as the promise and potential of an incipient golden age, cannot be comprehended.

The Teachings of the *Gupta Vidya* with regard to *manvantara* and *pralaya* are meant to be studied not merely out of intellectual interest or philosophic curiosity. They are intended for those who truly seek to become *yogins*: those who, by daily meditation, daily self-study and the daily renunciation of the fruits of action, seek self-consciously to bring about profound changes in their subtle vestures consonant with the present phase of evolution. Through the spiritual discipline of concentration, they aim at making the astral form coherent, and the mind controlled. In the context of such a regenerative discipline, the radical difference between psychic action – which works at the level of the molecular and the structural – and noetic action – which works at the level of the atomic – is vital. Here the term 'atomic' refers to that which is even more rudimentary than what science calls atomic or even subatomic. This cannot be apprehended unless a person experiences self-consciously the progressive refinement of magnetism, involving sub-hierarchies of colour and sound and yielding a percipient awareness of the most minute subdivisions of various classes of elementals.

The basic distinction between the psychic and the noetic applies not only to all the elements, but also to thoughts, and indeed to everything perceptible at any level of form. Through deep meditation, one may awaken the capacity to touch that golden Buddhic potency which is in everything, and thus bring about a beneficent alchemical transubstantiation. But one must first have attained to such a degree of disinterestedness that one can consciously assist and accelerate the processes of change, quickening the process of dispersion. Through meditation one must learn to cooperate intelligently with the atomic noetic potential of the higher Triad in a pralayic process of continuous dispersion and dissolution, refusing to allow any recoalescence of that which is dying, so as to sustain continuity of consciousness into that which is being born.

Unfortunately, through possessiveness, through enormous thirst for sensation, through reassertion of *ahankara* – the drives inherent in the Fourth Round, whose dominant principle is *kama* – most humans tend to solidify, to concretize the moribund residues of the past. This is analogous to the physical process, whereby creatures that lived in previous, more ethereal Rounds leave behind them fossils, concretized residues. If this process of consolidation applies to all the life-atoms that make up the astral form in its aspects linked to the physical body, it is also relevant to the subtler states of the astral vesture. To understand and assist the corresponding process of perpetual dissolution, or *nitya pralaya*, is to engage in a kind of letting go, that continual practice of dying which Plato depicts in Phaedo as central to the life of the true philosopher. Conscious and continuous dispersion of all the elements is inseparable from an equal sensitivity to constant and perpetual creation, or *nitya sarga*. The invisible creation at the primary causal level of nature which continually maintains the universe in motion. Taken together, *nitya pralaya* and *nitya sarga* are complementary aspects of the Great Breath. Meditation upon *pralaya* and *manvantara*, dissolution and creation, is linked with mastering spiritual and mental breathing. This involves not only their rhythm but also their attunement to the subtlest level of cosmic breathing.

The profound Teaching regarding *nitya pralaya* and *nitya sarga*, like everything else connected with spiritual self-transformation and self-regeneration, cannot be consciously applied unless one learns to work in terms of cycles of seven and fourteen years. One must prepare for that stage by thinking out to the core who one is, why one is alive, what one truly wants, and what it is one is prepared to live for. This requires a careful preparation in detachment, as well as the courage to face and fully accept one's karmic responsibilities in the realm of *Dharma*. These are the prerequisites of discipleship and practical occultism. Merely by thinking upon these ideas, individuals can tap soul-knowledge in relation to past lives, wherein this knowledge was direct and active. If a person is sufficiently compassionate, suffused with an authentic concern for the welfare of all that lives, determined to be vitally helpful to humanity in some future life – ten lives or a hundred lives from now – then he or she can sufficiently prepare for occult training by coming to understand now that which will come to one's aid at the moment of death. This self-conscious strengthening of the sutratmic thread will enhance the moment of birth in the next life, easing entry early in that life into the Bodhisattvic current.

In the nineteenth century H.P. Blavatsky sought to assure those who had retired from productive lives that even in old age they might prepare their mental luggage for the next life. Today many suffer from the opposite affliction. Through weak wills, frustrated ambitions or fearful eschatologies, they are resolved to do everything quickly or not at all. This is mental laziness, as well as a futile attempt at moral blackmail directed against the universe. Instead of such self-destructive cowardice, one should strive to be fearless in the metaphysical imagination, and dwell on the highest conceptions. One should be ready to look up to the boundless sky whilst addressing one's obligations on earth. Holding fast to a serene rhythm of selfless devotion, one should develop an ethical sensitivity to others, whilst maintaining an alert attentiveness to one's own obligations. One must refine a sense of balance, soaring to the empyrean in meditation, whilst controlling the quotidian details of ethical involvement. Thus metaphysics and ethics may be brought together, to create a steady, strong current of fervent aspiration. Thus too, the process of dissolution is quickened, the potential for continuous creation increased. By letting go, one cooperates with nature's archetypal rhythms.

Beyond these cyclic transformations lies the Triad of absolute abstract Space, Duration and Motion, the metaphysical basis for all continuity of consciousness. All three may be seen as aspects of the Three-in-One, expanding the conceptions of matter, time and motion into primordial substance, boundless eternity and divine thought. It is also helpful to concentrate on absolute abstract Motion as the One Life. This has a philosophical bearing upon one's notions of relative degrees of reality and unreality, of emptiness and illusion, of dependence and causality. The One Life comprises both light and electricity in all their cosmic manifestations and is equivalent to the universal soul or *Anima Mundi*. In Sanskrit it is the *Jivatman*, the analogue of the Platonic *Nous* or mundane cosmic intelligence, absolutely free from differentiated matter and ever-designing action. Through the invocation of the *Jivatman*, the ever-pulsating life-principle, infinite and all-transcendent, Aryan philosophy addresses itself to that perpetual motion which is beyond the distinction between consciousness and unconsciousness. Only through relation to a field of manifestation, relative to *Mahat* in *manvantara* and *pralaya*, can one speak of that which is conscious, self-conscious or unconscious. So entirely does *Jivatman* transcend all human conception that it may as well be spoken of as absolute unconsciousness as absolute consciousness.

If the One Life or *Jivatman* is beyond all these distinctions, this implies that absolute and abstract continuity of consciousness has nothing to do with the purposes and processes of manifestation. It could, for example, be confusing to speak as Hegel does of the Absolute seeking to attain self-consciousness, or, in Hindu terms, of *Parabrahm* having some motive in manifestation. The notion of pure being or absolute consciousness admits of no contrast or polarity, and can participate in no relativities whatsoever. Nor can it have anything to do with the infinite extension of any attribute of finite manifestation (even so subtle an attribute of manifestation as thought, which necessarily presupposes the differentiation of a field and its perceiver). If, then, one is going to meditate upon universal life as a boundless ocean of energy without frontier or finite purpose, one must be freed of all binding conceptions and limiting teleologies, and even all thought bound up with mental instantiation in time. One of the *Rishis* likened the Reality apprehended in *pralaya* to the depths of a boundless ocean of ceaseless energy.

In that fathomless divine abyss, everything is potential, but as a formless and fundamental rhythm or pulsation without reference to any worlds or to manifestation itself. It cannot be understood in relation to the absence of worlds. It is neither definable through affirmation nor through negation, neither through instantiation nor through privation. Cyclic or periodic existence, on the other hand, involves changes of form and state. Archetypally, this may be understood in terms of the potential of the seed, which gestates, then sprouts, then, as a tree with branches and limbs, bears in turn a myriad seeds. On an abstract level, this entire process contains an intrinsic reference to form and matter as it appears to minds that perceive it, and therefore, also a reference to variations of states of perceptive consciousness. These contrasts within manifested matter and consciousness are essential to cyclic existence but in no way characterize the impartite and boundless Reality beyond manifestation.

To every cycle there is a mayavic element, a veiling of that which is indestructible and entirely unaffected by transformation. The life potency that is in the seed in essence is a reflection of something on the akashic plane unaffected by the seed's sprouting. Some beings on this plane may worry whether seeds sprout, but in terms of the essence, the sprouting is of no significance. Once this idea is grasped, one can begin to understand how it is possible, through perception of formless spiritual essences, to change one's perspective in reference to any cycle or to relate the phases of one cycle to another. One may, for example, relate the seven days of the week to the seven planets, and both to the seven phases of human life. Thus one may discern both sequence and possibility, whilst stripping certain cycles of a portion of their limitation. The ability to do this at will depends upon the extent to which one's consciousness is freed from the clutches of *kama Manas*, desire, time and sensation. When the ray of the *Jivatman* is emancipated from the bondage of change, it can experience the universal pulsation of its omnipresent source. Thus it is possible to create a certain negative capability, in the Keatsian sense, a capacity for awareness of the unmanifest side of nature.

The greater this capacity, the more one can correct the natural tendency within incarnation of being caught up in the results and rancours of yesterday, today or tomorrow.

Authentic continuity of consciousness consists of unbroken self-conscious experience of the universality of the life-process, enjoying and relishing its unity amidst all the diversity. It is the ability to trace the Ariadne's thread of the One Life in all the seven kingdoms of nature amidst all the multitudinous forms, whilst at the same time reverencing it at its very root in a realm that is beyond manifestation, beyond the realm of form, exempt from change, undivided by subject and object. The purpose of all study of the sacred and secret science is to gain this freedom for the imagination and this depth for meditation, so that one may become better able to see to the core, and better able to discard that which obscures the Monadic spark. In practice, this means elevating, through daily discipline, one's ethical nature to the same level as one's metaphysical imagination.

One must reach a point where one's only desire or wish is on behalf of the whole, and where one's celebration of all human beings in one's own silent meditation is so real and so joyous that the boundaries of selfhood are shattered. Too often, the two wings of metaphysics and ethics are unbalanced, and spiritual aspirants find that they cannot convert metaphysics into magic. They lack the strength of mind and heart to void their sense of egoity and enclose all humanity within the vast continuity of universal self. Hence, the exercise of the metaphysical imagination must be strengthened daily through meditation, in the midst of the therapeutic practice of self-study and the cheerful performance of *Dharma*. When ethics and metaphysics retain a durable continuity, and flow with a graceful balance, they can be synthesized, to awaken *Buddhi-*Manasic wisdom and the soul-memory of the *sutratman*. Drawing upon that wisdom and sacrificing all strivings at its universal fire, one can make the requisite changes in consciousness, in the substance of the subtle vestures, and in one's magnetic field, so as to become effortless in the continual self-conscious enactment of the *AUM*.

Hermes, April 1983

THE FORWARD IMPULSE

Each class of Creators endows man with what it has to give: the one builds his external form; the other gives him its essence, which later on becomes the Human Higher Self owing to the personal exertion of the individual.... Where there is no struggle, there is no merit. Humanity, 'of the Earth earthy', was not destined to be created by the angels of the first divine Breath: therefore they are said to have refused to do so, and man had to be formed by more material creators.... The first humanity...was a pale copy of its progenitors; too material, even in its ethereality, to be a hierarchy of gods; too spiritual and pure to be MEN, endowed as it is with every negative (Nirguna) perfection. Perfection, to be fully such, must be born out of imperfection, the incorruptible must grow out of the corruptible, having the latter as its vehicle and basis and contrast.

The Secret Doctrine, ii 95

Since that which is absolute and real is boundless and inexhaustible, no realized degree of perfection by beings in any world or system of worlds can be considered as the final terminus. In every theatre of spiritual evolution there are some beings who represent the serene fulfilment of the impulse to growth from a prior period of evolution. There will be many others who must still struggle towards maturation and perfection. There will also be a few who represent the forward impulse of spiritual evolution, moving far beyond any degree of realized perfection ever known before. Like bright stars radiating from invisible centres in space, their hearts are centred upon unmanifest eternal wisdom, which they transmit and transmute into fresh opportunities for growth for every struggling being around them. Self-luminous with theurgic wisdom and therapeutic compassion, these are the *Agnishvatta*

Pitris, the Promethean *Asuras* who light up self-consciousness in human beings when the moment is right.

Before this sacred hour can strike, preparatory work must take place, guided by those intermediate hosts of fecund intelligences that represent realized degrees of perfection from the past. These are the efflorescent *Suras*, the pantheons of ethereal gods, who are mentally passive in relation to the possibilities of the future but still able to form and furnish the needed vestures of lower hosts of struggling monads. The substantial difference between the *Suras* and *Asuras* may be seen as the enormous difference between passive goodness or negative perfection, and the heroic capacity, which is quintessentially human, to take existing forms and inspire authentic spiritual creativity. All heroic strength arises out of this magical power of the majestic light of divine self-consciousness. It is the rare ability to see that which does not exist and the creative capacity to make real that which has never been realized before, but has ever subsisted in the latent realm of Eternal Ideation. This remarkable ability to bring the Unmanifest to bear upon the active realm of manifestation is the extraordinary gift of higher self-consciousness. It is the talismanic gift of creative courage that characterizes the *Agnishvatta Pitris*.

Self-consciousness enables them to become skilful transmitters of the divine light of supersensuous ether in a world of grossly differentiated matter. They have developed the infallible capacity to sift and select, to concentrate to the exclusion of other things, and the dialectical ability to analyse and reduce to basic elements what is otherwise nebulous and diffuse. These are distinct faculties that all human beings possess to some degree, but are rarely understood because rarely considered. All too often, people imagine that these potent faculties are to be used for making final judgements about the world, for fattening the predatory *kama rupa* and buttressing the insecure self. In reality, however, they exist solely for the sake of spiritual freedom. The seminal gifts of the *Agnishvatta Pitris* repose in the human mind for the sake of self-conscious mastery over the chaotic kingdom of inherited vestures.

Thus, any viable conception of perfectibility requires a sensitive, scrupulous care for the undeniable imperfections of flawed materials in the lunar vestures. These may be vitally affected if a vigilant individual generates fresh patterns of thought or feeling that can work like alchemy. It is certainly possible to change the polarity and quality of the life-atoms in the vestures by increasing the porosity of the elementals that comprise them. This is a creative and courageous task, and it can be carried out only if one faces the facts. One must always scrutinize and settle one's karmic accounts. One must be ever willing to look honestly where one really stands in relation to the moment of death. One must see through and beyond entire realms of appearances and so take a moral stand based on general principles. One must derive their deeper meanings and apt applications within the sacred sphere of one's duty. In short, one must cultivate one's own garden of Eden or Gethsemane.

This Promethean stance in relation to one's own spiritual evolution is crucial to the entire Theosophical philosophy of growth. It is supported by the ancient teaching, which was intuited by Leibniz, that every monad has inherent within it the potency of All-Force. Given typically truncated views of human nature, this is seldom understood by most human beings. As Mahatma K.H. explained in the last century:

> The great difficulty . . . lies in the liability to form more or less incomplete mental conceptions of the working of the one element, of its inevitable presence in every imponderable atom, and its subsequent ceaseless and almost illimitable multiplication of new centres of activity without affecting in the least its own original quantity.

He then intimated that from the beginning of a long sequence of manvantaric cycles, centred on a single point in abstract Space, proceeding through the development of a series of globes replete with genera, species and classes of beings, there is no loss of the original force or life-essence during the protracted evolution of their derivatives.

The force there is not transformed into something else . . . but with each development of a new centre of activity from within itself multiplies *ad infinitum* without ever losing a particle of its nature in quantity or quality. Yet acquiring as it progresses something plus in its differentiation. This 'force' so-called shows itself truly indestructible but does not correlate and is not convertible . . . but rather may be said to grow and expand into 'something else' while neither its own potentiality nor being are in the least affected by the transformation.

The extraordinary energy in the One Element, when correctly understood in relation to a complex doctrine of emanation, is capable of endless reproduction, expansion and innovation without taking away anything from that which was in the beginning. Since the ultimate ground of the One Element is inherently boundless and beyond all perceptible limitation, the entire process of differentiation leaves intact the whole potential in the impartite essence of that which was in the beginning.

The poet's observation that in love, "to divide is not to take away", is a profound intuition of a fundamental law of Nature which applies to all its operations, from the formation of worlds to the transformations of atoms. This supreme law of cosmic Eros (*Fohat*) governs all the processes whereby the one Universal Element differentiates to form manifest Nature, with its incredibly complex diversity of systems. In this recondite doctrine of recurring emanation there is a hidden continuity between that which was potentially present at the beginning and that which is fully developed at the end of any cycle. What is vital for alert human beings to realize, and what was so crucial to the Leibnizian doctrine, is that the monad contains within it this potent force of growth and development. But this seminal force cannot be separated from the whole, even in the name of spiritual individuation. It is not merely appropriate to any particular monad, but is itself all-potent on the plane of the One Element. Naturally enough, this force must be intelligently applied to the vast spectrum of possibilities within which the individual monad has to confront its own perceptions and apperceptions. Applying this mind-boggling idea to the monadic wave, working from the *devas* right down to the critical mineral kingdom, and onward and upward to the highest perfected human being, one can see that there is an incredible range and at the same time an extraordinary continuity. Always and everywhere this supreme principle of growth is at work, sustaining a myriad of processes of unfoldment and development, reform and regeneration.

In terms of human principles, this ubiquitous force of growth is objectively correlative with the *Atma-Buddhic* monad, the uncompounded thinking element that is the very essence of higher *Manas. Manas* itself may be thought of as a flame from the fire of *Mahat*. In man this flame is surrounded by dense smoke. That which is all-potent on the higher planes is obscured on the lower planes by inferior forces. That which is an extremely refined vibration on the higher planes, capable there of self-maintenance and perpetual motion, will be eclipsed when inserted into a context of harsher and grosser vibrations. This accounts for the tremendous gap in human beings between what they can touch and experience in deep sleep and what they can express in waking life. To understand this it is necessary to gain a dynamic sense of balance between the activation, on the deeper plane of ideation, of the all-potent force, and the dialectical difficulties of realizing its fullness in everyday life. To tap the noumenal power of growth in the human monad is to draw away from the so-called attraction of the lower realm of desire and become irradiated by the light of *Atman*. One must not fall prey to any false sense of obligation to express one's deepest thoughts or attempt to convince others. That will only serve to ensure disappointment, and it will never contribute to any significant improvement in the human condition.

Here one may profit from the teachings of the *Tao Te Ching*. Taoism emphasizes a cool appreciation of the eternal interplay of light and shadow, and also the importance of minimizing manifestation, expression and interference with others. To gain spiritual buoyancy in the realm of ideation, it is necessary to let go of that which weighs one down. This is not something that can be done all at once, but rather must be made a regular practice. As one contemporary philosopher puts it, one must initiate a "*samadhi* shift". Most individuals are so caught up in the fickle ego that they become tense and strained, like the child in Aesop's fable who caught the fox. Instead, one should appropriately pause and let go. If one is in a mad hurry to get somewhere and has a flat tire, one should not fret and fume, but pause to look around, shifting attention to that which has nothing to do with oneself. If nothing else, one can always look up at the sky, which, as Emerson said, is the great purifier. This is a kind of *samadhi* shift into a realm of ego-free experience. Once one has let go, released all tension, one can achieve much more and with much greater ease. One can begin to enjoy the world from a non-egocentric standpoint, seeing it through the eyes of children or old people, of strangers or friends. To see the world in ways that go beyond one's tyrannical ego is to restore, if only for a moment, some awareness of one's vast potential for growth and timely self-correction.

To sustain and make more continuous this noetic awareness, it is necessary to have a clear philosophical conception of the different modes of manifestation of the universal power of growth. All the animal and vegetable kingdoms possess this immense power of growth; indeed, they could not exist without it. Nevertheless, it exists in them in an instinctual mode quite different from that relevant to thinking beings, to moral agents and responsible choosers. *Gupta Vidya* expresses this constellation of skills in terms of sets of fires constituting the principles of Man and Nature.

> Man needs four flames and three fires to become one on Earth, and he requires the essence of the forty-nine fires to be perfect. It is those who have deserted the Superior Spheres, the Gods of Will, who complete the *Manu* of illusion. For the 'Double Dragon' has no hold upon the mere form. It is like the breeze where there is no tree or branch to receive and harbour it. It cannot affect the form where there is no agent of transmission (*Manas*, 'Mind') and the form knows it not.
>
> *The Secret Doctrine*, ii 57

Through this arcane doctrine of the three fires, the Occult Catechism expresses something of the extraordinary subtlety of the dynamic relationship between the higher and lower planes of existence. These three fires correspond to three sets of entities: gods, *Asuras* and human beings. In manifestation, however, there must be material ancestors or lunar *Pitris* before there can be cognitively self-conscious beings. These are responsible for the projection in ethereal matter of human beings in form. When they also have got the gifts that come from the higher classes of gods and *Asuras*, they become human beings in mind. The three fires are the solar fire of the gods, the electric fire of the *Pitris*, and the fire by friction of the *Asuras*. These three fires cannot be understood through mere physical analogies, but must be understood through deep meditation, through the subtle interplay of idea and image in the realm of creative imagination. Indeed, this alchemical process is itself intimately connected with the Hermetic awakening to self-conscious awareness of these three higher fires. Thus, it is difficult to convey the eternal light of the *Atman*, the sempiternal light of universal *Buddhi* or the supernal light of pure self-consciousness to contemporary human beings, in whom the three higher principles are merely an overbrooding presence.

In most human beings, *Manas* itself is only very partially incarnated, because all attention is given to the external sensory world, to eating and drinking, to the clamorous wants of the physical body, to getting and spending. People seem only too willing to become servants, sadly enslaved to the legions of lunar and sidereal elementals that occupy the lower quaternary. When human beings have thoughtlessly enlisted themselves in the service of these insatiable elementals – and making all their tortuous cerebration utilitarian, centred upon a furtive and shadowy personal ego – they cannot be given any meaningful conception of the real subjective life of the true man of meditation in whom *Atma, Buddhi* and higher *Manas* are fully active. It is no wonder that most human beings have some intense experience of higher conscious activity only in deep sleep or in *Devachan*. In the latter condition, it is solely the presence of the solar element of *Manas* that makes it a positive state of perception for the disembodied monad. In deep sleep and *Devachan*, the involuntary absence of the ego-centred lunar *manas* permits the activation of these higher powers of perception.

Clearly, the common difficulty in releasing the creative potential for growth lies in the absurd way so many people identify themselves wholly or largely with the shadowy psycho-physical vestures. This is, in fact, a direct inversion and costly misappropriation of the quintessential and defining principle of man – *Manas*. How one employs the creative mind in thinking of oneself is a potent talisman and, according to Shankara, the chief key to both bondage and liberation. In the wondrous cosmogony of the *Puranas*, Brahma is said to create by thinking of himself as the father of the world. As H.P. Blavatsky noted,

> This thinking of oneself as this, that, or the other, is the chief factor in the production of every kind of psychic or even physical phenomena. The words 'whosoever shall say to this mountain be thou removed and cast into the sea, and shall not doubt . . . that thing will come to pass', are no vain words. Only the word 'faith' ought to be translated by WILL. Faith without Will is like a wind-mill without wind – barren of results.
>
> *The Secret Doctrine, ii 59*

The capacity to think constructively of oneself is intimately connected with the mysterious power of *Kriyashakti,* and is crucial to the gaining of self-conscious immortality. Without vainly attempting to pry into arcane mysteries, anyone may begin to draw upon this sovereign power through mystic meditation. One may take the sublime portrait of the Self-Governed Sage – associating it, if one wishes, with an actual statue or picture – and think of the resplendent qualities of the Silent Sage, adoring and apprehending them, assimilating them in one's heart and mind. Thus can one actively and deliberately undertake a subtle process of transformation in one's own astral sphere.

The true aim of this esoteric practice of self-transformation is to engender the priceless seed of *bodhichitta*, which in the bloom of enlightenment becomes the Self-Governed Sage. By meditating upon, by adoring, by even thinking of oneself in relation to the Self-Governed Sage – intensely, persistently and with unconditional will, heart and mind – one may gestate the embryonic *Bodhisattva* in oneself. So it is that in the Deity Yoga of Tibetan *Buddhism*, detailed rules for meditation and purification are given in relation to the meticulous consecration of the field, the *mandala*, the magnetic sphere and the central image upon which the rapturous meditation is based. All are integral parts of a systematic discipline which can only be helpful if used with the assured guidance of an accredited *guru*, with an authentic spiritual lineage (*Guruparampara*).

In Deity Yoga, or indeed in any such arduous practice, it is vitally important to understand at some level the abstruse notion of voidness, of omnipresent Akashic Space. One must have the proven capacity, philosophically, to make real to oneself transcendental and absolute abstractions. As soon as one can do this, one becomes intensely aware of the tremendous richness, the unbounded potency, existing within metaphysical Space and also, therefore, within any enveloping matrix of ideation, even within one's own imperfect vestures. As one gains this sacred awareness, one will become effortlessly able to bring down the ineffable light of intense concentrated adoration. This is an extremely high and difficult practice, and certainly much too sacred to be spoken about. But if one truly thinks about it, and truly determines to do it for the highest motives, there is no looking back.

Until this point is reached, the neophyte must patiently engage in a long and arduous course of preparation, probation and purification, seeking to gain at least conceptual clarity with regard to the impersonal nature of inmost creativity. In ordinary speech the term 'creativity' is used much too loosely. In the context of spiritual life it has to do with compassionate meditation and metaphysical imagination. It is grounded in subjective realities that have nothing to do with anything external, though it may express itself in external ways. Spiritual creativity has to do with releasing the spiritual will, which is nothing less and nothing else than the light-energy of the *Atman*. It is universal, cosmic, unmodified and formless. Spiritual will is totally free. It is omnipotent. But it is also so universal that, like the light-energy of the *Atman*, it can be tapped only with complete mental purification.

It is necessary to create vital points of contact in the lower *manas* with higher *Manas*, centres for smooth transmission within one's Manasic field of the subliminal energies of *Buddhi* and *Atman*. This naturally implies a great deal of theurgic work upon oneself, virtually all of which must take place in reverential silence and noetic secrecy. Though the cosmic will may be compared to the rushing wind, and faith to a rustic windmill, nevertheless, when one thinks of spiritual will moving the windmill of human faith, one should not think of that will as blowing from outside. In reality, one is thinking here of a benevolent spiritual breath which is only experienced within the sanctum of indrawn consciousness, when there is a complete quiescence of physical and mental activity, coupled with a slowing down of the rate of breathing and a calm withdrawal of attention from the lesser vestures. Through deep study and daily meditation upon these seminal ideas, through honest self-examination and cheerful self-correction, one may gradually come to clarify, at least in one's habitual conceptions, one's misty apprehension of spiritual creativity.

The true treasure-house of all cosmic creativity is the supernal realm of Akashic ideation. Just as there are many modes of refinement and specialization of intelligence in the different Rounds and Races on this globe, there must be many more on other globes, not only in the Earth Chain, but in all the chains of planets throughout the solar system. There is an incredible wealth to all the iridescent patterns of ideation and activity within the solar system, not to mention even vaster spheres of existence. All these patterns and potentialities for the variegated expression of Divine Intelligence have a definite impact, through the diffused *Akasha*, upon the creative potential of human beings. Through the sacred gift of the *Agnishvatta Pitris*, all human beings can draw freely from the Akashic realm. Those who are hierophants consciously invoke the highest hierarchies, and know how to tap those energies so as to advance human good on this terrestrial plane.

This is an exact and definite knowledge, inseparable in its awesome mastery and timely expression from the heroic courage associated with the divine hosts of *Asuras*. It is a courage to go beyond known limits, a daring refusal to settle down, a Promethean urge to redeem the human condition. It is sometimes only experienced as a confused disaffection with the earthly realm of personal existence, but in its origins it is a consistent refusal to settle on any sacrosanct finalities, to consolidate any final conception of human good, human progress and human perfectibility. This invaluable gift of the *Asuras* is revolutionary in the highest sense. But it is a revolutionary urge that is accompanied by such potent and profound compassion for every living being that it can hardly be compared with modern, mythified revolutions. Terrestrial revolutions sometimes arise from the altruistic urges of a few, but these rapidly become inverted. They are not, therefore, real revolutions. True revolutions in human consciousness are those initiated by Buddha and earlier by Krishna; they represent a fundamental alteration in the horizon of human consciousness. They affect classes of souls who become capable of reflecting their regenerative spirit throughout a series of civilizations. Those who voluntarily participate in these Copernican revolutions become courageous pioneers, true helpers consecrated to universal welfare (*Lokasangraha*).

This is the highest spiritual and revolutionary urge in humanity, and its inmost essence may be likened to the fiery presence of the Dragon of Wisdom. Unlike the Double Dragon – whose breath cannot make any difference to the external world because of its immense distance from this plane – the Dragon of Wisdom, reposing in man as *Buddhi–Manas*, can effortlessly master this field of differentiated elements and imperfect instruments. It can provisionally accept them and partake of them, while at the same time freely acting in the midst of them, to create a current of mental purification and spiritual regeneration. From time immemorial this has been associated with Shiva, the *Mahayogin*. The symbolic wearing of sackcloth and ashes expresses the spiritual truth that human beings are capable of experiencing exalted modes of renunciation and transcendence, of *tapas* and penance, even in their toughest conditions. All beings can release a revolutionary courage that is capable of moving into the Akashic realm and eliciting from the *Akasha* the concept of a golden age, the kingdom of heaven, a new humanity.

Hermes, October 1986

THE MAHAMUDRA OF VOIDNESS

Thou has to study the voidness of the seeming full, the fullness of the seeming void. O fearless Aspirant, look deep within the well of thine own heart, and answer. Knowest thou of Self the powers, O thou perceiver of external shadows?

If thou dost not – then art thou lost.

For, on Path fourth, the lightest breeze of passion or desire will stir the steady light upon the pure white walls of Soul. The smallest wave of longing or regret for Maya's gifts illusive, along Antaskarana – the path that lies between thy Spirit and thy self, the highway of sensations, the rude arousers of Ahankara – a thought as fleeting as the lightning flash will make thee thy three prizes forfeit, the prizes thou hast won.

For know, that the ETERNAL *knows no change.*

The Voice of the Silence

True meditation upon emptiness depends upon a fullness of preparation through a series of stages of moral practice. Without proper preparation, authentic insight into the nature of voidness (*shunyata*) is impossible. It matters not how long this preparation takes; it must be honest and genuine, devised by each human being according to his or her own individual karmic agenda. Otherwise it is impossible to launch seriously into meditation, to enter into it with an inward assurance that one will never abandon it. Even after one has entered the path leading to *dhyana*, one will, inevitably, experience difficulties. Yet one's very presence upon that path must be based upon an immutable resolve. One's preparation for deep meditation upon emptiness must be rooted in a commitment that is irreversible, inalienable and irrevocable.

In Tibetan Buddhism this arduous course of preparation is understood as a necessary precondition for a further and even more fundamental transformation of consciousness that is the fruition of meditation upon emptiness. This quintessential transformation of consciousness is conveyed in a text composed by the First Panchen Lama as a *mahamudra*.

His teaching, first written down in the sixteenth century, derives from a series of oral instructions transmitted by Tsong-Kha-Pa, the founder of the Gelukpa Order in the fourteenth century. These teachings are said to have been received by Tsong-Kha-Pa ultimately from Manjushri, one of the *Dhyani Bodhisattvas* and an emanation from one of the *Dhyani Buddhas*. The First Panchen Lama crystallized an oral tradition around a central Teaching which he called a *mahamudra*.

According to a contemporary commentary upon this Teaching delivered by Geshe Rabten, a religious counsellor to the present Dalai Lama, a *mahamudra* may be understood as a great seal symbolizing an immutable realization of voidness. When one enters into a formal agreement, as in signing a contract, one puts down one's name or seals a document. Everyone knows what this means in statutory law. It is sacred and irrevocable. It is firm and binding. So, too, in a deeper and spiritual sense, one may seal one's entire consciousness irreversibly upon the path of *dhyana* – meditation. Ultimately, this is a direct subjective experience of voidness. Yet as Geshe Rabten's commentary points out, this fundamental transformation of consciousness cannot come about except as the sequel to a long and difficult period of preparation through moral practice, mental development and preliminary exercises in meditation. Even these, as set forth in the *Sutra Yana* teachings of Tibetan Buddhism, require resolves, vows and the development of an unshakeable determination that once one has begun upon this path, no matter what the difficulties, one will seek to become increasingly honest with oneself and strive ever harder to overcome them.

One must be committed in advance not to become infatuated with one's own difficulties, but rather to see beyond them and to persevere in one's course of self-induced and self-devised inner growth. As in all of Buddha's teachings, the only authentic basis of such resolve is a motivation to heal the suffering of humanity. Every time one is inclined to falter upon this path, one should think of the pain of human beings and the misery of human ignorance. Thinking of one's own share in the world's pain, one may realize one's obligation to lessen the burden of the world. To think about this deeply and in detail is to find the motivation necessary to carry on and to persist in a heroic search for deep meditation and the realization of truth or *satya*.

The primary means of preparation for the *mahamudra* meditation is taking refuge in the Buddha, the *Dharma* and the *Sangha*. As soon as one directs one's mind towards the supreme compassion and enormous sacrifice of Gautama Buddha and the entire Host of *Bodhisattvas*, one is filled with a tremendous purifying strength. By thinking of these beings, who have attained to the state of supreme enlightenment solely for the sake of humanity, one can gain the energy and strength to form an irreversible resolve. Thus all efforts at meditation should begin with an adoration of predecessors, a rejoicing in their very existence and in the reality of their deeds and their living presence. To this joyous practice each individual may bring devotion and an undivided seriousness entirely of his or her own choice. Thinking of the meaning of one's own life in relationship to the meaning of the lives of all, and in relation to the world's pain and need, one may contemplate the great work of the *Bodhisattvas*, inserting one's own resolve into the broader mission of building a rainbow bridge between the Host of *Dhyanis* and the world of *Myalba*. Taking refuge in the triple gem, one can find the courage in oneself to try to aid the earth with all its plight and pain, caused ultimately by a fundamental alienation from the true Self, an ignorance of the true destiny of humanity.

It is not possible to take refuge in the Buddha, the *Dharma* and the *Sangha* without prostrating oneself before their clearly visualized presence. In his commentary on the *mahamudra*, Geshe Rabten recommends performing one hundred thousand such prostrations, and acknowledges that even these may not be enough to bring about the necessary purification. In the East, physical prostration before objects of veneration comes naturally because of a pervasive sense of the sacred and heartfelt sentiments of gratitude towards ancestors and benefactors of every kind. But in the West, physical prostration is not something that everybody can readily undertake. It may come naturally, but one had better not simulate it, force it or fake it. Nonetheless, mental prostrations, an inward humility, and the surrendering of the personal will and the judgemental mind can be of great benefit. Nothing but good can come to a human being through the surrender of a divided and treacherous heart. The total prostration of one's being, as enjoined by Krishna in the fourth chapter of the *Bhagavad Gita*, is an essential mental posture preparatory for true meditation.

The Tibetan texts lay down for monks a series of *mantrams* to be chanted. As Geshe Rabten explains, the set of recitations and visualizations revolving around *vajrasattva* is intended to assist in the elimination of negative tendencies. This aspect of the *mahamudra* preparation is of particular significance to individuals who have yet to master the discipline and momentum of a mendicant. *Vajrasattva* represents the embodiment of the power of purification of all the Buddhas. Whilst Tibetan tradition lays down for monks specific modes for visualizing *vajrasattva* and specific *mantrams* to be chanted, these details are inappropriate and unnecessary for lay individuals outside the tradition. What is of crucial importance is to bring to bear from within oneself the purifying power of the Buddha-nature upon the whole assemblage of one's unholy modes of thought, feeling and will. There are, in every human being, a myriad such elements in a state of interconnection. These negative tendencies no doubt arose in former lives, and if they are not extinguished in this life, they will have their fruition in future lives of pain and suffering. The entire assemblage should be acknowledged so as to create a mental posture of total honesty.

To enter the Path, one must be free of all self-deception. Otherwise, as the *Sutras* teach, one will be arrested from further progress and thrown back from further growth. Such devices as prostration and chanting are intended to help one confront all one's errors, especially those that may have caused pain to other beings and which were avoidable, occasions when one knew better and yet acted wickedly. Purification in preparation for the path leading to meditation requires that all of these must be confronted. They must be collected together, brought to the forefront of one's attention, and then burnt out at the very root. Their force of persistence must be destroyed through a resolve in relation to the future and an honest recognition of their effects upon others.

This is, no doubt, a difficult practice and must be repeated again and again. Whichever purificatory chants one selects – whether it be from *The Voice of the Silence*, the *Bhagavad Gita* or *The Jewel in the Lotus* – these must all be taken as means that are helpful in confronting what is called the *papapurusha* – the assemblage of sins. It is this hideous aggregate of negative tendencies that forms the basis, at the moment of death, of the *kama rupa*. On average, it will take some one hundred and fifty years for this form to disintegrate. But if it is more tenacious, owing to a life of self-deception, dishonesty and spiritual pretension, it can last much longer, emitting a foul odour and precipitating crimes and even murders, recognized and unrecognized, on this earth. After-death consequences involving the *kama rupa* pertain to a plane of effects, but what one does in life pertains to the causal plane of human consciousness. If one is not vigilant, one may be gestating the energies that become powerfully coagulated into a tenacious *kama rupa*. All such entities are based, in Buddhist theory, upon the force of self-grasping, bound up with the false imputation of inherent existence to the personal ego. Naturally, the presence of such entities putrefying and disintegrating over many centuries throws an oppressive pall over humanity that puts a tremendous brake upon the aspirations of every single human being. Yet this should not be allowed to become a subject of fascination or speculation. Rather, one should recognize one's own liability to contribute to astral pollution and so one should resolve to purify oneself and one's emanations.

In describing the preparation for *mahamudra* meditation, Geshe Rabten compares these negative tendencies to seeds. It is as if one wished to build a beautiful building, but could not do so without preparing clean ground for its foundations. Before laying the foundations, one must clear away rocks and weeds, cleansing the ground of all obstructions and removing seeds that spring up and interfere with the building. At the same time, this work of purification must be coupled with the collection of materials that will be helpful in setting up the foundations. In the long run, one's fundamental attention must be directed towards the constructive end of serving universal enlightenment. There is little or no essential interest in the obstructions and tendencies that come in the way of the release of this higher motivation. All these tendencies can be classified into certain broad types which are, in the end, both banal and boring. Most of them have to do with attraction and aversion, anger and pride, greed and delusion, and, above all, a false conception of the self. Owing to this false conception of a fake ego, reinforcing it through unconscious habit and semi-conscious patterns of reaction, a persistent aggregate of tendencies has originated.

Instead of becoming preoccupied with the melodramatic history of this aggregate of tendencies, one should merely note them as they arise and mark them for elimination. They will inevitably appear when one starts to engage in meditation, and one should note them only with a view to removing them through the setting up of counter-tendencies drawn from positive efforts to visualize spiritual strengths. Hence the connection, in the Tibetan practice, between the visualization of *vajrasattva* and the elimination of negative tendencies. Each individual must learn to select the appropriate counter-forces necessary to negate the particular strong negative tendencies that arise. In drawing upon these counter-forces from within, one will discover that one can bring to one's aid many an element in one's own being that can serve to one's spiritual advantage. Every human being has a number of elements which represent a certain ease, naturalness, decency and honesty as a human being. Sometimes there is a debilitating tendency to overlook these or take them for granted. The spiritual path requires a progressively heightened degree of self-awareness. One should give oneself full credit for whatever positive tendencies one has, whether they have to do with outward energies on the physical plane, mental energies, moral tenacity or metaphysical insight. In order to find that in oneself which can work in one's favour, and can help in counteracting negative tendencies, one should engage in regular recitation and frequent reflection upon sacred scriptures. Thus one will discover points of resonance in one's individual karmic inheritance that can help release purifying energies flowing from the ideation of Buddhas and *Bodhisattvas*.

If this practice is going to prosper, one must bring to it a moral insight rooted in an understanding of metaphysics. The mind must be focussed upon general ideas. One must reflect upon the relationship of insight and compassion. Insight is not merely intellectual, but rather arises through the recognition of what skill in action means in specific contexts. Insight involves a perception of how wisdom is reflected within action, and which can come about only through a deep reflection upon the process of how such insight is released. On the other side, before one can truly generate a conscious current of compassion, one must create a state of calm abiding. One must find out one's resources and potentials for calmness and for generating the maximum field of patience, peacefulness, gentleness and steadfastness. Then one must combine in practice one's capacity for calmness with one's capacity for discerning what is essential. Inevitably, this will involve a protracted study lasting over lifetimes, and include enquiry into the fundamental propositions of *Gupta Vidya*, the study of karma and the study of what Buddhist thought refers to as the chain of dependent origination.

In essence, this entire course of study is aimed at bringing about a meta-psychological encounter with a false view of the self that must be confronted and dispelled. Ultimately, this complex matter goes to the core of the *mahamudra* meditation. But at a preliminary level and in the course of preparation for that meditation, one must come to grips with the confused notion of oneself that is identified with bodily desire, proclivities towards pleasure and avoidance of pain. At subtler levels one must confront one's conception of oneself that is bound up with the entire chaotic series of thoughts, all of which have particular histories and form associative chains of memory that have been built up over lifetimes of indulgence. All take a variety of forms and leave discernible tracks, all are connected with certain fantasies, wishes, hopes and expectations. They are designated in various ways in different analytic traditions, but always at the root there is the protean force of self-grasping. It is not easy either to confront or to abandon, and hence *The Voice of the Silence* warns that even when one is very close to attaining *dhyana*, one may be completely disrupted by a sudden eruption of self-grasping.

> "Ere the gold flame can burn with steady light, the lamp must stand well-guarded in a spot free from all wind." Exposed to shifting breeze, the jet will flicker and the quivering flame cast shades deceptive, dark and ever-changing, on the Soul's white shrine.
>
> And then, O thou pursuer of the truth, thy Mind-Soul will become as a mad elephant, that rages in the jungle. Mistaking forest trees for living foes, he perishes in his attempts to kill the ever-shifting shadows dancing on the wall of sunlit rocks.
>
> Beware, lest in the care of Self thy Soul should lose her foothold on the soil of Deva-knowledge.
>
> Beware, lest in forgetting SELF, thy Soul lose o'er its trembling mind control, and forfeit thus the due fruition of its conquests.
>
> Beware of change! For change is thy great foe. This change will fight thee off, and throw thee back, out of the Path thou treadest, deep into viscous swamps of doubt.
>
> *The Voice of the Silence*

This passage from *The Voice of the Silence* refers primarily to an extremely high state of consciousness and an advanced stage along the Path. It refers to a point at which the very core of self-grasping must be let go. Long before one has earned the privilege of such an archetypal confrontation with the false self, one will have to win many minor skirmishes with the force of self-grasping. For this purpose, *The Voice of the Silence* gives a specific recipe that is indispensable. It is emphasized in every authentic spiritual tradition and it is central to the New Cycle and the Aryanization of the West. It is put in terms of the metaphor of the mango fruit. One must become as tender as the pulp of the mango towards the faults of others, feeling with them their suffering and pain. Yet one must also learn to be as hard as the mango stone towards one's own faults. One must give no quarter to excuse-making or shilly-shallying. Instead, one must fully accept what one thinks to be one's own particular pain, while recognizing that it is, at its core, nothing but a manifestation of delusive self-grasping.

The mango metaphor sums up all the elements involved in the preparation for deep *dhyana* – continuous, uninterrupted meditation. Geshe Rabten points to a specific preparatory exercise called "taking and giving", which is a beautiful and profound instantiation of the mango metaphor. One begins by visualizing all the ignorance and all the suffering of the world. Then one must consciously take in with every inhalation of breath everything that is ugly, unsatisfactory, violent and disturbing. For the purpose of understanding and contemplation, the world's mess may be thought of as sticks of fuel burning with a thick black smoke. One must inhale this dense black smoke and let it flow through one's body, permeating every nerve and cell, penetrating to the centre of one's heart, where it destroys all traces of self-concern. Then as one exhales, one should visualize sending out light-energy towards all beings, acting through one's positive tendencies and serving to eliminate their sufferings.

This exercise of taking and giving should be conjoined with one's adoration and prostration before the Buddhas and before one's *Ishtaguru*. Indeed, *Guru Yoga* is the fifth and quintessential element of the preparation for *mahamudra* meditation. One may, at first, contemplate the *Ishtaguru* as a drop of light, or, at a more advanced stage, one may actually contemplate the essential form of the *Ishtaguru* in the space before one's mind. It is implicit in the very conception of the *Ishtaguru* that the individual must choose whichever form of contemplation will be most beneficial. Once a choice is made, however, it is crucial that one persistently and with full fidelity bring the distracted mind back, again and again, to the object of its contemplation. The test of this devotion is that one will find a deepening, and yet spontaneous, longing to be of service to others. More and more, one's motivation will be that the black smoke of human ignorance and suffering should pass through oneself and become converted, through persistence in *dhyana*, into a healing light that will radiate, brightening and helping the lives of others. In other words, one will become an instrument through which a great sacrifice is made consciously, a channel through which a great redemptive force can proceed. At that point, of course, there can be no separative self.

One must have become like an alabaster vase, pure and radiant, a translucent sphere mirroring the *Dhyanis* through *dhyana*. In the act of choosing one's *Ishtaguru* or *Ishtadevata* – whether it be under the form of Buddha or Krishna or some other *Avatar* – one will in fact have entered the ray of a particular *Dhyani*. One will have activated the potentiality of a Fohatic circuit through which may be drawn the beneficent energies of the entire Host of *Dhyanis*. One will infallibly recognize this because one's body and mind will be greatly lightened. So free does one become from any dependence upon anything outside that one can subsist upon the food of meditation. This is an extremely high stage which cannot be attained and maintained except by individuals who have early made the great renunciation spoken of in *The Voice of the Silence.*

Every neophyte can approach the threshold of that path and gain an intuition of that exalted condition. The entire practice of the *paramitas* at every level – cycling from *dana* through *virya* to *dhyana* and gaining a glimpse of *prajna* and coming back to the foundation of boundless charity in *dana* – will bring about an inevitable loosening and lightening of the tendency to grasp, to crave and even to think of oneself as separate from other beings. The entire preparatory course of the *paramitas* is summed up in Mahatma Gandhi's mantramic phrase: *one reduces oneself to a zero.* In mystical terms, one becomes a sphere of light.

As one treads the difficult path towards the *dhyana* haven of pure, uninterrupted meditation, one is sure to encounter distractions. According to Geshe Rabten, these may be broadly classified into two types that always work in one or another of two directions. On the one hand, distractions may work as a kind of excitement. On the other, they may operate as a kind of sinking or slackening. With either type, one is liable to become over-active and therefore agitated, and so lose concentration through exaltation in one's happiness or joy or sense of release, or one is likely to get sluggish, drowsy, enfeebled, and thereby lose the power of concentration. These two dangers will combine, recurring again and again. Everyone, therefore, must find out where his or her propensities lie. Different individuals at different times will be more or less liable to become distracted from a current of meditation by excitement or by sluggishness. If one tends to get distracted by excitement, it is suggested that one not close one's eyes during the practice of meditation, but rather keep them open and focussed upon a form that is representative of the object of meditation. Yet, if one is liable to get sluggish and fall prey to sinking, then one may benefit by focussing attention on the navel and taking one's breath from below. Different suggestions will be applicable to different people; in the end, propensities towards distractions are only significant in relation to a process of learning by trial and error.

As with all efforts to purify one's moral practice, the effort to establish a non-distracted mind must begin with a contemplation of the possibilities of a state of perfected meditation. In Tibetan tradition the state of mental quiescence needed for true meditation is represented by myriad analogies. Thus, for example, the clear cognitive nature of the mind may be represented by the image of the sun ablaze in a cloudless sky. There is light and luminosity throughout the field of the mind, giving a supreme clarity to all its operations. There is a simultaneous omnidirectional transmission of light, and, in relation to concentration on any specific object, there is a sharpening of the contours of existence and a heightened alertness to details in the phenomenal world. The cloudlessness signifies an absence of obstruction and confusion of the cognitive nature of the mind, but also a total suffusion of the mind by the overarching, refulgent light of the sun. As Geshe Rabten explains, this analogy represents the nature of the mind as clear cognition, and though it is not to be confused with a realization of the mind's ultimate nature as voidness, it is an authentic intimation of the future course of the *mahamudra* meditation.

Another analogy, perhaps more applicable to the situation of aspirants who are just beginning the practices leading to *dhyana*, is the sureness of the eagle soaring through the sky. The eagle glides gracefully through the sky, ascending without apparent effort, and only periodically flapping its wings. The gliding state represents the absorption of the mind in the object of meditation. The flapping of the wings represents the use of the analytic faculty to dispel a temporary distraction. Whilst it will be necessary in the initial stages to employ the analytic mind to confront and dispel a great variety of distractions, one should steadily move towards the ideal of an eagle's soaring flight. One must advance from a state that is essentially one of great distraction to a steady state, in which one may remain undistracted for relatively long periods of time. Then, when distracting thought currents arise, whether they involve excitation or sinking, they may be noticed, confronted and mastered without breaking the course of meditation any more than the eagle's flight is broken by a single flapping of its wings. In meditation one's basic concern is with the graceful glide, the smooth ascent, movement towards the One.

If one is able to take the standpoint that all human history is a series of successes and failures in preparation for meditation and for initiation into the Mysteries, one may understand that the seemingly burdensome accumulation of history is nothing but the collective residues of a series of over-reactions to distractions in meditation. Confronted honestly, the entire pseudo-drama of history is nothing but a mass of excuses for the inability to maintain concentration. Thus, if one truly wants to effect a fundamental transformation in consciousness so that one becomes incapable of falling back from the true path of *dhyana*, one must be willing to carry out the full course of preparation for that transformation. One must begin by honestly taking stock of oneself and learning to engage in a sufficient degree of self-surrender of the will, through humility, devotion, adoration and prostration, so that one may begin to attune oneself to the higher chords of one's being. Once one begins seriously to meditate, one may begin to visualize the meaning of a harmonic balance within oneself. Whether one pictures oneself as a fish swimming in the ocean of wisdom or as an eagle soaring in the heavens of light, one's emphasis must be upon developing a continuous current of meditative practice. One must develop those spontaneous reflexes whereby one confronts and dispels distracting thoughts without fascination or excess, bringing the mind back again to the main focus of attention. This must be done again and again at first, and one should never underestimate the tremendous effort involved in the beginning.

Every honest student of the path intimated in *The Voice of the Silence* will understand these difficulties. But a point must come in the practice of *dhyana* when there is a taste of the flow of uninterrupted contemplation, when there is a lightening of the load, when tension disappears – including the tension of striving – and when it becomes easier, subtler and more discriminating. Losing preoccupation with oneself, one begins to forget even the meditating self, and so becomes more aware of the vast, boundless expanse into which one proceeds. One will still be far from the summits of meditation and the accomplishment of the true *mahamudra*, whereby one permanently sets aside the bonds of delusion, but one will have embarked upon the authentic preparation for real meditation and sensed thereby the boundlessly buoyant life of the spirit.

Hermes, May 1985

DHYANA MARGA

Ere thou canst settle in Dhyana-Marga and call at thine, thy Soul has to become as the ripe mango fruit: as soft and sweet as its bright golden pulp for others' woes, as hard as that fruit's stone for thine own throes and sorrows, O Conqueror of Weal and Woe.

Make hard thy Soul against the snares of Self; deserve for it the name of 'Diamond-Soul'.

For, as the diamond buried deep within the throbbing heart of earth can never mirror back the earthly lights, so are thy mind and Soul; plunged in Dhyana-Marga, these must mirror nought of Maya's realm illusive.

The Voice of the Silence

Every authentic system of spiritual discipline indicates different stages upon the path of progressive mastery over the mind. The path of progressive awakening to supreme unconditional universal Truth is an arduous course of intensified practice leading to serene contemplation. *Dhyana Marga* – the Path of Meditation – is an inward fusion of mentality and morality that releases the mystical energies of enlightenment. Transcending ratiocinative analysis and ethical endeavour, though yielding to the full fruition of both, *dhyana* is the mysterious catalyst spoken of by Jesus which "leavens the whole". It is the living presence of the *Dhyani* energies vital to any lasting nucleus of universal brotherhood formed by sincere aspirants and neophytes on the Path. Like the fabulous wish-fulfilling gem or the pearl of great price, *dhyana* is one of the priceless treasures of the Path which must, at a certain stage of development, be earned by the disciple before there can be any further advance. If this is true of the cyclic process of individual growth, it is even more true of the evolutionary stream of humanity.

From the beginning of the New Cycle emphasis has been laid upon reaching beyond discursive reasoning and analytic study. Though skilful analysis can be helpful, it is no more efficacious than one wing of a bird in flight. The other wing is ethical practice, purification of motive and steadfastness in reference to one's deepest integrity and fidelity of commitment. The balance between these two aspects of development has been stressed from the start, but as in the life of a bird a definite stage comes at which further development of the wings is neither possible nor desirable, so too in the growth of a committed group of sincere individuals, many of whom have bound themselves by commitments to the spirit of the Pledge of Kwan-Yin. Touched by the potent vibration of the Cycle, a strong nucleus of seekers has persisted, despite ups and downs, in creating a distinct current of direction in their lives. In ways known and unknown to themselves, they have resonated to the current Seventh Cycle of the Theosophical Movement, the last of the series initiated by Tsong-Kha-Pa in the fifteenth century in Tibet. It is deeply fitting that all aspirants upon the path of *The Voice of the Silence* should now seek to become more firm and steadfast with regard to *dhyana* – meditation.

True meditation begins with intense concentration or *dharana* – bringing the mind to a clear focus, which then gives way to the uninterrupted contemplation that is the beginning of *dhyana*. In its full unfoldment it can lead to true wisdom – *prajna* – complete absorption in one's higher consciousness with universal self-consciousness, a state of being marked by the attunement of *Atma-Buddhi-Manas* to the Cosmic Triad. The actual level of attainment reached by anyone attempting this meditation and the pace of his or her development are relatively unimportant. Whatever doubts, anxieties or ambitions some may bring to such attempts are largely irrelevant. What is significant is that a definite and increasing number of human beings should make an attempt, at whatever pace, to learn the practice of true meditation. The simple fact that a number of human beings recognize this common undertaking and obligation, sensing the common joy in the quest for gaining greater proficiency in *dhyana*, is propitious and encouraging to the alchemical work of the Theosophical Movement. It is a positive contribution to the profound impact of the New Cycle, to the elevation of human consciousness in the world as a whole, and to the careful preparation of the ground for the Mystery Temples of the future.

The apprentice on the path of *Dhyana Marga* must learn that the senses are liars; it is precisely at that moment when one seems outwardly to be most alone and engaged in the difficult task of acquiring mental concentration that one is in fact most directly related to humanity. Once one sees this clearly, it becomes possible to insert one's honest and humble efforts in the practice of *dhyana* into a larger effort by a number of people. If they bind themselves together by invisible threads spun through firmness and contemplation and by a continuous current of meditation, they can leaven up the world, in the metaphor of Jesus. This has nothing to do with any individualistic accomplishment. Rather, through their meditation, they can create a magnetic field into which can be focussed the wisdom of Avalokiteshvara, the wisdom of the collective Hosts of *Dhyani* Buddhas, *Mahatmas* and *Bodhisattvas*. Metaphysically, it is the totality of actual and invisible wisdom behind the whole of this system of worlds, which is itself a partial emanation of the primal Adi-Buddha. The aggregate sum-total of actual and potential wisdom forming the radiant core of the system of worlds is nothing but a spark of that absolute and infinite ocean of purely transcendental Wisdom from which arises the possibility of all worlds and all periods of manifestation.

Wisdom is neither created nor destroyed, neither increased nor decreased, but is universal, inexhaustible and vast. It is already self-existent on a primordial plane and is in fact the very ground of the possibility of existence. It may be represented in thought and in collective manifestation as a Host of beings called the Army of the Voice. This is merely a metaphor to intimate something of the virtually inconceivable grandeur and precision of the array of divine elements and beings that constitute the living cosmos. It is possible to focus that light of universal wisdom, continual contemplation and eternal ideation within a matrix created by the love, unity and joint heroic efforts of a nucleus of human beings formed over a period of time. Thus, it is possible to bring down onto the plane of mundane human existence glimpses and rays, sparks and flashes, of that divine light of wisdom that is all-potent on its own plane but is otherwise latent and unavailable. Collectively, a group of human beings can become like a great lens for the drawing down of the light of unmanifest wisdom into our globe to meet the cries of pain, the hungers and the longings of myriads of minds and hearts.

To begin to become an apprentice of eternal wisdom in time, one must gain some minimal understanding of cycles. There can be no practice of concentration and meditation, *dharana* and *dhyana*, unless one can rise above the sequence of alternating states of consciousness involved in the breath, the pulse, sleeping and waking, the passage of seasons, septenates of years, life and death and rebirth. Whilst it would be a false and self-imposed burden to expect to comprehend complex evolutionary cycles, one may, nonetheless, bring a minimal sense of the marriage of continuity and detachment to one 's understanding of the collective human pilgrimage. The New Cycle of the Theosophical Movement, its Seventh Impulsion, marks its anniversary on November 17, a date that is significant not only in the nineteenth and twentieth centuries of the Christian era, but in relation to human consciousness on this earth in general. According to Clement of Alexandria, it was the true birthday of Jesus. Historically, it was the birthday of Pico della Mirandola, the light of the Renaissance. It is also the anniversary of many extraordinary events in history, both recorded and unrecorded. It is one of a series of occult points in the year that may be thought of as birthdays of the *Dhyanis*, points of intersection in cyclic time of aspects of Avalokiteshvara with manifested humanity. Thus, whilst the Seventh Impulsion of the Theosophical Movement is directly linked to this particular aspect of the manifestation of Avalokiteshvara, it cannot be separated from the other manifestations of the *Logos* present at other cyclic intervals.

The present period is one of those watersheds in human evolution that represent the end of a complex series of events in recorded history. It involves the end of the old monastic orders, including the Hindu, Tibetan, Chaldean, Egyptian, Jewish and Christian. All of these will disappear in their older forms. If one is attached to these forms, this will seem to be a great loss, a sort of spiritual discontinuity in human affairs. If, on the other hand, one is detached and therefore able to penetrate to the core of the cycle, one will understand the continuity of the transition and sense that which will tap the quintessence of these old orders and yet transcend them. At the end of every long epoch of human evolution, at the dawning of a new epoch, there is inevitably a night of disintegration. Even if one is able to overcome one's doubts, fears and anxieties in the face of the necessary dissolution of forms, it is still difficult to envisage in advance which of the inexhaustible possibilities of Divine Wisdom will be realized in a subsequent period of development. The wisest of beings are truly agnostic about the future. All neophytes would be wise in their turn not to attempt to extrapolate on the basis of what they think they know about recorded history and the tragedies of the twentieth century. Most human beings are so self-absorbed in their petty personal concerns that they know almost nothing even of the little story called recorded history over three thousand years, much less the broader global developments that have taken place in the first five thousand years of the *Kali Yuga*.

So long as one is worried about what has happened, is happening and will happen – so long as one is caught up in the illusions of the past, present and future – one cannot hope to understand or assimilate the perspective of meta-history. It is possible, nonetheless, in golden moments to glimpse the presence of the powerful vibration that was predominant in the golden age of humanity a million years ago at the dawn of the Fifth Root Race, an epoch hearkening back to that which existed eighteen and three-quarters million years ago in the Third Root Race. Manifestation itself is a complex-seeming superimposition of derivative vibrations upon the primal Soundless Sound. Moments in history such as the present should not be understood in terms of the seemingly static, though exceedingly ephemeral, images that waver on the surface of space but rather in terms of the vibrant impulsions behind these transitory forms. Thus, at present, the vibration of the Third Root Race may be felt as superimposed upon the process in which there is an inevitable end of all that has become degraded in recorded history. Everything in historical time eventually becomes unusable to the spirit, becomes warped and distorted, attracts lower elementals – forces bound up with human failure, greed, exploitation, self-righteousness, moralism and also universal human ignorance. Buddha put this simply in saying that existence is suffering. Put in another way, most human beings would agree that whatever specific form of happiness they might envisage, they will find it a torment to be condemned to the eternal experience of this form of happiness. Bondage to form is inconsistent with the freedom and immortality of the spirit; it is not in the order of Nature.

The vibration of the *Logos* associated with Hermes-Mercury-Budha which rejoices in the void anticipates, encompasses and transcends all historical parameters. This vibration represents the reverberation of *Brahma Vach*, unaffected and unmodified by the great vicissitudes of the historical process and the cycles of manifestation. It is archetypally and magnificently summed up in the figure of Sage Bhusunda in Valmiki's *Yoga Vasishtha*. When asked by Sage Vasishtha how he had remained untouched by the dissolution of worlds, Bhusunda replied:

> When at the end of a *kalpa* age the order of the world and the laws of Nature are broken and dissolved, we are compelled to forsake our abode, like a man departing from his best friend.

> We then remain in the air, freed from all mundane conceptions, the members of our bodies becoming devoid of their natural functions, and our minds released from all volitions.

> When the zodiacal suns blaze forth in their full vigour, melting down the mountains by their intense heat, I remain with intellect fixed in the Varuna *mantram*.

> When the diluvian winds burst with full force, shattering and scattering the huge mountains all around, it is by attending to the Parvati *mantram* that I remain as stable as a rock.

> When the earth with its mountains is dissolved into the waters, presenting the face of a universal ocean, it is by the volatile power of the Vayu *mantram* that I bear myself aloft.

> I then convey myself beyond this perceptible world and rest in the holy ground of Pure Spirit. I remain as if in profound sleep, unagitated in body or mind.

> I abide in this quiescence until the lotus-born *Brahma* is again employed in his work of creation, and then I re-enter the confine of the re-created world.

Yoga Vasishtha Maharamayana, Nirvana Prakarana XXI

Surveying vast worlds, epochs, civilizations and historical eras, Bhusunda stood apart, rooted in *dharana* and *dhyana*. He represents the eternal spectator, unaffected and unmodified by the vicissitudes of the process of history. It is this supreme detachment rooted in meditation that may be called the *Hermes* current. When that Logoic current is self-consciously sounded at the level of SAT – Truth-Wisdom – it becomes the mirroring in time, on the lower planes of manifested existence, of the eternal vibration of *Brahma Vach*. To understand this is to see that everything emerging from that *Hermes* current is a preparation for *dhyana* – irreversible and boundless meditation. Thus there is already in the rich resources of the New Cycle nourishment available for earnest souls eager to learn how to engage in deep, strong and firm meditation, so as to become lenses for the light of Divine Wisdom.

If this is the nature of the great undertaking of *dhyana*, and if some individuals confront many difficulties in rising to meet the opportunities of the Cycle, it ultimately must be due to a lack of sufficient motivation. No explanation of deficiency in meditation owing to this or that circumstance can ever be adequate. It is illogical to attempt to explain an inability to maintain continuity of consciousness in the formless realm by pointing to any collection of circumstances in the derivative regions of form. Hence there is strong emphasis in every authentic spiritual tradition upon the purification and cleansing of the heart. Before one can really master the mind, one must cleanse the heart. It is necessary to see all the distorted, complex and awkward elements in one's feeling nature. And yet there is hardly a human being alive who does not know what it is to care for another, who does not know what it is to suffer, and who does not want to relieve the suffering of others. In fact, the very sense of the hideousness of the deformities of one's feeling nature is nothing but a reflection of the soul's awareness of its intrinsic beauty and purity. Like a craftsman with the highest standard of excellence, the soul surveys its self-evolved vestures with an objective and critical eye.

Rather than becoming fascinated with that in oneself, much less in others, which must be let go because it does not measure up to the best in oneself, one must learn to hold fast to those authentic elements that represent, in every human heart, the vibration of a minute point of universal life, light and love. This *Dharma*-energy can be used to purify the heart so that one can bring not just part of oneself but the whole of one's being into line with a single strong motivation so as to be of help to all living beings. One may release the will to be of service in the relief of human ignorance and the alleviation of the deeper cause of all human pain that is the false notion of the self. One may begin to learn the positive joy of bringing down the light of wisdom and letting that light diffuse into as many beings as it possibly can. When such motivation begins to pervade one's being, becoming strong and firm, it gives a buoyancy and lightness, an incentive and resolve to keep going.

Once this current is established, one sees that one's past failures stemmed from either the inability to commit oneself completely and irrevocably to the quest, or a neglect of the detailed and difficult task of burning out every impure element in the heart. In any event, through the release of heart energy, one is prepared to begin burning out all the corrosive motivations that arise from fear, self-protection, body identification, identification with the astral form, with *tanha* – the clinging to forms in general. Clinging to the realm of sensations is at the root of the hardness and impermeability of the lower mind. Once one begins to understand how much pain obscurity of the mind produces within and without, one can bring a greater honesty and maturity, a greater intensity, to the task of self-purification. One will find it easier if one lets go of the notions of personal salvation, progress and enlightenment, discarding all elements of fascination with the ups and downs of the personal nature. All these represent only the outer rind of human life; they are of little consequence at the moment of death.

One must be willing to become fearless in the spirit of *virya*, the dauntless energy and unwavering courage to enter into the realm of unconditional Truth – SAT. The root teaching of voidness has to do with the emptiness of the notion of self-sufficiency and independence, the falsity of the notion that there is anything that is disconnected from the entire chain. All of this has got to be negated. It is a delusion that arises from linguistic tricks and convention, lax mental habits, refusal to confront the fact of death, unwillingness to confront the life process as it works in Nature. Ultimately, it is a refusal to recognize that conscious immortality means entering the light beyond all forms and conditions.

It is, as *The Secret Doctrine* shows, a fundamental abrogation of one's destiny as an evolving human being:

> ... as long as we enjoy our five senses and no more, and do not know how to divorce our all-perceiving Ego (the Higher Self) from the thraldom of these senses – so long will it be impossible for the personal Ego to break through the barrier which separates it from a knowledge of things in themselves (or Substance). That Ego, progressing in an arc of ascending subjectivity, must exhaust the experience of every plane. But not till the Unit is merged in the ALL, whether on this or any other plane, and Subject and Object alike vanish in the absolute negation of the Nirvanic State (negation, again, only from our plane), is scaled that peak of Omniscience – the Knowledge of things-in-themselves; and the solution of the yet more awful riddle approached, before which even the highest *Dhyan Chohan* must bow in silence and ignorance – the unspeakable mystery of that which is called by the Vedantins, the PARABRAHMAM.

> *The Secret Doctrine*, i 329-330

Only when one can prepare oneself through degrees of *dhyana* rooted in supreme detachment – *vairagya* – can one enter the light of unconditioned Truth or SAT and remain there in ceaseless contemplation. Wherever there is conditionality, there is the inevitability of discontinuity. Conditionality and discontinuity go together. Instead of becoming disturbed by them, however, one should rejoice in the lesson. The more one becomes unconditional, the more one can confront latent conditionality. Thus, one may begin to discern the persistent origins and causes of distortion, discontinuity and tension. The neophyte should understand at the outset that even when one attains to *dhyana* in its true sense, as a confirmed chela on the Path, there are still seven lives of the most vigorous self-training yet ahead. Once one understands this, one can let go of all the tension that comes from taking on false burdens. Instead of cluttering the mind with mere words and shadows, the undigested cuds of unchewed ideas, one should learn how to take a phrase, a sentence, an idea from the Teaching, and chew on it as thoroughly as possible. In every ancient tradition of *dhyana*, it is impossible to dispense with higher analysis. Skill lies in striking the right balance – neither too much nor too little. As one engages in the process of *dhyana*, various hard knots will emerge. It is necessary to stand back and subject them to analysis. One must see the components, the causes, the combinations that form the knot. Along *Dhyana Marga* there will be a periodic need for such analysis – a kind of self-administered open mind and open heart surgery. It can be done when the need arises if one has prepared adequately and honestly and if one is surcharged by a tremendous love of one's fellow beings and an ardent desire to become a meditator.

In time, one will begin to generate a continuous rhythm of meditation, broken occasionally by passing thoughts, but fundamentally flowing as ceaselessly as a current in the heart. When it is interrupted in a more serious way, one will immediately strive to repair one's foundations through some detailed analysis of the problem so that one may be purged and freed of a particular impediment. Once a momentum of meditation is established, these interruptions become a much rarer occurrence than expected. Depending upon one's earnestness in meditation, which can only be understood in relation to love of the whole human race, one's own so-called pain and difficulties will become trifling in relation to the world's pain. Unless one gets these balances right early on, one will have a distorted importance of the preparatory phase of one's own quest. That could stall the whole voyage. But once one is truly moved by that fire of universal feeling that exists in everyone, one will find the courage needed to maintain the quest. Taking advantage of the rhythms of the seasons, of Nature, of the Teachings and the Cycle, one will become more assured and so more able to stay, for longer periods, in an uninterrupted state of meditation.

One will probably not attain the higher stages of *dhyana* in waking meditation for quite a while, perhaps a lifetime. Nonetheless, one is invited to think about these stages, to visualize and resonate to them. This is extremely important and has to do with the release of the powers of the soul. One should completely forget about whether one can or cannot do some particular thing right now. One should not be afraid to contemplate any of the glorious possibilities of the very greatest human beings and Masters of meditation. One should take every opportunity to adore perfected human beings; in adoring them one will give life to the seeds and germs of *dhyana* in oneself. This does not amount to some mechanical and harsh doctrine of pseudo-equality. Rather, it depends upon recognizing that every human being has an exact karmic degree in relation to *dhyana* and *prajna*. Paradoxically, it is only by recognizing this that one can truly understand what it means to say that all human beings stand in the same sacred unmanifest ground of the unmodified, impartite Divine Spirit. Thus, as one grows in understanding of these soul powers, one may enjoy reflecting upon higher states of meditation, as represented by the portraits of perfected beings in the sacred texts and scriptures of all traditions. It is irrelevant and counter-productive to be bothered by the inevitable fact that one will not immediately experience these high states of consciousness.

One may, for example, reflect upon that state of *dhyana* likened to the calm depths of the ocean, recognizing in the metaphor the freedom of the universal Self. To abide in that is like remaining in the Egg of *Brahma* Though this high state of true self-government may seem very distant, one may nevertheless deeply reflect upon it. One may ask what it would be like to have a mind that is so oceanic and so cosmic, so profoundly expansive and inclusive of all things in all minds, that it is capable of reverberating to everything in the mind of Nature. Certainly one should include such lofty thoughts in one's horizon. In this way, one will come to recognize that what at first seemed a burdensome and laborious task is in fact a joyous working out, stage by stage, of clusters of karma. It is also a lightening and a loosening, in each context, so that there may be a flow from the subtler ethereal vestures into the grosser vestures. How this will actually affect the visible vesture in this life will vary from one individual to the next. Many meditators become wizened, but they have no regrets because they have no attachment to the external skin and shell. Instead, they rejoice in the inner purification that has taken place. Even one's perspective changes in regard to what is truly helpful to the immortal soul and what is harmful. Once one touches the current of this supreme detachment and begins to enter the light of the void through efforts at *dhyana*, one may begin to make one's own honest and yet heroic, courageous and cheerful way towards gaining greater continuity, control and proficiency in meditation. Blending the mind and heart, one may enter the way that leads to the *dhyana* haven:

> The *Dhyana* gate is like an alabaster vase, white and transparent; within there burns a steady golden fire, the flame of *Prajna* that radiates from *Atma*.
>
> Thou art that vase.

The Voice of the Silence

What is it the aspirant of Yoga *Vidya* strives after if not to gain *Mukti* by transferring himself gradually from the grosser to the next more ethereal body, until all the veils of *Maya* being successively removed his *Atma* becomes one with *Paramatma*? Does he suppose that this grand result can be achieved by a two or four hours' contemplation? For the remaining twenty or twenty-two hours that the devotee does not shut himself up in his room for meditation – is the process of the emission of atoms and their replacement by others stopped? If not, then how does he mean to attract all this time – only those suited to his end? From the above remarks it is evident that just as the physical body requires incessant attention to prevent the entrance of a disease, so also the inner man requires an unremitting watch, so that no conscious or unconscious thought may attract atoms unsuited to its progress. This is the real meaning of contemplation. The prime factor in the guidance of the thought is WILL.

D.K. Mavalankar

Hermes, April 1985

DEGREES OF ENLIGHTENMENT

The names of the deities of a certain mystic class change with every Manvantara. Thus the twelve great gods, Jayas, created by Brahma to assist him in the work of creation in the very beginning of the Kalpa, and who, lost in Samadhi, neglected to create – whereupon they were cursed to be repeatedly born in each Manvantara, till the seventh – are respectively called Ajitas, Tushitas, Satyas, Haris, Vaikunthas, Sadhyas and Adityas: they are Tushitas (in the second Kalpa) and Adityas in this Vaivasvata period, besides other names for each age. But they are identical with the Manasa or Rajasas, and these with our incarnating Dhyan Chohans. They are all classes of the Gnana-devas.... There are real Devagnanams, and to these classes of Devas belong the Adityas, the Vairajas, the Kumaras, the Asuras, and all those high celestial beings whom Occult teaching calls Manaswin, the Wise, foremost of all.

The Secret Doctrine, ii 90

According to the ancient *Puranas* the first gods were the *Virajas*, the *Agnishvatta Pitris*, the gods and fathers of the gods. Beheld by *Brahma* with the all-seeing eye of yoga, the *Agnishvattas* inhabit the eternal sphere called Virajaloka. From these incorporeal *Pitris*, unshadowed by any astral phantom, come all the Hosts of the *Manasas*, the spiritual ancestors who endowed nascent humanity with the potency of self-conscious thought over eighteen million years ago. The recognition and realization of this divine heredity is essential to the seminal work of the Theosophical Movement, which was, is and ever shall be the progressive elevation of the *Buddhi* and *Manas* of the human race. All human beings are pristine rays of *Mahat*, universal mind, and therefore all human beings are inherently capable of universal self-consciousness, transcending every object and every subject. The *Buddhi*-Manasic potential of humanity is not, in principle, limited by any field that requires the focussing of consciousness upon any specific class of particulars. Divine self-consciousness has not only the effortless capacity for intense interior concentration upon any class of objects, but also the assured capacity for freeing itself from confinement through any class of particulars. Human consciousness is intrinsically capable of conceiving all possible as well as all actual beings, all possible and actual subjects and objects. Through the joyous awareness of their essentially divine nature, human beings are capable not only of seeing humanity and the entirety of manifested Nature in terms of all that may be known about the present and the past, but also of visualizing the vast range of possibilities constituting the future of Nature and Man.

It was the divine intent of the solar ancestors of the human race that humanity should awaken and master this latent capacity for *kriyashakti*. This would naturally encompass the ability to visualize the future development of flora and fauna and of the elemental kingdoms, as well as the mineral, vegetable and animal kingdoms. In particular, far-sighted individuals may fearlessly extend the horizon of human powers and possibilities, and imagine what fully self-conscious human beings might be like in the far distant future. This sovereign capacity of human beings to go far beyond any particular set of facts is not a matter of mere idle speculation or sporadic invention. If this sacred activity of calmly visualizing the future is sustained with deep concentration that transcends the realm of memory and sensation, it will penetrate with depth and intensity into a much subtler plane of existence, wherein all matter is undifferentiated, primordial and fiery. This is the plane of the supersensuous ether, the *Akasha*, which is exceedingly subtle, plastic and pliable to persistent ideation.

Through such intense concentration, human beings may actually help fashion the noumenal prototypes of the future. This is a sacred theurgic activity, and to be able to sustain it one would not only have to become practised and proficient in deep meditation, but also to become dispassionate and detached towards the existing world of objects and subjects. Certainly, one would have to free oneself from the crude memory of cursory events that impinge, mostly through sensation, pleasure and pain. upon the agitated personality. In fact, one would have to disengage oneself from all the chaotic affinities that one has formed in the astral body with ephemeral events, meretricious attractions and concretizing tendencies. To engage in this profound self-purification, one must learn to stay in a meditative state of voidness, experiencing what St. John of the Cross called the dark night of the soul. After purging all the lower affinities and supplanting them with finer tendencies originating in the higher Self, one may gradually become directly conscious of the higher affinities of the immortal soul. It is at this point that the awakened soul may become immediately aware of the different classes of hierarchies and creators involved in the spiritual lineage of humanity. Among the myriad classes of creators, human beings have a special affinity with highly evolved divine intelligences allied with the *sukshma sharira*, what might be called the subliminal aspect of the astral form. Every human being has recognizable affinities with the myriad gods, and with all the divine intelligences that endlessly circulate within the supersensuous ether of Space. Potentially, human consciousness may inhabit not merely spaces on and around the earth, but also interplanetary spaces, intrasolar spaces and spaces extending even to those that circle round the nucleus of the central Spiritual Sun.

The profound nature and enormous range of human potential is hardly comprehensible to most ordinary human beings. Even a partial incarnation of true *Buddhi*-Manasic genius will produce a highly sensitive individual capable of remarkable flashes of genius, extraordinary vision and divine intuition. Mozart was one such genius, a shining example of a free spirit who inhabited a world that has no relationship to the world as we know it. These rare souls may be expansively buoyant in their relationships to human beings and also be daringly outspoken and maddeningly unorganized in a worldly sense. For such a kaleidoscopic mind, replete with musical vibrations – the endless permutations, patterns and resonances of Akashic sound – it is very difficult to make a practical accommodation to ordinary human consciousness. Instead, such boisterous beings are in continual communication with the *devas*, with divine beings and divine intelligences, and are effortlessly capable of experiencing the music of the spheres as well as the divine dance (*lila*) of the noumenal plane.

Even such souls, however, can scarcely give a sufficient indication of the immense range of creative ideation. It flourishes freely in a realm impossible to map, impossible to delimit or even to define. Whether one talks in the language of comparison and contrast, or in terms of individuation and universalization, no category can convey enough about the inexhaustible range of possible conceptions that belong to the vast realm of seminal ideation. Yet if one begins to discern something of the nature of these wondrous possibilities, it becomes clear that there can be conscious alterations, by controlled ideation, in human beings, which not only transcend *kama Manas* – the brain-mind caught up in the volatile and ever-changing realm of sensory particulars – but may even gain a skilful mastery at some level over hosts of elementals, and then delegate many of the functions that belong to the lower quaternary to a trained set of elementals.

Everyone has some experience, at a preliminary level, of such training. An extremely experienced cook, even an experienced driver, may have some sense of being involved with intelligences or elementals that seem to function without constant guidance. These entities have been programmed, one might say, to respond flexibly and to become extremely sensitive to all the actual and possible features of a situation. Whilst one may gain some elementary sense of this from such ordinary examples, it is inadequate to convey a full sense of the complete mastery over elementals that one finds, for example, in Shakespeare's The Tempest. Prospero the Magus has in Ariel a highly skilled controller over the elemental field who is at the same time a perfect instrument of Prospero. This entirely realistic example reveals the ever-present possibility in human ideation of delegating whole classes of functions through trained elementals. In practice, this requires a transformed relationship between the Lunar *Pitris* – who have given humanity all the elements of its lower quaternary – and the Solar *Pitris* – who have lit up in humanity the flame of self-consciousness. Only by forming self-conscious affinities with the *Agnishvatta Pitris*, who are responsible for all the *Manasas*, may one gain such mastery.

To establish that relationship one must move to a realm of meta-ethics and of noetic magic, far removed from all ordinary conceptions. What in other people are involuntary and compulsive tendencies can, in fact, be brought together in ways in which there is a precision in the orchestration of elemental intelligences in the performance of a wide variety of activities. All these activities would be commanded by the astral shadow of the Lunar *Pitris*, which itself has become highly responsible and wholly responsive to the Solar *Dhyani* who has become more fully incarnated. Here it is helpful to draw an analogy with the macro-processes of evolution, which may be put in terms of the following stages:

> Three stages in the elemental side; the mineral kingdom; three stages in the objective physical side – these are the seven links of the evolutionary chain. A descent of spirit into matter, equivalent to an ascent in physical evolution; a re-ascent from the deepest depths of materiality (the mineral) towards its status quo ante, with a corresponding dissipation of concrete organisms up to Nirvana – the vanishing point of differentiated matter.

Five Years of Theosophy

The progressive descent of spirit into matter involves an increasing obscuration of spirit. To be able to elaborate, extend and experience the matrix of matter, there must be a temporary loss of conscious access to innate, timeless and unbounded spirituality. On the other side of the evolutionary arc, to be able to free the spiritual will is to reduce and refine, to concentrate and reshape matter, so that one becomes less involved with gross life-atoms and more capable of dealing with the most sensitive, refined and supersensuous life-atoms. These in turn are capable of responding as naturally and as reliably to the spiritual will as a fine musical instrument to the hands of a master. Such a maestro is not focussed upon either instrument or script, but having mastered them both, creates and re-creates sound through his own metaphysical imagination.

Long before this can happen to human beings in general, long before the beginning of the Sixth Race, there must be a conscious development, within the Fifth Sub-Race of the Fifth Race, of an impartial, impersonal and universal sense of justice in the moral realm. This can only come from a freedom from all possible roles and a capacity to enact them freely, while at the same time being able to see beyond them. The vanguard of the Fifth Root Race in the Fifth Sub-Race arose essentially in Europe and Scandinavia, going back to ancient Nordic conceptions of law, self-respect, honour and freedom. Later, the whole range of Germanic peoples, coming down to the Mediterranean world, and above all the rich heritage of England and France, contributed to this remarkable development. The greatest creative geniuses over thousands of years in that part of the world have created complex languages and also a scintillating spectrum of conceptual possibilities that is still to be fully assimilated by many human beings. Unfortunately, most human beings, especially in the last hundred years, have become mentally slavish and morally parasitic, subsisting only because of mass education and mass culture. Strutting and posturing, they cling to copies upon copies of the shadows of shadows of the original insights of the greatest minds. Even the better products of contemporary culture scarcely have even an indirect awareness of secondary and third-order reflections of the seminal ideation of the vanguard of the Fifth Sub-Race. To break this destructive cycle of degradation, it is necessary to go beyond the outward ephemera of contemporary culture by developing the power of meditation with a degree of continuity and skill that is paralleled by the development of a responsible detachment, rooted in the fact that one had discharged all one's duties. Only when one fulfils all one's familiar obligations in many spheres can one become truly detached – free to contemplate and free to go beyond the claims of the world – and also free to give full support to an arduous programme of systematic and continuous spiritual meditation.

This theurgic activity, which is now so crucial to the Fifth Sub-Race, was laid down in its essentials in the First Sub-Race of the Fifth Root Race in India. Here in the New Cycle one may be helped through a variety of sacred texts, especially through the *Yoga Vasishtha*. Even though it might have been written down relatively recently (namely, in the last two thousand years), it actually records the Teachings given a million years ago in the time of Rama by the Sage Vasishtha. The *Yoga Vasishtha* sets forth the holy discourses given by the Sage in the court of Rama, the great King-Initiate and incarnated Avatar who was no other than the being who later became Krishna. Rama invited the *Rishi*, who was beyond time, outside history and representative of the realm of the transcendent, to transmit the quintessence of the highest wisdom in regard to the Self, in regard to mind, error, happiness, virtue, and also in regard to the highest exemplification of living liberation, the *Jivanmuktas*. The Sage offered disquisition upon disquisition, repeatedly and in diverse modes, using rich and telling metaphors, but always reverting to certain central questions based upon the relation between the real and the unreal. Here the terms 'real' and 'unreal' are not applied merely to the world of fugitive sense-perceptions, but to immense periods of time, to entire worlds and *manvantaras*. From that elevated standpoint, one is asked to generate an active sense of reality which is more fundamental, more durable and much more meaningful, and which therefore can be carried over millions upon millions of years. That is the exalted philosophical level at which Vasishtha speaks. At the core of his Teachings are profound questions about the relation of the unmanifest to the manifest.

In the *Yoga Vasishtha* the supreme basis of a consecrated life of conscious immortality and ceaseless contemplation was provided at the beginning, as also in the later climactic development, of the Fifth Root Race. To rise in consciousness to this level, much less go beyond it, is to develop a radically new attitude towards the whole concept of conquest and control, a heightened sense of the invisible world of elementals and an entirely new conception of noetic magic involving the exercise of *kriyashakti*, creative visualization. This requires the sovereign capacity to alchemize and transform all one's lower vestures. And it is the testimony of the Sage that this is possible only if one can activate potentials in the subtlest vestures. It is essential to awaken certain higher subdivisions of *Manas* in relation to specific subdivisions of *Buddhi* and to bring them together.

This daring programme, which goes directly to the heart of the Theosophical Movement, is really a concerted effort to stimulate the metaphysical imagination of thinking beings who have the courage and freedom to see beyond the limits of their environment, beyond the parameters of their parochial, familial and cultural affinities. Those who can go beyond these customary limitations, and who can truly adopt a universal perspective of the human heritage, will be able to see behind all the great myths of all humanity certain inspiring central conceptions which throw light not only upon the forgotten language of dreams and visions, but also upon the world as it is. A true awakening of spiritual imagination inevitably and wholly changes one's view of what it is to be alive and who one is. It also generates a rich inner life, joyous and serene, but rooted in a relaxed mastery over all the obligations of one's outer life. Whilst accomplishing all of these with ease, completing them with only a portion of oneself, one will keep free the rest of oneself to continue to gestate the highest conceptions.

The effortless performance of every obligation, whilst established in transcendence of the outer world, involves a rethinking of the fundamental nature of attention to good and evil, to right and wrong. This would also be connected with a reconceptualization of what are seen as limitation and imperfection, suffering and misfortune, in the so-called real world. Through a meditative metaphysical awareness of the *Agathon* outside space and time, one must develop a compassionate and therapeutic understanding of the moral opposites in manifestation.

> Good and Evil are twins, the progeny of Space and Time, under the sway of *Maya*. Separate them, by cutting off one from the other, and they will both die. Neither exists *per se*, since each has to be generated and created out of the other, in order to come into being; both must be known and appreciated before becoming objects of perception, hence, in mortal mind, they must be divided.
>
> *The Secret Doctrine*, ii 96

Good and evil as an inseparable pair of opposites may be thought of in terms of the relationship of manifested and differentiated light and shadow. Here one is speaking not of noumenal light, not of that which originates from the centre of the hexagon, the light of *Daiviprakriti*, nor even of *Fohat*, which is the synthesis of all phenomenal light-energies. Rather, one is addressing a level that is much below the level of primordial manifestation and is concerned with the world of chaos and contrast, the realm of highly concretized perceptions. Generally, human beings have a narrowly limited view of light and, therefore, also of shadow. As the human instruments are imperfect, they give a dull and distorted conception of light and shadow. This is the inevitable outcome of the limited spatio-temporal horizon which engages consciousness in the sensorium. It operates especially strongly in memory and sensation, through the notion of the past and through expectations focussed upon a concretized and foreshortened future. All these perceptions and conceptions are under the sway of *maya*. There is, therefore, an element of unreality and exaggeration, an element of deception, in all moral concepts derived from such consciousness.

This may be seen at work in many ways. One might belong to a particular family, a certain class or to some specific community. Within such a context, it might appear that there is an extraordinary difference between human beings, such that they are clearly divided between 'the good guys' and 'the bad guys'. Some insight into the deceptive nature of contrast may be found in the work of the novelist Claude Houghton, who specialized most of his life in studying criminals and defending them. Moving in the underworld of London, he won the respect of a large number of criminals. He discovered in that underworld many senior police officers whose whole task was to befriend the most important of the crooks. He thus discovered a very complicated kind of understanding between both sets of individuals. Behind the facade of social life and its facile generalizations, he saw there were innumerable unexpected and complicated shades and blendings of goodness and evil, of strength and weakness, of courage and timidity, that mocked any exaggerated contrast of good and evil. Some of the authentic complexity of human beings can also be seen in Shakespearian plays, where every character has an element of absurdity and a possibility of transcendence; everyone is changing all the time, and by the end may, in unexpected ways, be elevated.

Seen from the objective standpoint of a great dramatist, the entire gamut of human character is so great that one must begin to accept that any sort of harsh contrast between good and evil is subjective and deceptive. Such contrasts are based upon external signs and are limited owing to the habitually limited contexts in consciousness in which people ordinarily move. Yet it is precisely these limitations which impose upon individuals tremendous burdens of fear and expectation, as well as induce them to indulge in judgementalism. From the exalted standpoint of an enlightened being, as Buddha once said, all differences between all human beings are as nothing compared to the tremendous difference between the enlightened and the unenlightened. Once one registers the huge abyss separating the great benefactors and divine ancestors of the human race from ordinary human beings, one can clearly see the relativity of one's perceptions regarding good and evil, right and wrong. Even more is required if one is going to be not merely an objective observer or a sympathetic judge, but a mature being responsible for others. Again, one may be helped by examples – a wise mother with a large family made up of difficult and easy children, or a wise schoolteacher, who truly wants to release the potential and do the best for a large class of different people. One might also think of a wise healer, a shaman, who must not only diagnose but also cure a great variety of suffering individuals. But whilst such examples can help clarify the nature of compassion, they serve only as dim approximations of the boundless compassion and beatific grace of the enlightened.

The only way to move towards that distant goal is through practical altruism now. If one truly desires to awaken *Buddhi*, one must begin to learn how to act nonjudgementally and responsibly on behalf of others. Human beings who are not merely concerned with judging, let alone absolutizing, the differences between human beings, but who want to help human beings to change their condition, have to engage, either semi-consciously or with full self-consciousness, in a kind of spiritual alchemy. They must first help to change the vocabulary of people. They must minimize the use of the words 'cannot' and 'impossible'. They must discourage the phrase 'I won't'. They must stress what can be done here and now. Instead of saying that nothing can be done, people must be encouraged to discover the first step that can be taken right now. This requires an alchemical alteration in one's view of what is bad. That which is bad is that which is still alterable. Inflexibility resides purely on the plane of effects. Considered on the plane of causes, it is based upon a false idea which, though persistent and therefore strong, can nevertheless be modified and qualified. In time, indeed, it can be replaced by the true idea of which it is a distorted reflection or even a polar opposite.

To be able to assist others in altering their perception of what is limited or limiting, to be able to help others to see opportunities where they would otherwise feel blanked out, is an alchemical art. It involves being able to see the dynamic relationship between limited goods and limited evils. Potentials of the greater good often lie within limited evils, just as the dangers of shadows often lie in prospects that seem to offer the greater good. This alchemical art is difficult to describe because it can only be learnt through daily practice. Put simply, no one can really know anything about human nature if he or she becomes an expert in human weakness. At best, one can only become a candidate for maleficent magic, or sorcery. To have any authentic knowledge of human nature and to help human beings grow, one has to become an ingenious expert on the inherent good in human beings. One must be able to put the case for any and every human being on earth.

If one truly wishes to help humanity, one must, like a good physician, be willing to recognize illnesses for what they are and call things by their proper names. One cannot soft-pedal or deny the existence of extreme and unnatural selfishness.

> Spirituality is on its ascending arc, and the animal or physical impedes it from steadily progressing on the path of its evolution only when the selfishness of the personality has so strongly infected the real inner man with its lethal virus, that the upward attraction has lost all its power on the thinking reasonable man. In sober truth, vice and wickedness are an abnormal, unnatural manifestation, at this period of our human evolution – at least they ought to be so. The fact that mankind was never more selfish and vicious than it is now, civilized nations having succeeded in making of the first an ethical characteristic, of the second an art, is an additional proof of the exceptional nature of the phenomenon.
>
> *The Secret Doctrine,* ii 110

There is nothing more horrifying than the kamarupic portrait of an extremely selfish personality. There is nothing more ugly than *tanha,* the desperate clinging to the physical body. These common evils are, in fact, much more difficult to dispel than the so-called dramatic examples of evil that so fascinate popular culture.

The wise individual who truly wants to gain a greater knowledge of human nature must grow deaf to the chaotic sounds that emerge from the hollow sounding-box of the insecure personality. He must see every person from the profound standpoint of the indwelling ray of the immortal soul, the trapped ray of universal mind. Those who are in right earnest in wanting to work actively for the humanity of the future must experience a good deal of what one of the *Mahatmas* characterized as "swimming in *adversus flumen*". To be able to gain a dynamic and therapeutic view of human nature, they must go far beyond any absolutizing or relativistic conceptions of good and evil. They must, on behalf of the future, restore a consciousness of the ineffable presence within themselves, and all humanity, of that which was in the beginning, the divine light of *Mahat*, the sacred lineage of the *Agnishvatta Pitris*.

Hermes, November 1986

YOGA SUTRAS – BOOK I
SAMADHI PADA

AUM atha yoganushasanam

1. OM. Now begins instruction in yoga. (1)

yogash chitta-vritti-nirodhah

2. Yoga is the restraint of the modifications of the mind. (2)

tada drashtuh svarupe 'vasthanam

3. Then the Seer is established in his own essential nature. (3)

vritti-sarupyam itaratra

4. Otherwise, there is self-identification with the mental modifications. (4)

vrittayah panchatayyah klishtaklishtah

5. The mental modifications are fivefold and are painful or pleasurable. (5)

pramana-viparyaya-vikalpa-nidra-smritayah

6. These are correct cognition, misconception, fantasy, sleep and memory. (6)

pratyakshanumanagamah pramanani

7. Correct cognition is based on direct perception, valid inference and verbal testimony. (7)

viparyayo mithya-jnanam atad-rupa-pratishtham

8. Misconception is illusory knowledge based upon what is other

than itself. (8)

shabda-jnananupati-vastu-shunyo vikalpah

9. Fantasy, empty of substance, is engendered by words and concepts. (9)

abhava-pratyayalambana vrittir nidra

10. Sleep is the modification engendered by the abeyance and absence of mental contents. (10)

anubhuta-vishayasanpramosha smritih

11. Memory is the not letting go of an object or image of subjective experience. (11)

abhyasa-vairagyabhyam tan-nirodhah

12. The restraint of these mental modifications comes from assiduous practice (*abhyasa*) and through dispassionate detachment (*vairagya*). (12)

tatra sthitau yatno 'bhyasah

13. Practice (*abhyasa*) is the continuous effort to abide in a steady state. (13)

sa tu dirgha-kala-nairantarya-satkarasevito dridha-bhumih

14. This is indeed firmly grounded when it is persistently exercised for a long time, without interruption, and with earnest, reverential attention and devotion. (14)

drishtanushravika-vishaya-vitrishnasya vashikara-sanjna vairagyam

15. Dispassionate detachment (*vairagya*) is the consciousness of perfect mastery in one who has ceased to crave for objects, seen or unseen. (15)

tat param Purusha-khyater guna-vaitrishnayam

16. That is the supreme dispassion when there is cessation of all craving for the attributes (*gunas*), owing to discernment of the Self (*Purusha*). (16)

vitarka-vicharanandasmitanugamat sanprajnatah

17. Cognitive contemplation is accompanied by reasoning, deliberation, bliss and the awareness of pure being (*asmita*). (17)

virama-pratyayabhyasa-purvah sanskara-shesho 'nyah

18. Another sort of contemplation comes through the previous practice, the cessation of all mental contents, residual potencies alone remaining. (18)

bhava-pratyayo videha-prakritilayanam

19. It is caused by phenomenal existence in the case of the disembodied and of those absorbed into Nature (*prakriti*). (19)

shraddha-virya-smriti-Samadhi-prajnapurvaka itaresham

20. In the case of others, it is preceded by faith (*shraddha*), energy (*virya*), attentiveness (*smriti*), and the intellectual insight (*prajna*) needed for meditative absorption (*Samadhi*). (20) (20)

tivra-sanveganam asannah

21. It is close at hand for those with vehement intensity. (21)

mridu-madhyadhimatratvat tato 'pi visheshah

22. There is also a further differentiation – mild, moderate and intense. (22)

ishvara-pranidhanad va

23. Or by devoted self-surrender to the Lord. (23)

klesha-karma-vipakashayair aparamrishtah purushavishesha ishvarah

24. *Ishvara* is a distinct spirit (*Purusha*), untouched by troubles, actions and their results, and latent impressions. (24)

tatra niratishayam sarvajna-bijam

25. In *Ishvara* the seed of omniscience becomes infinite. (25)

sa purvesham api guruh kalenanavachchedat

26. *Ishvara* is the preceptor even of the Ancients, for He is not fettered by time. (26)

tasya vachakah pranavah

27. His designation is OM. (27)

tajjapas tad-artha-bhavanam

28. Let there be constant chanting of OM and meditation on its meaning. (28)

tatah pratyak-chetanadhigamo 'py antaraya-bhavash cha

29. From that comes the turning inward of consciousness and the removal of hindrances. (29)

vyadhi-styana-sanshaya-pramadalasyavirati-bhranti-darshanalabdhabhumikatvanavasthitatvani chitta-vikshepas te 'ntarayah

30. The hindrances which cause mental distractions are disease, dullness, doubt, heedlessness, indolence, addiction to sense-objects, distorted perception, failure to find a footing and instability in any state. (30)

duhkha-daurmanasyangamejayatva-shvasa-prashrasa vikshepa-sahabhuvah

31. These distractions are accompanied by sorrow, depression, bodily restlessness and spasmodic breathing. (31)

tat-pratishedhartham eka-tattvabhyasah

32. To check these, there should be constant practice of one truth or principle (*eka-tattva*). (32)

maitri-karuna-muditopekshanam sukha-duhkha-punyapunya-vishayanam bhavanatash chitta-prasadanam

33. The mind becomes purified through the practice of friendliness, compassion, gladness and indifference respectively towards happiness, sorrow, virtue and vice, (33)

prachchardana-vidharanabhyam va pranasya

34. Or by expulsion and retention of breath (*prana*). (34)

vishayavati va pravrittir utpanna manasah sthiti-nibandhani

35. The awakening of subtle sensory vision can hold the mind in a state of steadiness, (35)

vishoka va jyotishmati

36. Or a state of serene luminosity, (36)

vita-raga-vishayam va chittam

37. Or the mind is fixed on one free from craving, (37)

svapna-nidra-jnanalambanam va

38. Or by dwelling on insights gained in dreams and dreamless sleep, (38)

yathabhimata-dhyanad va

39. Or by meditating on that which is deeply desired. (39)

paramanu-parama-mahattvanto 'sya vashikarah

40. Thus, his mastery extends from the minutest atom to the ultimate infinitude. (40)

kshina-vritter abhijatasyeva maner grahitri-grahana-grahyeshu tatstha-tadanjanata samapattih

41. When the modifications of the mind vanish, it becomes like a transparent crystal, attaining the power of transformation (*samapatti*), taking on the colour of what it rests on, whether it be the cognizer, the cognized or the act of cognition. (41)

tatra shabdartha-jnana-vikalpaih sankirna savitarka

42. Whenever the construction of words and meanings is confused and uncertain, the mind wavers in a polemical and chaotic state (*sankirna savitarka*). (42)

smriti-parishuddhau svarupa-shunyevartha-matra-nirbhasa nirvitarka

43. When the memory is purified, when the mind is void of its own form, it is luminous with true knowledge of its sole object, attaining to an unclouded state (*nirvitarka*). (43)

etayaiva savichara nirvichara cha sukshma-vishaya vyakhyata

44. Also, by this process, the deliberative and non-deliberative states concerning subtle elements (*sukshma-vishaya*) are explained. (44)

sukshma-vishayatvam chalinga-paryavasanam

45. And the subtle elements extend up to the noumenal, primordial and undifferentiated (*alinga*). (45)

ta eva sabijah samadhih

46. They are only the basis of meditation with its seed. (46)

vichara-vaisharadye 'dhyatma-prasadah

47. On attaining the utmost purity of the non-deliberative state, there is the dawning of spiritual light, the gracious peace and luminosity of the supreme Self. (47)

ritambhara tatra prajna

48. Therein is direct cognition (*prajna*), which carries and holds the unalloyed Truth. (48)

shrutanumana-prajnabhyam anya-vishaya vishesharthatvat

49. Direct cognition is essentially different from testimony and inference, owing to its focus upon a specific object, Truth itself. (49)

taj-jah sanskaro 'nya sanskara-pratibandhi

50. The impress engendered therefrom supersedes all other latent impressions. (50)

tasyapi nirodhe sarva-nirodhan nirbijah samadhih

51. On the stoppage of even that, all else being eliminated, there arises meditation without a seed (*nirbijah Samadhi*). (51)

Hermes, May 1987

YOGA SUTRAS – BOOK II

SADHANA PADA

tapah-svadhyayeshvara-pranidhanani kriya-yogah

1. Austerity, self-study and devoted self-surrender to the Lord constitute the practice of yoga. (52)

Samadhi-bhavanarthah klesha-tanukaranarthash cha

2. This is for the sake of shrinking afflictions and inducing meditative absorption (*Samadhi*). (53)

avidyasmita-raga-dveshabhiniveshah kleshah

3. The afflictions are ignorance, egoism, attachment, aversion and the tenacious clinging to existence. (54)

avidya kshetram uttaresham prasupta-tanu-vichchinnodaranam

4. Ignorance is the originating field for the others, whether they be dormant, tenuous, dispersed or activated. (55)

anityashuchi-duhkhanatmasu nitya-shuchi-sukhatmakhyatir avidya

5. Ignorance is the belief that the impermanent, the impure, the painful, are the permanent, the pure, the pleasurable, that the non-Self is the Self. (56)

drig-darshana-shaktyor ekatmatevasmita

6. Egoism (*asmita*) is the delusive or apparent identification of the potency of the Seer with the power of sight. (57)

sukhanushayl ragah

7. Attachment accompanies and pursues pleasure. (58)

duhkhanushayi dveshah

8. Aversion accompanies and dwells upon pain. (59)

svarasavahi vidusho 'pi tatha rudho 'bhiniveshah

9. The tenacious clinging to existence, sustained by its own energy, is so rooted even in the learned. (60)

te pratiprasava-heyah sukshmah

10. These subtle afflictions can be destroyed by inverse propagation (*pratiprasava*), involution or reabsorption into their causal origins. (61)

dhyana-heyas tad-vrittayah

11. Their mental modifications are destroyed by deep meditation (*dhyana*). (62)

klesha-mulah karmashayo drishtadrishta-janma-vedaniyah

12. The mental deposits of *karma* have their roots in the afflictions (*kleshas*) and their fruitage in experiences seen in this life, or in a future life now unseen. (63)

sati mule tad-vipako jaty-ayur-bhogah

13. So long as the roots remain, there must be their fructification in the form of class, length of life and the experience of pleasures and pains. (64)

te hlada-paritapa-phalah punyapunya-hetutvat

14. They have joy or sorrow as their fruit, by reason of virtue or vice. (65)

parinama-tapa-sanskara-duhkhair guna-vritti-virodhach cha
duhkham eva sarvam vivekinah

15. To the discerning, all is sorrowful owing to the miseries brought by change, anxiety and acquired impressions, and also because of the conflict between the propensities (*gunas*) of Nature and mental modifications (*vritti*). (66)

heyam duhkham anagatam

16. The misery which has not yet come must be avoided. (67)

drashtri-drishyayoh sanyogo heya-hetuh

17. The conjunction of the Seer and the seen is the cause of that which is to be avoided. (68)

prakasha-kriya-sthiti-shilam bhutendriyatmakam
bhogapavargarthem drishyam

18. Having the properties of luminosity, motion and inertia, the objective world of visible Nature consists of the elements and the sense-organs, all for the sake of experience and emancipation. (69)

visheshavishesha-lingamatralingani gunaparvani

19. The states and stages of the propensities (*gunas*) are the particularized, the archetypal, the distinctly differentiated, and the signless, irresolvable, undifferentiated. (70)

drashta dristhimatrah shuddho 'pi pratyayanupashyah

20. The Seer is simply pure vision, and yet, though pure, he perceives ideas seemingly through the mind. (71)

tad-artha eva drishyasyatma

21. The very essence of the visible is that it exists for the sake of the Seer, the Self alone. (72)

kritartham prati nashtam apy anashtam tad-anya-sadharanatvat

22. Although it has vanished for him whose purpose is accomplished, it has not ceased to be for others, owing to its very commonality. (73)

sva-svami-shaktyoh svarupopalabdhi-hetah sanyogah

23. The conjunction of the potencies of the Seer and the seen is the reason for the apprehension of his own form and his experience of the true nature of things seen. (74)

tasya hetur avidya

24. Its effective cause is ignorance. (75)

tad-abhavat sanyogabhavo hanam tad drisheh kaivalyam

25. In its absence, the conjunction disappears, and its avoidance is the real remedy; that is the isolation and liberation, the absolute freedom (*kaivalya*), of the Seer. (76)

viveka-khyatir aviplava hanopayah

26. Unbroken discriminative cognition is the means of emancipation. (77)

tasya saptadha pranta-bhumih prajna

27. His awakening of perfect cognition is sevenfold, attained in successive stages. (78)

yoganganushthanad ashuddhikshaye jnanadiptir a viveka-khyateh

28. Through the practice of the component parts of yoga, as impurity is gradually destroyed, the light of wisdom shines forth, leading to discriminative cognition of Reality. (79)

yama-niyamasana-pranayama-pratyahara-dharana-dhyana-samadhyayo 'shtavangani

29. Restraint (*yama*), binding observance (*niyama*), posture (*asana*), regulation of breath (*pranayama*), abstraction and sense-withdrawal (*pratyahara*), concentration (*dharana*), contemplation (*dhyana*) and perfect meditative absorption (*Samadhi*) are the eight limbs of yoga. (80)

tatra ahimsa-satyasteya-brahmacharyaparigraha yamah

30. Of these, non-violence (*ahimsa*), truthfulness (*satya*), non-stealing (*asteya*), continence (*brahmacharya*) and non-possessiveness (*aparigraha*) are the five forms of restraint (*yamas*). (81)

ete jati-desha-kala-samayanavachchimah sarvabhauma mahavratam

31. These are not conditioned or qualified by class or country, time or circumstance, and apply to all spheres and stages, thus constituting the Great Vow. (82)

shaucha-santosha-tapah-svadhyayeshvara-pranidhanani niyamah

32. Purity, contentment, austerity, self-study and devoted self-surrender to the Lord are the five observances (*niyamas*). (83)

vitarka badhane pratipaksha bhavanam

33. When the mind is oppressed by perverse thoughts, it must summon and sustain their opposites. (84)

vitarka himsadayah krita-karitanumodita lobha-krodha-moha-purvaka mridu-madhyadhimatra duhkhajnananantaphala iti pratipaksha-bhavanam

34. Perverse thoughts of a violent and destructive nature, whether enacted, abetted or endorsed, whether induced by avarice, anger or delusion, whether mild, moderately present or intensely indulged, result in endless misery and folly; consequently, their opposites must be nurtured and nourished. (85)

ahimsa-pratishthayam tat-sanniddhau vairatyagah

35. When one is firmly grounded in non-violence (*ahimsa*), all hostility is given up in one's presence. (86)

satya-pratishthayam kriya-phalashrayatvam

36. When one is firmly grounded in truth (*satya*), all acts gestated bear fruit dependably. (87)

asteya-pratishthayam sarva-ratnopasthanam

37. When one is firmly grounded in non-stealing (*asteya*), all sorts of precious jewels present themselves. (88)

brahmacharya-pratishthayam virya-labhah

38. When one is firmly grounded in celibacy in consciousness and conduct (*brahmacharya*), one gains vigour, vitality and strength. (89)

aparigraha-sthairye janma-kathanta-sanbodhah

39. When one is established in non-possessiveness (*aparigraha*), one gains luminous insight in relation to the process and purposes, the meaning and significance, of the succession of births. (90)

shauchat svanga-jugupsa parair asansargah

40. Through internal purity and external purification, one gains bodily protection and freedom from pollution in contacts with others. (91)

sattvashuddhi-saumanasyaikagryendriyajayatma-darshana-yogyatvani cha

41. Through the cleansing of consciousness and purity of motivation, one gains mental serenity, one-pointedness, control of the sense-organs, as well as fitness for soul-vision and direct apprehension of the Self. (92)

santoshad anuttamah sukha-labhah

42. Through joyous contentment, one gains supreme happiness. (93)

kayendriya-siddhir ashuddhi-kshayat tapasah

43. Through the elimination of pollution, the practice of penance (*tapas*) brings about the perfection of the body and the sense-organs. (94)

svadhyayad ishta-devata-sanprayogah

44. Through self-study comes communion with the chosen deity. (95)

Samadhi-siddhir ishvara-pranidhanat

45. Through persevering devotion to the Lord comes perfection in meditative absorption (*Samadhi*). (96)

sthira-sukham asanam

46. The posture must be firm and pleasant. (97)

prayatna-shaithilyananta-samapattibhyam

47. This is gained by release of tension and serene contemplation upon the boundless infinite. (98)

tato dvandvanabhighatah

48. Thus arises freedom from assault by the pairs of opposites. (99)

tasmin sati shvasa-prashvasayor gativichchedah pranayamah

49. When this is attained, there comes *pranayama*, the regulation of breath, the restraint of inhalation and exhalation. (100)

*bahyabhyantara-stambha-vrittir deshakala-sankhyabhih
paridrishto dirghasukshmah*

50. These modifications are external, internal or wholly suspended; they are regulated according to space, time or number, whether protracted or attenuated. (101)

bahyabhyantara-vishayakshepi chaturthah

51. The fourth modification goes beyond the external-internal range. (102)

tatah kshiyate prakashavaranam

52. Thus is worn away the veil which obscures the light. (103)

dharanasu cha yogyata manasah

53. And thus the mind gains fitness for concentration. (104)

sva-vishayasanprayoge chitta-svarupanukara ivendriyanam pratyaharah

54. *Pratyahara*, abstraction or dissociation, is the disjoining of the sense-organs from their respective objects, assuming, as it were, the nature of the mind itself. (105)

tatah parama vashyatendriyanam

55. Thence comes supreme control of the senses. (106)

Hermes, June 1987

YOGA SUTRAS – BOOK III

VIBHUTI PADA

desha-bandhash chittasya dharana

1. *Dharana*, concentration, is the fixing or focussing of consciousness on a particular point or place. (107)

tatra pratyayaikatanata dhyanam

2. *Dhyana*, meditation, is the continuous, uninterrupted flow of consciousness towards the chosen object. (108)

tad evarthamatra-nirbhasam svarupa-shunyam iva samadhih

3. *Samadhi*, meditative absorption or ecstasy, arises when the object of meditation shines forth alone, as if emptied of the form of the agent. (109)

trayam ekatra sanyamah

4. The three together constitute *sanyama*, constraint. (110)

taj-jayat prajnalokah

5. Through mastery of it comes the light of cognitive insight (*prajna*). (111)

tasya bhumishu viniyogah

6. Its application is by stages. (112)

trayam antarangam purvebhyah

7. The three together are more interior than the preceding. (113)

tad api bahirangam nirbijasya

8. Even these are exterior to seedless *Samadhi*, or soul vision. (114)

vyutthana-nirodha-sanskarayor abhibhava-pradhurbhavan nirodha-kshana-chittanvayo nirodha-parinamah

9. *Nirodhaparinama* is that mental transformation through restraint wherein the consciousness becomes permeated by that condition which intervenes momentarily between fading impressions and emerging potencies. (115)

tasya prashanta-vahita sanskarat

10. Its flow becomes serene and steady through habituation. (116)

sarvarthataikagratayoh kshayodayau chittasya Samadhi-parinamah

11. *Samadhiparinama*, meditative transformation, is the dwindling of distractions and the emergence of unitary consciousness or one-pointedness (*ekagrata*). (117)

tatah punah shantoditau tulya-pratyayau chittasyaikagrata-parinamah

12. Thence again comes *ekagrataparinama*, the development of one-pointedness, wherein the two states of consciousness, the quiescent or subsided and the active or uprisen, are exactly similar and balanced. (118)

etena bhutendriyeshu dharma-lakshanavastha-parinama vyakhyatah

13. Thus are explained the transformations of intrinsic properties, secondary qualities and states of being in the objective elements and instrumental sense-organs. (119)

shantoditavyapadeshya-dharmanupati dharmi

14. The substratum is that which is common to the properties, whether quiescent, active or unmanifest. (120)

kramanyatvam parinamanyatve hetuh

15. The variation in sequence or succession is the cause of the difference and distinctness in transformation. (121)

parinama-traya-sanyamad atitanagata-jnanam

16. Through *sanyama*, perfectly concentrated meditative constraint, comes knowledge of past and future. (122)

shabdartha-pratyayanam itaretaradhyasat sankaras tat-pravibhaga-sanyamat sarva-bhuta-ruta-jnanam

17. The sound, the meaning and the idea called up by a word are confounded owing to their indistinct superimposition. Through *sanyama* on their separation and resolution there comes a cognitive comprehension of the sounds uttered by all sentient beings. (123)

sanskara-sakshatkaranat purva-jatijnanam

18. By bringing latent impressions into consciousness there comes the knowledge of former births. (124)

pratyayasya para-chitta-jnanam

19. Through concentrated perception of mental images comes the knowledge of other minds. (125)

na cha tat salambanam tasyavishayi-bhutatvat

20. The mental supports are not perceived, for that is not the object of observation. (126)

*kaya-rupa-sanyamat tad-grahya-shakti-stambhe chakshuh-
prakashasanprayoge 'ntardhanam*

21. Through *sanyama* on the form and colour of the body,
    by suspending its power of perceptibility and thereby
    disconnecting the light from the body and the sight of others,
    there comes the power to make the body invisible. (127)

etena sthabdady antardhanam uktam

22. Thus can also be explained the power of concealment of sound,
    touch, taste and smell. (128)

*sopakramam nirupakramam cha karma tat-sanyamad aparanta-
jnanam arishtebhyo va*

23. Through *sanyama* on *karma*, which is either fast or slow in
    fruition, active or dormant, one gains knowledge of the time of
    death and also of omens and portents. (129)

maitry-adishu balani

24. Through *sanyama* on kindliness (*maitri*) and similar graces one
    gains mental, moral and spiritual strength. (130)

baleshu hasti-baladini

25. Through *sanyama* on various powers one gains the strength of an
    elephant. (131)

pravritty-aloka-nyasat sukshma-vyavahita-viprakrishta-jnanam

26. Through *sanyama* on the shining, effulgent light one gains
    knowledge of the small and subtle, the hidden and veiled, and
    the remote. (132)

bhavana-jnanam surye sanyamat

27. Through *sanyama* on the sun there comes knowledge of the solar
    system, cosmic evolution and involution. (133)

chandre tara-vyuha-jnanam

28. Through *sanyama* on the moon there comes knowledge concerning the arrangement of stars. (134)

dhruve tad-gati-jnanam

29. Through *sanyama* on the pole-star comes knowledge of the relative motions and positions of the stars. (135)

nabhi-chakre kaya-vyuha-jnanam

30. Through *sanyama* on the solar plexus comes knowledge of the structure and organization of the body. (136)

kantha-kupe kshut-pipasa-nivrittih

31. Through *sanyama* on the pit of the throat there comes cessation of hunger and thirst. (137)

kurma-nadyam sthairyam

32. Through *sanyama* on the nerve-centre called the 'tortoise' duct there comes steadiness. (138)

murdha-jyotishi siddha-darshanam

33. Through *sanyama* on the light in the head comes the vision of perfected beings. (139)

pratibhad va sarvam

34. Through *sanyama* on the effulgent light of intuition comes all knowledge. (140)

hridaye chitta-sanvit

35. Through *sanyama* on the heart comes knowledge of cosmic intellection. (141)

*sattva-purushayor atyantasankirnayoh pratyayavishesho bhogah
pararthat svartha-sanyamat Purusha-jnanam*

36. Indulgence in experience is the result of the inability to
distinguish between the Self (*Purusha*) and the principle of
understanding (*sattva*), though they are utterly distinct. Self-
knowledge results from *sanyama* on the Self-existent, which is
apart from the non-self. (142)

tatah pratibha-shravana-vedanadarshasvada-vartta jayante

37. Thence are produced intuitional, extra-sensory hearing, touch,
sight, taste and smell. (143)

te samadhav upasarga vkyutthane siddhayah

38. They are obstacles to meditative absorption (*sanyama*) but are
powerful aids when the mind is turned outwards. (144)

*bandha-karana-shaithilyat prachara-sanvedanach cha chittasya
para-shariraveshah*

39. The mind can enter another's body through the suspension of
the causes of bondage and through knowledge of the mental
channels. (145)

udana-jayaj jala-panka-kantakadishvasanga utkrantisth cha

40. Through mastery over the vital energy called *udana* comes
imperviousness to water and mud, thorn and the rest, levitation
and victory over death. (146)

samana-jayaj jvalanam

41. Through mastery over the vital energy called *sanyama* comes
blazing radiance. (147)

shrotrakashayoh sanbandha-sanyamad divyam shrotram

42. Through *sanyama* on the connection between the ear and the

ether (*Akasha*) comes divine hearing. (148)

kayakashayoh sanbandha-sanyamat laghu-tula-samapattesth chakashagamanam

43. Through *sanyama* on the connection between the body and the ether (*Akasha*) comes lightness like cotton and the attainment of levitation in space. (149)

bahir akalpita vrittir maha-videha tatah prakashavarana-kshayah

44. *Mahavideha* is the power of invoking the incorporeal state of consciousness which is beyond the intellect and therefore inconceivable. Thus is destroyed the obscuring veil over the light. (150)

sthula-svarupa-sukshmanvayarthavattva-sanyamad bhuta-jayah

45. Through *sanyama* on gross matter, its essential form, its subtle qualities, its concomitant compounds and molecules and their functions, comes mastery over the elements. (151)

tato 'nimadi-pradurbhavah kaya-sanpat tad-dharmanabhighatash cha

46. Thence comes the manifestation of the powers of minuteness and the rest, as well as the perfection of the body and the realization of the indestructibility of the elements. (152)

rupa-lavanya-bala-vajra-sanhananatvani kaya-sanpat

47. Perfection of the body consists in beauty, grace, strength and adamantine hardness. (153)

grahana-svarupasmitanvayarthavattva-sanyamad indriya-jayah

48. Mastery over the sense-organs comes through *sanyama* on their power of apprehension, their real nature, egoism, concomitance and specific functions. (154)

tato manojavitam vikarana-bhavah pradhana-jayash cha

49. Thence comes instantaneous cognition, independent of instruments, and the complete mastery of *pradhana*, the chief common principle throughout Nature. (155)

sattva-purushanyata-khyati-matrasya sarvabhavadhishthatritvam sarvajnatritvam cha

50. Only through the knowledge of the distinction between the principle of understanding (*sattva*) and the Self (*Purusha*) comes supremacy over all states of existence and omniscience. (156)

tad-vairagyad api dosha-bija-kshaye kaivalyam

51. Through non-attachment even to that comes the destruction of the seeds of bondage and the state of emancipation (*kaivalya*). (157)

sthany-upanimantrane sangha-smayakaranam punar anishta-prasangat

52. There must be avoidance of attachment or amazement on encountering celestial beings, owing to the possible recurrence of the undesirable. (158)

kshana-tat-kramayoh sanyamad vivekajam jnanam

53. Through *sanyama* on indivisible moments and their order of succession comes discriminative knowledge. (159)

jati-lakshana-deshair anyatanavachchedat tulyayos tatah pratipattih

54. Therefrom comes the discernment of two similar events and of things whose distinctness cannot be measured or distinguished by class, property or position. (160)

tarakam sarva-vishayam sarvatha-vishayam akramam cheti vivekajam jnanam

55. Transcendental discriminative knowledge is that which simultaneously encompasses all objects and all possible processes, reaching beyond all endings. (161)

sattva-purushayoh shuddhi-samye kaivalyam

56. Emancipation (*kaivalya*) is attained when there is equalization of purity between the principle of understanding (*sattva*) and the Self (*Purusha*). (162)

Hermes, July 1987

YOGA SUTRAS - BOOK IV

KAIVALYA PADA

janmaushadhi-mantra-tapah-samadhijah siddhayah

1. Spiritual powers (*siddhis*) are inborn and activated by herbs, incantations, austerities or meditative absorption (*Samadhi*). (163)

jaty-antara-parinamah prakrity-apurat

2. Transformation from one species or state of existence into another is made possible through the overflow of natural tendencies and forces. (164)

nimittam aprayojakam prakritinam varanabhedas tu tatah kshetrikavat

3. The instrumental cause does not produce the essential modification or movement of natural tendencies; it merely pierces through obstructions, just like the farmer in the field. (165)

nirmana-chittany asmita-matrat

4. Many minds are produced solely by the power of egoism or selfhood. (166)

pravritti-bhede prayojakam chittam ekam anekesham

5. The one mind is directing many minds in their multiple activities. (167)

tatra dhyanajam anashayam

6. Of these, the mind born of meditation is devoid of mental deposits or latent impressions. (168)

karmashuklakrishnam yoginas trividham itaresham

7. The actions of *yogins* are neither white nor black, while those of others are of three kinds. (169)

tatas tad-vipakanugunanam evabhivyaktir vasananam

8. From these, only those tendencies are manifested for which the conditions are favourable for fruition. (170)

jati-desha-kala-vyavahitanam apy anantaryam smriti-sanskarayor ekarupatvat

9. Although separated by class, locality and time, there is an immediate succession of memories and tendencies which are identical in form. (171)

tasam anaditvam chashisho nityatvat

10. And there is no temporal beginning for those tendencies, owing to the constant persistence of desire or the will to live. (172)

hetu-phalashrayalambanaih sangrihitatvad esham abhave tad-abhavah

11. As they are bound together by cause and effect, substratum and support, they cease to exist when these disappear. (173)

atitanagatam svarupato 'sty adhva-bhedad dharmanam

12. The past and the future subsist in their true nature, while the variation in properties is owing to differences of phase and direction. (174)

te vyakta-sukshmah gunatmanah

13. They, whether manifest or unmanifest, are of the nature of *gunas* or potencies. (175)

parinamaikatvad vastu-tattvam

14. The essential nature of the object consists in the identity and uniqueness of the transformation. (176)

vastu-samye chitta-bhedat tayor vibhaktah panthah

15. Though the object is the same, the cognition is different, owing to the diversity and distinctness of states of being. (177)

na chaika-chitta-tantram vastu tad-apramanakam tada kim syat

16. Nor is an object dependent on one mind. What would become of it when not cognized by that mind? (178)

tad-uparagapekshitvach chittasya vastu jnatajnatam

17. An object is known or not known according as the mind is coloured and attracted by it or not. (179)

sada jnatasth chitta-vrittayas tat-prabhoh
purushasyaparinamitvat

18. The modifications of the mind are always known to its master, owing to the immutability of the Self (*Purusha*). (180)

na tat svabhasam drishyatvat

19. Nor is the mind self-luminous, since it can be seen as an object. (181)

eka-samaye chobhayanavadharanam

20. Nor can it be both cognizer and cognized at the same time. (182)

chittantara-drishye Buddhi-buddher atiprasangah smriti-
sanskarah cha

21. If the mind were to be seen by another within, there would be an endless series of perceiving minds and a commingling of memories. (183)

chiter apratisankramayas tad-akarapattau svabuddhi-sanvedanam

22. Knowledge of its own nature through self-cognition comes when consciousness assumes that form in which it does not move from place to place. (184)

drashtri-drishyoparaktam chittam sarvartham

23. Consciousness, coloured by the Seer and the seen, is all-comprehensive. (185)

tad asankhyeya-vasanabhish chitram api parartham sanhatya-karitvat

24. Though variegated by countless impressions, the mind exists for another (*Purusha*), for it acts in association. (186)

vishesha-darshina atma-bhava-bhavana-vinivrittih

25. For the discerning Seer there is complete cessation of identification of mental states with the consciousness of the Self (*atman*). (187)

tada hi viveka-nimnam kaivalya-pragbharam chittam

26. Verily, then, the mind becomes serenely bent towards discrimination and is borne onwards towards total emancipation (*kaivalya*). (188)

tach-chidreshu pratyayantarani sanskarebhyah

27. During intervals other thoughts will arise through the force of former impressions. (189)

hanam esham kleshavad uktam

28. Their removal is like that of the afflictions (*kleshas*) already mentioned. (190)

prasankhyane 'py akusidasya sarvatha viveka-khyater dharma-

meghah samadhih

29. From constant and continuous discriminative knowledge, without any selfish attachment even towards the highest illumination, comes the meditative absorption (*Samadhi*) known as the rain-cloud of righteousness (*dharma-megha*). (191)

tatah klesha-karma-nivrittih

30. Then comes the cessation of afflictions (*kleshas*) and works (*karma*). (192)

tada sarvavarana-malapetasya jnanasyanantyaj jneyam alpam

31. Then all veils and stains being removed, his knowledge becoming infinite, little remains to be known. (193)

tatah kritarthanam parinama-krama-samaptir gunanam

32. Then the three *gunas* having fulfilled their purpose, the process of transformation comes to an end. (194)

kshana-pratiyogi parinamaparanta-nirgrahyah kramah

33. Succession is the uninterrupted sequence of moments and is fully apprehended at the final stage. (195)

purushartha-shunyanam gunanam pratiprasavah kaivalyam svarupa-pratishtha va chiti-shakter iti

34. Emancipation (*kaivalya*) comes when the *gunas*, becoming devoid of any motive for action for the Self (*Purusha*), are reabsorbed into latency. In this state the Self (*Purusha*) is established in its own nature, which is the energy of pure consciousness or cosmic ideation. (196)

kaivalya nirvanayoh purnaikyam

35. There is complete identity of emancipation (*kaivalya*) and supreme peace (*nirvana*). (197)

kaivalyam dharman dharminah purushasya

36. Emancipation (*kaivalya*) is the state which subsists in the Self (*Purusha*). (198)

kaivalye akhile vishve Purusha-darshanam purushe chakhila vishva-darshanam

37. In the state of emancipation there is the vision of the Self in the entire cosmos and of the cosmos in the Self. (199)

sagunam satchidanandam nirgunam chatatah param tatvam iti

38. Absolute Existence, Consciousness and Bliss constitute the plenitude of the Self, and beyond these is the Attributeless Self. (200).

Hermes, August 1987

THE SIX DHARSHANAS

To contemplate these things is the privilege of the gods and to
do so is also the aspiration of the immortal soul of men generally
– though only in a few cases is such aspiration realized.

Plato

I – THEORIA AND PRAXIS

Throughout its long and largely unrecorded history, Indian thought preserved its central concern with ontology and epistemology, with noetic psychology as the indispensable bridge between metaphysics and ethics, employing introspection and self- testing as well as logical tools, continually confronting the instruments of cognition with the fruits of contemplation. Through its immemorial oral teachings and a vast variety of written texts, the fusion of *theoria* and *praxis*, theory and practice, was never sacrificed to the demands of academic specialization or the compartmentalization of human endeavour. Diverse schools of thought shared the conviction that true understanding must flow from the repeated application of received truths. Coming to know is a dynamic, dialectical process in which thought stimulates contemplation and regulates conduct, and in turn is refined by them. Although an individual who would be healthy and whole thinks, feels and acts, gnosis necessarily involves the fusion of thought, will and feeling, resulting in *metanoia*, a radically altered state of being. The Pythagorean conception of a philosopher as a lover of wisdom is close to the standpoint of an earnest seeker of truth in the Indian tradition.

Indian thought did not suffer the traumatic cognitive disruption caused by the emergence of ecclesiastical Christianity in the Mediterranean world, where an excessive concern with specification of rigid belief, sanctioned and safeguarded by an institutional conception of religious authority and censorship, sundered thought and action to such an extent that it became common to think one way and act in another with seeming impunity. The chasms which opened up between thought, will and feeling provided fertile soil for every kind of psychopathology, in part because such a fragmentation of the human being engenders inversions, obsessions and even perversities, and also in part because for a thousand years it has been virtually impossible to hold up a credible paradigm of the whole and healthy human being. The philosophical quest became obscured in the modern West by the linear succession of schools, each resulting from a violent reaction to its predecessors, each claiming to possess the Truth more or less exclusively, and often insisting upon the sole validity of its method of proceeding. The slavish concern with academic respectability and the fear of anathemization resulted in the increasing alienation of thought from being, of cognition from conduct, and philosophical disputation from the problems of daily life.

Indian thought did not spurn the accumulated wisdom of its ancients in favour of current fashions and did not experience a violent disruption of its traditional hospitality to multiple standpoints. The so-called *astika* or orthodox schools found no difficulty in combining their veneration of the Vedic hymns with a wide and diverse range of views, and even the *nastika* or heterodox schools, which repudiated the canonical 'authority' of the *Vedas*, retained much of Vedic and Upanishadic metaphysics and almost the whole of their psychology and ethics. Indian philosophical schools could not see themselves as exclusive bearers of the total Truth. They emerged together from a long-standing and continuous effort to enhance our common understanding of God, Man and Nature, and they came to be considered as *darshanas* or paradigmatic standpoints shedding light from different angles on noumenal and phenomenal realities. They refrained from claiming that any illumination which can be rendered in words – or even in thoughts – can be either final or complete.

II – THE SIX SCHOOLS

It may be pointed out here that a system of philosophy however lofty and true it may be should not be expected to give us an absolutely correct picture of the transcendent truths as they really exist. Because philosophy works through the medium of the intellect and the intellect has its inherent limitations, it cannot understand or formulate truths which are beyond its scope.... We have to accept these limitations when we use the intellect as an instrument for understanding and discovering these truths in the initial stages. It is no use throwing away this instrument, poor and imperfect though it is, because it gives us at least some help in organizing our effort to know the truth in the only way it can be known – by Self-realization.

I. K. Taimni

The ageless and dateless *Vedas*, especially the exalted hymns of the *Rig Veda*, have long been esteemed as the direct expression of what gods and divine seers, *rishis* or immortal sages, saw when they peered into the imperishable centre of Being which is also the origin of the entire cosmos. The *Upanishads* (from *upa, ni* and *sad*, meaning 'to sit down near' a sage or *guru*), included in the *Vedas*, constitute the highest transmission of the fruits of illumination attained by these *rishis*. Often cast in the form of memorable dialogues between spiritual teachers and disciples, they represent rich glimpses of truth, not pieced together from disparate intellectual insights, but as they are at once revealed to the divine eye, *divya chakshu*, which looks into the core of Reality, freely intimated in idioms, metaphors and *mantras* suited to the awakening consciousness and spiritual potentials of diverse disciples. However divergent their modes of expression, they are all addressed to those who are ready to learn, willing to meditate deeply, and seek greater self-knowledge through intensive self- questioning. The *Upanishads* do not purport to provide discursive knowledge, conceptual clarification or speculative dogmas, but rather focus on the fundamental themes which concern the soul as a calm spectator of the temporal succession of states of mind from birth to death, seeking for what is essential amidst the ephemeral, the enduring within the transient, the abiding universals behind the flux of fleeting appearances.

From this standpoint, they are truly therapeutic in that they heal the sickness of the soul caused by passivity, ignorance and delusion. This ignorance is not that of the malformed or malfunctioning personality, maimed by childhood traumas or habitual vices. It is the more fundamental ignorance (*avidya*) of the adroit and well-adapted person who has learnt to cope with the demands of living and fulfil his duties in the world at a certain level without however, coming to terms with the causes of his longings and limitations, his dreams and discontinuities, his entrenched expectations and his hidden potentials. The sages spoke to those who had a measure of integrity and honesty and were willing to examine their presuppositions, but lacked the fuller vision and deeper wisdom that require a sustained search and systematic meditation. For such an undertaking, mental clarity, moral sensitivity, relaxed self-control and spiritual courage are needed, as well as a willingness to withdraw for a period from worldly concerns. The therapeutics of self-transcendence is rooted in a recondite psychology which accommodates the vast spectrum of self- consciousness, different levels of cognition and degrees of development, reaching up to the highest conceivable self- enlightenment.

Upanishadic thought presupposed the concrete and not merely conceptual continuity of God, Nature and Man. Furthermore, Man is the self-conscious microcosm of the macrocosm, where the part is not only inseparably one with the whole but also reflects and resonates with it. Man could neither be contemplated properly nor fully comprehended in any context less than the entirety of visible and invisible Nature, and so too, ethics, logic and psychology could not be sundered from metaphysics. 'Is', the way things are, is vitally linked to 'must', the ways things must be, as well as to 'ought', the way human beings should think and act, through 'can', the active exploration of human potentialities and possibilities, which are not different, save in scope and degree, from cosmic potencies. A truly noetic psychology bridges metaphysics and ethics through a conscious mirroring of *Rta*, ordered cosmic harmony, in *dharma*, righteous human conduct that freely acknowledges what is due to each and every aspect of Nature, including all humanity, past, present and future.

The ancient sages resolved the One-many problem at the mystical, psychological, ethical and social levels by affirming the radical metaphysical and spiritual unity of all life, whilst fully recognizing (and refusing to diminish through any form of reductionism) the immense diversity of human types and the progressive awakenings of human consciousness at different stages of material evolution and spiritual involution. The immemorial pilgrimage of humanity can be both universally celebrated and act as a constant stimulus to individual growth. Truth, like the sun shining over the summits of a Himalayan range, is one, and the pathways to it are as many and varied as there are people to tread them.

As if emulating the sculptor's six perspectives to render accurately any specific form in space, ancient Indian thinkers stressed six *darshanas*, which are sometimes called the six schools of philosophy. These are *astika* or orthodox in that they all find inspiration in different ways in the *Vedas*. And like the sculptor's triple set of perspectives – front-back, left side-right side, top- bottom – the six *darshanas* have been seen as three complementarities, polarized directions that together mark the trajectory of laser light through the unfathomable reaches of ineffable wisdom. Each standpoint has its integrity and coherence in that it demands nothing less than the deliberate and radical reconstitution of consciousness from its unregenerate and unthinking modes of passive acceptance of the world. Yet none can claim absoluteness, finality or infallibility, for such asseverations would imply that limited conceptions and discursive thought can capture ultimate Reality. Rather, each *darshana* points with unerring accuracy towards that cognition which can be gained only by complete assimilation, practical self-transformation and absorption into it. At the least, every *darshana* corresponds with a familiar state of mind of the seeker, a legitimate and verifiable mode of cognition which makes sense of the world and the self at some level.

All genuine seekers are free to adopt any one or more of the *darshanas* at any time and even to defend their chosen standpoint against the others but they must concede the possibility of synthesizing and transcending the six standpoints in a seventh mode which culminates in *taraka*, transcendental, self-luminous gnosis, the goal of complete enlightenment often associated with the secret, incommunicable way of *buddhiyoga* intimated in the fourth, seventh and eighteenth chapters of the *Bhagavad Gita*.

Although scholars have speculated on the sequential emergence of the *darshanas*, and though patterns of interplay can be discerned in their full flowering, their roots lie in the ancient texts and they arise together as distinctive standpoints. It has also been held that the six schools grew out of sixty-two systems of thought lost in the mists of antiquity. At any rate, it is generally agreed that each of the later six schools was inspired by a sage and teacher who struck the keynote which has reverberated throughout its growths refinement and elaboration. As the six schools are complementary to each others they are traditionally viewed as the six branches of a single tree. All six provide a theoretical explanation of ultimate Reality and a practical means of emancipation. The oldest are Yoga and *Sankhya*, the next being *Vaishesika* and *Nyaya*, and the last pair are *Purva Mimamsa* and *Vedanta* (sometimes called Uttara *Mimamsa*). The founders of these schools are considered to be Patanjali of *Yoga*, Kapila of *Sankhya*, Kanada of *Vaishesika*, Gautama of *Nyaya*, Jaimini of Purva *Mimamsa* and Vyasa of *Vedanta*, though the last is also assigned to *Badarayana*. All of them propounded the tenets of their philosophical systems or schools in the form of short *sutras*, whose elucidation required and stimulated elaborate commentaries. Since about 200 C.E., a vast crop of secondary works has emerged which has generated some significant discussions as well as a welter of scholastic disputation and didactic controversies, moving far away from *praxis* into the forests of *theoria*, or reducing *praxis* to rigid codes and *theoria* to sterile formulas. At the same time, there has remained a remarkable vitality to most of these schools, owing to their transmission by long lineages which have included many extraordinary teachers and exemplars. This cannot be recovered merely through the study of texts, however systematic and rigorous, in a philosophical tradition which is essentially oral, even though exceptional powers of accurate recall have been displayed in regard to the texts.

Nyaya and *Vaishesika* are schools primarily concerned with analytic approaches to the objects of knowledge, using carefully tested principles of logic. The word *Nyaya* suggests that by which the mind reaches a conclusion, and since the word also means 'right' or 'just', *Nyaya* is the science of correct thinking. The founder of this school, Gautama, lived about 150 B.C.E., and its source-book is the *Nyaya Sutra*. Whilst knowledge requires an object, a knowing subject and a state of knowing, the validity of cognition depends upon *pramana*, the means of cognition. There are four acceptable *pramanas*, of which *pratyaksha* – direct perception or intuition – is most important. Perception requires the mind, *manas*, to mediate between the self and the senses, and perception may be determinate or indeterminate. Determinate perception reveals the class to which an object of knowledge belongs, its specific qualities and the union of the two. Indeterminate perception is simple apprehension without regard to genus or qualities. In the *Nyaya* school, indeterminate perception is not knowledge but rather its prerequisite and starting-point.

Anumana or inference is the second *pramana* or means of cognition. It involves a fivefold syllogism which includes a universal statement, an illustrative example and an application to the instance at hand. *Upamana* is the apt use of analogy, in which the similarities which make the analogy come alive are essential and not superficial. *Shabda*, sound or verbal expression, is the credible testimony of authority, which requires not uncritical acceptance but the thoughtful consideration of words, meanings and the modes of reference. As the analytic structure of *Nyaya* logic suggests, its basic approach to reality is atomistic, and so the test of claims of truth is often effectiveness in application, especially in the realm of action. Typically, logical discussion of a proposition takes the form of a syllogism with five parts: the proposition (*pratijna*) the cause (*hetu*), the exemplification (*drishtanta*), the recapitulation (*upanaya*) and the conclusion (*nigamana*).

However divergent their views on metaphysics and ethics, all schools accept and use *Nyaya* canons of sound reasoning. A thorough training in logic is required not only in all philosophical reasoning, exposition and disputation, but it is also needed by those who seek to stress mastery of *praxis* over a lifetime and thereby become spiritual exemplars. This at once conveys the enormous strength of an immemorial tradition as well as the pitiable deficiencies of most professors and pundits, let alone the self-styled so-called exoteric *gurus* of the contemporary East. Neither thaumaturgic wonders nor mass hypnosis can compensate for mental muddles and shallow thinking; indeed, they become insuperable obstacles to even a good measure of gnosis and noetic theurgy, let alone authentic enlightenment and self-mastery.

The *Vaishesika* school complements *Nyaya* in its distinct pluralism. Its founder, Kanada, also known as Kanabhaksha, lived around 200 C.E., and its chief work is the *Vaishesika Sutra*. Its emphasis on particulars is reflected in its name, since *vishesha* means 'particularity', and it is concerned with properly delineating the categories of objects of experience. These objects of experience, *padarthas*, are six: substance (*dravya*), quality (*guna*), and *karma* or movement and activity (forming the triplicity of objective existence), and generality (*samanya*), particularity (*vishesha*) and *samavayi* or inherence (forming a triad of modes of intellectual discernment which require valid logical inference). A seventh object of experience, non-existence (*shunya*), was eventually added to the six as a strictly logical necessity. The *Vaishesika* point of view recognizes nine irreducible substances: earth, water, air, fire, aether (*Akasha*), time, space, self and mind, all of which are distinct from the qualities which inhere in them. The self is necessarily a substance – a substrate of qualities – because consciousness cannot be a property of the physical body, the sense-organs or the brain-mind. Although the self as a substance must be everywhere pervasive, its everyday capacity for feeling, willing and knowing is focussed in the bodily organism.

Since the self experiences the consequences of its own deeds, there is, according to *Vaishesika*, a plurality of souls, each of which has its *vishesha*, individuality or particularity. What we experience is made up of parts, and is non-eternal, but the ultimate components – atoms – are eternal. Individuality is formed by imperceptible souls and certain atoms, which engender the organ of thought. At certain times, during immense cosmogonic cycles, nothing is visible, as both souls and atoms are asleep, but when a new cycle of creation begins, these souls reunite with certain atoms. Gautama asserted that even during incarnated existence, emancipation may be attained through ascetic detachment and the highest stages of contemplative absorption or *Samadhi*. Though the *Vaishesika* school wedded an atomistic standpoint to a strict atheism, over time thinkers accepted a rationalistic concept of Deity as a prime mover in the universe, a philosophical requisite acceptable to *Nyaya*. The two schools or systems were combined by Kusumanjali of *Udayana* about 900 C.E. in his proof of the existence of God. Since then, both schools have been theistic. The Jains claim early parentage for the *Vaishesika* system, and this merely illustrates what is very common in the Indian tradition, that innovators like Gautama and Kanada were reformulating an already ancient school rather than starting *de novo*.

The *Purva Mimamsa* of Jaimini took as its point of departure neither knowledge nor the objects of experience, but *dharma*, duty, as enjoined in the *Vedas* and *Upanishads*. As the accredited sources of *dharma*, these sacred texts are not the promulgations of some deity who condescended to step into time and set down principles of correct conduct. Rather, the wisdom in such texts is eternal and uncreate, and true *rishis* have always been able to see them and to translate that clear vision into mantramic sounds and memorable utterances. Hence *Mimamsa* consecrates the mind to penetrating the words which constitute this sacred transmission. Central to the *Mimamsa* school is the theory of self-evidence – *svata pramana:* truth is its own guarantee and the consecrated practice of faith provides its own validation. Repeated testings will yield correct results by exposing discrepancies and validating real cognitions. There is a recognizable consensus amidst the independent visions of great seers, and each individual must recognize or rediscover this consensus by proper use and concentrated enactment of *mantras* and hymns. Every sound in the fifty-two letters of Sanskrit has a cosmogonic significance and a theurgic effect. Inspired *mantras* are exact mathematical combinations of sounds which emanate potent vibrations that can transform the magnetic sphere around the individual as well as the magnetosphere of the earth. Self-testing without self-deception can become a sacred activity, which is *sui generis.*

From the *Mimamsa* perspective, every act is necessarily connected to perceptible results. One might say that the effects are inherent in the act, just as the fruit of the tree is in the seed which grew and blossomed. There is no ontological difference between act and result, for the apparent gap between them is merely the consequence of the operation of time. Since the fruit of a deed may not follow immediately upon the act, or even manifest in the same lifetime, the necessary connection between act and result takes the form of *apurva*, an unseen force which is the unbreakable link between them. This testable postulate gives significance to the concept of *dharma* in all its meanings – 'duty', 'path', 'teaching', 'religion', 'natural law', 'righteousness', 'accordance with cosmic harmony' – but it cannot by itself secure complete liberation from conditioned existence. Social duties are important, but spiritual duties are even more crucial, and the saying "To thine own self be true" has an array of meanings reaching up to the highest demands of soul-tendance. In the continual effort to work off past karma and generate good karma, there is unavoidable tension between different duties, social and spiritual. The best actions, paradigmatically illustrated in Vedic invocations and rituals, lead to exalted conditions, even to some heavenly condition or blissful state. Nonetheless, as the various *darshanas* interacted and exchanged insights, *Mimamsa* came to consider the highest action as resulting in a cessation of advances and retreats on the field of merit, whereby *dharma* and *adharma* were swallowed up in a sublime and transcendental state of unbroken awareness of the divine.

In striving to penetrate the deepest arcane meaning of the sacred texts, *Mimamsa* thinkers accepted the four *pramanas* or modes of knowledge set forth in *Nyaya*, and added two others: *arthapatti* or postulation, and *abhava* or negation and non-existence. They did this in part because, given their view of the unqualified eternality of the *Vedas*, they held that all cognition is valid at some level and to some degree. There can be no false knowledge; whatever is known is necessarily true. As a consequence, they saw no reason to prove the truth of any cognition. Rather, they sought to demonstrate its falsity, for if disproof were successful, it would show that there had been no cognition at all. The promise of gnosis rests upon the sovereign method of falsifiability rather than a vain attempt to seek total verification in a public sense. Shifting the onus of proof in this way can accommodate the uncreate *Vedas*, which are indubitably true and which constitute the gold standard against which all other claims to truth are measured. *Mimamsa* rests upon the presupposition of the supremacy of Divine Wisdom, the sovereignty of the Revealed Word and the possibility of its repeated realization. Even among those who cannot accept the liturgical or revelatory validity and adequacy of the *Vedas*, the logic of disproof can find powerful and even rigorous application. As a method, it became important to the philosophers of *Vedanta*.

Vedanta, meaning 'the end or goal of the *Vedas*', sometimes also called *Uttara Mimamsa*, addresses the spiritual and philosophical themes of the *Upanishads*, which are considered to complete and form the essence of the *Vedas*. Badarayana's magisterial *Brahma Sutras* ordered the Upanishadic Teachings in a logically coherent sequence which considers the nature of the supreme *brahman*, the ultimate Reality, and the question of the embodiment of the unconditioned Self. Each of the five hundred and fifty-five *sutras* (literally, 'threads') are extremely short and aphoristic, requiring a copious commentary to be understood. In explaining their meaning, various commentators presented Vedantic doctrines in different ways. Shankaracharya, the chief of the commentators and perhaps the greatest philosopher in the Indian tradition, espoused the *advaita,* non-dual, form of *Vedanta,* the purest form of monism, which has never been excelled. He asked whether in human experience there is anything which is impervious to doubt. Noting that every object of cognition – whether dependent on the senses, the memory or pure conceptualization – can be doubted, he recognized in the doubter that which is beyond doubt of any kind. Even if one reduces all claims to mere avowals – bare assertions about what one seems to experience – there nonetheless remains that which avows. It is proof of itself, because nothing can disprove it. In this, it is also different from everything else, and this difference is indicated by the distinction between subject and object. The experiencing Self is subject; what it experiences is an object. Unlike objects, nothing can affect it: it is immutable and immortal.

For Shankara, this Self (*atman*) is *sat-chit-ananda,* being or existence, consciousness or cognition, and unqualified bliss. If there were no world, there would be no objects of experience, and so although the world as it is experienced is not ultimately real, it is neither *abhava,* non-existent, nor *shunya,* void. Ignorance is the result of confusing *atman,* the unconditioned subject, with *anatman,* the external world. From the standpoint of the cosmos, the world is subject to space, time and causality, but since these categories arise from nascent experience, they are inherently inadequate save to point beyond themselves to the absolute, immutable, self-identical *brahman,* which is absolute Being (*sat*). *Atman* is *brahman,* for the immutable singularity of the absolute subject, the Self, is not merely isomorphic, but radically identical with the transcendent singularity of the ultimate Reality. Individuals who have yet to realize this fundamental truth, which is in fact the whole Truth, impose out of ignorance various attitudes and conceptions on the world, like the man who mistakes an old piece of rope discarded on the trail for a poisonous serpent. He reacts to the serpent, but his responses are inappropriate and cause him to suffer unnecessarily, because there is no serpent on the trail to threaten him. Nonetheless, the rope *is* there. For Shankara, the noumenal world is real, and when a person realizes its true nature, gaining wisdom thereby his responses will be appropriate and cease to cause suffering. He will realize that he *is* the *atman* and that the *atman* is *brahman*.

Although *brahman* is ultimately *nirguna*, without qualities, the aspirant to supreme knowledge begins by recognizing that the highest expression of *brahman* to the finite mind is *Ishvara*, which is *saguna brahman*, Supreme Reality conceived through the modes of pure logic. Taking *Ishvara*, which points beyond itself to That (*Tat*), as his goal and paradigm, the individual assimilates himself to *Ishvara* through the triple path of ethics, knowledge and devotion – the *karma, jnana* and *bhakti yogas* of the *Bhagavad Gita* – until *moksha*, emancipation and self-realization, is attained. For Shankara, *moksha* is not the disappearance of the world but the dissolution of *avidya*, ignorance.

Ramanuja, who lived much later than Shankara, adopted a qualified non-dualism, *Vishishtadvaita Vedanta*, by holding that the supreme *brahman* manifests as selves and matter. For him, both are dependent on *brahman*, and so selves, not being identical with the Ultimate, always retain their separate identity. As a consequence, they are dependent on *brahman*, and that dependency expresses itself self-consciously as *bhakti* or devotion. In this context, however, the dependence which is manifest as *bhakti* is absurd unless *brahman* is thought to be personal in some degree, and so *brahman* cannot be undifferentiated. Emancipation or freedom is not union with the divine, but rather the irreversible and unwavering intuition of Deity. The Self is not identical with *brahman*, but its true nature is this intuition, which is freedom. Faith that *brahman* exists is sufficient and individual souls are parts of *brahman*, who is the creator of universes. Yet *brahman* does not create anything new; what so appears is merely a modification of the subtle and the invisible to the gross which we can see and sense. Because we can commune with this God by prayer, devotion and faith, there is the possibility of human redemption from ignorance and delusion. The individual is not effaced when he is redeemed; he maintains his self-identity and enjoys the fruits of his faith.

About a century and a half after Ramanuja, Madhava promulgated a dualistic (*dvaita*) *Vedanta*, in which he taught that *brahman*, selves and the world are separate and eternal, even though the latter two depend forever upon the first. From this standpoint, *brahman* directs the world, since all else is dependent, and is therefore both transcendent and immanent. As that which can free the self, *brahman* is identified with Vishnu. Whereas the ultimate Reality or *brahman* is neither independent (*svatantra*) nor dependent (*paratantra*), God or Vishnu is independent, whereas souls and matter are dependent. God did not cause the cosmos but is part of it, and by his presence keeps it in motion. Individual souls are dependent on *brahman* but are also active agents with responsibilities which require the recognition of the omnipresence and omnipotence of God. For the individual self, there exists either the bondage which results from ignorance and the karma produced through acting ignorantly, or release effected through the adoration, worship and service of Deity. The self is free when its devotion is pure and perpetual. Although the later forms of *Vedanta* lower the sights of human potentiality from the lofty goal of universal self-consciousness and conscious immortality taught by Shankaracharya, they all recognize the essential difference between bondage and freedom. The one is productive of suffering and the other offers emancipation from it. But whereas for Shankara the means of emancipation is wisdom (*jnana*) as the basis of devotion (*bhakti*) and *nishkama karma* or disinterested action, the separation between *atman* and *brahman* is crucial for Ramanuja and necessitates total *bhakti*, whilst for Madhava there are five distinctions within his dualism – between God and soul, God and matter, soul and matter, one form of matter and another, and especially between one soul and another – thus requiring from all souls total obeisance to the omnipresent and omnipotent God.

Suffering is the starting point of the *Sankhya darshana* which provides the general conceptual framework of Yoga philosophy. Patanjali set out the *Taraka Raja Yoga* system, linking transcendental and self-luminous wisdom (*taraka*) with the alchemy of mental transformation, and like the exponents of other schools, he borrowed those concepts and insights which could best delineate his perspective. Since he found *Sankhya* metaphysics useful to understanding, like a sturdy boat used to cross a stream and then left behind when the opposite bank has been reached, many thinkers have traditionally presented *Sankhya* as the theory for which Yoga is the practice. This approach can aid understanding, providing one recognizes from the first and at all times that *yoga* is the path to metaconsciousness, for which no system of concepts and discursive reasoning, however erudite, rigorous and philosophical, is adequate. More than any other school or system, Yoga is essentially experiential, in the broadest, fullest and deepest meaning of that term.

Hermes, June 1988

THE SANKHYA DARSHANA

The term 'Sankhya' is ultimately derived from the Sanskrit root *khya*, meaning 'to know', and the prefix *san*, 'exact'. Exact knowing is most adequately represented by *Sankhya*, 'number', and since the precision of numbers requires meticulous discernment, *Sankhya* is that *darshana* which involves a thorough discernment of reality and is expressed through the enumeration of diverse categories of existence. Philosophically, *Sankhya* is dualistic in its discernment of the Self (*Purusha*) from the non-self (*prakriti*). In distinguishing sharply between *Purusha*, Self or Spirit, on the one hand, and *prakriti*, non-self or matter, on the other, the *Sankhya* standpoint requires a rigorous redefinition of numerous terms used by various schools. Even though later *Sankhya* freely drew from the Vedic-Upanishadic storehouse of wisdom which intimates a rich variety of philosophical views, its earliest concern does not appear to have been philosophical in the sense of delineating a comprehensive conceptual scheme which describes and explains reality. Early *Sankhya* asked, "What is real?" and only later on added the question, "How does it all fit together?"

Enumerations of the categories of reality varied with individual thinkers and historical periods, but the standard classification of twenty-five *tattvas* or fundamental principles of reality is useful for a general understanding of the *darshana*. Simply stated, *Sankhya* holds that two radically distinct realities exist: *Purusha*, which can be translated 'Spirit', 'Self' or 'pure consciousness', and *mulaprakriti*, or 'pre-cosmic matter', 'non-self' or 'materiality'. Nothing can be predicated of *Purusha* except as a corrective negation; no positive attribute, process or intention can be affirmed of it, though it is behind all the activity of the world. It might be called the Perceiver or the Witness, but, strictly speaking, no intentionality can be implied by these words, and so *Purusha* cannot be conceived primarily as a knower. *Mulaprakriti*, however, can be understood as pure potential because it undergoes ceaseless transformation at several levels. Thus, of the twenty-five traditional *tattvas*, only these two are distinct. The remaining twenty-three are transformations or modifications of *mulaprakriti*. *Purusha* and *mulaprakriti* stand outside conceptual cognition, which arises within the flux of the other *tattvas*. They abide outside space and time, are simple, independent and inherently unchanging, and they have no relation to one another apart from their universal, simultaneous and mutual presence.

Mulaprakriti is characterized by three qualities or *gunas: sattva* or intelligent and noetic activity, *rajas* or passionate and compulsive activity, and *tamas* or ignorant and impotent lethargy, represented in the *Upanishads* by the colours white, red and black. If *mulaprakriti* were the only ultimate reality, its qualities would have forever remained in a homogeneous balance, without undergoing change, evolution or transformation. Since *Purusha* is co-present with *mulaprakriti*, the symmetrical homogeneity of *mulaprakriti* was disturbed, and this broken symmetry resulted in a progressive differentiation which became the world of ordinary experience. True knowledge or pure cognition demands a return to that primordial stillness which marks the utter disentanglement of Self from non-self. The process which moved the *gunas* out of their perfect mutual balance cannot be described or even alluded to through analogies, in part because the process occurred outside space and time (and gave rise to them), and in part because no description of what initiated this universal transformation can be given in the language of logically subsequent and therefore necessarily less universal change. In other words, all transformation known to the intellect occurs in some context – minimally that of the intellect itself – whilst the primordial process of transformation occurred out of all context, save for the mere co-presence of *Purusha* and *mulaprakriti*.

This imbalance gave rise, first of all, logically speaking, to *mahat* or *Buddhi*. These terms refer to universal consciousness, primordial consciousness or intellect in the classical and neo-Platonic sense of the word. *Mahat* in turn gave rise to *ahankara*, the sense of 'I' or egoity. (*Ahankara* literally means 'I-making'.) Egoity as a principle or *tattva* generated a host of offspring or evolutes, the first of which was *manas* or mind, which is both the capacity for sensation and the mental ability to act, or intellectual volition. It also produced the five *buddhindriyas* or capacities for sensation: *shrota* (hearing), *tvac* (touching), *chaksus* (seeing), *rasana* (tasting) and *ghrana* (smelling). In addition to sensation, *ahankara* gave rise to their dynamic and material correlates, the five *karmendriyas* or capacities for action, and the five *tanmatras* or subtle elements. The five *karmendriyas* are *Vach* (speaking), *pani* (grasping), *pada* (moving), *payu* (eliminating) and *upastha* (procreating), whilst the five *tanmatras* include *shabda* (sound), *sparsha* (touch), *rupa* (form), *rasa* (taste) and *gandha* (smell). The *tanmatras* are called 'subtle' because they produce the *mahabhutas* or gross elements which can be perceived by ordinary human beings. They are *Akasha* (aether or empirical space), *vayu* (air), *tejas* (fire, and by extension, light), *ap* (water) and *prithivi* (earth).

This seemingly elaborate system of the elements of existence (*tattvas*) is a rigorous attempt to reduce the kaleidoscope of reality to its simplest comprehensible components, without either engaging in a reductionism which explains away or denies what does not fit its classification, or falling prey to a facile monism which avoids a serious examination of visible and invisible Nature. Throughout the long history of *Sankhya* thought, enumerations have varied, but this general classification has held firm. Whilst some philosophers have suggested alternative orders of evolution, for instance, making the subtle elements give rise to the capacities for sensation and action, Ishvarakrishna expressed the classical consensus in offering this classification of twenty-five *tattvas*.

Once the fundamental enumeration was understood, *Sankhya* thinkers arranged the *tattvas* by sets to grasp more clearly their relationships to one another. At the most general level, *Purusha* is neither generated nor generating, whilst *mulaprakriti* is ungenerated but generating. *Buddhi*, *ahankara* and the *tanmatras* are both generated and generating, and *manas*, the *buddhindriyas*, *karmendriyas* and *mahabhutas* are generated and do not generate anything in turn. In terms of their mutual relationships, one can speak of kinds of *tattvas* and indicate an order of dependence from the standpoint of the material world.

No matter how subtle and elaborate the analysis, however, one has at best described ways in which consciousness functions in *prakriti*, the material world. If one affirms that *Purusha* and *prakriti* are radically and fundamentally separate, one cannot avoid the challenge which vexed Descartes: how can *res cogitans*, thinking substance, be in any way connected with *res extensa*, extended (material) substance? *Sankhya* avoided the most fundamental problem of Cartesian dualism by willingly admitting that there can be no connection, linkage or interaction between *Purusha* and *prakriti*. Since consciousness is a fact, this exceptional claim involved a redefinition of consciousness itself. Consciousness is necessarily transcendent, unconnected with *prakriti*, and therefore it can have neither cognitive nor intuitive awareness, since those are activities which involve some centre or egoity and surrounding field from which it separates itself or with which it identifies. Egoity or perspective requires some mode of action, and all action involves the *gunas*, which belong exclusively to *prakriti*. Consciousness, *Purusha*, is mere presence, *sakshitva*, without action, dynamics or content. Awareness, *chittavritti*, is therefore a function of *prakriti*, even though it would not have come into being – any more than anything would have evolved or the *gunas* would have become unstable – without the universal presence of *Purusha*. Thus it is said that *Purusha* is unique in that it is neither generated nor generating, whereas all other *tattvas* are either generating, generated or both.

In this view, mind is material. Given its capacity for awareness, it can intuit the presence of *Purusha*, but it is not that *Purusha*. All mental functions are part of the complex activity of *prakriti*. Consciousness is bare subjectivity without a shadow of objective content, and it cannot be said to have goals, desires or intentions. *Purusha* can be said to exist (*sat*) – indeed, it necessarily exists – and its essential and sole specifiable nature is *chit*, consciousness. Unlike the Vedantin *atman*, however, it cannot also be said to be *ananda*, bliss, for *Purusha* is the pure witness, *sakshi*, with no causal connection to or participation in *prakriti*. Yet it is necessary, for the *gunas* could not be said to be active save in the presence of some principle of sentience. Without *Purusha* there could be no *prakriti*. This is not the simple idealistic and phenomenological standpoint summarized in Berkeley's famous dictum, *esse est percipi*, "to be is to be perceived". Rather, it is closer to the recognition grounded in Newtonian mechanics that, should the universe achieve a condition of total entropy, it could not be said to exist, for there would be no possibility of differentiation in it. Nor could its existence be denied. The presence of *Purusha*, according to *Sankhya*, is as necessary as is its utter lack of content.

Given the distinction between unqualified, unmodified subjectivity as true or pure consciousness, and awareness, which is the qualified appearance of consciousness in the world, consciousness appears as what it cannot be. It appears to cause and initiate, but cannot do so, since *Purusha* cannot be said to be active in any sense; it appears to entertain ideas and chains of thought, but it can in reality do neither. Rather, the action of the *gunas* appears as the activity of consciousness until the actual nature of consciousness is realized. The extreme break with previous understanding resulting from this realization – that consciousness has no content and that content is not conscious – is emancipation, the freeing of *Purusha* from false bondage to *prakriti*. It is akin to the Vedantin realization of *atman* free of any taint of *maya*, and the Buddhist realization of *shunyata*. Philosophical conceptualization is incapable of describing this realization, for pure consciousness can only appear, even to the subtlest cognitive understanding, as nothing. For *Sankhya*, *Purusha* is not nothing, but it is nothing that partakes of *prakriti* (which all awareness does).

Sankhya's unusual distinction between consciousness and what are ordinarily considered its functions and contents implies an operational view of *Purusha*. Even though no properties can be predicated of *Purusha*, the mind or intellect intuits the necessity of consciousness behind it, as it were. That is, the mind becomes aware that it is not itself pure consciousness. Since this awareness arises in individual minds, *Purusha* is recognized by one or another egoity. Without being able to attribute qualities to *Purusha*, it must therefore be treated philosophically as a plurality. Hence it is said that there are literally innumerable *purushas*, none of which have any distinguishing characteristics. The Leibnizian law of the identity of indiscernibles cannot be applied to *Purusha*, despite the philosophical temptation to do so, precisely because philosophy necessarily stops at the limit of *prakriti*. *Purusha* is outside space and time, and so is also beyond space-time identities. Since the minimum requirements of differentiation involve at least an indirect reference to either space or time, their negation in the concept of indiscernibility also involves such a reference, and cannot be applied to *Purusha*. Even though *Sankhya* affirms a plurality of *purushas*, this stance is less the result of metaphysical certitude than of the limitations imposed by consistency of method. The plurality of *purushas* is the consequence of the limits of understanding.

Within the enormous and diverse history of Indian thought, the six *darshanas* viewed themselves and one another in two ways. Internally, each standpoint sought clarity, completeness and consistency without reference to other *darshanas*. Since, however, the *darshanas* were committed to the proposition that they were six separate and viable perspectives on the same reality, they readily drew upon one another's insights and terminology and forged mutually dependent relationships. They were less concerned with declaring one another true or false than with understanding the value and limitations of each in respect to a complete realization of the ultimate and divine nature of things. Whilst some Western philosophers have pointed to the unprovable Indian presupposition that the heart of existence is divine, the *darshanas* reverse this standpoint by affirming that the core of reality is, almost definitionally, the only basis for thinking of the divine. In other words, reality is the criterion of the divine, and no other standard can make philosophical sense of the sacred, much less give it a practical place in human psychology and ethics. In their later developments, the *darshanas* strengthened their internal conceptual structures and ethical architectonics by taking one another's positions as foils for self-clarification. Earlier developments were absorbed into later understanding and exposition. Historically, *Sankhya* assimilated and redefined much of what had originally belonged to *Nyaya* and *Vaishesika*, and even *Mimamsa*, only to find much of its terminology and psychology incorporated into Vedanta, the most trenchantly philosophical of the *darshanas*. At the same time, later *Sankhya* borrowed freely from Vedantin philosophical concepts to rethink its own philosophical difficulties.

Despite *Sankhya's* unique distinction between consciousness and awareness, which allowed it to preserve its fundamental dualism in the face of monistic arguments – and thereby avoid the metaphysical problems attending monistic views – it could not avoid one fundamental philosophical question: What is it to say that *prakriti* is dynamic *because* of the presence of *Purusha*? To say that *prakriti* reflects the presence of *Purusha*, or that *Purusha* is reflected in *prakriti*, preserves a rigid distinction between the two, for neither an object reflected in a mirror nor the mirror is affected by the other. But *Sankhya* characterizes the ordinary human condition as one of suffering, which is the manifest expression of the condition of *avidya*, ignorance. This condition arises because *Purusha* falsely identifies with *prakriti* and its evolutes. Liberation, *Mukti*, is the result of *viveka*, discrimination, which is the highest knowledge. Even though *viveka* might be equated with pure perception as the *sakshi* or Witness, the process of attaining it suggests either an intention on the part of *Purusha* or a response on the part of *prakriti*, if not both. How then can *Purusha* be said to have no relation, including no passive relation, to *prakriti*? Even Ishvarakrishna's enchanting metaphor of the dancer before the host of spectators does not answer the question, for there is a significant relationship between performer and audience.

Such questions are worthy of notice but are misplaced from the *Sankhya* standpoint. If philosophical understanding is inherently limited to the functions of the mind (which is an evolute of *prakriti*), it can encompass neither total awareness (*Purusha*) nor the fact that both *Purusha* and *prakriti* exist. This is the supreme and unanswerable mystery of *Sankhya* philosophy, the point at which *Sankhya* declares that questions must have an end. It is not, however, an unaskable or meaningless question. If its answer cannot be found in philosophy, that is because it is dissolved in *Mukti*, freedom from ignorance, through perfect *viveka*, discrimination. In *Sankhya* as in *Vedanta*, philosophy ends where realization begins. Philosophy does not resolve the ultimate questions, even though it brings great clarity to cognition. Philosophy prepares, refines and orients the mind towards a significantly different activity, broadly called 'meditation', the rigorous cultivation of clarity of discrimination and concentrated, pellucid insight. The possibility of this is provided for by *Sankhya* metaphysics through its stress on the asymmetry between *Purusha* and *prakriti*, despite their co-presence. *Prakriti* depends on *Purusha*, but *Purusha* is independent of everything; *Purusha* is pure consciousness, whilst *prakriti* is unself-conscious. *Prakriti* continues to evolve because individual selves in it do not realize that they are really *Purusha* and, therefore, can separate themselves from *prakriti*, whilst there can never be complete annihilation of everything or of primordial matter.

Whereas *Yoga* accepted the postulates of *Sankhya* and also utilized its categories and classifications, all these being in accord with the experiences of developed *yogins,* there are significant divergences between *Yoga* and *Sankhya*. The oldest *Yoga* could have been agnostic in the sense implicit in the *Rig Veda* Hymn to Creation, but Patanjali's *Yoga* is distinctly theistic, diverging in this way from atheistic *Sankhya*. Whilst *Sankhya* is a speculative system, or at least a conceptual framework, *Yoga* is explicitly experiential and therefore linked to an established as well as evolving consensus among advanced *yogins*. This is both illustrated and reinforced by the fact that whereas *Sankhya* maps out the inner world of disciplined ideation in terms of thirteen evolutes – *Buddhi, ahankara, manas* and the ten *indriyas* – Patanjali's *Yoga* subsumes all these under *chitta* or consciousness, which is resilient, elastic and dynamic, including the known, the conceivable, the cosmic as well as the unknown. Whereas *Sankhya* is one of the most self-sufficient or closed systems, *Yoga* retains, as a term and in its philosophy, a conspicuously open texture which characterizes all Indian thought at its best. From the Vedic hymns to even contemporary discourse, it is always open-ended in reference to cosmic and human evolution, degrees of adeptship and levels of initiatory illumination. It is ever seeing, reaching and aspiring, beyond the boundaries of the highest thought, volition and feeling; beyond worlds and rationalist systems and doctrinaire theologies; beyond the limits of inspired utterance as well as all languages and all possible modes of creative expression. Philosophy and mathematics, poetry and myth, idea and icon, are all invaluable aids to the image-making faculty, but they all must point beyond themselves, whilst they coalesce and collapse in the unfathomable depths of the Ineffable, before which the best minds and hearts must whisper *neti neti,* "not this, not that". There is only the Soundless Sound, the ceaseless *AUM* in Boundless Space and Eternal Duration.

Hermes, July 1988

PATANJALI AND THE YOGA SUTRAS

Almost nothing is known about the sage who wrote the *Yoga Sutras*. The dating of his life has varied widely between the fourth century B.C.E. and the sixth century C.E., but the fourth century B.C.E. is the period noted for the appearance of aphoristic literature. Traditional Indian literature, especially the *Padma Purana*, includes brief references to Patanjali, indicating that he was born in Illavrita Varsha. Bharata Varsha is the ancient designation of Greater India as an integral part of Jambudvipa, the world as conceived in classical topography, but Illavrita Varsha is not one of its subdivisions. It is an exalted realm inhabited by the gods and enlightened beings who have transcended even the rarefied celestial regions encompassed by the sevenfold Jambudvipa. Patanjali is said to be the son of Angira and Sati, to have married Lolupa, whom he discovered in the hollow of a tree on the northern slope of Mount Sumeru, and to have reduced the degenerate denizens of Bhotabhandra to ashes with fire from his mouth. Such legendary details conceal more than they reveal and suggest that Patanjali was a great *Rishi* who descended to earth in order to share the fruits of his wisdom with those who were ready to receive it.

Some commentators identify the author of the *Yoga Sutras* with the Patanjali who wrote the *Mahabhashya* or *Great Commentary* on Panini's famous treatise on Sanskrit grammar sometime between the third and first centuries B.C.E. Although several scholars have contended that internal evidence contradicts such an identification, others have not found this reasoning conclusive. King Bhoja, who wrote a well-known commentary in the tenth century, was inclined to ascribe both works to a single author, perhaps partly as a reaction to others who placed Patanjali several centuries C.E. owing to his alleged implicit criticisms of late Buddhist doctrines. A more venerable tradition, however, rejects this identification altogether and holds that the author of the *Yoga Sutras* lived long before the commentator on Panini. In this view, oblique references to Buddhist doctrines are actually allusions to modes of thought found in some *Upanishads*.

In addition to our lack of definite knowledge about Patanjali's life, confusion arises from contrasting appraisals of the *Yoga Sutras* itself. There is a strong consensus that the *Yoga Sutras* represents a masterly compendium of various *Yoga* practices which can be traced back through the *Upanishads* to the *Vedas*. Many forms of *Yoga* existed by the time this treatise was written, and Patanjali came at the end of a long and ancient line of *yogins*. In accord with the free-thinking tradition of *shramanas*, forest recluses and wandering mendicants, the ultimate vindication of the *Yoga* system is to be found in the lifelong experiences of its ardent votaries and exemplars. The *Yoga Sutras* constitutes a practitioner's manual, and has long been cherished as the pristine expression of *Raja Yoga*. The basic texts of *Raja Yoga* are Patanjali's *Yoga Sutras*, the *Yogabhashya* of Vyasa and the *Tattvavaisharadi* of Vachaspati Mishra. *Hatha Yoga* was formulated by Gorakshanatha, who lived around 1200 C.E. The main texts of this school are the *Goraksha Sutaka*, the *Natha Yoga Pradipika* of Yogindra of the fifteenth century, and the later *Shivasamhita*. Whereas *Hatha Yoga* stresses breath regulation and bodily discipline, *Raja Yoga* is essentially concerned with mind control, meditation and self-study.

The *Yoga Sutras* of Patanjali is universal in the manner of the *Bhagavad Gita*, including a diversity of standpoints whilst fusing *Sankhya* metaphysics with *bhakti* or self-surrender. There is room for differences of emphasis, but every diligent user of Patanjali's aphorisms is enabled to refine aspirations, clarify thoughts, strengthen efforts, and sharpen focus on essentials in spiritual self-discipline. Accommodating a variety of exercises – mind control, visualization, breath, posture, moral training – Patanjali brings together the best in differing approaches, providing an integrated discipline marked by moderation, flexibility and balance, as well as degrees of depth in meditative absorption. The text eludes any simple classification within the vast resources of Indian sacred literature and *a fortiori* among the manifold scriptures of the world. Although it does not resist philosophical analysis in the way many mystical treatises do, it is primarily a practical aid to the quest for spiritual freedom, which transcends the concerns of theoretical clarification. Yet like any arcane science which necessarily pushes beyond the shifting boundaries of sensory experience, beyond conventional concepts of inductive reasoning and mundane reality, it reaffirms at every point its vital connection with the universal search for meaning and deliverance from bondage to shared illusions. It is a summons to systematic self-mastery which can aspire to the summits of gnosis.

The actual text as it has come down to the present may not be exactly what Patanjali penned. Perhaps he reformulated in terse aphoristic language crucial insights found in time-honoured but long-forgotten texts. Perhaps he borrowed terms and phrases from diverse schools of thought and training. References to breath control, *pranayama*, can be found in the oldest *Upanishads*, and the lineaments of systems of *Yoga* may be discerned in the *Maitrayana*, *Shvetashvatara* and *Katha Upanishads*, and veiled instructions are given in the 'Yoga' *Upanishads* – *Yogatattva*, *Dhyanabindu*, *Hamsa*, *Amritanada*, *Shandilya*, *Varaha*, *Mandala Brahmana*, *Nadabindu* and *Yogakundali* – though a leaning towards *Sankhya* metaphysics occurs only in the *Maitrayana*. The *Mahabharata* mentions the *Sankhya* and the *Yoga* as ancient systems of thought. *Hiranyagarbha* is traditionally regarded as the propounder of *Yoga*, just as Kapila is known as the original expounder of *Sankhya*. The *Ahirbudhnya* states that *Hiranyagarbha* disclosed the entire science of *Yoga* in two texts – the *Nirodha Samhita* and the *Karma Samhita*. The former treatise has been called the *Yoganushasanam*, and Patanjali also begins his work with the same term. He also stresses *nirodha* in the first section of his work.

In general, the affinities of the *Yoga Sutras* with the texts of *Hiranyagarbha* suggest that Patanjali was an adherent of the *Hiranyagarbha* school of *Yoga*, and yet his own manner of treatment of the subject is distinctive. His reliance upon the fundamental principles of *Sankhya* entitle him to be considered as also belonging to the *Sankhya Yoga* school. On the other hand, the significant variations of the later *Sankhya* of Ishvarakrishna from older traditions of proto-*Sankhya* point to the advantage of not subsuming the *Yoga Sutras* under broader systems. The author of *Yuktidipika* stresses that for Patanjali there are twelve capacities, unlike Ishvarakrishna's thirteen, that egoity is not a separate principle for Patanjali but is bound up with intellect and volition. Furthermore, Patanjali held that the subtle body is created anew with each embodiment and lasts only as long as a particular embodiment, and also that the capacities can only function from within. Altogether,

Patanjali's work provides a unique synthesis of standpoints and is backed by the testimony of the accumulated wisdom derived from the experiences of many practitioners and earlier lineages of teachers.

Some scholars and commentators have speculated that Patanjali wrote only the first three *padas* of the *Yoga Sutras*, whilst the exceptionally short fourth *pada* was added later. Indeed, as early as the writings of King Bhoja, one verse in the fourth *pada* (IV. 16) was recognized as a line interpolated from Vyasa's seventh commentary in which he dissented from *Vijnanavadin* Buddhists. Other interpolations may have occurred even in the first three *padas*, such as III. 22, which some classical commentators questioned. The fact that the third *pada* ends with the word *iti* ('thus', 'so', usually indicating the end of a text), as it does at the end of the fourth *pada*, might suggest that the original contained only three books. However, the philosophical significance of the fourth *pada* is such that the coherence of the entire text need not be questioned on the basis of inconclusive speculations.

Al-Biruni translated into Arabic a book he called *Kitab Patanjal* (*The Book of Patanjali*), which he said was famous throughout India. Although his text has an aim similar to the *Yoga Sutras* and uses many of the same concepts, it is more theistic in its content and even has a slightly Sufi tone. It is not the text now known as the *Yoga Sutras*, but it may be a kind of paraphrase popular at the time, rather like the *Dnyaneshwari*, which stands both as an independent work and a helpful restatement of the *Bhagavad Gita*. The *Kitab* translated by al-Biruni illustrates the pervasive influence of Patanjali's work throughout the Indian subcontinent.

For the practical aspirant to inner tranquillity and spiritual realization, the recurring speculations of scholars and commentators, stimulated by the lack of exact historical information about the author and the text, are of secondary value. Whatever the precise details regarding the composition of the treatise as it has come down through the centuries, it is clearly an integrated whole, every verse of which is helpful not only for theoretical understanding but also for sustained practice. The *Yoga Sutras* constitutes a complete text on meditation and is invaluable in that every *sutra* demands deep reflection and repeated application. Patanjali advocated less a doctrinaire method than a generous framework with which one can make experiments with truth, grow in comprehension and initiate progressive awakenings to the supernal reality of the *Logos* in the cosmos.

The word *Yoga* is derived from the Sanskrit verbal root *yuj*, 'to yoke' or 'to join', related to the Latin *jungere*, 'to join', 'to unite'. In its broadest usages it can mean addition in arithmetic; in astronomy it refers to the conjunction of stars and planets; in grammar it is the joining of letters and words. In *Mimamsa* philosophy it indicates the force of a sentence made up of united words, whilst in *Nyaya* logic it signifies the power of the parts taken together. In medicine it denotes the compounding of herbs and other substances. In general, *Yoga* and *viyoga* pertain to the processes of synthesis and analysis in both theoretical and applied sciences. Panini distinguishes between the root *yuj* in the sense of concentration (*Samadhi*) and *yujir* in the sense of joining or connecting. Buddhists have used the term *Yoga* to designate the withdrawal of the mind from all mental and sensory objects. Vaishesika philosophy means by *Yoga* the concentrated attention to a single subject through mental abstraction from all contexts. Whereas the followers of Ramanuja use the term to depict the fervent aspiration to join one's *ishtadeva* or chosen deity, *Vedanta* chiefly uses the term to characterize the complete union of the human soul with the divine spirit, a connotation compatible with its use in *Yoga* philosophy. In addition, Patanjali uses the term *Yoga* to refer to the deliberate cessation of all mental modifications.

Every method of self-mastery, the systematic removal of ignorance and the progressive realization of Truth, can be called *Yoga*, but in its deepest sense it signifies the union of one's apparent and fugitive self with one's essential nature and true being, or the conscious union of the embodied self with the Supreme Spirit. The *Maitrayana Upanishad* states:

> Carried along by the waves of the qualities darkened in his imagination, unstable, fickle, crippled, full of desires, vacillating, he enters into belief, believing I am he, this is mine, and he binds his self by his self as a bird with a net. Therefore a man, being possessed of

will, imagination and belief, is a slave, but he who is the opposite is free. For this reason let a man stand free from will, imagination and belief. This is the sign of liberty, this is the path that leads to *brahman*, this is the opening of the door, and through it he will go to the other shore of darkness.

Thus, *Yoga* refers to the removal of bondage and the consequent attainment of true spiritual freedom. Whenever *Yoga* goes beyond this and actually implies the fusion of an individual with his ideal, whether viewed as his real nature, his true self or the universal spirit, it is gnostic self-realization and universal self-consciousness, a self-sustaining state of serene enlightenment. Patanjali's metaphysical and epistemological debt to *Sankhya* is crucial to a proper comprehension of the *Yoga Sutras*, but his distinct stress on *praxis* rather than *theoria* shows a deep insight of his own into the phases and problems that are encountered by earnest practitioners of *Yoga*. His chief concern was to show how and by what means the spirit, trammelled in the world of matter, can withdraw completely from it and attain total emancipation by transforming matter into its original state and thus realize its own pristine nature. This applies at all levels of self-awakening, from the initial cessation of mental modifications, through degrees of meditative absorption, to the climactic experience of spiritual freedom.

Patanjali organized the *Yoga Sutras* into four *padas* or books which suggest his architectonic intent. *Samadhi Pada*, the first book, deals with concentration of mind (*Samadhi*), without which no serious practice of *Yoga* is possible. Since *Samadhi* is necessarily experiential, this *pada* explores the hindrances to and the practical steps needed to achieve alert quietude. Both restraint of the senses and of the discursive intellect are essential for *Samadhi*. Having set forth what must be done to attain and maintain meditative absorption, the second book, *Sadhana Pada*, provides the method or means required to establish full concentration. Any effort to subdue the tendency of the mind to become diffuse, fragmented or agitated demands a resolute, consistent and continuous practice of self-imposed, steadfast restraint, *tapas*, which cannot become stable without a commensurate disinterest in all phenomena. This relaxed disinterestedness, *vairagya*, has nothing to do with passive indifference, positive disgust, inert apathy or feeble-minded *ennui* as often experienced in the midst of desperation and tension in daily affairs. Those are really the self-protective responses of one who is captive to the pleasure-pain principle and is deeply vulnerable to the flux of events and the vicissitudes of fortune. *Vairagya* implies a conscious transcendence of the pleasure-pain principle through a radical reappraisal of expectations, memories and habits. The pleasure-pain principle, dependent upon passivity, ignorance and servility for its operation, is replaced by a reality principle rooted in an active, noetic apprehension of psycho-spiritual causation. Only when this impersonal perspective is gained can the *yogin* safely begin to alter significantly his psycho-physical nature through breath control, *pranayama*, and other exercises.

The third book, *Vibhuti Pada*, considers complete meditative absorption, *sanyama*, its characteristics and consequences. Once calm, continuous attention is mastered, one can discover an even more transcendent mode of meditation which has no object of cognition whatsoever. Since levels of consciousness correspond to planes of being, to step behind the uttermost veil of consciousness is also to rise above all manifestations of matter. From that wholly transcendent standpoint beyond the ever-changing contrast between spirit and matter, one may choose any conceivable state of consciousness and, by implication, any possible material condition. Now the *yogin* becomes capable of tapping all the *siddhis* or theurgic powers. These prodigious mental and moral feats are indeed magical, although there is nothing miraculous or even supernatural about them. They represent the refined capacities and exalted abilities of the perfected human being. Just as any person who has achieved proficiency in some specialized skill or knowledge should be careful to use it wisely and precisely, so too the *yogin* whose spiritual and mental powers may seem practically unlimited must not waste his energy or misuse his hard-won gifts. If he were to do so, he would risk getting entangled in worldly concerns in the myriad ways from which he had sought to free himself. Instead, the mind must be merged into the inmost spirit, the result of which is *kaivalya*, steadfast isolation or eventual emancipation from the bonds of illusion and the meretricious glamour of terrestrial existence.

In *Kaivalya Pada*, the fourth book which crowns the *Yoga Sutras*, Patanjali conveys the true nature of isolation or supreme spiritual freedom insofar as it is possible to do so in words. Since *kaivalya* is the term used for the sublime state of consciousness in which the enlightened soul has gone beyond the differentiating sense of 'I am', it cannot be characterized in the conceptual languages that are dependent on the subject-object distinction. Isolation is not nothingness, nor is it a static condition. Patanjali throws light on this state of gnosis by providing a metaphysical and metapsychological explanation of cosmic and human intellection, the operation of karma and the deep-seated persistence of the tendency of self-limitation. By showing how the suppression of modifications of consciousness can enable it to realize its true nature as pure potential and master the lessons of manifested Nature, he intimates the immense potency of the highest meditations and the inscrutable purpose of cosmic selfhood.

The metapsychology of the *Yoga Sutras* bridges complex metaphysics and compelling ethics, creative transcendence and critical immanence, in an original, inspiring and penetrating style, whilst its aphoristic method leaves much unsaid, throwing aspirants back upon themselves with a powerful stimulus to self-testing and self-discovery. Despite his sophisticated use of *Sankhya* concepts and presuppositions, Patanjali's text has a universal appeal for all ardent aspirants to Raja *Yoga*. He conveys the vast spectrum of consciousness, diagnoses the common predicament of human bondage to mental ailments, and offers practical guidance on the arduous pathway of lifelong contemplation that could lead to the summit of self-mastery and spiritual freedom.

Hermes, January 1989

SAMADHI PADA

*Through yoga let one concentrate on study. By perfection in study
and in yoga, the Supreme Soul shines forth clearly.*

Vyasa

The classic text of Patanjali opens with the simplest statement: "*atha
yoganushasanam*", "Now begins instruction in *yoga*." The typical reader
today might well expect this terse announcement to be followed by
a full explanation of the term *yoga* and its diverse meanings, perhaps
a polemical digression on different schools of thought and some
methodological guidance concerning the best way to use the text. None
of this occurs. Rather, Patanjali set down his most famous words: "*yogash
chitta-vritti-nirodhah*": "*Yoga* is the restraint of the modifications of the
mind." He stated the essential meaning of *yoga* without any argument
or illustration, as if he were providing a basic axiom. He thus showed
at the very start that he was concerned with practical instruction rather
than theoretical exposition. He thereby took for granted that the user
of the text already had some understanding of the task of *yoga* and was
ready to undergo a demanding daily discipline.

Yoga psychology differs radically from more recent, and especially
post-Freudian, schools of thought in its stress on self-emancipation
rather than on self-acceptance in relation to social norms or psychic
tensions. Most modern varieties of psychology, including even the
recent humanistic preoccupation with self-actualization as propounded
by Abraham Maslow and elaborated in different directions by
Carl Rogers and Rollo May, essentially aim at an integration and
harmonizing of otherwise disparate and conflicting elements in a person
in contemporary society. For Patanjali, all these identifiable elements
– thoughts, feelings, intentions, motives and desires (conscious and
unconscious) – are *chittavrittis*, mental modifications which must be seen
as hindrances to contemplative calm. Even if they are deftly balanced
and fully integrated, the individual would at best be a mature person
marked by thoughtful and creative responses in a world of suffering

and ignorance. Conquering, not coping, transcending, not reconciling, were Patanjali's chief concerns. For him, the latter were by-products of the former, and never the reverse. The psychology of self-emancipation means the deliberate and self-conscious restraint of everything that is productive of mental confusion, weakness and pain.

Patanjali's stipulative definition of *yoga* might seem dogmatic, but this reaction springs from ignorance of his central purpose and unstated presuppositions. Patanjali wrote not from the standpoint of revealed scripture, academic scholarship or of theoretical clarification, but from the standpoint of concrete experience through controlled experiment. If truth is ontologically bound up and intimately fused with self-transcendence, then what from the standpoint of self-emancipation is a stark description is, from the standpoint of the unenlightened, an arbitrary prescription. What would be the naturalistic fallacy on a single plane of manifested Nature becomes a necessary line of thought when multiple planes of unmanifested Nature are taken into account. The ability to alter states of consciousness presupposes the capacity to emulate the architectonics of a higher and less differentiated plane on a lower and more fragmented plane of percepts and concepts. In other words, *yoga* is that science in which the descriptions of reality necessarily function as prescriptions for those who have not experienced it. The analogy would be closer to music or mathematics than to the visual arts or the empirical sciences as normally understood.

Skilful methods are those which provide apt descriptions, giving the instructional guidance needed. Hence, in the hands of a spiritual master, the actual method to be pursued varies with each aspirant, for it is the vital and original link between the adept's transcendent *(taraka)* wisdom and the disciple's mental temperament and devotion *(bhakti)*. There is a reciprocal interaction between the readiness to receive and the mode of giving – of disciple and master. For Patanjali, the true nature of *chitta,* the mind, can be known only when it is not modified by external influences and their internal impresses. For as long as modifications persist without being deliberately chosen for a purpose, the mind unwittingly identifies with them, falling into passivity, habitude, and the pain which results from a state of fragmentation and self-alienation.

Since mental modifications ramify in myriad directions, their root causes need to be grasped clearly if they are to be firmly removed. The essential principle to be understood is central to the second and third of Gautama Buddha's Four Noble Truths. Those persistent misconceptions which, directly or indirectly, produce discontent and suffering have a distinctive set of causes which, if eliminated, inevitably ensure the cessation of their concomitant effects. Patanjali pointed to five *chittavrittis* which are distinct and yet share the common tendency to be pleasurable or painful. Whilst *yoga* psychology fully acknowledges the strength of the pleasure principle – the propensity to be drawn towards pleasurable sensations as if by a magnet and to be repelled by painful ones – it denies its relevance to real individuation as a moral agent, a *Manushya*, whose name comes from *manas*, 'mind', the root of which is *man*, 'to think'. Self-emancipation, the culmination in *yoga* of self-transcendence, requires the complete subordination of the pleasure-pain principle to the reality principle. Reality, in this view, has nothing to do with involuntary change, the inherent propensity of *prakriti*, matter, and not *Purusha*, spirit, whilst pleasure and pain are necessarily bound up with conditioning and change. This is why the most attractive states of mind seem so readily and recurrently to alter into the most repugnant states. In general, mental modifications obscure and obstruct the intrinsically blissful nature of pure consciousness, the serene state of mind of the "spectator without a spectacle."

The five types of mental modifications are: *correct cognition,* based on direct perception, valid inference and verbal testimony; *misconception,* based upon something other than itself, namely the five *kleshas* or sources of sorrow – ignorance, egoism, attachment, hate and the fear of death, according to the *Yogabhashya; fantasy,* engendered by words and concepts, when and to the degree that they do not refer to reality; *sleep,* which occurs when other modifications cease and the mind is emptied of mental contents; and *memory,* which is the result of clinging to, or at least not letting go of, objects or images of subjective experiences. The *chittavrittis* can be diagrammatically depicted as follows:

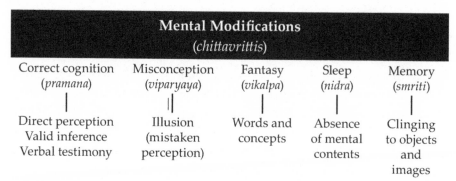

Although this array of mental modifications is easy to outline, its implications are extensive and radical. When Patanjali included correct cognition amongst the mental modifications, he was adhering to strict theoretical and practical consistency. He was concerned to deny that mundane insight, discursive thought and even scriptural authority can free the mind from bondage to delusion and suffering. Yet without a preliminary apprehension of *yoga* philosophy, how could one adopt its methods and hope to achieve its aims? In part the answer lies in a proper grasp of the pervasiveness of *maya* or illusion. If everything that conceals the changeless Real is *maya,* then the human being who seeks to know the Real by conventional methods is trapped in some sort of metaphysical split or even schizophrenia. Philosophers from the pre-Socratics and Platonists to Descartes and Spinoza recognized that a substance cannot become what it is not. To say that human beings are intrinsically capable of attaining *kaivalya,* self-emancipation or transcendence of *maya,* is to affirm that they are quintessentially what they seek. Their inmost nature is one with the Real. On the other hand, to say that they have to strive in earnest to realize fully what they essentially are implies that they have allowed themselves to become captive to *maya* through persistent self-limitation.

Given this delusive condition, the mere temporary cessation of modifications, such as occurs in sleep, will not help to liberate man's immortal spirit. As *maya* is pervasive illusion, humanity as it knows itself is a part of it. Ignorant or involuntary withdrawal from its action only makes it unconscious, and this is why sleep is classed as one of the *chittavrittis.* Rather, one has to master the rules of *maya* and learn how to extricate oneself gradually from it. Otherwise, one only makes random moves, embedding oneself in deeper ignorance and greater suffering. Patanjali taught that deliverance can only come through *abhyasa*, assiduous practice, and *vairagya*, dispassionate detachment. *Abhyasa is* the active opposite of passive sleep, and *vairagya* frees one from all attachments, including the *kleshas*, which induce misconceptions. Together, these two mirror in the world of change that which is changeless beyond it. In the language of the *Isha Upanishad*, one has to find the transcendent in the immanent, and for Patanjali, *abhyasa* and *vairagya* constitute exactly that mode of awareness.

For Patanjali, however, *abhyasa* is not just striving to *do* something; it is rather the effort to *be* something. "*Abhyasa* is the continuous effort to abide in a steady state." According to the *Yogabhashya*, *abhyasa* is the attempt to preserve *prashantavahita*, continuity of mind or consciousness which is both fully awake and without fluctuations. Like all such spiritual exercises, *abhyasa* becomes richer, more refined and more relaxed with persistence that comes from repeated effort, moral earnestness and joyous devotion. *Abhyasa* is the constant criterion for all effort, and the indispensable tool, whenever and however taken up.

Vairagya cannot be merely passive disinterest in the content of experience any more than sleep can substitute for wakeful serenity. It is true detachment whilst being fully aware of the relative significance of objects, and this element of self-conscious maintenance of calm detachment is exactly what makes it real *vairagya*. Through *vairagya*, one comes to know the world for what it is because one recognizes that every object of sense, whether seen or unseen, is an assemblage of evanescent attributes or qualities *(gunas)* of *prakriti*, whereas the enduring reality, from the standpoint of the seeker for emancipation, is *Purusha*, the Self of all. Shankaracharya stated: "The seer of *Purusha* becomes one who is freed from rejecting or accepting anything.... Detachment is extreme clarity of cognition."

Abhyasa and *vairagya* are fused in the intense yet serene mental absorption known as *Samadhi*. Patanjali characterized *Samadhi* (which means 'concentration', 'contemplation' and 'meditation', depending on the context) in relation to a succession of stages, for if *Samadhi* signifies a specific state, the contemplative seeker would either abide in it or fail to do so. But Patanjali knew that no one can suddenly bridge the gap between fragmented, distracted consciousness and wholly unified meditation. Rather, concentration *(Samadhi)* proceeds by degrees for one who persists in the effort, because one progressively overcomes everything that hinders it. In the arduous ascent from greater degrees of relative *maya* towards greater degrees of reality, the transformation of consciousness requires a calm apprehension of those higher states. The conscious descent from exalted planes of being requires the capacity to bring down a clearer awareness of reality into the grosser regions of *maya*. Continuous self-transformation on the ascent must be converted into confident self-transmutation on the descent.

Patanjali saw in the evolving process of meditation several broad but distinct levels of *Samadhi*. The first is *sanprajnata Samadhi*, cognitive contemplation, in which the meditator is aware of a distinction between himself and the thought he entertains. This form of meditation is also called *sabija Samadhi*, or meditation with a seed *(bija)*, wherein some object or specific theme serves as a focal point on which to settle the mind in a steady state. Since such a point is extrinsic to pure consciousness, the basic distinction between thinker and thought persists. In its least abstracted form, *sanprajnata Samadhi* involves *vitarka* (reasoning), *vichara* (deliberation), *ananda* (bliss) and *asmita* (the sense of ' I '). Meditation is some sort of *bhavana*, or becoming that upon which one ponders, for consciousness identifies with, takes on and virtually becomes what it contemplates. Meditation on a seed passes through stages in which these types of conditioning recede and vanish as the focal point of consciousness passes beyond every kind of deliberation and even bliss itself, until only *asmita* or the pure sense of 'I' remains. Even this, however, is a limiting focus which can be transcended.

Asanprajnata Samadhi arises out of meditation on a seed though it is itself seedless. Here supreme detachment frees one from even the subtlest cognition and one enters *nirbija Samadhi*, meditation without a seed, which is self-sustaining because free of any supporting focalization on an object. From the standpoint of the succession of objects of thought

– the type of consciousness all human beings experience in a chaotic or fragmentary way and a few encounter even in meditation on a seed – *nirbija Samadhi* is nonexistence or emptiness, for it is absolutely quiescent consciousness. Nonetheless, it is not the highest consciousness attainable, for it is the retreat of mind to a neutral *(laya)* centre from which it can begin to operate on a wholly different plane of being. This elevated form of pure consciousness is similar to a state experienced in a disembodied condition between death and rebirth, when consciousness is free of the involvement with vestures needed for manifestation in differentiated matter. Just as an individual becomes unconscious when falling into deep dreamless sleep, because consciousness fails to remain alert except in conditions of differentiation, so too consciousness in a body becomes unconscious and forgetful of its intrinsic nature on higher planes. *Samadhi* aims to restore that essential awareness self-consciously, making the alert meditator capable of altering planes of consciousness without any loss of awareness.

For earnest practitioners, Patanjali taught, *Samadhi* is attained in several distinct but interrelated ways – through *shraddha* (faith), *virya* (energy), *smriti* (retentiveness) and *prajna* (intellectual insight) – which are vital prerequisites for the metapsychological *yoga* of *Samadhi*. *Shraddha* is the calm and confident conviction that *yoga* is efficacious, coupled with the wholehearted orientation of one's psychic, moral and mental nature towards experiential confirmation. Undistracted *shraddha* of this sort leads naturally to *virya*, energy which releases the resolve to reach the goal and the resourceful courage needed to persist in seeking it. In *The Voice of the Silence*, an ancient text of spiritual discipline, *virya* is viewed as the fifth of seven keys required to unlock seven portals on the path to wisdom. In this text, *virya* follows upon *dana, shila, kshanti* and *viraga (vairagya)* – charity, harmony in conduct, patience, and detachment in regard to the fruits of action – all suggesting the hidden depths of *shraddha* which can release dauntless energy in the pursuit of Truth.

Smriti implies the refinement of memory which helps to extract the essential lesson of each experience without the needless elaboration of irrelevancies. It requires the perception of significant connections and the summoning of full recollection, the soul memory stressed by Plato wherein one awakens powers and potentialities transcending the experiences of a lifetime. *Prajna,* released by such inner awakenings, enables consciousness to turn within and cognize the deeper layers of oneself. Seen and strengthened in this manner, one's innate soul-wisdom becomes the basis of one's progressive understanding of the integral connection between freedom and necessity. In time, the 'is' of external facticity becomes a vital pointer to the 'ought' of the spiritual Path and the 'can' of one's true self-hood.

Supreme meditation, the most complete *Samadhi,* is possible for those who can bring clarity, control and imaginative intensity to daily practice. Yet Patanjali's instructions, like those of an athletic coach who guides the gifted but also aids those who show lesser promise, apply to every seeker who sincerely strives to make a modest beginning in the direction of the highest *Samadhi* as well as to those able to make its attainment the constant target of their contemplations. He spoke explicitly of those whose progress is rapid but also of those whose efforts are mild or moderate. An individual's strivings are stimulated to the degree they recognize that they are ever reaching beyond themselves as they have come to think of themselves through habit, convention, weakness and every form of ignorance. Rather than naively thinking that one is suddenly going to surmount every obstacle and obscuration in one's own nature, one can sedulously foster *bhakti*, total devotion and willing surrender to *Ishvara*, the Supreme Spirit immanent in all souls, even if one has hardly begun to grasp one's true self-hood. Such sustained devotion is *ishvarapranidhana,* the potent invocation of the Supreme Self through persistent surrender to It, isomorphic on the plane of consciousness with abnegation of the fruits of all acts to Krishna on the plane of conduct, as taught in the *Bhagavad Gita.*

Ishvara is *saguna brahman,* the supreme repository of all resplendent qualities, in contrast to *nirguna brahman,* the attributeless Absolute. *Ishvara* is *Purusha,* "untouched by troubles, actions and their results" (I.24), immanent in all *prakriti*. Cherishing the one source of all is the means by which one moves through degrees of *Samadhi,* culminating in the complete union of the individual and the cosmic, the state of *kaivalya* or isolation. Like *Kether*, the crown in the *Kabbalah*, *Ishvara* is at once the single motivating force behind the cosmic activity of *prakriti* and the utterly transcendent *(nirguna) Purusha* or pure spirit. What exists in each human soul as the latent bud of omniscience is awakened and it expands into the realm of infinitude in *Ishvara* itself. Untouched by time and therefore untrammelled by ordinary consciousness which is time-bound, *Ishvara* is the supreme Initiator of all, from the ancient *Rishis* to the humble disciple sitting in meditation. *Ishvara* is OM, the primal sound, the basic keynote of all being, the source of the music of the spheres, mirrored in the myriad manifestations of *prakriti*. Surrender to *Ishvara* is aided by the silent repetition of the sacred OM and by deep meditation upon its mystery and meaning. When *bhakti* flows freely in this rapturous rhythm, consciousness readily turns inward and removes all hindrances to progress in *Samadhi*.

Surrender to the luminous core of one's consciousness, which is more powerful than one's strongest proclivities, initiates a mighty countervailing force against the cumulative momentum generated by the *chittavrittis*. As the mind has grown accustomed to indulge, identify with and even cherish ceaseless modifications, any attempt to check those modifications runs against the self-reproducing tenacity of long established habits, impressions and tendencies. The *chittavrittis* are virtually infinite in their discrete manifestations and yet are amenable to broad classification on the basis of essential traits. The hindrances which aggravate mental distraction, fragmented consciousness and continual modification are disease, dullness, doubt, heedlessness, indolence, addiction to objects of sense, distorted perception, and failure to stabilize the mind in any particular state. Though distinct from each other, these distractions are all accompanied by sorrow *(duhkha)*, depression, bodily agitation and irregular breathing. They can, however, be most effectively eliminated through *abhyasa*, or constant practice of a single truth or principle. Whilst any profound truth which deeply moves one can be chosen, to the degree that it is true – and so to the degree that it is efficacious over time – it is *ekatattva*, the one principle, which in *Sankhya* philosophy is *Purusha* or pure spirit.

Overcoming mental obstructions through *abhyasa* in respect to one principle requires the progressive purification of the mind, freeing it from the froth and dross of old patterns fostered by feeble and fickle attention. Most seekers typically find easiest and most effective a concerted effort to expand the feeling of friendliness towards all beings, compassion for every creature, inward gladness and a cool detachment in regard to pleasure and pain, virtue and vice. On the physical plane of human nature, one can learn to make one's breathing calm and even, steady and rhythmical. Through intense concentration, one can begin to awaken subtler perceptions which are not subject to hindrances in the way the ordinary sense-organs are, to an almost grotesque extent. One may even activate a spark of *Buddhi,* pure insight and deep penetration, sensing the vast ocean of supernal cosmic light which interpenetrates and encloses everything. Some seekers will find it more feasible to contemplate the lustrous splendour of a mythic, historical or living being who is a paragon of supreme self-mastery. Others may benefit by brooding on flashes of reminiscence that recur in dreams or come from deep dreamless sleep. Patanjali also pointed out that one could gain mental stability by meditating intently upon what one most ardently desired. In the words of Charles Johnston, "Love is a form of knowledge", when it is profound and sacrificial, constant and unconditional.

All such efforts to surmount the hindrances which distract the mind are aids to deep meditation, and when they have fully worked their benevolent magic, the becalmed mind becomes the effortless master of everything which comes into the horizon of consciousness, from the atomic to the infinite. When all the hindrances disappear, mental modifications cease and the mind "becomes like a transparent crystal, attaining the power of transformation, taking on the colour of what it rests on, whether it be the cognizer, the cognized or the act of cognition" (I.41). When the mind is distracted through discursive trains of thought, it tends to oscillate between passive disorientation and aggressive attempts to conceal its ignorance through contentious and partisan fixations. But when the memory is purged of external traces and encrusted conditionality, and the mind is withdrawn from all limiting conceptions – including even its abstract self-image, thus focussed solely on *ekatattva*, truth alone – it is free from obscuration, unclouded (*nirvitarka*), and sees each truth as a whole. It notices the subtle elements behind shifting appearances, including the noumenal, primordial and undifferentiated sources and causes of all mental modifications. This serene self-emancipation of consciousness is called sabija *Samadhi*, meditation with a seed, the fulcrum for gaining all knowledge. In this sublime condition, the mind has become as pellucid as crystal and mirrors the spiritual light of *Purusha*, whence dawns direct insight (*prajna*) into the ultimate Truth.

Unlike other methods of cognizing truth – which concern this or that and hence are involved with *samvritti satya*, relative truths, though truths nonetheless – *prajna* has but one single object for its focus, the Supreme Truth itself (*paramartha satya*). Its power displaces and transcends all lesser forms of truth, exiling them permanently from consciousness. Beyond this lies only that indescribable state called *nirbija Samadhi*, meditation without a seed, wherein the mind lets go of even Truth itself as an object. When the mind ceases to function, the *Yogabhashya* teaches, *Purusha* becomes isolated, pure and liberated. Mind has become the pure instrument that guides the soul ever closer to that threshold where, when reached, spirit steps from false finitude into inconceivable infinitude, leaving the mind behind, passing into *kaivalya*, total isolation or supreme freedom. The last psychic veil is drawn aside and the spiritual man stands with unveiled vision. As M.N. Dvivedi commented, "The mind thus having nothing to rest upon exhausts itself. . . and *Purusha* alone shines in perfect bliss and peace." "The Light", I.K. Taimni remarked, "which was up to this stage illuminating other objects now illuminates Itself, for it has withdrawn beyond the realm of these objects. The Seer is now established in his own Self."

Having depicted the entire path leading from ignorance and bewilderment to beatific illumination, Patanjali saw only two tasks remaining: (1) to explain in detail the diverse means for attaining concentration and meditation, and (2) to elucidate the idea of *kaivalya* or isolation, insofar as it is possible to convey it through words.

Hermes, February 1989

SADHANA PADA

A person without self-discipline cannot attain perfection in Yoga. An undisturbed course of self-purificatory conduct should be practised.

Yogabhashya

Patanjali initiated his teaching concerning *praxis* by calling attention to the three chief elements in the discipline of *Yoga: tapas*, austerity, self-restraint and eventually self-mastery; *svadhyaya*, self-study, self-examination, including calm contemplation of *Purusha*, the Supreme Self; and *ishvarapranidhana*, self-surrender to the Lord, the omnipresent divine spirit within the secret heart. The threefold practice or *Sadhana* can remove the *kleshas* or afflictions which imprison *Purusha* and thus facilitate *Samadhi* or meditative absorption. This arduous alchemical effort was summed up succinctly by Shankaracharya: "Right vision *(samyagdarshana)* is the means to transcendental aloneness *(kaivalya)*.... *Yoga* practice, being the means to right vision, comes before it.... Ignorance is destroyed when directly confronted by right vision." The *kleshas*, though varied in their myriad manifestations, are essentially five: *avidya*, ignorance; *asmita*, egoism; *raga*, attachment; *dvesha*, aversion; and *abhinivesha*, tenacious clinging to mundane existence. Ignorance, however, is the broad field in which all the other *kleshas* arise, because they are no more than distinct specializations of ignorance.

Ignorance is a fundamental inverted confusion which mistakes *prakriti* for *Purusha*, the false for the true, the impure for the pure, and the painful for the pleasurable a persisting malaise which might have been difficult to comprehend in the past but which is now a familiar condition in contemporary psychology. Springing from fundamental ignorance, egoism (asmita) confuses the potency of the Seer *(Purusha)* with the power of sight *(Buddhi)*. Attachment *(raga)* is the pursuit of what is mistaken to be pleasurable, whilst aversion *(dvesha)* flees from what is believed to be painful. These two constitute the primary pair of opposites on the psychological level in the field of ignorance, and all other pairs of opposites are derived from them. Clinging to phenomenal existence (*abhinivesha*) is the logical outcome of the operation of ignorance, and once aroused is self-sustaining through the inertia of habit, so that countervailing measures are needed to eradicate it, together with the other *kleshas*.

Through ignorance (*avidya*) there is an obscuration of the cosmic Self (*Purusha*), a fundamental misidentification of what is real, a persistent misconception which carries its own distinct logic within the complex dialectic of *maya*:

> Since the *kleshas* are engendered by a persistent error, at root mistaking *prakriti* for *Purusha*, or attributing the essential characteristics of *Purusha* to one or another aspect of *prakriti*, they can be eliminated only by a radical reversal of the downward tendency of alienation and retreat from truth. This fundamental correction, as far reaching as the entrenched habit of inversion which necessitates it, is *dhyana*, meditation, together with the mental and moral exercises which strengthen it. To say, as Hindu and Buddhist thinkers alike assert, that *karma* is rooted in *avidya* is to imply that the ramifying results of karma now experienced, or yet to be experienced in a future incarnation, are all rooted in the *kleshas*.

In the graphic language of spiritual physiology, the *kleshas* constitute a psychic colouring or peculiar obsession which forms a persisting matrix of *karma*, the results of which must eventually be experienced, and also creates mental deposits which channel mental energies into repeatedly reinforcing the *kleshas*. *Dhyana* alone can effectively eradicate these mental deposits while providing the clear detachment (*vairagya*) and cool patience (*kshanti*) to exhaust and dissolve the karmic matrix over time. As long as the *kleshas* remain, involuntary incarnation into bodies captive to the pleasure pain principle is inescapable. Elation and depression are the inevitable effects of such embodiment. Since these are the product of egoism and the polarity of attraction and aversion, rooted in ignorance and resulting in the tenacious clinging to mundane existence, the discerning *yogin* comes to see that the truth of spiritual freedom and the rapture of limitless love transcend the *kleshas* entirely.

All *karma* brings discord and distress, including the insistent pains of loss and gain, growth and decay.

Karma means *parinama*, change, and this invariably induces the longing to recover what is receding, to enhance what is emerging, or to sustain a static balance where no thing can endure. To be drawn to some objects and conditions and to be disinclined towards others is indeed to foster *tapa*, anxious brooding over what might be lost or what one might be forced to encounter. All experiences leave residual impressions, *samskaras*, which agitate the mind and stimulate desires to have or to avoid possible future experiences. In general, the *gunas* or root qualities of *prakriti* – *sattva*, *rajas* and *tamas*: luminosity, action and inertia; purity, restlessness and languor; or harmony, volatility and fixity persist in ceaselessly shifting permutations which continually modify the uncontrolled mind. For these reasons, Patanjali taught, all life without spiritual freedom is fraught with sorrow. Through *Yoga*, it is not possible to avoid consequences already set in motion, but it is feasible to destroy the *kleshas* and thereby remove the causal chain of suffering.

Metaphysically, *Buddhi*, intuitive intellect, is closer to *Purusha* than any other aspect of *prakriti*. Nonetheless, *Buddhi* is still what is seen by *Purusha*, the Perceiver, and it is through confounding the Perceiver with what is perceived at the super-sensuous level that suffering arises. *Prakriti*, consisting of the *gunas*, is the entire field, enclosing the objective world and the organs of sensation. It exists solely for the sake of the soul's education and emancipation. The *Yogabhashya* teaches that identification of the Perceiver with the seen constitutes experience, "whilst realizing the true nature of *Purusha* is emancipation." In the realm of *prakriti*, wherein the Perceiver is captive to the ever-changing panorama of Nature, the *gunas*, which may be construed as the properties of perceptible objects but which are really propensities from the standpoint of psycho-mental faculties, act at every level of conscious awareness.

At the level of differentiated consciousness, *vitarka*, wherein the mind scrutinizes specific objects and features, the *gunas* are particularized (*vishesha*). When consciousness apprehends archetypes, laws and abstract concepts (*vichara*), the *gunas* are archetypal (*avishesha*). When the *gunas* are discerned as signs and signatures *(linga)*, objects are resolved into symbols of differentiation in a universal field of complete objectivity, and consciousness experiences ecstasy *(ananda)*. Though discrete, objects are no longer distinguished in contrast to one another or through divergent characteristics; they are distinct but seen as parts of a single whole. They are apprehended through *Buddhi* or intuitive insight.

The *gunas* are *alinga* – signless, irresolvable, undifferentiated – and lose their distinction from consciousness itself when objects dissolve in the recognition that consciousness and its modifications alone constitute the noumenal and phenomenal world. Hence, pure consciousness *(lingamatra)*, which is the simple, unqualified sense of 'I', subsists in a pristine noumenal condition *(alinga)* wherein it does not witness the ceaseless operation of the *gunas*. This divine consciousness is the highest state of meditative absorption, beyond which lies complete emancipation, *Purusha* without any tincture of *prakriti*. The Perceiver is pure vision, apprehending ideas seemingly through the mind. Once final emancipation, which is the ultimate aim and purpose of all experience, is attained, *Purusha* no longer encounters the confusion of spirit and matter through mental modifications. As experience, correctly understood, culminates in eventual self-emancipation, *kaivalya*, Patanjali held that "the very essence of the visible is that it exists for the sake of the Seer, the Self alone" (II.21).

The world does not vanish for all others when a man of meditation attains *kaivalya*; they remain in confusion until they also attain the same utterly transcendent state of awareness. Here *Yoga* philosophy exhausts its conceptual and descriptive vocabulary. Whether one asserts that there is an indefinite number of *purushas*, each capable of attaining *kaivalya*, or one states that *Purusha* attains *kaivalya* in this instance but not that, is a matter of indifference, for one perforce invokes enumeration, time and space terms properly applying to *prakriti* alone to characterize a wholly transcendent reality. The pervasive existential fact is that *prakriti* persists so long as there are beings trapped through ignorance, and the vital psychological truth is that no being who attains the transcendent *(taraka)* reality of unqualified, pure *Purusha* can do so vicariously for another. Through their hard-won wisdom and compassion, emancipated seers and sages can point the way with unerring accuracy. They know how to make their magnanimous guidance most effective for every human being, but each seeker must make the ascent unaided.

If the cosmos as considered in contemporary physics resolved itself into a condition of undisturbed entropy, or if, in the language of *Sankhya*, the *gunas* achieved total and enduring equilibrium, Nature *(prakriti)* would cease to exist, since there would be nothing to be perceived. Ignorance and its inseparable concomitant, suffering, arise from a broken symmetry in Nature. In contemporary thought there is no adequate explanation for the origin of that 'cosmic disaster', for the emergence of sentience is said to occur *within* the broken symmetry. If the scientific community were trained to use the language of *Sankhya* and *Yoga* philosophy, it would have to speak of the origin of *Purusha*, consciousness, within the evolutionary permutations and convolutions of *prakriti. Sankhya* and *Yoga* teach, however, that *Purusha*, sempiternal and independent, perceives *prakriti* and indirectly gives rise to the broken symmetry itself, the anti-entropic condition which is the activity of the *gunas.* For Patanjali, *prakriti* must necessarily exist, for it is through experience conjunction with *prakriti* that *Purusha* knows itself as it is. But when *Purusha* wrongly apprehends *prakriti*, as it must until it knows itself truly as it is, ignorance and all the entangling *kleshas* arise. When *Purusha* attains *kaivalya*, emancipation, it sees without error, and this is gained through experience in self-correction and self-mastery. From the highest standpoint, this means that *Purusha* preserves its freedom and intrinsic purity by avoiding mistaken assumptions and false conclusions. From the standpoint of any individual involved in *prakriti*, unbroken discriminative cognition *(vivekakhyati)* is the sole means to emancipation, for it releases the abiding sense of reality *(Purusha)* in him. The dual process of removing the *kleshas* and reflecting on the Self *(Purusha)* assures the progressive and climactic attainment of emancipation *(kaivalya)* such that ignorance does not arise again.

Having delineated the path to *kaivalya*, Patanjali discoursed in some detail on the seven successive stages of *Yoga* which lead to *Samadhi*, full meditative absorption, but he insisted that, even though each stage must be passed in succession, truth and wisdom dawn progressively upon the aspirant to stimulate his endeavour. *Yoga* is successive, gradual and recursive, the path of ascent which alone leads from darkness to light, from ignorance to transcendental wisdom, from death and recurring rebirth to conscious immortality and universal self-consciousness. Although the stages through which consciousness must ascend are sequential in one sense, the practice of *Taraka Raja Yoga* involves eight limbs or aspects which are logically successive but ethically and psychologically simultaneous. In fact, one can hardly pursue one part of Patanjali's eight-limbed *Yoga (ashtangayoga)* without also attending to its other divisions. Just as a human being, despite his ignorance, is an integrated whole, so too *ashtangayoga,* despite its logical sequence, is an integral unity. Patanjali enumerated the eight *(ashta)* limbs *(anga)* of this *Taraka Raja Yoga* as five which concern *karma* and lay the foundation for meditation, and three which constitute meditation itself: restraint *(yama)*, binding observance *(niyama)*, posture *(asana)*, regulation of breath *(pranayama)*, abstraction and withdrawal from the senses *(pratyahara)*; concentration *(dharana)*, contemplation *(dhyana)* and complete meditative absorption *(Samadhi)*.

The *yamas* or restraints are five, constituting a firm ethical foundation for spiritual growth, starting with *ahimsa* (nonviolence) and including *satya* (truth), *asteya* (nonstealing), *brahmacharya* (continence) and *aparigraha* (nonpossession). Shankaracharya held that *ahimsa* – nonviolence, harmlessness, defencelessness in Shelley's phrase – is the most important of the *yamas* and *niyamas*, and is the root of restraint. Like all constraints and observances, *ahimsa* must not be interpreted narrowly but should be seen in its widest sense. For Shankaracharya, this meant that *ahimsa* should be practised in body, speech and mind so that one avoids harming others in any way, even through an unkind thought. *Ahimsa* can be taken to include the classical Greek sense of *sophrosyne*, a sense of proportion which voids all excess, the state of mind which can avoid even unintentional harm to a single being in the cosmos. In employing *ahimsa* as a talismanic tool of political and social reform, Gandhi exemplified the central importance and far-reaching scope of *ahimsa*. For Patanjali, however, *ahimsa* and the other *yamas* and *niyamas* constitute the daily moral discipline needed to pursue *Taraka Raja Yoga*. *Taraka Raja Yoga* is not a narrowly technical or specialized practice to be added to other instrumental activities in the world; it is rather the indispensable means for radically transforming one's essential perception of, and therefore one's entire relation to, the world. From the standpoint of Self-knowledge, which is ultimate gnosis, there are no greater disciplines. Hence the *yamas* are not altered by condition and circumstance, social class or nationality, nor by time nor the actual level of spiritual attainment. Together they constitute the awesome *mahavrata* or Great Vow, the first crucial step to true spiritual freedom.

The *niyamas* or binding observances are also five, constituting the positive dimension of ethical probity. They are *shaucha* (purity), *santosha* (contentment), *tapas* (austerity, self-discipline), *svadhyaya* (self-study) and *ishvarapranidhana* (surrender to the Lord). Like the *yamas*, the *niyamas* cannot be fully grasped as specific and bounded concepts. First of all, they should be seen as evolving conceptions – for example, purity of thought is deepened through purity of conduct – and then they will rapidly unfold subtler levels of meaning as the aspirant attains more intensive depths of meditation. Purity of volition is thus ever enriched and refined. The greatest obstacles to the restraints and binding observances are those thoughts which run in the opposite direction – thinking of impure things or acts, wishing to do harm for a perceived injustice, self-indulgence, self-deception and self-assertion. Such illicit and destructive thoughts are perverse precisely because they belie and defeat the initial commitment to the *yamas* and *niyamas*. Instead of suppressing such scattered thoughts or wallowing in hideous self-pity, one must firmly and deliberately insert into the mind their potent opposites – love for hate, tenderness for temerity, sweetness for spite, virile confidence for the devilry of self-doubt, authentic self-conquest for compulsive self-indulgence. Thus what begins as a shrewd defence against deleterious thoughts becomes a deft substitution of one kind of thought for another and results in sublimation, the skilful transformation of the tonality and texture of consciousness. Strict and consistent measures are needed to deal with subversive thoughts, not in order to repress them or to hide guilt for having them, but only because they induce depression and self-loathing, with predictable and pathetic consequences. Facing unworthy thoughts firmly, and thereby exorcising them, is to free oneself from their nefarious spell.

When any object is forcibly confined, it exerts crude pressure against its external constraints. In the ethical realm, effortless self-restraint produces a powerful glow of well-being which others can appreciate and even emulate. When, for example, one is established in *ahimsa*, others do become aware of an encompassing and inclusive love, and latent or overt hostility dissolves around one's radius of benevolence. *Satya*, truth, is the path of least resistance amongst the shifting ratios of the *gunas*, and when one is clearly established in truth, the predictable consequences of thought, word and deed are constructive and consistent. Similarly, strengthening oneself through *asteya* (nonstealing), one desists from every form of misappropriation, even on the plane of thought and feeling, and discovers what is apposite on all sides. Nature protects and even provides for those who do not appropriate its abundant resources. *Brahmacharya*, selfless continence in thought and conduct, fosters vitality and vigour. *Aparigraha*, nonpossessiveness, promotes noetic insight into the deeper meaning and purpose of one's probationary sojourn on earth.

Expansiveness too has its compelling effects. *Shaucha*, inward and outer purity, protects the mind and body from moral and magnetic pollution, and prevents one from tarnishing or misusing others. One acquires a dependable degree of serenity, control of the senses and one-pointedness in concentration, thus preparing oneself for the direct apprehension of *Purusha*, the Self. *Santosha*, deep contentment, assures satisfaction not through the gratification of wants (which can at most provide a temporary escape from frustration), but rather through the progressive cessation of craving and its prolific yearnings and regrets. *Tapas*, austerity, penance or self-discipline, removes pollution inherited from one's own past and releases the full potentials of mind, senses and body, including those psychic faculties mistakenly called supernormal only because seldom developed. *Svadhyaya*, self-study, calls for careful study and calm reflection, including the diligent recitation and deep contemplation of texts, thus giving voice to potent *mantras* and sacred utterances. It achieves its apotheosis through direct communion with the *ishtadevata*, the chosen deity upon whom one has concentrated one's complete attention, will and imagination. This exalted state readily leads to *ishvarapranidhana*, one-pointed and single-hearted devotion to the Lord. Such devotion soon deepens until one enters the succeeding stages of meditative absorption *(Samadhi)*.

With the firm foundation of *yamas* and *niyamas,* one can begin to benefit from the noetic discipline of intense meditation and become modestly proficient in it over a lifetime of service to humanity. Since the untrained mind is easily distracted by external and internal disturbance, real meditation is aided by an alert and relaxed bodily vesture. To this end, a steady posture *(asana)* is chosen, not to indulge the acrobatic antics of the shallow *Hatha Yogin,* but rather to subdue and command the body, whilst retaining its alertness and resilience. The correct posture will be firm and flexible without violating the mind's vigorous concentration and precise focus. Once the appropriate *asana* is assumed by each neophyte, the mind is becalmed and turned towards the Infinite, becoming wholly impervious to bodily movement and change, immersed in the boundless space of the akashic empyrean. Thus the impact of the oscillating pairs of opposites upon the volatile brain mind, captivated by sharp contrasts and idle speculations, and the agitation of the body through recurring sensations are at least temporarily muted. In this state of serene peace, the effortless regulation of rhythmic breath *(pranayama)* becomes as natural as floating on the waters of space. Just as the mind and body are intimately interlinked at every point, such that even holding a firm physical posture aids the calming of the mind, so too *pranayama* points to silent mental breathing as well as smooth respiration.

Prana, which includes the solar life-breath, is the efflux of the constant flow of cosmic energy, regulated by the ideation of *Purusha* and radiating from the luminous substance of pure *prakriti.* From the *nadabrahman* the Divine Resonance and perpetual motion of absolute Spirit and the global respiration of the earth reverberating at its hidden core, its slowly rolling mantle and its shifting crust, to the inspiration and expiration of every creature in the cosmos, the ocean of *prana* permeates and purifies all planes of being. In the human constitution, irregular, spasmodic or strained, uneven breathing can disturb the homeostatic equilibrium of the body and cause fragmented, uncoordinated modes of awareness. Proper breathing oxygenates the physical system optimally, and also aids the mind in maintaining a steady rhythm of unbroken ideation, fusing thought, will and energy. *Pranayama* begins with deliberate exhalation, so that the lungs are generously emptied and the unusable matter expelled into them is made to exit the bodily temple. Thereupon, slow inbreathing invites oxygen to permeate the entire lung system and penetrate the blood, arteries, nerves and cells. Holding the breath in a benevolent pause permits the respiratory system to adjust gently to the next phase of oxygenation and detoxification. When these rhythmic movements are marked by due measure and proportion, mantramically fused into the inaudible OM, there is a distinct improvement in psychophysical health and a remarkable increase of vigilance and vigour.

The fourth step in *pranayama* transcends the physiological dimensions of respiration for which they are a preparation. The highest *pranayama* becomes possible when one has gained sufficient sensitivity through the earlier stages of *pranayama* to sense and direct the divine flow of *prana* throughout one's entropic psychophysical system. Then one may, through mental volition alone, fuse mental serenity and single-mindedness with psychophysical equilibrium, and also convey subtle pranic currents, charged with selfless ideation, to various *padmas* or vital centres (*chakras*) in the body. Since each of the seven *padmas* is precisely correlated with the corresponding state of concentrated consciousness, the fearless equipoise needed to activate these magnetic centres and the benevolent *siddhis* or theurgic powers thereby released requires the commensurate and controlled alteration in the tonality and texture of consciousness. When the highest *padma* is effortlessly and gently touched by mind-directed *prana*, nonviolent consciousness simultaneously attains full *Samadhi*. "Thus is worn away," said Patanjali, "the veil which obscures the light" (II. 52), thereby pointing to the subduing of the *kleshas* and the neutralization of *karma* through the progressive awakening of discriminative insight and intuitive wisdom.

The process of purification is not an end in itself, but the necessary condition to prepare the mind for *dharana*, complete concentration. *Pranayama*, delusive and dangerous when misappropriated for selfish purposes pursued through subtle enslavement by the *kleshas*, is hereby integrated into Patanjali's eight-fold *Yoga* as a preliminary step towards subduing the restless mind, freeing it to become the servant of the immortal soul, seeking greater wisdom, self-mastery and universal self-consciousness. *Pratyahara,* abstraction and disassociation of sensory perception from sense-objects, is now accessible. Withdrawal of the senses from their objects of attraction does not destroy them. Rather, the subtler senses take on the plastic and fluidic nature of the serene mind itself. Without the myriad distractions of familiar and strange sense-objects, the senses become subtilized and pliant, no longer pulling consciousness towards internal images, external objects or captivating sense data. Instead, the noetic mind firmly expels images and subdues impulses, gaining sovereign mastery over them. Patanjali ended the second *pada* here, having shown the pathway to proper preparation for profound meditation. The significance of the last three interconnected *angas* or stages of *Yoga* is indicated by the fact that Patanjali set them apart in the third *pada* for his authoritative exposition.

The preparatory discipline or *Sadhana* of the second *pada* has been thus strikingly extolled by Rishi Vasishtha:

> He engaged in the practice of Raja Yoga, remaining silent and graceful in countenance. He abstracted his senses from their objects as the oil is separated from the sesamum seed, withdrawing their organs within himself as the turtle contracts his limbs under his hard shell.
>
> With his steady mind he cast all external sensations far off from himself, as a rich and brilliant gem, shedding a coating of dust, then scattered its rays to a distance. Without coming in contact with them, he compressed his sensations within himself, as a tree in the cold season compresses its sap within its bark . . . .
>
> He confined his subdued mind in the cave of his heart, as a great elephant is imprisoned in a cavern of the Vindhya Mountain when it has been brought by stratagem under subjection. When his soul had gained its clarity, resembling the serenity of the autumnal sky, it forsook all unsteadiness, like the calm ocean una*Git*ated by any winds.

> *Yoga Vasishtha Maharamayana*

VIBHUTI PADA

Attention is the first and indispensable step in all knowledge.
Attention to spiritual things is the first step to spiritual knowledge.

Charles Johnston

Patanjali commenced the third *pada* of the *Yoga Sutras* with a compelling distinction between three phases of meditation. *Dharana* is full concentration, the focussing of consciousness on a particular point, which may be any object in the world or a subject chosen by the mind. The ability to fix attention is strengthened by the practice of the first five *angas* of Patanjali's *ashtangayoga*, for without some cultivation of them the mind tends to meander and drift in every direction. *Dhyana* is meditation in the technical sense of the term, meaning the calm sustaining of focussed attention. In *dhyana*, consciousness still encounters some modifications, but they all flow in one direction and are not disturbed by other fluctuations of any sort. Rather like iron – consisting of molecules clustered together in various ways, their axes oriented in different directions – undergoes a shift of alignment of all molecules in a single direction when magnetized, so too consciousness can become unidirectional through experiencing a current of continuity in time.

Samadhi, broadly characterized as 'meditative absorption' or 'full meditation', signifies the deepening of *dhyana* until the chosen object of meditation stands alone and consciousness is no longer aware of itself as contemplating an object. In *Samadhi* consciousness loses the sense of separateness from what is contemplated and, in effect, becomes one with it. Like a person wholly lost in their work, "the object stands by itself," in the words of the *Yogabhashya*, as if there were only the object itself. Although these three phases can be viewed as separate and successive, when they occur together in one simultaneous act they constitute *sanyama*, serene constraint or luminous concentration. The novice who nonetheless is capable of entering *Samadhi* may take a long time to move from *dharana* to deep *Samadhi*, because he experiences the entire movement as a radical change in consciousness. But the adept in *sanyama* can include all three in a virtually instantaneous act, thus arousing the ability to move from one object of contemplation to another almost effortlessly.

Prajna, cognitive insight, the resplendent light of wisdom, or intuitive apprehension, comes as a result of mastering *sanyama*. Although *prajna is* the highest level of knowledge to which philosophy can aspire, it is not the supreme state, for it halts at the threshold of *vivekakhyati*, pristine awareness of Reality, which can be neither articulated nor elucidated. *Sanyama*, Patanjali taught, is not completely mastered all at once. Rather, once *sanyama is* attained, it is strengthened in stages by deft application to different objects and levels of being. Each such application reveals the divine light as it manifests in that context, until the adept practitioner of exalted *sanyama* can focus entirely on *Purusha* itself. In *sanyama* the patient aspirant glimpses the divine radiance, the resplendent reflection of *Purusha*, wherever he focusses attention, but in time he will behold only *Purusha*. In the *Bhagavad Gita*, Krishna asked Arjuna to see Himself in all things, but in the climactic cosmic vision, Arjuna witnessed the cosmic form *(vishvarupa)* of the Lord. *Sanyama is* wholly internal, whilst the first five *yoga* practices are external. Though all the *angas* are crucial to *yoga*, the last three, harmoniously synthesized in *sanyama*, constitute *yoga* proper. Since this is the central aim of everything stated so far in the *Yoga Sutras*, *sanyama* received considerable emphasis from Patanjali.

Nirodha, restraint, cessation or interception, is essential to *sanyama* because it is concerned neither with different states nor objects of consciousness, but chiefly with the process of transformation or replacement of the contents of consciousness. In *sanyama* the definite shift from one object of attention to another – and these can be wholly abstract and mental objects – involves a change of mental impression. As an object fades from mental view, another appears on the mental horizon to take its place. But like the pregnant moment just before dawn, when night is fleeing and the first light of day is sensed but has not yet shown itself, there is a suspended moment when what is fading has receded and the new object of focus is yet to appear. This is *nirodhaparinama*, the moment, however fleeting, between successive modifications when, according to the *Yogabhashya*, "the mind has nothing but subliminal impressions" (III.9). Should the mind lose its alertness at just that point, it would fall into a somnolent state, for in *sanyama*, consciousness is wholly absorbed in the object of consciousness, whilst in *nirodhaparinama* that object has vanished. But if it remains fully awake, it gains a powerful glimpse of the tranquil state of nonmodification, and may thus pass through the *laya* or still point of equilibrium to enter into a higher plane. With sufficient practice, the *yogin* learns to extend *nirodha* and abide in it long enough to initiate this transition. The less accomplished, if they do not get caught in the torpor of the penultimate void, may notice the passage of *nirodha* as a missed opportunity. With persistent effort, the *yogin* learns to remain in *nirodha*, relishing the peaceful, smooth flow of cosmic consciousness and reaching the highest *Samadhi*.

Samadhiparinama, meditative transformation, occurs when *nirodha* is experienced not simply as a negation of objects of consciousness but rather as a positive meditation on nothingness. One-pointedness of consciousness has been so mastered through the progressive displacement of all distractions that *ekagrata*, one-pointedness, alone subsists, and this becomes *ekagrataparinama*, total one-pointedness. It is as if the seed of meditation, first sought and recovered every single time the mind wandered and was sharply brought back to a focus, then firmly fixed in focus, had been split asunder until nothing remained but the empty core upon which the mind settles peacefully. Here the besetting tendency to fluctuate has become feeble, whilst the propensity to apply restraint is strong. Since all states of consciousness are necessarily correlated with states of matter, both being products of the *gunas* stimulated to action by the presence of *Purusha*, the depiction of consciousness also pertains to matter. The powerful transformation of consciousness is precisely matched in the continual transformations of matter, though the ordinary eye fails to apprehend the critical states in the transformation of matter, just as it remains largely unaware of *nirodha*. Nonetheless, there is a single substratum, *dharmin*, which underlies all change, whether in consciousness or in matter, and this is *prakriti*, the primeval root of all phenomena. For Patanjali, this means that all transformations are phenomenal in respect to *prakriti* the *prima materia* in its essential nature, and, like *Purusha*, ever unmodified. The ceaseless fluctuations of mind and world are merely countless variations of succession owing to alterations of cause. Realizing this, the *yogin* who has mastered *sanyama*, and thereby controls the mind at will, can equally control all processes of gestation and growth.

Having elucidated the nature of concentration as the sole means for discovering and transforming consciousness at all levels, Patanjali turned to the remarkable phenomenal effects possible through *sanyama*. Any fundamental change in consciousness initiates a corresponding change in and around one's vestures. A decisive shift in the operation and balance of the *gunas*, in thought, focus and awareness, reverberates throughout the oscillating ratios between the *gunas* everywhere. Since any significant refocussing of the mind produces dazzling insights and diverse phenomena, Patanjali conveyed their range and scope. For *yoga* they are not important in themselves because the goal is *kaivalya*, liberation, but they are vitally important as aids or obstacles on the way to achieving the goal. Patanjali could not dismiss or overlook them, since they are real enough and inescapable, and so he delineated them clearly, knowing fully that all such arcane information can be abused. One who willingly uses such knowledge to stray off the arduous path to emancipation brings misery upon himself. One who would use this knowledge wisely needs to understand the many ways one can be misled into wasting the abundant resources accessible to the *yogin*. Profound alterations in states of consciousness through *sanyama* can bring about awakened powers called *siddhis*, attainments, many of which may seem to be supernatural and supernormal to the average person. They are, however, neither miraculous nor supernatural, since they suspend, circumvent or violate no laws. Rather, they merely indicate the immense powers of controlled consciousness within the perspective of great Nature, powers that are largely latent, untapped and dormant in most human beings. They are suggestive parameters of the operation of the vast scope and potency of consciousness in diverse arenas of *prakriti*.

Sanyama, the electric fusion of *dharana*, *dhyana* and *Samadhi*, can release preternatural knowledge of past and future; the *yogin* gains profound insight into the metaphysical mystery of time. The future is ever conditioned by the past, and the past is accurately reflected in every aspect of the future. The present is strictly not a period of time; it is that ceaselessly moving point which marks the continual transition from future to past. Comprehending causality, seeing the effect in the cause, like the tree in the seed, the *yogin* perceives past and future alike by concentrating on the three phases of transformation experienced in the present and which, at the critical points of transformation, indicate the eternal, changeless substratum hidden behind them. Once conscious awareness is fixed beyond the temporal succession of states of consciousness, causality ceases to be experienced as a series of interrelated events – since the succession is itself the operation of past *karma* – and is perceived as an integrated whole in the timeless present. Thus past and future are seen from the same transcendent perspective as the timeless present. Freeing oneself from captivity to the mechanical succession of moments in clock time, one can rise beyond temporality and grasp causality noetically rather than phenomenally.

Although language is often viewed as an arbitrary and conventional system of communication, interpersonal understanding and mental telepathy as well as rapport between receptive and congenial minds are based on more than mere convention. Just as time is experienced as internal to the subject when the mind is mechanical, whilst causality is not necessarily time-bound, the evolution of language cannot dispense with intersubjectivity, shared clusters of concepts, rites and rituals, habits and customs, races and cultures. The deepest meaning of sounds is subtle and elusive, dissolving meanings and expectations. The linkage connected to the possibility of speech as well as to the potency of the primordial OM, the secret name of *Ishvara*, is *sphota*, the ineffable and inscrutable meaning intimated by sounds and speech. Through *sanyama*, the *yogin* can so deftly discern sound, meaning and idea that he instantly grasps the meaning, whatever the utterance of any person. Not only does he readily understand what is said by anyone, however awkward, disingenuous or deceptive the utterance, but he also apprehends the meaning of any sound uttered by any sentient being, whether birds and beasts, insects; trees or aquatic creatures.

The focussing power of *sanyama* enables the *yogin* to explore the subtlest impressions retained on the mental screen, and in so doing he can summon them into the light of consciousness. In this way, he can examine his entire mental inheritance and even discern previous lives. Knowing the exact correlations between states of consciousness and external conditions, he can recognize the linkage between latent memories and the traumas they induce, as well as the integral connection between past impressions and their inevitable karmic effects, thereby recollecting the patterns of previous incarnations. Similarly, by directing his yogic focus on the *pratyaya* or content of any mind functioning through a set of vestures, he can cognize that mental condition. Since all such mental contents are mirrored in the features and gestures of another, he can read the thoughts of another by looking at the person, and he can make the same determination by examining any portion of the expressed thought of another. Rather like a hologram, each and every aspect of an individual reflects the evolving structure of the whole being. Through *sanyama*, any facet of the person can reveal his psychic and mental make-up. Such attention will not, however, unveil the underlying structure of another's deepest consciousness, since that is hidden even to the person scrutinized. To discover the inward depths of the person, the *yogin* has to take the subject as the sole object of his sustained concentration and not merely that subject's mental contents. The ultimate question "Who are you?" can be resolved only in the way the question "Who am I?" is taken as a theme of intense meditation.

For Patanjali, as for different schools of Indian thought and for Plato (*Republic*, Book VI), seeing is a positive act and not merely a passive reception of light refracted from an object in the line of sight. Seeing involves the confluence of light (an aspect of *sattvaguna*) from the object of sight and the light from the eye of the seer, an active power (another aspect of *sattva*). The *yogin* can direct *sanyama* to the form and colour of his own body and draw in the light radiating from it, centring it wholly within his mind, *manas,* so that the *sattva* from the eye of another cannot fuse with it. Thus the body of the *yogin* cannot be seen, for he has made himself invisible. Similarly, by meditation upon the ultimate basis of any sensory power, the element essential to that sense, and its corresponding sense-organ, the *yogin* can become soundless, intangible and beyond the limited range of all the bodily senses. With the proper inversion of the process, he can dampen or delete any sense image, like glaring lights or background noise, either converting them into mild sensations or blanketing them entirely.

If the *yogin* should choose to practise *sanyama* on his past *karma*, he can obtain unerring insight into every causal chain he once initiated. Recognizing which tendencies are being expended and at what rates, as well as those lines of force which cannot bear fruit in this life, he may discern the time of his death – that point wherein the fruition of *karma* ensures the complete cessation of vital bodily functions. At the same time, such knowledge readily gives warnings of future events, all of which are the inevitable fruition of *karma*, and thus the *yogin* readily sees in each moment signs and portents of the future. He does not perceive, in such instances, something that is present only to his penetrating gaze. Rather, he is only reading correctly the futurity which ever lurks in present events, just as gold ore inheres in the dull rock even though only the trained eye of the prospector can see it and know it for what it is. Whilst such practical wisdom allows the *yogin* to foresee mental and physical conditions, he can also discern more fundamental changes which are due to the inexorable working of overlapping cycles, and, even more, he can focus on those critical points which trace the curve of potentiality for permanent spiritual change, or *metanoia*.

By focussing on *maitri*, kindliness, or any similar grace of character, the *yogin* can fortify that virtue in himself, thereby increasing his mental and moral strength and becoming the shining exemplar and serene repository of a host of spiritual graces. The *yogin* can activate and master any power manifest in Nature and mirrored in the human microcosm, refining its operation through his vestures, honing his inward poise and inimitable timeliness in its benevolent use. Thus, by contemplating the *sattva* or light within, discarding the reflected lights imperfectly and intermittently transmitted through the sensory apparatus, the *yogin* can investigate and come to cognize every subtle thing, whether small, hidden, veiled or very distant. He can discern the atom *(anu)* by deploying the light within, for all light is ultimately one. Should he choose to practise *sanyama* in respect to the sun, he can come to know the harmonies of the solar system from the standpoint of its hidden structure as a matrix of solar energies. Further, he can know all solar systems by analogy with ours, and so his comprehension of cosmic forces expressed in, through and around the sun is more than mere familiarity with the structure of a physical system. He also grasps the architectonics – psychic, mental and spiritual – of all such systems. Similarly, his concentration on the moon yields insights into the intricate arrangements of the stars, since, like the moon, they are all in motion around multiple centres. By concentrating on the pole-star – whose arcane significance is far more than what is commonly assumed on the basis of its visible locus in the sidereal vault – he discerns the motions of the stars in relation to one another, not just on the physical plane but also as the shimmering veil of *Ishvara*, the manifested *Logos* of the cosmos.

Directing the power of *sanyama* upon the soul's vestures, the *yogin* can calmly concentrate on the solar plexus, connected with the pivotal *chakra* or psycho-spiritual centre in the human constitution, and thus thoroughly grasp the structure and dynamics of the physical body. By concentrating on the pit of the throat, connected with the trachea, he can control hunger and thirst. Since hunger and thirst are physical expressions at one level of being which have corresponding correlates and functions at every level, his concentration can also affect mental and psychic cravings, since he has mastered the *prana* or vital energy flowing from this particular *chakra*. More specifically, by concentrating on the *nadi*, or nerve centre called the 'tortoise', below the trachea, the *yogin* gains mental, psychic and physical steadiness, facilitating enormous feats of strength.

If *sanyama* is directed to the divine light in the head, the *yogin* can come to see *siddhas*, perfected beings. This supple light is hidden in the central *sushumna* nerve in the spinal column, and emanates that pristine vibration (*suddhasattva*) which is magnetically linked to the sun and is transmitted through the moon. Concentrating on that supernal light, the *yogin* can perceive those perfected beings whose luminous and translucent vestures are irradiated by the light of the *Logos* (*daiviprakriti*). Similarly, concentration on the laser light of spiritual intuition, *kundalini* released by *Buddhi*, results in flashes of inward illumination. This light emanates from *pratibha*, the pure intellect which is self-luminous and omnidirectional, constant and complete, unconnected with earthly aims and objects. Focussing on its radiance releases *taraka jnana*, the transcendental gnosis which has been aptly termed 'the knowledge that saves'. This primeval wisdom is wholly unconditioned by any temporal concern for self or the external world, is self-validating and self-shining, the ultimate goal of *Taraka Raja Yoga*. It puts one in close communion with *Ishvara* whilst preserving a vital link, like a silver thread, with the world of woe, illusion and ignorance. *Pratibha* is that crystalline intellection exemplified by *Bodhisattvas* who have transcended all conditionality, yet seek to serve ceaselessly all souls trapped in the chains of bondage. By concentration on the secret, spiritual heart – the *anahata chakra* – the *yogin* becomes attuned to cosmic intellection, for the *anahata* is man's sacred connection with cosmic consciousness, reverberating until near death with the inaudible yet ever pulsating OM.

Should the *yogin* master all these marvellous *siddhis*, he would still remain ensnared in the world which is pervaded by pain and nescience, until he is prepared to take the next, absolutely vital step in the mastery of *taraka jnana*. Any individual involuntarily participates in the stream of sensory experience by blindly assenting to the pleasure-pain principle. This will last as long as he cannot discriminate between *Purusha*, the cosmic Self, and the individuating principle of spiritual insight, *sattva*. Even the subtlest light shining in the incomprehensible darkness of pure Spirit, *Purusha*, must be transcended. The *Yogabhashya* states the central issue: "It has therefore been asked in the *Upanishad*: By what means can the Knower be known?" *Sanyama* must be entirely directed *to Purusha* so that it is perfectly mirrored in the serene light of noetic understanding (*sattva*). *Buddhi*, that intuitive faculty of divine discernment through which the highest *sattva* expresses itself, becomes a pellucid mirror for *Purusha*. Just as *Purusha*, cosmically and individually, penetrates and comprehends *prakriti*, so too the highest *prakriti* now becomes the indispensable means for apprehending *Purusha*. This is the basis for *svasamvedana*, ultimate self-knowledge, the paradigm for all possible self-study at any and every level of consciousness and being. Once this fundamental revolution has occurred, self-consciousness can turn back to the world of objects – which once plunged it into a state of delusion and later gave rise to a series of obstacles to be surmounted – and adopt a steadfast, universal standpoint flowing from all-potent, pure awareness. What once needed various mental and psychophysical mechanisms can now be accomplished without adventitious aids, thereby dispensing altogether with all conditionality and systemic error.

In practice, the *yogin* can now freely and directly exercise the powers commonly connected with the lower sense-organs, without dependence on sensory data. Hence his sight, hearing, smell, taste and especially touch are extrasensory, far greater in range and reach than ever before, precisely because there is no longer reliance on imperfect sensory mechanisms conditioned by physical space and psychological time. What were once obstructions to the deepest meditation (*Samadhi*) can now serve as talismanic aids in benefitting both Nature and Humanity. The *yogin* can, for example, choose at will to enter another's body with full consent, because his mind is no longer entangled with a physical or astral vesture and because he knows the precise conduits through which minds are tethered to bodies. Having risen above any and all temptation to gratify the thirst for sensation or the craving for experience, he can employ his extraordinary powers and extra-sensory faculties solely for the sake of universal enlightenment and the welfare of the weak.

Having gained complete self-mastery, the *yogin* can now exercise benevolent control over invisible and visible Nature (*prakriti*) for the *Agathon*, the greatest good of all. Since even his own vestures are now viewed as external to him, his relation to them has become wholly isomorphic with his conscious connection to the vital centres in the Great Macrocosm. By mastering *udana*, one of the five currents of *prana*, chiefly connected with vertical motion, the *yogin* makes his body essentially impervious to external influences, including the presence of gravity and the inevitability of death. By mastering *samana*, the current of *prana* which governs metabolic and systemic processes, he can render his body self-luminous and radiant, as Jesus did during his climactic transfiguration and as Moses is said to have done during his salvific descent from Mount Sinai. Knowing the integral connection between the inner ear and *Akasha*, the supple light and etheric empyrean in invisible space, the trained *yogin* can hear anything that ever impressed itself, however distantly, upon that universal, homogeneous and supersensuous medium. Similarly, knowing the vital connection between the astral body and *Akasha*, he can make his body light and even weightless, and also as pliable and versatile as a superb musical instrument.

From the standpoint of self-consciousness, the *yogin* who has mastered *taraka jnana* can practise *mahavideha*, the power of making the mind wholly incorporeal, so that it abides in pure and perfect awareness beyond even *Buddhi*. Such a state of cosmic consciousness is indescribable, though it can be identified as that exalted condition in which no light anywhere is absent from his mental horizon. From the standpoint of Nature, the perfected *yogin* has total control of matter and can fully comprehend it in its subtlest and most minute forms. He can manifest through his vestures the entire spectrum of possibilities of universal self-consciousness and effortless control over matter – merging into the atom, magnifying himself into the galactic sphere, making the human temple worthy of every perfection, including grace, beauty, strength, porosity, malleability and rock-like hardness. Controlling the seven sense-organs, the masterly *yogin* knows precisely how they function on the spiritual, mental, moral and physical planes, and he can instantaneously cognize anything he chooses. Comprehending and controlling *pradhana*, the common principle and substratum of invisible Nature, he can direct every change and mutation in material *prakriti*. He is no longer subject to the instruments he employs, for the entire cosmos has become his aeolian harp and sounding-board.

The *yogin's* total grasp of the elusive and ever-shifting distinction between *Purusha* and *prakriti*, especially between the universal Self and the individuating principle of understanding *(sattva)*, between subject and object at all levels, becomes the basis for his unostentatious sovereignty over every possible state of existence. His complete comprehension of the Soundless Sound (OM), of the Sound in the Light and the Light in the Sound, results in what is tantamount to serene omnipotence and silent omniscience. Yet although the perfected *yogin* is a Magus, a Master of gnosis, wholly lifted out of the sphere of *prakriti* and supremely free, self-existent and self-conquered, he does not allow even the shadow of attachment to transcendental joy to stain his sphere of benevolence to all. Complete and invulnerable non-attachment, *vairagya*, can destroy the lurking seeds of self-concern and susceptibility to delusion, and he may thus approach the threshold of *kaivalya*, supreme self-emancipation. If, however, he is enthralled by the glorious deities and celestial wonders he encounters in the spiritual empyrean, he could rekindle the dormant yearning for terrestrial life, with its fast-proliferating chain of earthly entanglements. But if he steadfastly practises *sanyama* on the *kalachakra*, the Wheel of Time, and even more, penetrates the last veil of *kala*, the mystery of Being, Becoming and Beness, the infinitude of the Eternal Now hidden within the infinitesimal core of the passing moment, he can dissolve without trace the divine *yogamaya* of conditioned space-time. Such unfathomable depths of consciousness transcend the very boundaries of gnosis and cannot be conveyed in any language, conceptual or ontological.

The purest and most perfect awareness is indistinguishable from the direct apprehension of ultimate Reality wherein, in the words of Shankaracharya, the very distinctions between seer, seeing and sight, or knower, knowing and known, wholly vanish. Here, for example, the Leibnizian principle of the identity of indiscernibles collapses in thought and language. Knowing eternity in time in its irreducible moments, even indistinguishable events or objects can be instantaneously separated in an ecstatic, simultaneous apprehension of the One without a second, of the One mirrored in the many, of the many co-present in the One, of the tree of knowledge within the tree of life. And yet nothing is known by species, genus or class: each thing is known by its instantaneous co-presence. *Taraka jnana* is thus not only omniscient in its range but simultaneous in its scope. The *yogin* knows at once all that can possibly be known, in a world of commonalities, comparisons and contrasts, and infinitesimal parts within infinite wholes.

Supreme emancipation, *kaivalya*, dawns only when *Purusha* shines unhindered and *sattva* receives the full measure of light. *Purusha* is no longer veiled, obscured or mirrored by the faculties and functions of *prakriti* and *Buddhi* becomes unconditional, untainted by any teleological or temporal trace. There is no more any consciousness of seeking the light, which the aspirant legitimately entertains, or of radiating the light, which the recently omniscient *yogin* experiences. There is now solely the supernal and omnipresent, ever-existing light of *Purusha*, abiding in its intrinsic splendour of supreme freedom, and this is *kaivalya*, the supreme state of being "aloof and unattached, like *Akasha*" (*Srimad Bhagavatam VI*). Since this is the ultimate goal of *Taraka Raja Yoga*, in terms of which each spiritual potency, skill and striving must be calibrated, Patanjali devoted the concluding fourth *pada* to this exalted theme.

In the memorable words of the Sage Kapila to Devahuti, the daughter of *Manu*:

> The moment his mind ceases to discriminate, by reason of the activities of the senses, between objects which are not intrinsically different, looking upon some as pleasant, on others as not, that moment he sees with his own mind his own SELF, equable and self-luminous, free from likes and dislikes, and completely aloof, serenely established in the intuition of transcendental rapture. Pure Consciousness is spoken of variously as *parabrahm, Paramatman, Ishvara* or *Purusha.* The Lord, the One without a second, masquerades as the multiplicity of seer, seen and so on. The one goal of all *yoga*, practised perfectly with all its ancillary disciplines, is the attainment by the *yogin* of total detachment from the world.... At the same time he should learn to see the SELF in all creatures, and all creatures in the SELF, making no difference between them, even as in all creatures he recognizes the presence of the gross elements. Just as fire looks different in the diverse logs that it burns, owing to the difference between the logs, so too does the SELF seem different in the varied bodies it indwells. The *yogin*, vanquishing thus the inscrutable *maya* of the Lord, which deludes the *jiva* and is the cause of the phenomenal world, rests secure in his own true state.
>
> *Srimad Bhagavatam*

Hermes, April 1989

KAIVALYA PADA

With the fulfillment of their twofold purpose, the experience and
the emancipation of the SELF, and with the cessation of mutations,
the gunas cannot manifest even for a moment.

Yogabhashya

Patanjali provided a vast perspective on consciousness and its varied levels, as well as the necessary and sufficient conditions for sustained meditation. He set forth the essential prerequisites to meditation, the persisting obstacles to be overcome by the conscientious seeker, and the awesome powers and exhilarating experiences resulting from the progressive attainment of *Samadhi*. In the fourth *pada*, the heart of which is *kaivalya*, the ultimate aim and transcendental culmination of the discipline of *Taraka Raja Yoga*, Patanjali epitomized the entire process from the standpoint of the adept *yogin* in meditation. He was thus able to offer a rounded exposition which might otherwise remain obscure. The *Yoga Sutras* is for daily use, and not dilettantish perusal. Its compelling logic is intrinsically self validating as well as capable of continuous self testing. Its reasonableness and efficacy are endorsed by a long succession of accredited seers and seekers.

The *siddhis*, or arcane, supernormal and spiritual powers, may be inborn in any incarnation. Although they may appear spontaneous or superfluous to the superficial eye, they are strictly the products of profound meditations in previous lives, as they depend for their development on mastery of the mind and its myriad correlations amongst the manifold elements in the cosmos. Since individual consciousness may have undergone such strenuous discipline in prior incarnations but not in the present life, the imprint of these practices in the immortal soul can be retained without conscious remembrance of the fact. If, however, it is not supported and strengthened by conscious discipline (*abhyasa*) in this life, the manifestation of unusual mental capacities and uncommon *siddhis* may be sporadic, relatively uncontrolled and precariously inconstant. Furthermore, because all knowledge is recollection, in a Platonic sense, and the residues of the past linger in the present, *siddhis* can sometimes be stimulated by hallucinogenic drugs and herbs like verbena, or by sacred chants and time honoured incantations, although the effects of external aids are notoriously uneven and ever unpredictable. Systematic austerities (*tapas*) may also release something of the attainments of previous incarnations, but true *Samadhi* alone provides the rigorous, progressive and reliable pathway to self-mastery and sovereignty over the subtle forces of Nature. With such complete command of the *gunas* or modes of *prakriti* as it manifests in the mind and in the external world, the adept *yogin* can alter his nature from one class of being (the human) to another (a *deva* or god, in a broad sense of the term), if the karmic conditions in life are congenial and conducive to rapid development. Even then, the wise practitioner would not pursue this discipline except from the highest of motives, for anything less would hinder *prakrityapurat*, the 'flow of *prakriti*' needed for its safe and smooth accomplishment.

No significant change of human nature would be possible if it merely depended upon instrumental causes, for these can only rearrange components or unveil hidden but pre-existent features. Hence, doing good deeds cannot transform one's composite nature, nor need they bear that burden, for one's inmost nature is *Purusha*, Self alone, and this is reflected by pure consciousness, *Buddhi*. Right conduct on the moral and mental planes can remove various obstructions to the rapid unfoldment of the vast potential of consciousness and that complete realization of *Purusha* known as self-emancipation (*kaivalya*). To the *yogin*, his mind serves as the director of any number of mental matrices or emanated minds which can carry out semi-independent functions under its supervision. Just as the presence of *Purusha* quickens and facilitates the fertile expansion of consciousness, so too the controlled mind of the *yogin* stimulates intellection everywhere. The *yogin* can work through the receptive minds of mature disciples, aiding all humanity by strengthening its spiritual aspirations. Whether mental aspects of the *yogin* or the sympathetic minds of others, no matrix of consciousness is free of *samskaras* or mental deposits, save the *yogin's* mind born of meditation. Only the consciousness integrated by pure *dhyana* is devoid of all impediment.

The *yogin* is above good and evil acts, not because he has become indifferent to the consequences of action, but rather because he is naturally disposed to remove all obstructions and mental deposits. Good conduct as well as bad bears fruit for the doer, but the *yogin* acts in such complete accord with Nature that what he does responds to necessity, being neither pure (*sattva*) nor polluted (*tamas*) nor mixed, like that of most human beings. His conduct follows a fourth course, that of *nishkama* or desirelessness, so that he cannot be said to do what he wishes, but rather he only does what needs to be done. *Nishkama karma*, the fruition of pure desireless action, neither returns nor clings to the *yogin*. Being one with Nature, he ceases to be a separative centre of focus or agency, and his actions, strictly speaking, are no longer 'his', being the spontaneous play of *prakriti* before *Purusha*. Hence, he leaves no impressions or residues in his consciousness even whilst doing his duty with single minded precision, since he acts as the willing instrument of *Purusha* immanent in *prakriti*. He has only former mental deposits, resulting from past *karma*, which he meticulously removes to attain total freedom.

The *yogin's* assiduously nurtured capacities disallow the emergence of fresh *karma*, the results of which could adhere to him because he is no longer subject to *vasana*, the force of craving and the unchecked impulse for life in form, with its attendant consequences. But he cannot instantly dissolve *karma* generated long ago, for whatever was the result of *vasana* in the past must inevitably linger, although the *yogin* is aware of its antecedents and does not become distracted or discouraged by it. In addition to the results that are already manifest, the force of craving and the *vasanas* (identifiable traces of unfulfilled longings and the cumulative *karma* they rapidly engender) deposit unconscious residues in the mind. These are more difficult to discern, for they are not recurring modifications of consciousness such as those induced by specific objects of desire, but are subtle tinctures or discolorations in the lens of cognition, hard to detect, recognize and remove. Being unconscious, and unknown to the thinker, they will appear only when conditions are ripe, and the *yogin* must patiently wait for their emergence in order to eliminate them. Even though immense periods of time and many incarnations may intervene between the initial insertion of the *vasanas* into consciousness and their eventual emergence, they are neither dissolved nor transformed, for they are retained in a stream of soul reminiscence which is not brain dependent, and which indeed provides a basis of continuity. This stream of latent reminiscence is revealed in the sometimes sudden appearance of surprising tendencies that seem out of character, but are nonetheless inescapable in the strict operation of *karma*.

Although any specific *vasana* could, in principle, be traced to a particular point in time – some previous incarnation – when the stream of consciousness encountered a similar cluster of thoughts, feelings or acts, *vasana* or desire in general is atemporal. It is coeval with mind (*chitta*) and with the cosmos. Whilst any distinct *vasana* could first appear only when a congenial psychophysical structure arose to make its manifestation possible, *vasana* as a force is an inextricable element in the matrices of differentiated matter. Just because the propensity to enjoyment or self-indulgence is an integral aspect of the cosmic process – the captivating dance of *prakriti* before *Purusha* – the overcoming of all such propensities demands a deliberate choice maintained over time through *Taraka Raja Yoga*, the discipline of transcendental detachment. *Vasana* finds its support in the mutable mind, which is the action of *prakriti* owing to the proximity of *Purusha*. Only when the mind is fully awake, wholly focussed and serenely steadfast will *vasana* vanish. This is equivalent to the potential ability of *prakriti* to behold *Purusha* qua *Purusha* without wavering, and this is only possible as a deliberate act – *Buddhi* reflecting *Purusha* without distortion or fluctuation.

Considered from the temporal standpoint, the protracted continuity of *vasana* as a strong force and the specific *vasanas* as persisting matrices of memory suggest the arbitrariness of the divisions of time into past, present and future. Each *vasana* is but a seed which inevitably grows into a plant and bears appropriate fruit: knowing the seed, one can cognize all future states of development. In the present lie latent the past and the future, just as the present was contained in the future and will remain until it slides speedily into the past. The underlying reality cannot be understood without seeing the present as no more than a moving phase through the limitless continuum of time, all of which is latent save for the swiftly passing moment. When all the *vasanas* have been consigned to the past, and when even the very basis of desire ceases to bother consciousness, *kaivalya* alone abides. All continuous change and the ramifying consequences of change are the tumultuous activity of the *gunas*, and when that relentless activity belongs to the past, no longer swaying the mind of the *yogin*, the *gunas* have ceased their incessant interplay in the stream of consciousness. Becoming latent, they have ceased to manifest and have become dormant or homogeneous, leaving intact the luminous vision of serene self emancipation *(kaivalya)*.

An object is what it is not because of some unique substratum, for the ultimate substratum of everything is the same. An object is distinct only because of the complex configuration of the *gunas*, the ceaseless interplay of which constitutes its nature. The fluid geometry of Nature, with the shifting ratios of *gunas*, permits some objects to persist longer than others, but the principle remains the same and endurance is merely relative. Even though an object survives for a time, the mutual activity of the *gunas* which constitutes each mind is different and alters at varying rates. Hence each person cognizes the object distinctively. The object is independent of each and every mind, though all apprehension of the object is entirely mind-dependent. Whether an object is known or not is the result of whether or not a particular mind is attracted to it. *Purusha*, however, cannot be a mental object. Rather, it is seen directly when the mind remains focussed upon it and does not move. Significantly, direct awareness of *Purusha* occurs when the mind ceases to act, which in *Sankhya* philosophy is equivalent to saying that the mind ceases to be what it is. *Purusha* witnesses all mental modifications and is the true Knower precisely because it does not alter or waver.

The mind is not self-luminous and cannot know itself by its own effort. Subject to change, it can be seen as an object by another, and ceaselessly changing, it cannot know itself, for change cannot discern change, just as relativities cannot calibrate relativities. *Purusha*, the ever changeless, is alone the Knower, whose reflection is cast upon consciousness, which then knows derivatively. Since the mind moves from moment to moment, it cannot both function as that which cognizes and that which is cognized. Hence, that which cognizes the mind whilst it cognizes objects (and so undergoes modification) is above the mind. Since consciousness operates on many levels, the level of awareness which apprehends consciousness necessarily transcends the level of the apprehended consciousness. Ultimately, *Purusha* comprehends all consciousness. One cannot speak of one mind knowing another within itself, as if the human being were constituted by many minds – an erroneous view encouraged by the limitations of descriptive and conceptual languages; one would have to posit an infinite regress of such minds, each knowing the one 'below' or 'in front of' itself, since none could know itself. The absurdity of an infinite series of minds within the consciousness of each individual is shown clearly by the problem of memory. Which mind would then remember? All of them? An infinitude of interacting memories would result in utter confusion of consciousness.

Self-cognition is possible when the relativating nature of the mind – its constant fluctuation which is the activity of the *gunas* – ceases. Pure consciousness desists from deploying the mind and so can know it, and when it does so, it ceases to be involved in any sort of movement from moment to moment. "The self-knowledge spoken of here", W. Q. Judge wrote, "is that interior illumination desired by all mystics, and is not merely a knowledge of self in the ordinary sense." Likening consciousness to light and the mind to a globe, I. K. Taimini suggested a striking metaphor: "If a light is enclosed within a translucent globe, it reveals the globe. If the globe is removed, the light reveals itself." This revelation is not knowledge in any ordinary sense, because within it there is no subject/object distinction, no separation of perceiver, perceived and perception; there is only the eternal Reality of the Self-illuminated *Purusha*. Although the mind, acted upon by the *gunas* and so consisting wholly of *prakriti*, is not consciousness, it is tinctured by *Purusha* and receives its luminous hue from it, even whilst suffused with the gaudier colours of the world of objects. It seems to be both conscious and nonconscious, and so those who do not know *Purusha* but experience its effects in *prakriti* mistake the mind, an instrument, for consciousness itself, when in fact the true cognizer of objects impressed upon the mind is *Purusha*. This root error – mistaking the organ of perception for the power of perception – is the origin of all ignorance, illusion and sorrow.

The mind, which is essentially an assemblage," the *Yogabhashya* teaches, "cannot act on its own to serve its own interests" (IV.24). Modified by a chaotic series of new impressions and weighed down by myriad deposits from past impressions, the mind cannot act for itself even though it thinks it does. From a teleological standpoint, the mind exists solely for *Purusha*, and despite an individual's deep-seated, ignorant confusion – the inexorable cause of sorrow – all mental activity arises in association with the Self, which it unknowingly seeks. Impressions engender a *maya* of independent activity which is dispelled in *Samadhi* wherein the nature of the mind is discerned. When the Perceiver, *Purusha*, sees beyond the confusion of ordinary cerebrations, there is no identification of the power of sight with the instrument of seeing, and it is entirely unaffected by the attributes, tendencies and images of the mind. The fully awakened, alert and tranquil mind, settled in the supreme stillness of *Samadhi*, speedily learns correct cognition and moves steadily in the direction of *kaivalya*, self-emancipation. In fact, it is *Purusha* hidden behind the gossamer veils of intellection whose light illumines the way, but, in the apt analogy of I. K. Taimini, like the magnet attracting iron filings, the mind seems to move towards the magnetic *Purusha*, when in truth the invisible power of *Purusha* draws the mind to itself. At this exalted stage, the individual seeks nothing except the total freedom of self emancipation. Even when the mind, like a guided missile locked on to its target, moves without the slightest wavering or change of course towards the luminous *Purusha*, old impressions will cyclically reassert themselves, owing to their unspent momentum. They can be eliminated by the same methods developed for dissolving the *kleshas* or afflictions, except that here the *yogin* knows them already for what they are and can instantaneously destroy them, or return them to complete dormancy, through undisturbed discernment (*vivekakhyati*) of the True Self (*Purusha*).

When the *yogin* abides in this peaceful state wherein *Purusha* alone stands at the focal point of his entire consciousness, he verges on *prasankhyana*, omniscience or complete illumination. Since any lurking attachment can be a hindrance to self realization, he must renounce even the desire for the highest illumination, save insofar as it may elevate all existence. From the inception of his spiritual quest in lives long past, *viveka* (discrimination) and *vairagya* (detachment) have been crucial to his endeavours. As *viveka* culminates in *vivekakhyati* (discernment of the Real), so too *vairagya* culminates in *paravairagya*, supreme detachment towards the highest conceivable fruit of effort, *prasankhyana*. When this occurs, *Samadhi* becomes *dharmamegha*, the rain cloud of righteousness, which is perpetual discernment of *Purusha* or unending enlightenment. The circle is closed, the line returns upon itself, and the *yogin* passes from linear time into the omnidirectional realization of *Purusha*, the Self, rising above time to the Eternal Now which transcends every moment though implicit in temporal succession. All the residues of the afflictions (*kleshas*) simply drop away as water runs off an impervious surface, and the *yogin* finds self-emancipation even in embodied life. *Dharmamegha Samadhi* destroys the residuum of *karma* and the *kleshas* at the root, so that they can never arise again. The *yogin* has attained that supreme felicity from which there is no falling away.

The *yogin's* cognition becomes infinite and without any limit whatsoever, for of the three *gunas*, *rajas* and *tamas* have ceased to be active. But even this cognition is transcended, for the stilling of *rajas* and *tamas* deprives *sattva* of a contrasting field for expression, and so all three *gunas* become quiescent. This can be conceived as their merger into homogeneous latency or as their cessation, for they no longer sustain the process of ceaseless transformation. Without such transformation, there is no existence as evident in Nature (*prakriti*), and yet since they remain latent they still exist for all those who live in ignorance. As all knowledge depends upon transformations of consciousness which occur through the succession of moments (*kshanas*), knowledge is limited by the discontinuity of moments. For the *yogin* who has reached the threshold of *kaivalya*, the succession of moments is seen as a discrete continuum and is wholly transcended. His knowledge is no longer bound by temporal succession because he beholds the process as a whole. Rather than being subject to the transformations of the world, he sees them as an endless succession of discrete states, whilst his transcendental (*taraka*) knowledge is continuous and complete. He is now the Perceiver (*Purusha*), utterly unaffected by the passing show of phenomenal Nature (*prakriti*).

The *gunas*, no longer stirred to activity by the presence of *Purusha*, are reabsorbed into absolute latency, and *Purusha* abides in its own essential nature, without any trace of ignorance, misconception, confusion and sorrow. For the *yogin*, experience comes to an end, for he has become one with his true nature, which is *Purusha*, the energy of pure consciousness – devoid of moments – which is cosmic ideation, upon which all noumena and phenomena depend. This is complete emancipation, *kaivalya*, and supreme peace, *nirvana*. *Kaivalya* is the ineffable state of stillness – though such terms are wholly inadequate, metaphysically and metapsychologically – which is the self-existence of *Purusha* in and as itself. The *yogin* is no longer captive to the central duality postulated in *Sankhya* philosophy, for he beholds *Purusha*, which is himself, in the entire cosmos, and the entire cosmos, which is also himself, in *Purusha*. For him, as in *Mahayana* mysticism, *nirvana* is *samsara* and vice versa. Since there is no separation between the two, there is no room for even the subtlest error, and so sin and sorrow vanish forever. *Sat-chit-ananda*, Being, Consciousness and Bliss, constitute for him the fullness of *Purusha*, which nonetheless abides beyond them as the attributeless Self.

What, one might ask, does the *yogin* do now? Does he abide forever in unalloyed bliss? Such questions cannot be raised, for the *yogin* is no longer a creature of time and space. Rather than being now or doing then, he always was, is and will be, for he lives in the Eternal Now. Even though consciousness, bound by time, change and error, makes of such an inconceivable condition a frozen ecstasy, no picture of it can be anything but a fantasy rooted in ignorance. The *yogin* is entirely free and moves through sublime states of awareness which the unenlightened mind can neither imagine nor articulate, and therefore Patanjali, a true Sage, remained silent. When the *yogin* ceases to be a part of the temporal process and becomes indistinguishable from it – on the principle of the identity of indiscernibles – he becomes its creator. He was there in the beginning and he is its *eschaton*, the end and goal beyond which there is only Silence.

In the memorable words of *Shrimad Bhagavatam*, Book XI:

> The *yogin*, having discarded the notions of 'good' and 'bad', though experiencing the objects of the senses in all their diversity, is no more addicted to them than the wind to the places where it happens to blow. The *yogin* who has realized the SELF, though he seems to identify

with the properties of the material vesture he inhabits, is no more attached to them than the breeze is attached to the fragrant scent it carries. Even whilst remaining in the body, the Sage should think of his soul as unattached to the body and the like, and unlimited just as the sky is, not only because it is present in all Nature, animate and inanimate, as the invariable concomitant, but being identical with the Supreme, it is also all pervading . . . .

Pure and kind-hearted by nature, the Sage is like water, in that he is a sanctifying influence in the lives of those who purify themselves by seeing, touching or speaking of him. Radiating power, enhanced by austerities, possessing nothing, yet imperturbable, the *yogin* who has steadied his mind remains unsoiled like the fire, regardless of what he may consume. While the creation and destruction of the bodies that the SELF assumes proceeds every moment at the hands of Time, which rushes like a swift stream, the SELF remains unnoticed, like the emergence and subsidence of tongues of flame in a burning fire.

Hermes, May 1989

THEOSOPHICAL GLOSSARY

Meditation and Self-Study

A

Absoluteness. When predicated of the UNIVERSAL PRINCIPLE, it denotes an abstract noun, which is more correct and logical than to apply the adjective "absolute " to that which has neither attributes nor limitations, nor can IT have any.

Adam (Heb.). In the *Kabalah* Adam is the "only-begotten", and means also "red earth". (See "Adam-Adami" in the *S.D.* II p. 452.) It is almost identical with *Athamas* or *Thomas*, and is rendered into Greek by *Didumos*, the "twin"– Adam, "the first", in chap. 1 of *Genesis*, being shown, "male-female."

Adam Kadmon *(Heb).* Archetypal Man; Humanity. The "Heavenly Man" not fallen into sin; Kabalists refer it to the Ten Sephiroth on the plane of human perception. [w.w.w.]

In the *Kabalah* Adam Kadmon is the manifested Logos corresponding to our *Third* Logos; the Unmanifested being the first paradigmic ideal Man, and symbolizing the Universe in *abscondito*, or in its "privation" in the Aristotelean sense. The First Logos is the "Light of the World", the Second and the Third – its gradually deepening shadows.

Adept *(Lat.).* *Adeptus,* "He who has obtained." In Occultism one who has reached the stage of Initiation, and become a Master in the science of Esoteric philosophy.

Âditi (*Sk.*). The Vedic name for the *Mûlaprakriti* of the Vedantists; the abstract aspect of Parabrahman, though both unmanifested and unknowable. In the *Vedas* Âditi is the "Mother-Goddess", her terrestrial symbol being infinite and shoreless space.

Adwaita (*Sk.*). A Vedânta sect. The non-dualistic (A-dwaita) school of Vedântic philosophy founded by Sankarâchârya, the greatest of the historical Brahmin sages. The two other schools are the Dwaita (dualistic) and the Visishtadwaita; all the three call themselves Vedântic.

Adwaitin (*Sk.*). A follower of the said school.

Æther (*Gr.*). With the ancients the divine luminiferous substance which pervades the whole universe, the "garment" of the Supreme Deity, Zeus, or

301

Jupiter. With the moderns, Ether, for the meaning of which in physics and chemistry see Webster's *Dictionary* or any other. In esotericism Æther is the third principle of the Kosmic Septenary; the Earth being the lowest, then the Astral light, Ether and *Âkâsa* (phonetically *Âkâsha*) the highest.

Agathodæmon (*Gr.*). The beneficent, good Spirit as contrasted with the bad one, Kakodæmon. The "Brazen Serpent" of the Bible is the former; the flying serpents of fire are an aspect of Kakodæmon. The Ophites called Agathodæmon the Logos and Divine Wisdom, which in the Bacchanalian Mysteries was represented by a serpent erect on a pole.

Agathon (*Gr.*). Plato's Supreme Deity. Lit., "The Good", our ALAYA, or "Universal Soul".

Agni (*Sk.*). The God of Fire in the Veda; the oldest and the most revered of Gods in India. He is one of the three great deities: Agni, Vâyu and Sûrya, and also all the three, as he is the triple aspect of fire; in heaven as the Sun; in the atmosphere or air (Vâyu), as Lightning; on. earth, as ordinary Fire. Agni belonged to the earlier Vedic *Trimûrti* before Vishnu was given a place of honour and before Brahmâ and Siva were invented.

Agnishwattas (*Sk.*). A class of Pitris, the creators of the first ethereal race of men. Our solar ancestors as contrasted with the *Barhishads,* the "lunar" Pitris or ancestors, though otherwise explained in the *Purânas.*

Aham (*Sk.*). "I" – the basis of *Ahankâra*, Self-hood.

Ahankâra (*Sk.*). The conception of "I", Self-consciousness or Self- identity; the "I", the egotistical and *mâyâvic* principle in man, due to our ignorance which separates our "I" from the Universal ONE-SELF Personality, Egoism.

Ain Soph (*Heb.*). The "Boundless" or Limitless; Deity emanating and extending. [w.w.w.]

Ain Soph is also written *En Soph* and *Ain Suph*, no one, not even Rabbis, being sure of their vowels. In the religious metaphysics of the old Hebrew philosophers, the ONE Principle was an abstraction, like Parabrahmam, though modern Kabbalists have succeeded now, by dint of mere sophistry and paradoxes, in making a "Supreme God" of it and nothing higher. But with the early Chaldean Kabbalists Ain Soph is "without form or being", having "no likeness with anything else" (Franck, *Die Kabbala*, p. 126). That Ain Soph has never been considered as the "Creator" is proved by even such an orthodox Jew as Philo calling the "Creator" the *Logos*, who stands next the "Limitless One", and the "Second God". "The Second God is its (Ain Soph's) wisdom", says Philo (*Quaest. et Solut.*). Deity is NO-THING; it is nameless, and therefore called Ain Soph; the word *Ain* meaning NOTHING. (See Franck's *Kabbala*, p. 153 ff.)

Aitareya (*Sk.*). The name of an Aranyaka (Brâhmana) and a Upanishad of the *Rig Veda*. Some of its portions are purely Vedântic.

Akâsa (*Sk.*). The subtle, supersensuous spiritual essence which pervades all space; the primordial substance erroneously identified with Ether. But it is to Ether what Spirit is to Matter, or *Âtmâ* to *Kâma-rûpa*. It is, in fact, the Universal Space in which lies inherent the eternal Ideation of the Universe in its ever-changing aspects on the planes of matter and objectivity, and from which radiates the *First Logos*, or expressed thought. This is why it is stated in the *Purânas* that Âkâsa has but one attribute, namely sound, for sound is but the translated symbol of Logos – "Speech" in its mystic sense. In the same sacrifice (*the Jyotishtoma Agnishtoma*) it is called the "God Âkâsa". In these sacrificial mysteries Âkâsa is the all-directing 'and omnipotent Deva who plays the part of Sadasya, the superintendent over the magical effects of the religious performance, and it had its own appointed Hotri (priest) in days of old, who took its name. The Âkâsa is the indispensable agent of every *Krityâ* (magical performance) religious or profane. The expression "to stir up the Brahmâ", means to stir up the power which lies latent at the bottom of every magical operation, Vedic sacrifices being in fact nothing if not ceremonial magic. This power is the Âkâsa – in another aspect, *Kundalini* – occult electricity, the alkahest of the alchemists in one sense, or the universal solvent, the same *anima mundi* on the higher plane as the *astral light* is on the lower. "At the moment of the sacrifice the priest becomes imbued with the spirit of Brahmâ, is, for the time being, Brahmâ himself". (*Isis Unveiled*).

Alaya (*Sk.*). The Universal Soul (See *Secret Doctrine* Vol. I. pp. 47 *et seq.*). The name belongs to the Tibetan system of the contemplative *Mahâyâna* School. Identical with *Âkâsa* in its mystic sense, and with *Mulâprâkriti*, in its essence, as it is the basis or root of all things.

Amânasa (*Sk.*). The " Mindless', the early races of this planet; also certain Hindu gods.

Ambhâmsi (*Sk.*). A name of the chief of the Kumâras Sanat-Sujâta, signifying the "waters". This epithet will become more comprehensible when we remember that the later type of Sanat-Sujâta was Michael, the Archangel, who is called in the Talmud "the Prince of *Waters*", and in the Roman Catholic Church is regarded as the patron of gulfs and promontories. Sanat-Sujâta is the immaculate son of the immaculate mother (Ambâ or Aditi, chaos and space) or the "waters" of limitless space. (See *Secret Doctrine-*, Vol. I., p. 460.)

Androgyne Ray (*Esot.*). The first differentiated ray; the Second Logos; Adam Kadmon in the *Kabalah*; the "male and female created he them", of the first chapter of *Genesis*.

Anima Mundi (*Lat.*). The"Soul of the World", the same as the *Alaya* of the Northern Buddhists; the divine essence which permeates, animates and informs all, from the smallest atom of matter to man and god. It is in a sense the "seven-skinned mother" of the stanzas in the *Secret Doctrine*, the essence of seven planes of sentience, consciousness and differentiation, moral and physical. In its highest aspect it is *Nirvâna*, in its lowest Astral Light. It was feminine with the Gnostics, the early Christians and the Nazarenes; bisexual with other sects, who considered it only in its four lower planes. Of igneous, ethereal nature in the objective world of form (and then ether), and divine and spiritual in its three higher planes. When it is said that every human soul was born by detaching itself from the *Anima Mundi*, it means, esoterically, that our higher Egos are of an essence identical with **It,** which is a radiation of the ever unknown Universal ABSOLUTE.

Annamaya Kosha (*Sk.*). A Vedantic term. The same as *Sthûla Sharîra* or the physical body. It is the first "sheath" of the *five* sheaths accepted by the Vedantins, a sheath being the same as that which is called "principle" in Theosophy.

Anoia (*Gr.*). "Want of understanding", "folly". *Anoia* is the name given by Plato and others to the lower Manas when too closely allied with Kâma, which is irrational (*agnoia*). The Greek word agnoia is evidently a derivation from and cognate to the Sanskrit word *ajnâna* (phonetically, *agnyana*) or ignorance, irrationality, absence of knowledge. (See "Agnoia" and "Agnostic".)

Antahkarana (*Sk.*)., or Antaskarana. The term has various meanings, which differ with every school of philosophy and sect. Thus Sankârachârya renders the word as "understanding"; others, as "the internal instrument, the Soul, formed by the thinking principle and egoism"; whereas the Occultists explain it as the *path* or bridge between the Higher and the Lower Manas, the divine *Ego*, and the *personal* Soul of man. It serves as a medium of communication between the two, and conveys from the Lower to the Higher Ego all those personal impressions and thoughts of men which can, by their nature, be assimilated and stored by the undying Entity, and be thus made immortal with it, these being the only elements of the evanescent *Personality* that survive death and time. It thus stands to reason that only that which is noble, spiritual and divine in man can testify in Eternity to his having lived.

Anthropomorphism (*Gr.*). From "anthropos" meaning man. The act of endowing god or gods with a human form and human attributes or qualities.

Anugîtâ (*Sk.*). One of the *Upanishads*. A very occult treatise. (*See The sacred Books of the East.*)

Anupâdaka (*Sk.*). Anupapâdaka, also Aupapâduka; means parentless", "self-existing", born without any parents or progenitors. A term applied to certain self-created gods, and the Dhyâni Buddhas.

Arjuna (*Sk.*) Lit., the "white". The third of the five Brothers Pandu or the reputed Sons of Indra (esoterically the same as Orpheus). A disciple of Krishna, who visited him and married Su-bhadrâ, his sister, besides many other wives, according to the allegory. During the fratricidal war between the *Kauravas* and the *Pândavas*, Krishna instructed him in the highest philosophy, while serving as his charioteer. (*See Bhagavad Gîtâ.*)

Arûpa (*Sk.*). "Bodiless", formless, as opposed to *rûpa*, "body", or form.

Arvâksrotas (*Sk.*). The *seventh* creation, that of man, in the *Vishnu Purâna*.

Âryasangha (*Sk.*) The Founder of the *first* Yogâchârya School. This Arhat, a direct disciple of Gautama, the Buddha, is most unaccountably mixed up and confounded with a personage of the same name, who is said to have lived in Ayôdhya (Oude) about the fifth or sixth century of our era, and taught Tântrika worship in addition to the Yogâchârya system. Those who sought to make it popular, claimed that he was the same Âryasangha, that had been a follower of Sâkyamuni, and that he was 1,000 years old. Internal evidence alone is sufficient to show that the works written by him and translated about the year 600 of our era, works full of Tantra worship, ritualism, and tenets followed now considerably by the "red-cap" sects in Sikhim, Bhutan, and Little Tibet, cannot be the same as the lofty system of the early Yogâcharya school of pure Buddhism, which is neither northern nor southern, but absolutely esoteric. Though none of the genunine Yogâchârya books (the *Narjol chodpa*) have ever been made public or marketable, yet one finds in the *Yogâchârya Bhûmi Shâstra* of the *pseudo*-Âryasangha a great deal from the older system, into the tenets of which he may have been initiated. It is, however, so mixed up with Sivaism and Tantrika magic and superstitions, that the work defeats its own end, notwithstanding its remarkable dialectical subtilty. (See the *Theosophical Glossary*)

Asakrit Samâdhi (Sk.). A certain degree of ecstatic contemplation. A stage in *Samâdhi*.

Âsana (*Sk.*). The third stage of *Hatha Yoga*, one of the prescribed postures of meditation.

Ashta Siddhis (*Sk.*). The eight consummations in the practice of Hatha Yoga.

Astral Body, or Astral "Double". The ethereal counterpart or shadow of man or animal. The **Linga Sharira**, the "Doppelgäinger". The reader must not confuse it with the ASTRAL SOUL, another name for the lower Manas, or Kama-Manas so-called, the reflection of the HIGHER EGO.

Astral Light (*Occult*) The invisible region that surrounds our globe, as it does every other, and corresponding as the second Principle of Kosmos (the third being Life, of which it is the vehicle) to the *Linga Sharira* or the Astral

Double in man. A subtle Essence visible only to a clairvoyant eye, and the lowest but one (*viz.*, the earth), of the Seven Akâsic or Kosmic Principles. Eliphas Levi calls it the great Serpent and the Dragon from which radiates on Humanity every evil influence. This is so; but why not add that the Astral Light gives out nothing but what it has received; that it is the great terrestrial crucible, in which the vile emanations of the earth (moral and physical) upon which the Astral Light is fed, are all converted into their subtlest essence, and radiated back intensified, thus becoming epidemics – moral, psychic and physical. Finally, the Astral Light is the same as the *Sidereal Light* of Paracelsus and other Hermetic philosophers. "Physically, it is the ether of modern science. Metaphysically, and in its spiritual, or occult sense, ether is a great deal more than is often imagined. In occult physics, and alchemy, it is well demonstrated to enclose within its shoreless waves not only Mr. Tyndall's 'promise and potency of every quality of life', but also the *realization* of the potency of every quality of spirit. Alchemists and Hermetists believe that their *astral*, or sidereal ether, besides the above properties of sulphur, and white and red magnesia, or *magnes*, is the *anima mundi*, the workshop of Nature and of all the Kosmos, spiritually, as well as physically. The 'grand magisterium' asserts itself in the phenomenon of mesmerism, in the 'levitation' of human and inert objects; and may be called the ether from its spiritual aspect. The designation *astral* is ancient, and was used by some of the Neo-platonists, although it is claimed by some that the word was coined by the Martinists. Porphyry describes the celestial body which is always joined with the soul as 'immortal, luminous, and star-like'. The root of this word may be found, perhaps, in the Scythic *Aist-aer* – which means star, or the Assyrian *Istar*, which, according to Burnouf has the same sense." (*Isis Unveiled.*)

Asuras (*Sk.*). Exoterically, elementals and evil, gods – considered maleficent; demons, and *no* gods. But esoterically – the reverse. For in the most ancient portions of the *Rig Veda*, the term is used for the Supreme Spirit, and therefore the Asuras are spiritual and divine It is only in the last book of the *Rig Veda*, its latest part, and in the *Atharva Veda*, and the *Brâhmanas*, that the epithet, which had been given to Agni, the greatest Vedic Deity, to Indra and Varuna, has come to signify the reverse of gods. *Asu* means breath, and it is with his breath that Prajâpati (Brahmâ) creates the Asuras. When ritualism and dogma got the better of the Wisdom religion, the initial letter **a** was adopted as a negative prefix, and the term ended by signifying "not a god", and Sura only a deity. But in the Vedas the Suras have ever been connected with *Surya*, the sun, and regarded as *inferior* deities, devas.

Aswattha (*Sk.*) The **Bo-tree**, the tree of knowledge, *ficus religiosa*.

Atmâ (or **Atman**) (*Sk.*). The Universal Spirit, the divine Monad, the 7th Principle, so-called, in the septenary constitution of man. The Supreme Soul.

Atma-bhu (*Sk.*). Soul-existence, or existing as soul. (See "*Alaya*".)

Atmabodha (*Sk.*). Lit., "Self-knowledge"; the title of a Vedantic treatise by Sankârachârya.

Atma-jnâni (*Sk.*) The Knower of the World-Soul, or Soul in general.

Atma Vidyâ (*Sk.*). The highest form of spiritual knowledge; lit., "Soul-knowledge".

Atri, Sons of (*Sk.*). A class of Pitris, the "ancestors of man", or the so-called Prâjapâti, "progenitors"; one of the seven Rishis who form the constellation of the Great Bear.

Attavada (*Pali*). The sin of personality.

Aum (*Sk.*). The sacred syllable; the triple-lettered unit; hence the trinity in One.

Avalokiteswara (*Sk.*) "The on-looking Lord" In the exoteric interpretation, he is Padmapâni (the lotus bearer and the lotus-born) in Tibet, the first divine ancestor of the Tibetans, the complete incarnation or Avatar of Avalokiteswara; but in esoteric philosophy Avaloki, the "on-looker", is the Higher Self, while Padmapâni is the Higher Ego or Manas. The mystic formula "Om mani padme hum" is specially used to invoke their joint help. While popular fancy claims for Avalokiteswara many incarnations on earth, and sees in him, not very wrongly, the spiritual guide of every believer, the esoteric interpretation sees in him the Logos, both celestial and human. Therefore, when the Yogâchârya School has declared Avalokiteswara as Padmâpani "to be the Dhyâni Bodhisattva of Amitâbha Buddha", it is indeed, because the former is *the spiritual reflex in the world of forms* of the latter, both being one – one in heaven, the other on earth.

Avatâra (*Sk.*) Divine incarnation. The descent of a god or some exalted Being, who has progressed beyond the necessity of Rebirths, into the body of a simple mortal. Krishna was an avatar of Vishnu. The Dalai Lama is regarded as an avatar of Avalokiteswara, and the Teschu Lama as one of Tson-kha-pa, or Amitâbha. There are two kinds of avatars: those born from woman, and the parentless, the *anupapâdaka*.

Avidyâ (*Sk.*). Opposed to *Vidyâ*, Knowledge. Ignorance which proceeds from, and is produced by the illusion of the Senses or *Viparyaya*.

B.

Barhishad (*Sk.*). A class of the "lunar" Pitris or "Ancestors", Fathers, who are believed in popular superstition to have kept up in their past incarnations the household sacred flame and made fire-offerings. Esoterically the Pitris who evolved their shadows or *chhayas* to make there-with the first man. (See *Secret Doctrine*, Vol. II.)

Bhagavad-Gita (*Sk.*). Lit., "the Lord's Song". A portion of the Mahabharata, the great epic poem of India. It contains a dialogue wherein Krishna—the "Charioteer"—and Arjuna, his Chela, have a discussion upon the highest spiritual philosophy. The work is pre-eminently occult or esoteric.

Bhagavat (*Sk.*). A title of the Buddha and of Krishna. "The Lord" literally.

Bhâshya (*Sk*) A commentary.

Bodhisattva (*Sk).* Lit., "he, whose essence (*sattva*) has become intelligence (*bodhi*)"; those who need but one more incarnation to become perfect Buddhas, i.e., to be entitled to Nirvâna. This, as applied to *Manushi* (terrestrial) Buddhas. In the metaphysical sense, *Bodhisattva* is a title given to the sons of the celestial *Dhyâni* Buddhas.

Brahma (*Sk.*). The student must distinguish between Brahma the neuter, and Brahmâ, the male creator of the Indian Pantheon. The former, Brahma or Brahman, is the impersonal, supreme and uncognizable Principle of the Universe from the essence of which all emanates, and into which all returns, which is incorporeal, immaterial, unborn, eternal, beginningless and endless. It is all-pervading, animating the highest god as well as the smallest mineral atom. Brahmâ on the other hand, the male and the alleged Creator, exists periodically in his manifestation only, and then again goes into pralaya, i.e., disappears and is annihilated.

Brahmâ's Day. A period of 2,160,000,000 years during which Brahmâ having emerged out of his golden egg (*Hiranyagarbha*), creates and fashions the material world (being simply the fertilizing and creative force in Nature). After this period, the worlds being destroyed in turn, by fire and water, he vanishes with objective nature, and then comes Brahmâ's Night.

Brahmâ's Night. A period of equal duration, during which Brahmâ. is said to be asleep. Upon awakening he recommences the process, and this goes on for an AGE of Brahmâ composed of alternate "Days", and "Nights", and lasting 100 years (of 2,160,000,000 years each). It requires fifteen figures to express the duration of such an age; after the expiration of which the *Mahapralaya* or the Great Dissolution sets in, and lasts in its turn for the same space of fifteen figures.

Brahmâ Vâch (*Sk.*) Male and female Brahmâ. Vâch is also some-times called the female logos; for Vâch means Speech, literally. (See *Manu* Book I., and *Vishnu Purâna.*)

Brahma Vidyâ (*Sk.*) The knowledge, the esoteric science, about the two Brahmas and their true nature.

Brahmâ Virâj (*Sk.*) The same: Brahmâ separating his body into two halves, male and female, creates in them Vâch and Virâj. In plainer terms and *esotericlly* Brahmâ the Universe, differentiating, produced thereby material nature, Virâj, and spiritual intelligent Nature, Vâch – which is the *Logos* of Deity or the manifested expression of the eternal divine Ideation.

Brâhman (*Sk.*) The highest of the four castes in India, one supposed or rather fancying himself, as high among men, as Brahman, the ABSOLUTE of the Vedantins, is high among, or above the gods.

Brahmâputrâs (*Sk.*) The Sons of Brahmâ.

Buddha (*Sk.*). Lit., "The Enlightened". The highest degree of knowledge. To become a Buddha one has to break through the bondage of sense and personality; to acquire a complete perception of the REAL SELF and learn not to separate it from all otherselves; to learn by experience the utter unreality of all phenomena of the visible Kosmos foremost of all; to reach a complete detachment from all that is evanescent and finite, and live while yet on Earth in the immortal and the everlasting alone, in a supreme state of holiness.

Buddhi (*Sk.*). Universal Soul or Mind. *Mahâbuddhi* is a name of Mahat (see "Alaya"); also the spiritual Soul in man (the sixth principle), the vehicle of Atmâ exoterically the seventh.

Buddhism. Buddhism is now split into two distinct Churches : the Southern and the Northern Church. The former is said to be the purer form, as having preserved more religiously the original teachings of the Lord Buddha. It is the religion of Ceylon, Siam, Burmah and other places, while Northern Buddhism is confined to Tibet, China and Nepaul. Such a distinction, however, is incorrect. If the Southern Church is nearer, in that it has not departed, except perhaps in some trifling dogmas due to the many councils held after the death of the Master, from the public or *exoteric* teachings of Sâkyamuni – the Northern Church is the outcome of Siddhârta Buddha's esoteric teachings which he confined to his elect Bhikshus and Arhats. In fact, Buddhism in the present age, cannot he justly judged either by one or the other of its exoteric popular forms. Real Buddhism can be appreciated only by blending the philosophy of the Southern Church and the metaphysics of the Northern Schools. If one seems too iconoclastic and stero:, and the other too metaphysical and transcendental, even to being overgrown with the weeds of Indian exotericism – many of the gods of its Pantheon having been transplanted under new names to Tibetan soil – it is entirely due to the popular expression of Buddhism in both Churches. Correspondentially they stand in their relation to each other as Protestantism to Roman Catholicism. Both err by an excess of zeal and erroneous interpretations, though neither the Southern nor the Northern Buddhist clergy have ever departed from truth consciously, still less have they acted under the dictates of *priestocracy*, ambition, or with an eye to personal gain and power, as the two Christian Churches have.

C

Causal Body. This "body", which is no body either objective or subjective, but *Buddhi*, the Spiritual Soul, is so called because it is the direct cause of the Sushupti condition, leading to the *Turya* state, the highest state of *Samadhi*. It is called *Karanopadhi*, "the basis of the Cause", by the Târaka Raja Yogis; and in the Vedânta system it corresponds to both the *Vignânamaya* and *Anandamaya Kosha*, the latter coming next to Atma, and therefore being the vehicle of the universal Spirit. Buddhi alone could not be called a "Causal Body ", but becomes so in conjunction with Manas, the incarnating Entity or EGO.

Chakra (*Sk.*) A wheel, a disk, or the circle of Vishnu generally. Used also of a cycle of time, and with other meanings.

Chaldeans, or *Kasdim*. At first a tribe, then a caste of learned Kabbalists. They were the *savants*, the magians of Babylonia, astrologers and diviners. The famous Hillel, the precursor of Jesus in philosophy and in ethics, was a Chaldean. Franck in his *Kabbala* points to the close resemblance of the "secret doctrine" found in the *Avesta* and the religious metaphysics of the Chaldees.

Chelâ (*Sk.*) A disciple, the pupil of a Guru or Sage, the follower of some adept of a school of philosophy (*lit.*, child).

Chhâyâ (*Sk.*) "Shade" or " Shadow". The name of a creature produced by Sanjnâ, the wife of Surya, from herself (astral body). Unable to endure the ardour of her husband, Sanjnâ left Chhâyâ in her place as a wife, going herself away to perform austerities. Chhâyâ is the astral image of a person in esoteric philosophy.

Chhaya loka (*Sk.*) The world of Shades; like Hades, the world of the *Eidola* and *Umbræ*. We call it *Kâmaloka*.

Chidâkâsam (Sk); The field, or basis of consciousness.

Chohan (*Tib.*) "Lord" or "Master" ; a chief; thus **Dhyan-Chohan** would answer to "Chief of the Dhyanis", or celestial Lights – which in English would be translated Archangels.

Chréstos (*Gr.*) The early Gnostic form of Christ. It was used in the fifth century B.C. by Æschylus, Herodotus, and others. The *Manteumata pythochresta*, or the "oracles delivered by a Pythian god" "through a pythoness, are mentioned by the former (*Choeph.*901). *Chréstian* is not only "the seat of an oracle", but an offering to, or for, the oracle.

Chréstés is one who explains oracles, "a prophet and soothsayer", and Chrésterios one who serves an oracle or a god. The earliest Christian writer, Justin Martyr, in his first *Apology* calls his co-religionists Chréstians. It is only through ignorance that men call themselves Christians instead of Chréstians," says Lactantius (lib. iv., cap. vii.). The terms Christ and Christians, spelt originally Chrést and Chréstians, were borrowed from the Temple vocabulary of the Pagans. Chréstos meant in that vocabulary a disciple on probation, a candidate for hierophantship. When he had attained to this through initiation, long trials, and suffering, and had been "*anointed*" (i.e., "rubbed with oil", as were Initiates and even idols of the gods, as the last touch of ritualistic observance), his name was changed into Christos, the "purified", in esoteric or mystery language. In mystic symbology, indeed, *Christés*, or *Christos,* meant that the "Way", the Path, was already trodden and the goal reached ; when the fruits of the arduous labour, uniting the personality of evanescent clay with the indestructible INDIVIDUALITY, transformed it thereby into the immortal EGO. "At the end of the Way stands the *Chréstes*", the *Purifier,* and the union once accomplished, the *Chrestos,* the "man of sorrow", became *Christos* himself. Paul, the Initiate, knew this, and meant this precisely, when he is made to say, in bad translation : "I travail in birth again until Christ be formed in you" (Gal. iv.19), the true rendering of which is . . . "until ye form the Christos within yourselves" But the profane who knew only that Chréstés was in some way connected with priest and prophet, and knew nothing about the hidden meaning of Christos, insisted, as did Lactantius and Justin Martyr, on being called *Chréstians* instead of Christians. Every good individual, therefore, may find Christ in his "inner man" as Paul expresses it (Ephes. iii. 16,17), whether he be Jew, Mussulman, Hindu, or Christian. Kenneth Mackenzie seemed to think that the word *Chréstos* was a synonym of Soter, "an appellation assigned to deities, great kings and heroes," indicating "Saviour," – and he was right. For, as he adds:"It has been applied redundantly to Jesus Christ, whose name Jesus or Joshua bears the same interpretation. The name Jesus, in fact, is rather a title of honour than a name – the true name of the Soter of Christianity being Emmanuel, or God with us (*Matt*.i, 23.).Great divinities among all nations, who are represented as expiatory or self-sacrificing, have been designated by the same title." *(R. M. Cyclop.)* The Asklepios (or Æsculapius) of the Greeks had the title of *Soter.*

Cosmic Gods. Inferior gods, those connected with the formation of matter.

Cosmic ideation (*Occult.*) Eternal thought, impressed on substance or spirit-matter, in the eternity ; thought which becomes active at the beginning of every new life-cycle.

Cycle. From the Greek *Kuklos.* The ancients divided time into end less cycles, wheels within wheels, all such periods being of various durations, and each marking the beginning or the end of some event either cosmic, mundane, physical or metaphysical. There were cycles of only a few years, and cycles of immense duration, the great Orphic cycle, referring to the ethnological change of races, lasting 120,000 years, and the cycle of Cassandrus of 136,000, which brought about a complete change in planetary influences and their correlations between men and gods – a fact entirely lost sight of by modern astrologers.

D

Dæmon (*Gr.*) In the original Hermetic works and ancient classics it has a meaning identical with that of "god", "angel" or "genius". The Dæmon of Socrates is the incorruptible part of the man, or rather the real inner man which we call Nous or the rational divine Ego. At all events the Dæmon (or Daimon of the great Sage was surely not the demon of the Christian Hell or of Christian orthodox theology. The name was given by ancient peoples, and especially the philosophers of the Alexandrian school, to all kinds of spirits, whether good or bad, human or otherwise. The appellation is often synonymous with that of gods or angels. But some philosophers tried, with good reason, to make a just distinction between the many classes.

Daitya Guru (*Sk.*) The instructor of the giants, called *Daityas* (*q.v.*) Allegorically, it is the title given to the planet Venus-Lucifer, or rather to its indwelling Ruler, *Sukra*, a male deity (See *Sec. Doct.*. ii. p. 30).

Daityas (*Sk.*) Giants, Titans, and exoterically demons, but in truth identical with certain Asuras, the intellectual gods, the opponents of the useless gods of ritualism and the enemies of *puja* sacrifices.

Daksha (*Sk.*) A form of Brahmâ and his son in the Purânas But the *Rig Veda* states that "Daksha sprang from Aditi, and Aditi from Daksha", which proves him to be a personified correlating Creative Force acting on *all the planes*. The Orientalists seem very much perplexed what to make of him; but Roth is nearer the truth than any, when saying that Daksha is the spiritual power, and at the same time the male energy that generates the gods in eternity, which is represented by Aditi. The Purânas as a matter of course, anthropomorphize the idea, and show Daksha instituting "sexual intercourse on this earth", after trying every other means of procreation. The generative Force, spiritual at the commencement, becomes of course at the most material end of its evolution a procreative Force on the physical plane ; and so far the Purânic allegory is correct, as the Secret Science teaches that our present mode of procreation began towards the end of the third Root-Race.

Dangma (*Sk.*) In Esotericism a purified Soul. A Seer and an Initiate; one who has attained full wisdom.

Darsanas (*Sk.*) The Schools of Indian philosophy, of which there are six; *Shad-darsanas* or six demonstrations.

Day of Brahmâ. See "Brahmâ's Day" etc.

Demiurgic Mind. The same as "Universal Mind". Mahat, the first "product" of Brahmâ, or himself.

Demiurgos (*Gr*) The Demiurge or Artificer; the Supernal Power which built the universe. Freemasons derive from this word their phrase of "Supreme Architect ". With the Occultists it is the third manifested Logos, or Plato's "second god", the second logos being represented by him as the "Father", the only Deity that he dared mention as an Initiate into the Mysteries.

Demon est Deus inversus (*Lat*) A Kabbalistic axiom; lit., "the devil is god reversed"; which means that there is neither evil nor good, but that the forces which create the one create the other, according to the nature of the materials they find to work upon.

Deva (*Sk.*). A god, a "resplendent" deity. Deva-Deus, from the root *div* "to shine". A Deva is a celestial being – whether good, bad, or indifferent. Devas inhabit "the three worlds", which are the *three planes* above us. There are 33 groups or 330 millions of them.

Deva Sarga (*Sk.*). Creation: the origin of the principles, said to be Intelligence born of the qualities or the attributes of nature.

Devachan (*Sk.*). The "dwelling of the gods". A state intermediate between two earth-lives, into which the EGO (Atmâ-Buddhi-Manas, or the Trinity made One) enters, after its separation from Kâma Rupa, and the disintegration of the lower principles on earth.

Devajnânas (*Sk.*). or *Daivajna*. The higher classes of celestial beings, those who possess divine knowledge.

Deva-lôkas (*Sk.*). The abodes of the Gods or Devas in superior spheres. The seven celestial worlds above Meru.

Devamâtri (*Sk.*). Lit., "the mother of the gods". A title of Aditi, Mystic Space.

Dhârana (*Sk*). That state in Yoga practice when the mind has to be fixed unflinchingly on some object of meditation.

Dhâranî (*Sk.*). In Buddhism—both Southern and Northern—and also in Hinduism, it means simply a *mantra* or *mantras*—sacred verses from the *Rig Veda*. In days of old these mantras or Dhâranî were all considered mystical and practically efficacious in their use. At present, however, it is the Yogâchârya school alone which proves the claim in practice. When chanted according to given instructions a **Dhâranî** produces wonderful effects. Its occult power, however, does not reside in the *words* but in the inflexion or accent given and the resulting sound originated thereby. (See "Mantra" and "Akasa").

Dharma (*Sk.*). The sacred Law; the Buddhist Canon.

Dharmachakra (*Sk.*). Lit., The turning of the "wheel of the Law". The emblem of Buddhism as a system of cycles and rebirths or reincarnations.

Dharmakâya (*Sk*). Lit., "the glorified spiritual body" called the "Vesture of Bliss". The third, or highest of the *Trikâya* (Three Bodies), the attribute developed by every "Buddha", i.e., every initiate who has crossed or reached the end of what is called the "fourth Path" (in esotericism the sixth "portal" prior to his entry on the seventh). The highest of the *Trikâya*, it is the *fourth* of the *Buddhakchêtra*, or Buddhic planes of consciousness, represented figuratively in Buddhist asceticism as a robe or vesture of luminous Spirituality. In popular Northern Buddhism these vestures or robes are: (1) Nirmanakâya (2) Sambhogakâya (3) and Dharmakâya the last being the highest and most sublimated of all, as it places the ascetic on the threshold of Nirvâna. (See, however, the *Voice of the Silence,* page 96, *Glossary,* for the true *esoteric* meaning.)

Dhyan Chohans (*Sk*). Lit., "The Lords of Light". The highest gods, answering to the Roman Catholic Archangels. The divine Intelligences charged with the supervision of Kosmos.

Dhyâna (*Sk.*). In Buddhism one of the six Paramitas of perfection, a state of abstraction which carries the ascetic practising it far above this plane of sensuous perception and out of the world of matter. Lit., "contemplation". The six stages of Dhyan differ only in the degrees of abstraction of the personal Ego from sensuous life.

Dhyani Bodhisattyas (*Sk.*). In Buddhism, the five sons of the Dhyani-Buddhas. They have a mystic meaning in Esoteric Philosophy.

Dhyani Buddhas (*Sk.*). They "of the Merciful Heart"; worshipped especially in Nepaul. These have again a secret meaning.

Dianoia (*Gr.*). The same as the Logos. The eternal source of thought, "divine ideation", which is the root of all thought. (See "Ennoia.")

Djnâna (*Sk*), or *Jnâna.* Lit., Knowledge; esoterically, "supernal or divine knowledge acquired by Yoga". Written also *Gnyana.*

Drakôn (*Gr.*) or Dragon. Now considered a "mythical" monster, perpetuated in the West only on seals,. &c., as a heraldic griffin, and the Devil slain by St. George, &c. In fact an extinct antediluvian monster In Babylonian antiquities it is referred to as the "scaly one" and connected on many gems with Tiamat the sea. "The Dragon of the Sea" is repeatedly mentioned. In Egypt, it is the star of the Dragon (then the North Pole Star), the origin of the connection of almost all the gods with the Dragon. Bel and the Dragon, Apollo and Python, Osiris and Typhon, Sigur and Fafnir, and finally St. George and the Dragon, are the same. They were all solar gods, and wherever we find the Sun there also is the Dragon, the symbol of Wisdom—Thoth-Hermes. The Hierophants of Egypt and of Babylon styled themselves "Sons of the Serpent-God" and "Sons of the Dragon". "I am a Serpent, I am a Druid", said the Druid of the Celto-Britannic regions, for the Serpent and the Dragon were both types of Wisdom, Immortality and Rebirth. As the serpent casts its old skin only to reappear in a new one, so does the immortal Ego cast off one personality but to assume another.

Dwapara Yuga (*Sk.*). The third of the "Four Ages" in Hindu Philosophy; or the second age counted from below.

Dynasties. In India there are two, the Lunar and the Solar, or the *Somavansa* and the *Suryavansa*. In Chaldea and Egypt there were also two distinct kinds of dynasties, the *divine* and the *human*. In both countries people were ruled in the beginning of time by Dynasties of Gods. In Chaldea they reigned one hundred and twenty Sari, or in all 432,000 years; which amounts to the same figures as a Hindu Mahayuga 4,320,000 years. The chronology prefacing the *Book of Genesis* (English translation) is given "Before Christ, 4004". But the figures are a rendering by solar years. In the original Hebrew, which preserved a lunar calculation, the figures are 4,320 years. This "coincidence" is well explained in Occultism.

Dzyan or Dzyn (*Tib.*). Written also *Dzen*. A corruption of the Sanskrit Dhyan and *jnâna* (or *gnyâna* phonetically) – Wisdom, divine knowledge. In Tibetan, learning is called *dzin*.

E

Ego (*Lat.*). " Self" ; the consciousness in man "I am I" – or the feeling of "I-am-ship". Esoteric philosophy teaches the existence of two Egos in man, the mortal or personal, and the Higher, the Divine and the Impersonal, calling the former "personality" and the latter "Individuality Egoity. From the word "Ego". Egoity means "individuality", never "personality", and is the opposite of egoism or "selfishness", the characteristic par excellence of the latter.

Elementals. Spirits of the Elements. The creatures evolved in the four Kingdoms or Elements – earth, air, fire, and water. They are called by the Kabbalists, Gnomes (of the earth), Sylphs (of the air), Salamanders (of the fire), and Undines (of the water). Except a few of the higher kinds, and their rulers, they are rather forces of nature than ethereal men and women. These forces, as the servile agents of the Occultists, may produce various effects; but if employed by" Elementaries" (*q.v.*)_in which case they enslave the mediums – they will deceive the credulous. All the lower invisible beings generated on the 5th 6th, and 7th planes of our terrestrial atmosphere, are called Elementals Peris, Devs,

Djins, Sylvans, Satyrs, Fauns, Elves, Dwarfs, Trolls, Kobolds, Brownies, Nixies, Goblins, Pinkies, Banshees, Moss People, White Ladies, Spooks, Fairies, etc., etc., etc.

Elementaries. Properly, the disembodied souls of the depraved; these souls having at some time prior to death separated from themselves their divine spirits, and so lost their chance for immortality; but at the present stage of learning it has been thought best to apply the term to the spooks or phantoms of disembodied persons, in general, to those whose temporary habitation is the Kâma Loka. Eliphas Lévi and some other Kabbalists make little distinction between elementary spirits who have been men, and those beings which people the elements, and are the blind forces of nature. Once divorced from their higher triads and their bodies, these souls remain in their *Kâma-rupic* envelopes, and are irresistibly drawn to the earth amid elements congenial to their gross natures. Their stay in the Kâma Loka varies as to its duration; but ends invariably in disintegration, dissolving like a column of mist, atom by atom, in the surrounding elements.

Elohîm (*Heb.*). Also *Alhim*, the word being variously spelled. Godfrey Higgins, who has written much upon its meaning, always spells it *Aleim*. The Hebrew letters are *aleph, lamed, hé,yod, mem,* and are numerically 1, 30, 5, 10, 40 = 86. It seems to be the plural of the feminine noun *Eloah*, ALH, formed by adding the common plural form IM, a masculine ending; and hence the whole seems to imply the emitted active and passive essences. As a title it is referred to "Binah" the Supernal Mother, as is also the fuller title IHVH ALHIM, Jehovah Elohim. As Binah leads on to seven succeedent Emanations, so " Elohim" has been said to represent a sevenfold power of godhead. [w.w. w.]

Emanation *the Doctrine of.* In its metaphysical meaning, it is opposed to Evolution, yet one with it. Science teaches that evolution is physiologically a mode of generation in which the germ that develops the foetus pre-exists already in the parent, the development and final form and characteristics of that germ being accomplished in nature; and that in cosmology the process takes place blindly through the correlation of the elements, and their various compounds. Occultism answers that this is only the **apparent** mode, the real process being Emanation, guided by intelligent Forces under an immutable LAW. Therefore, while the Occultists and Theosophists believe thoroughly in the doctrine of Evolution as given out by Kapila and Manu, they are *Emanationists* rather than *Evolutionists*. The doctrine of Emanation was at one time universal. It was taught by the Alexandrian as well as by the Indian philosophers, by the Egyptian, the Chaldean and Hellenic Hierophants, and also by the Hebrews (in their Kabbala, and even in *Genesis).* For it is only owing to deliberate mistranslation that the Hebrew word asdt has been translated "angels" from the Septuagint, when it means *Emanations, Æons,* precisely as with the Gnostics. Indeed, in

Deuteronomy (xxxiii., 2) the word *asdt* or *ashdt* is translated as" fiery law", whilst the correct rendering of the passage should be "from his right hand went [not a fiery law, but a fire according to law "; viz., that the fire of one flame is imparted to, and caught up by another like as in a trail of inflammable substance. This is precisely emanation. As shown in Isis Unveiled : "In Evolution, as it is now beginning to he understood, there is supposed to be in all matter an impulse to take on a higher form – a supposition clearly expressed by Manu and other Hindu philosophers of the highest antiquity. The philosopher's tree illustrates it in the case of the zinc solution. The controversy between the followers of this school and the Emanationists may he briefly stated thus The Evolutionist stops all inquiry at the borders of ' the Unknowable "; the Emanationist believes that nothing can be evolved – or, as the word means, unwombed or born – except it has first been involved, thus indicating that life is from a spiritual potency above the whole."

En (or **Ain**) **Soph** (*Heb.*). The endless, limitless and boundless. The absolute deific Principle, impersonal and unknowable. It means literally "no-thing" i.e., nothing that could be classed with anything else. The word and ideas are equivalent to the Vedantic conceptions of Parabrahmn. [w.w.w.]

Some Western Kabbalists, however, contrive to make of IT, a personal "He", a male deity instead of an impersonal deity.

Epimetheus (*Gr.*). Lit., "He who takes counsel *after*" the event. A brother of Prometheus in Greek Mythology.

Epinoia (*Gr.*). Thought, invention, design. A name adopted by the Gnostics for the first passive Æon.

Eros (*Gr.*). Hesiod makes of the god Eros the third personage of the Hellenic primordial Trinity composed of Ouranos, Gæa and Eros. It is the personified procreative Force in nature in its abstract sense, the propeller to "creation" and procreation. Exoterically, mythology makes of Eros the god of lustful, animal desire, whence the term *erotic* esoterically, it is different. (See " Kâma".)

Esoteric (*Gr.*). Hidden, secret. From the Greek *esotericos*, "inner" concealed.

Esoteric Bodhism. Secret wisdom or intelligence from the Greek *esotericos* "inner", and the Sanskrit *Bodhi*, "knowledge", intelligence – in contradistinction to *Buddhi*, "the *faculty* of knowledge or intelligence" and *Buddhism*, the philosophy or Law of Buddha (the Enlightened). Also written " Budhism", from *Budha* (Intelligence and Wisdom) the Son of Soma.

Ether. Students are but too apt to confuse this with Akâsa and with Astral Light. It is neither, in the sense in which ether is described by physical Science. Ether is a material agent, though hitherto undetected by any physical apparatus;

whereas Akâsa is a distinctly spiritual agent, identical, in one sense, with the Anima Mundi, while the Astral Light is only the seventh and highest principle of the terrestrial atmosphere, as undetectable as Akâsa and real Ether, because it is something quite on another plane. The seventh principle of the earth's atmosphere, as said, the Astral Light, is only the second on the Cosmic scale. The scale of Cosmic Forces, Principles and Planes, of Emanations – on the metaphysical – and Evolutions – on the physical plane – is the Cosmic Serpent biting its own tail, the Serpent reflecting the Higher, and reflected in its turn by the lower Serpent. The Caduceus explains the mystery, and the four-fold Dodecahedron on the model of which the universe is said by Plato to have been built by the manifested Logos – synthesized by the unmanifested First-Born – yields geometrically the key to Cosmogony and its microcosmic reflection – our Earth.

Evolution. The development of higher orders of animals from lower. As said in *Isis Unveiled*: "Modern Science holds but to a one-sided physical evolution, prudently avoiding and ignoring the higher or spiritual evolution, which would force our contemporaries to confess the superiority of the ancient philosophers and psychologists over themselves. The ancient sages, ascending to the UNKNOWABLE, made their starting- point from the first manifestation of the unseen, the unavoidable, and, from a strictly logical reasoning, the absolutely necessary creative Being, the Demiurgos of the universe. Evolution began with them from pure spirit, which descending lower and lower down, assumed at last a visible and comprehensible form, and became matter. Arrived at this point, they speculated in the Darwinian method, but on a far more large and comprehensive basis." (See "Emanation".)

Exoteric. Outward, public; the opposite of esoteric or hidden.

F

First Point. Metaphysically the first point of manifestation, the germ of primeval differentiation, or the point in the infinite Circle "whose centre is everywhere, and circumference nowhere". The Point is the Logos.

Fire (*Living*). A figure of speech to denote deity, the "One" life. A theurgic term, used later by the Rosicrucians. The symbol of the *living fire* is the sun, *certain of whose rays develope the fire of life in a diseased body, impart the knowledge of the future* to the sluggish mind, and stimulate to active function a certain psychic and generally dormant faculty in man. The meaning is very occult.

Fohat (*Tib.*). A term used to represent the active (male) potency of the Sakti (female reproductive power) in nature. The essence of cosmic electricity. An occult Tibetan term for *Daiviprakriti* primordial light: and in the universe of manifestation the ever-present electrical energy and ceaseless destructive and formative power. Esoterically, it is the same, Fohat being the universal propelling Vital Force, at once the propeller and the resultant.

G

Gautama (*Sk.*) The Prince of Kapilavastu, son of Sudhôdana, the Sâkya king of a small realm on the borders of Nepaul, born in the seventh century B.c., now called the "Saviour of the World". Gautama or Gôtama was the sacerdotal name of the Sâkya family, and Sidhârtha was Buddha's name before he became a Buddha. Sâkya Muni, means the Saint of the Sâkya family. Born a simple mortal he rose to Buddhaship through his own personal and unaided merit. A man—verily greater than any god!

Gayâtri (*Sk.*) also *Sâvitri*. A most sacred verse, addressed to the Sun, in the Rig -Veda, which the Brahmans have to repeat mentally every morn and eve during their devotions.

Genii (*Lat.*) A name for Æons, or angels, with the Gnostics. The names of their hierarchies and classes are simply legion.

Gnâna (*Sk.*) Knowledge as applied to the esoteric sciences.

Gnân Devas (*Sk.*) Lit., "the gods of knowledge". The higher classes of gods or devas; the "mind-born" sons of Brahmâ, and others including the Manasa-putras (the Sons of Intellect). Esoterically, our reincarnating Egos.

Gnânasakti (*Sk.*) The power of true knowledge, one of the seven great forces in Nature (*six,* exoterically).

Gnôsis (*Gr.*) Lit., "knowledge". The technical term used by the schools of religious philosophy, both before and during the first centuries of so-called Christianity, to denote the object of their enquiry. This Spiritual and Sacred Knowledge, the *Gupta Vidya* of the Hindus, could only be obtained by Initiation into Spiritual Mysteries of which the ceremonial "Mysteries" were a type.

Gnostics (*Gr.*) The philosophers who formulated and taught the Gnôsis or Knowledge (*q.v.*). They flourished in the first three centuries of the Christian era: the following were eminent, Valentinus, Basilides, Marcion, Simon Magus, etc. [w.w. w.]

Golden Age. The ancients divided the life cycle into the Golden, Silver, Bronze and Iron Ages. The Golden was an age of primeval purity, simplicity and general happiness.

Great Age. There were several "great ages" mentioned by the ancients. In India it embraced the whole Maha-manvantara, the "age of Brahmâ", each "Day" of which represents the life cycle of a chain – i.e. it embraces a period of seven Rounds. (See *Esoteric Buddhism*, by A. P. Sinnett.) Thus while a "Day" and a "Night" represent, as Manvantara and Pralaya, 8,640,000,000 years, an "age" lasts through a period of 311,040,000,000,000 years; after which the Pralaya, or dissolution of the universe, becomes universal. With the Egyptians and Greeks the "great age" referred only to the tropical or sidereal year, the duration of which is 25,868 solar years. Of the complete age – that of the gods – they say nothing, as it was a matter to he discussed and divulged only in the Mysteries, during the initiating ceremonies. The "great age" of the Chaldees was the same in figures as that of the Hindus.

Grihastha (*Sk.*) Lit., "a householder", "one who lives in a house with his family". A Brahman " family priest" in popular rendering, and the sarcerdotal hierarchy of the Hindus.

Guardian Wall. A suggestive name given to the host of translated adepts (Narjols) or the Saints collectively, who are supposed to watch over, help and protect Humanity. This is the so-called "Nirmanâkâya" doctrine in Northern mystic Buddhism. (See *Voice of the Silence*, Part III.)

Guhya Vidyâ(*Sk.*) The secret knowledge of mystic Mantras.

Gunas (*Sk*) Qualities, attributes (See" Triguna") ; a thread, also a cord.

Gupta Vidyâ (*Sk.*) The same as Guhya Vidyâ; Esoteric or Secret Science; knowledge.

Guru (*Sk.*) Spiritual Teacher; a master in metaphysical and ethical doctrines; used also for a teacher of any science.

Guru Deva (*Sk.*) Lit., "divine Master".

H

Hatha Yoga (*Sk.*) The lower form of Yoga practice; one which uses physical means for purposes of spiritual self-development The opposite of *Râja Yoga*.

Hermaphrodite (*Gr.*). Dual-sexed; a male and female Being, whether man or animal.

Hermes Trismegistus (*Gr.*). The "thrice great Hermes", the Egyptian. The mythical personage after whom the Hermetic philosophy was named. In Egypt the God Thoth or Thot. A generic name of many ancient Greek writers on philosophy and Alchemy. Hermes Trismegistus is the name of Hermes or Thoth in his human aspect, as a god he is far more than this. As *Hermes-Thoth-Aah*, he is Thoth, the moon, i.e., his symbol is the bright side of the moon, supposed to contain the essence of creative Wisdom, "the elixir of Hermes ". As such he is associated with the Cynocephalus, the dog-headed monkey, for the same reason as was Anubis, one of the aspects of Thoth. (See " Hermanubis".)

The same idea underlies the form of the Hindu God of Wisdom, the elephant-headed Ganesa, or Ganpat, the son of Parvati and Siva. (See "Ganesa".) When he has the head of an *ibis*, he is the sacred scribe of the gods; but even then he wears the crown *atef* and the lunar disk. He is the most mysterious of gods. As a serpent, Hermes Thoth is the divine creative 'Wisdom. The Church Fathers speak at length of Thoth-Hermes. (See "Hermetic".)

Hermetic. Any doctrine or writing connected with the esoteric teachings of Hermes, who, whether as the Egyptian Thoth or the Greek Hermes, was the God of Wisdom with the Ancients, and, according to Plato, "discovered numbers, geometry, astronomy and letters". Though mostly considered as spurious, nevertheless the Hermetic writings were highly prized by St. Augustine, Lactantius, Cyril and others. In the words of Mr. J. Bonwick, " They are more or less touched up by the Platonic philosophers among the early Christians (such as Origen and Clemens Alexandrinus) who sought to substantiate their Christian arguments by appeals to these heathen and revered writings, though they could not resist the temptation of making them say a little too much. Though represented by some clever and interested writers as teaching pure monotheism, the Hermetic or Trismegistic books are, nevertheless, purely pantheistic. The Deity referred to in them is defined by Paul as that in *which* "we live, and move and have our being" – notwithstanding the "in Him" of the translators.

Hierophant. From the Greek "Hierophantes"; literally, "One who explains sacred things ". The discloser of sacred learning and the Chief of the Initiates. A title belonging to the highest Adepts in the temples of antiquity, who were the teachers and expounders of the Mysteries and the Initiators into the final great Mysteries. The Hierophant represented the Demiurge, and explained to the postulants for Initiation the various phenomena of Creation that were produced for their tuition. " He was the sole expounder of the esoteric secrets and doctrines. It was forbidden even to pronounce his name before an uninitiated person. He sat in the East, and wore as a symbol of authority a golden globe suspended from the neck. He was also called *Mystagogus*" (Kenneth R. H. Mackenzie, ix., F.T.S., in *The Royal Masonic cyclopædia*). In Hebrew and Chaldaic the term was *Peter*, the opener, discloser; hence the Pope as the successor of the hierophant of the ancient Mysteries, sits in the Pagan chair of St. Peter.

Higher Self. The Supreme Divine Spirit overshadowing man. The crown of the upper spiritual Triad in man – Atmân.

Hochmah (*Heb*.). See "Chochmah".

Hotri (*Sk*.). A priest who recites the hymns from the *Rig Veda*, and makes oblations to the fire.

Hotris (*Sk*). A symbolical name for the *seven* senses called, in the *Anugita* "the Seven Priests". "The senses supply the fire of mind (i.e., desire) with the oblations of external pleasures." An occult term used metaphysically.

Humanity. Occultly and Kabbalistically, the whole of mankind is symbolised, by Manu in India; by Vajrasattva or Dorjesempa, the head of the Seven Dhyani, in Northern Buddhism; and by Adam Kadmon in the Kabbala. All these represent the totality of mankind whose beginning is in this androgynic protoplast, and whose end is in the Absolute, beyond all these symbols and myths of human origin. Humanity is a great Brotherhood by virtue of the sameness of the material from which it is formed physically and morally. Unless, however, it becomes a Brotherhood also intellectually, it is no better than a superior genus of animals.

I

Ichchha (*Sk.*). Will, or will-power.

Ichchha Sakti (*Sk.*). Will-power; force of desire; one of the occult Forces of nature. That power of the will which, exercised in occult practices, generates the nerve-currents necessary to set certain muscles in motion and to paralyze certain others.

Illusion. In Occultism everything finite (like the universe and all in it) is called illusion or *maya*.

Illuminati (*Lat.*). The "Enlightened", the initiated adepts.

Image. Occultism permits no other image than that of the living image of divine man (the symbol of Humanity) on earth. The *Kabbala* teaches that this divine Image, the copy of the *sublime and holy upper Image* (the Elohim) has now changed into *another similitude*, owing to the development of men's sinful nature. It is only the *upper divine Image* (the Ego) which is the same; the lower (personality) has changed, and man, now fearing the wild beasts, has grown to bear on his face the similitude of many of them. (*Zohar* I. fol. 71a.) In the early period of Egypt there were no images; but later, as Lenormand says, "In the sanctuaries of Egypt they divided the properties of nature and consequently of Divinity (the Elohim, or the Egos), into seven abstract qualities, characterised each by an emblem, which are matter, cohesion, fluxion, coagulation, accumulation, station and division ". These were all attributes symbolized in various images.

Incarnations (*Divine*) or *Avatars*. The Immaculate Conception is as pre-eminently Egyptian as it is Indian. As the author of *Egyptian Belief* has it: "It is not the vulgar, coarse and sensual story as in Greek mythology, but refined, moral and spiritual "; and again the incarnation idea was found revealed on the wall of a Theban temple by Samuel Sharpe, who thus analyzes it: "First the god Thoth . . . as the messenger of the gods, like the Mercury of the Greeks (or the Gabriel of the first Gospel), tells the *maiden* queen Mautmes, that she is to give birth to a son, who is to be king Amunotaph III. Secondly, the god Kneph, the Spirit . . . . and the goddess Hathor (Nature) both take hold of the queen by the hands and put into her mouth the character for life, a cross, which is to be the life of the coming child", etc., etc. Truly divine incarnation, or the *avatar* doctrine, constituted the grandest mystery of every old religious system!

Individuality. One of the names given in Theosophy and Occultism to the Human Higher EGO. We make a distinction between the immortal and divine Ego, and the mortal human Ego which perishes. The latter, or "personality" (personal Ego) survives the dead body only for a time in the Kama Loka; the Individuality prevails forever.

Initiate. From the Latin *Initiatus.* The designation of anyone who was received into and had revealed to him the mysteries and secrets of either Masonry or Occultism. In times of antiquity, those who had been initiated into the arcane knowledge taught by the Hierophants of the Mysteries; and in our modern days those who have been initiated by the adepts of mystic lore into the mysterious knowledge, which, notwithstanding the lapse of ages, has yet a few real votaries on earth.

Initiation. From the same root as the Latin *initia,* which means the basic or first principles of any Science. The practice of initiation or admission into the sacred Mysteries, taught by the Hierophants and learned priests of the Temples, is one of the most ancient customs. This was practised in every old national religion. In Europe it was abolished with the fall of the last pagan temple. There exists at present but one kind of initiation known to the public, namely that into the Masonic rites. Masonry, however, has no more secrets to give out or conceal. In the palmy days of old, the Mysteries, according to the greatest Greek and Roman philosophers, were the most sacred of all solemnities as well as the most beneficent, and greatly promoted virtue. The Mysteries represented the passage from mortal life into finite death, and the experiences of the disembodied Spirit and Soul in the world of subjectivity. In our own day, as the secret is lost, the candidate passes through sundry meaningless ceremonies and is initiated into the solar allegory of Hiram Abiff, the "Widow's Son".

Inner Man. An occult term, used to designate the true and immortal Entity in us, not the outward and mortal form of clay that we call our body. The term applies, strictly speaking, only to the Higher Ego, the "astral man" being the appellation of the Double and of Kâma Rupa (*q.v.*) or the surviving *eidolon*.

Intercosmic gods. The Planetary Spirits, Dhyan-Chohans, Devas of various degrees of spirituality, and "Archangels" in general.

Isis. In Egyptian *Issa,* the goddess Virgin-Mother; personified nature. In Egyptian or Koptic *Uasari,* the female reflection of *Uasar* or Osiris. She is the "woman clothed with the sun" of the land of Chemi. Isis Latona is the Roman Isis.

Iswara *(Sk.).* The "Lord" or the personal god – *divine Spirit in man. Lit.,* sovereign (independent) existence. A title given to Siva and other gods in India. Siva is also called Iswaradeva, or sovereign deva.

J

Jhâna *(Sk.)* or *Jnana.* Knowledge; Occult Wisdom.

Jiva *(Sk.).* Life, as the Absolute; the Monad also or "Atma-Buddhi".

Jivanmukta *(Sk.).* An adept or yogi who has reached the ultimate state of holiness, and separated himself from matter; a Mahatma, or *Nirvânee,* a "dweller in bliss" and emancipation. Virtually one who has reached Nirvâna during life.

Jivatma *(Sk.).* The ONE universal life, generally; but also the divine Spirit in Man.

Jnânam *(Sk.).* The same as "Gnâna", etc., the same as "Jhâna" *(q.v.).*

Jnânendriyas *(Sk.).* The five channels of knowledge.

Jnâna Sakti *(Sk.).* The power of intellect.

K

Kadmon *(Heb.).* Archetypal man. See."Adam Kadmon".

Kaliyuga *(Sk.).* The fourth, the black or iron age, our present period, the duration of which us 432,000 years. The last of the ages into which the evolutionary period of man is divided by a series of such ages. It began 3,102 years B.C. at the moment of Krishna's death, and the first cycle of 5,000 years will end between the years 1897 and 1898.

Kalpa *(Sk.).* The period of a mundane revolution, generally a cycle of time, but usually, it represents a "day" and "night" of Brahmâ, a period of 4,320,000,000 years.

Kama *(Sk.)* Evil desire, lust, volition; the cleaving to existence. Kama is generally identified with *Mara* the tempter.

Kamadeva *(Sk.).* In the popular notions the god of love, a Visva-deva, in the Hindu Pantheon. As the *Eros* of Hesiod, degraded into Cupid by exoteric law, and still more degraded by a later popular sense attributed to the term, so is Kama a most mysterious and metaphysical subject. The earlier Vedic description of Kama alone gives the key-note to what he emblematizes. Kama is the first conscious, *all embracing desire* for universal good, love, and for all that lives and feels, needs help and kindness, the first feeling of infinite tender compassion and mercy that arose in the consciousness of the creative ONE Force, as soon as it came into life and being as a ray from the ABSOLUTE. Says the *Rig Veda*, "Desire first arose in IT, which was the primal germ of mind, and which Sages, searching with their intellect, have discovered in their heart to be the bond which connects Entity with non-Entity", or *Manas* with pure *Atma-Buddhi*. There is no idea of sexual love in the conception. Kama is pre-eminently the divine desire of creating happiness and love; and it is only ages later, as mankind began to materialize by anthropomorphization its grandest ideals into cut and dried dogmas, that Kama became the power that gratifies desire on the animal plane. This is shown by what every *Veda* and some *Brahmanas* say. In the *Atharva Veda*, Kama is represented as the Supreme Deity and Creator. In the Taitarîya Brahmana, he is the child of Dharma, the god of Law and Justice, of Sraddha and faith. In another account he springs from the heart of Brahmâ. Others show him born from water, i.e., from primordial chaos, or the "Deep". Hence one of his many names, *Irâ-ja*, "the water-born"; and *Aja*, "unborn" ; and *Atmabhu* or "Self-existent". Because of the sign of *Makara* (Capricornus) on his banner, he is also called " Makara Ketu". The allegory about Siva, the "Great Yogin ", reducing Kama to ashes by the fire from his *central* (or third) *Eye*, for inspiring the Mahadeva with thoughts of his wife, while he was at his devotions – is very suggestive, as it is said that he thereby reduced Kama to his primeval spiritual form.

Kamaloka *(Sk.).* The *semi*-material plane, to us subjective and invisible, where the disembodied "personalities", the astral forms, called *Kamarupa* remain, until they fade out from it by the complete exhaustion of the effects of the mental impulses that created these eidolons of human and animal passions and desires; (See "Kamarupa".) It is the Hades of the ancient Greeks and the Amenti of the Egyptians, the land of Silent Shadows; a division of the first group of the *Trailôkya*. (See "Kamadhâtu".)

Kamarupa *(Sk.).* Metaphysically, and in our esoteric philosophy, it is the subjective form created through the mental and physical desires and thoughts in connection with things of matter, by all sentient beings, a form which survives the death of their bodies. After that death three of the seven "principles" – or let us say planes of senses and consciousness on which the human instincts and ideation act in turn – viz., the body, its astral prototype and physical vitality, – being of no further use, remain on earth; the three higher principles, grouped into one, merge into the state of Devachan *(q.v.)*, in which state the Higher Ego will remain until the hour for a new reincarnation arrives; and the *eidolon* of the ex-Personality is left alone in its new abode. Here, the pale copy of the man that was, vegetates for a period of time, the duration of which is variable and according to the element of materiality which is left in it, and which is determined by the past life of the defunct. Bereft as it is of its higher mind, spirit and physical senses, if left alone to its own senseless devices, it will gradually fade out and disintegrate. But, if forcibly drawn back into the terrestrial sphere whether by the passionate desires and appeals of the surviving friends or by regular necromantic practices – one of the most pernicious of which is medium-ship – the "spook" may prevail for a period greatly exceeding the span of the natural life of its body. Once the Kamarupa has learnt the way back to living human bodies, it becomes a vampire, feeding on the vitality of those who are so anxious for its company. In India these *eidolons* are called *Pisâchas*, and are much dreaded, as already explained elsewhere.

Kapila Rishi (*Sk.*). A great sage, a great adept of antiquity; the author of the Sankhya philosophy.

Karabtanos (*Gr.*). The spirit of blind or animal desire; the symbol of Kama-rupa. The Spirit "without sense or judgment" in the Codex of the Nazarenes. He is the symbol of matter and stands for the father of the seven spirits of concupiscence begotten by him on his mother, the "Spiritus" or the Astral Light.

Kârana (*Sk.*). Cause (metaphysically).

Kârana Sarîra (*Sk.*). The "Causal body". It is dual in its meaning. Exoterically, it is Avidya, ignorance, or that which is the cause of the evolution of a human ego and its reincarnation ; hence the lower Manas esoterically – the causal body or Kâranopadhi stands in the Taraka Raja yoga as corresponding to Buddhi and the Higher " Manas," or Spiritual Soul.

Kâranopadhi (*Sk.*). The basis or *upadhi* of Karana, the "causal soul". In Taraka Rajayoga, it corresponds with both *Manas* and *Buddhi*. See Table in the *Secret Doctrine*, Vol. I, p. 157.

Karma (*Sk.*). Physically, action: metaphysically, the LAW OF RETRIBUTION, the Law of cause and effect or Ethical Causation. Nemesis, only in one sense, that of bad Karma. It is the eleventh *Nidana* in the concatenation of causes and effects in orthodox Buddhism ; yet it is the power that controls all things, the resultant of moral action, the meta physical *Samskâra*, or the moral effect of an act committed for the attainment of something which gratifies a personal desire. There is the Karma of merit and the Karma of demerit. Karma neither punishes nor rewards, it is simply *the one* Universal LAW which guides unerringly, and, so to say, blindly, all other laws productive of certain effects along the grooves of their respective causations. When Buddhism teaches that "Karma is that moral kernel (of any being) which alone survives death and continues in transmigration ' or reincarnation, it simply means that there remains nought after each Personality but the causes produced by it ; causes which are undying, i.e., which cannot be eliminated from the Universe until replaced by their legitimate effects, and wiped out by them, so to speak, and such causes – unless compensated during the life of the person who produced them with adequate effects, will follow the reincarnated Ego, and reach it in its subsequent reincarnation until a harmony between effects and causes is fully reestablished. No "personality" – a mere bundle of material atoms and of instinctual and mental characteristics – can of course continue, as such, in the world of pure Spirit. Only that which is immortal in its very nature and divine in its essence, namely, the Ego, can exist for ever. And as it is that Ego which chooses the personality it will inform, after each Devachan, and which receives through these personalities the effects of the Karmic causes produced, it is therefore the Ego, that *self* which is the "moral kernel" referred to and embodied karma, "which alone survives death."

Kartikeya *(Sk)*, or *Kartika*. The Indian God of War, son of Siva, born of his seed fallen into the Ganges. He is also the personification of the power of the Logos. The planet Mars. Kartika is a very occult personage, a nursling of the Pleiades, and a Kumâra. (See *Secret Doctrine*.)

Kasyapa *(Sk.)*. A Vedic Sage; in the words of *Atharva Veda*, "The self-born who sprang from Time". Besides being the father of the Adityas headed by Indra, Kasyapa is also the progenitor of serpents, reptiles, birds and other walking, flying and creeping beings.

Kosmos *(Gr.)*. The Universe, as distinguished from the world, which may mean our globe or earth.

Krishna *(Sk.)*.. The most celebrated avatar of Vishnu, the "Saviour" of the Hindus and their most popular god. He is the- eighth Avatar, the son of Devaki, and the nephew of Kansa, the Indian King Herod, who while seeking for him among the shepherds and cow-herds who concealed him, slew thousands of their newly-born babes. The story of Krishna's conception, birth, and childhood are the exact prototype of the New Testament story. The missionaries, of course, try to show that the Hindus stole the story of the Nativity from the early Christians who came to India.

Krita-Yuga *(Sk.)*. The first of the four Yugas or Ages of the Brahmans; also called *Satya-Yuga*, a period lasting 1,728,000 years.

Kriyasakti (Gk.). The power of thought; one of the seven forces of Nature. Creative potency of the *Siddhis* (powers) of the full Yogis.

Kronos *(Gr.)*. Saturn. The God of Boundless Time and of the Cycles.

Kshanti (*Sk.*). Patience, one of the *Paramîtas* of perfection.

Kshetrajna or *Kshetrajneswara* (*Sk.*). Embodied spirit, the Conscious Ego in its highest manifestations; the reincarnating Principle; the "Lord" in us.

Kumâra (*Sk.*). A virgin boy, or young celibate. The first Kumâras are the seven sons of Brahmâ born out of the limbs of the god, in the so-called ninth creation. It is stated that the name was given to them owing to their formal refusal to "procreate their species", and so they "remained Yogis", as the legend says.

Kundalini Sakti (*Sk.*). The power of life; one of the Forces of Nature; that power that generates a certain light in those who sit for spiritual and clairvoyant development. It is a power known only to those who practise concentration and Yoga.

L

Lanoo (*Sk.*). A disciple, the same as "chela".

Laya or *Layam* (*Sk.*). From the root *Li* "to dissolve, to disintegrate" a point of equilibrium (*zero-point*) in physics and chemistry. In occultism, that point where substance becomes homogeneous and is unable to act or differentiate.

Lha (*Tib.*). Spirits of the highest spheres, whence the name of Lhassa, the residence of the Dalaï-Lama. The title of Lha is often given in Tibet to some *Narjols* (Saints and Yogi adepts) who have attained great occult powers.

Lhamayin (*Tib.*). Elemental sprites of the lower terrestrial plane. Popular fancy makes of them demons and devils.

Linga or *Lingam* (*Sk.*). A sign or a symbol of abstract creation. Force becomes the organ of procreation only on this earth. In India there are 12 great Lingams of Siva, some of which are on mountains and rocks, and also in temples. Such is the *Kedâresa* in the Himalaya, a huge and shapeless mass of rock. In its origin the Lingam had never the gross meaning connected with the phallus, an idea which is altogether of a later date. The symbol in India has the same meaning which it had in Egypt, which is simply that the creative or procreative Force is divine. It also denotes who was the dual Creator – male and female, Siva and his Sakti. The gross and immodest idea connected with the phallus is not Indian but Greek and pre-eminently Jewish. The Biblical *Bethels* were real priapic stones, the " Beth-el" (phallus) wherein God dwells. The same symbol was concealed within the ark of the Covenant, the "Holy of Holies". Therefore the "Lingam" even as a phallus is not "a symbol of Siva" only, but that of every "Creator" or creative god in every nation, including the Israelites and their "God of Abraham and Jacob".

Linga Purâna (*Sk*.). A scripture of the Saivas or worshippers of Siva. Therein *Maheswara*, "the great Lord", concealed in the Agni Linga explains the ethics of life – duty, virtue, self-sacrifice and finally liberation by and through ascetic life at the end of the *Agni Kalpa* (the Seventh Round). As Professor Wilson justly observed "the Spirit of the worship (phallic) is as little influenced by the character of the type as can well be imagined. *There is nothing like the phallic orgies of antiquity; it is all mystical and spiritual.*"

Linga Sharîra (*Sk*.). The "body", i.e., the aerial symbol of the body. This term designates the *döppelganger* or the "astral body" of man or animal. It is the *eidolon* of the Greeks, the vital and *prototypal* body; the reflection of the men of flesh. It is born *before* and dies or fades out, with the disappearance of the last atom of the body.

Lipikas (*Sk*.). The celestial recorders, the "Scribes", those who record every word and deed, said or done by man while on this earth. As Occultism teaches, they are the agents of KARMA – the retributive Law.

Logos (*Gr*.). The manifested deity with every nation and people; the outward expression, or the effect of the cause which is ever concealed. Thus, speech is the Logos of thought; hence it is aptly translated by the "Verbum" and "Word" in its metaphysical sense.

Loka (*Sk*.). A region or circumscribed place. In metaphysics, a world or sphere or plane. The Purânas in India speak incessantly of seven and fourteen Lokas, above, and below our earth; of heavens and hells.

Lotus (*Gr*.). A most occult plant, sacred in Egypt, India and else where; called "the child of the Universe bearing the likeness of its mother in its bosom". There was a time "when the world was a golden lotus" (*padma*) says the allegory. A great variety of these plants, from the majestic Indian lotus, down to the marsh-lotus (bird's foot trefoil) and the Grecian "Dioscoridis", is eaten at Crete and other islands. It is a species of nymphala, first introduced from India to Egypt to which it was-not indigenous. See the text of *Archaic Symbolism* in the Appendix Viii. "The Lotus, as a Universal Symbol".

Lucifer (*Lat*.). The planet Venus, as the bright "Morning Star". Before Milton, Lucifer had never been a name of the Devil. Quite the reverse, since the Christian Saviour is made to say of himself in *Revelations* (xvi. 22.) "I am . . . the bright morning star" or Lucifer. One of the early Popes of Rome bore that name; and there was even a Christian sect in the fourth century which was called the *Luciferians*.

Lunar Pitris (Gods). Called in India the Fathers, "Pitris" or the lunar ancestors. They are subdivided, like the rest, into seven classes or Hierarchies, In Egypt although the moon received less worship than in Chaldea or India, still

Isis stands as the representative of Luna-Lunus, "the celestial Hermaphrodite". Strange enough while the modern connect the moon only with lunacy and generation, the ancient nations, who knew better, have, individually and collectively, connected their "wisdom gods" with it. Thus in Egypt the lunar gods are Thoth-Hermes and Chons; in India it is Budha, the Son of *Soma*, the moon; in Chaldea Nebo is the lunar god of Secret Wisdom, etc., etc. The wife of Thoth, *Sifix*, the lunar goddess, holds a pole with five rays or the five-pointed star, symbol of man, the Microcosm, in distinction from the Septenary Macrocosm. As in all theogonies a goddess precedes a god, on the principle most likely that the chick can hardly precede its egg, in Chaldea the moon was held as older and more venerable than the Sun, because, as they said, darkness precedes light at every periodical rebirth (or "creation") of the universe. Osiris although connected with the Sun and a Solar god is, nevertheless, born on Mount *Sinai*, because *Sin* is the Chaldeo-Assyrian word for the moon; so was Dio-Nysos, god of Nyssi or *Nisi*, which latter appelation was that of Sinai in Egypt, where it was called Mount Nissa. The *crescent* is not – as proven by many writers – an ensign of the Turks, but was adopted by Christians for their symbol before the Mahommedans. For ages the crescent was the emblem of the Chaldean Astarte, the Egyptian Isis, and the Greek Diana, all of them Queens of Heaven, and finally became the emblem of Mary the Virgin. "The Greek Christian Empire of Constantinople held it as their palladium. Upon the conquest by the Turks, the Sultan adopted it . . . and since that, the crescent has been made to oppose the idea of the *cross*". (*Eg. Belief.*)

M

Macrocosm (*Gr.*). The "Great Universe" literally, or Kosmos.

Macroprosopus (*Gr.*). A Kabalistic term, made of a compound Greek word: meaning the Vast or Great Countenance (See "Kabalistic Faces"); a title of Kether, the Crown, the highest Sephira. It is the name of the Universe, called *Arikh-Anpin*, the totality of that of which Microprosopus or *Zauir-Anpin* "the lesser countenance", is the part and antithesis. In its high or abstract metaphysical sense, Microprosopus is Adam Kadmon, the *vehicle of Ain-Suph*, and the crown of the Sephirothal Tree, though since Sephira and Adam Kadmon are in fact one under two aspects, it comes to the same thing. Interpretations are many, and they differ.

Madhyama (*Sk.*). Used of something beginningless and endless. Thus Vâch (Sound, the female Logos, or the female counterpart of Brahmâ is said to exist in several states, one of which is that of *Mâdhyama*, which is equivalent to saying that Vâch is *eternal* in one sense "the Word (Vâch) was with God, and *in* God", for the two are one.

Mâdhyamikas (Sk.). A sect mentioned in the *Vishnu Purâna*. Agreeably to the Orientalists, a "Buddhist sect, which is an anachronism. It was probably at first a sect of Hindu atheists. A later school of that name, teaching a system of sophistic nihilism, that reduces every proposition into a thesis and its antithesis, and then denies both, has been started in Tibet and China. It adopts a few principles of Nâgârjuna, who was one of the founders of the esoteric Mahayâna systems, not their *exoteric* travesties. The allegory that regarded Nâgârjuna's "Paramartha" as a gift from the *Nâgas* (Serpents) shows that he received his teachings from the secret school of adepts, and that the real tenets are therefore kept secret.

Mahâ Buddhi (*Sk.*). *Mahat*. The Intelligent Soul of the World. The seven *Prakritis* or seven "natures" or planes, are counted from Mahâbuddhi downwards.

Mahâ Chohan (*Sk.*). The chief of a spiritual Hierarchy, or of a school of Occultism; the head of the trans-Himalayan mystics.

Mahâ Deva (*Sk.*). Lit., "great god"; a title of Siva.

Mahâ Guru (*Sk.*). Lit., "great teacher". The Initiator.

Mahâ Kâla (*Sk.*). "Great Time". A name of Siva as the "Destroyer", and of Vishnu as the "Preserver".

Mahâ Kalpa (*Sk.*). The "great age".

Mahâ Manvantara (*Sk.*). Lit., the great interludes between the "Manus". The period of universal activity. Manvantara implying here simply a period of activity, as opposed to Pralaya, or rest – without reference to the length of the cycle.

Mahâ Mâyâ (*Sk.*). The great illusion of manifestation. This universe, and all in it in their mutual relation, is called the great Illusion or *Mahâmâyâ* It is also the usual title given to Gautama the Buddha's Immaculate Mother – Mayâdêvi, or the "Great Mystery", as she is called by the Mystics.

Mahâ Pralaya (*Sk.*). The opposite of Mahâmanvantara, literally "the great Dissolution", the "Night" following the "Day of Brahmâ". It is the great rest and sleep of all nature after a period of active manifestation; orthodox Christians would refer to it as the "Destruction of the World".

Mahâ Vidyâ (*Sk.*). The great esoteric science. The highest Initiates alone are in possession of this science, which embraces almost universal knowledge.

Mahâ Yogin (*Sk.*). The "great ascetic". A title of Siva.

Mahâ Yuga (*Sk.*). The aggregate of four *Yugas* or ages, of 4,320,000 solar years; a "Day of Brahmâ", in the Brahmanical system ; lit., "the great age".

Mahat (*Sk.*). Lit., "The great one". The first principle of Universal Intelligence and Consciousness. In the Purânic philosophy the first product of root-nature or *Pradhâna* (the same as Mulaprakriti); the producer of *Manas* the thinking principle, and of *Ahankâra*, egotism or the feeling of "I am I" (in the lower Manas).

Mahâtma. Lit., "great soul". An adept of the highest order. Exalted beings who, having attained to the mastery over their lower principles are thus living unimpeded by the "man of flesh", and are in possession of knowledge and power commensurate with the stage they have reached in their spiritual evolution. Called in Pali Rahats and Arhats.

Maitreya Buddha (*Sk.*). The same as the *Kalki Avatar* of Vishnu (the "White Horse" Avatar), and of Sosiosh and other Messiahs. The only difference lies in the dates of their appearances. Thus, while Vishnu is expected to appear on his white horse at the end of the present *Kali Yuga* age "for the final destruction of the wicked, the renovation of creation and the restoration of purity", Maitreya is expected earlier. Exoteric or popular teaching making slight variations on the esoteric doctrine states that Sakyamuni (Gautama Buddha) visited him in Tushita (a celestial abode) and commissioned him to issue thence on earth as his successor at the expiration of five thousand years after his (Buddha's) death. This would be in less than 3,000 years hence. Esoteric philosophy teaches that the next Buddha will appear during the seventh (sub) race of this Round. The fact is that Maitreya was a follower of Buddha, a well-known Arhat, though not his direct disciple, and that he was the founder of an esoteric philosophical school. As shown by Eitel (*Sanskrit-Chinese Dict.*), "statues were erected in his honour as early as B.C. 350".

Manas (*Sk.*). Lit., "the mind", the mental faculty which makes of man an intelligent and moral being, and distinguishes him from the mere animal; a synonym of *Mahat*. Esoterically, however, it means, when unqualified, the Higher EGO, or the sentient reincarnating Principle in man. When qualified it is called by Theosophists *Buddhi-Manas* or the Spiritual Soul in contradistinction to its human reflection – *Kâma-Manas*.

Manas, Kâma (*Sk.*). Lit., "the mind of desire." With the Buddhists it is the *sixth* of the Chadâyatana (*q.v.*), or the six organs of knowledge, hence the highest of these, synthesized by the seventh called *Klichta*, the spiritual perception of that which defiles this (lower) Manas, or the "Human-animal Soul", as the Occultists term it. While the Higher Manas or the Ego is directly related to *Vijnâna* (the 10th of the 12 Nidânas) – which is the perfect knowledge of all forms of knowledge, whether relating to object or subject in the nidânic concatenation of causes and effects; the lower, the Kâma Manas is but one of the *Indriya* or organs (roots) of Sense. Very little can be said of the dual Manas here, as the doctrine that treats of it, is correctly stated only in esoteric works. Its mention can thus be only very superficial.

Manas Sanyama (*Sk.*). Perfect concentration of the mind, and control over it, during Yoga practices.

Manas Taijasi (*Sk.*). Lit., the "radiant" Manas; a state of the Higher Ego, which only high metaphysicians are able to realize and comprehend.

Mânasa or *Manaswin* (*Sk.*). "The efflux of the *divine* mind," and explained as meaning that this efflux signifies the *manasa* or divine sons of Brahmâ-Virâj. Nilakantha who is the authority for this statement, further explains the term "manasa" by *manomâtrasarira*. These Manasa are the *Arupa* or incorporeal sons of the Prajâpati Virâj, in another version. But as Arjuna Misra identifies Virâj with Brahmâ, and as Brahmâ is Mahat, the universal mind, the exoteric blind becomes plain. The Pitris are identical with the Kumâra, the Vairaja, the Manasa-Putra (mind sons), and are finally identified with the human "Egos".

Mânasa Dhyânis (*Sk.*). The highest Pitris in the *Purânas*; the Agnishwatthas, or Solar Ancestors of Man, those who made of Man a rational being, by incarnating in the senseless forms of semi-ethereal flesh of the men of the third race. (See Vol. II. of *Secret Doctrine.*)

Mânasas (*Sk.*). Those who endowed humanity with *manas* or intelligence, the immortal EGOS in men. (See "Manas".)

Mantrika Sakti (*Sk.*). The power, or the occult potency of mystic words, sounds, numbers or letters in these Mantras.

Manus (*Sk.*). The fourteen Manus are the patrons or guardians of the race cycles in a Manvantara, or Day of Brahmâ. The primeval Manus are seven, they become fourteen in the *Purânas*.

Manushi or *Manushi Buddhas* (*Sk.*). Human Buddhas, Bodhisattvas, or incarnated Dhyan Chohans.

Manvantara (*Sk.*). A period of manifestation, as opposed to Pralaya (dissolution, or rest), applied to various cycles, especially to a Day of Brahmâ, 4,320,000,000 Solar years – and to the reign of one Manu – 308,448,000. (See Vol. II. of the *Secret Doctrine*, p. 68 *et. seq.*) Lit., *Manuantara* – between Manus.

Mârga (*Sk.*). "The "Path', The *Ashthânga mârga*, the "holy" or sacred path is the one that leads to Nirvâna. The eight-fold path has grown out of the seven-fold path, by the addition of the (now) first of the eight Marga; *i.e.*, "the possession of orthodox views"; with which a *real Yogâcharya* would have nothing to do.

Mârttanda (*Sk.*). The Vedic name of the Sun.

Mâyâ (*Sk.*). Illusion ; the cosmic power which renders phenomenal existence and the perceptions thereof possible. In Hindu philosophy that alone which is changeless and eternal is called *reality* ; all that which is subject to change through decay and differentiation and which has therefore a begining and an end is regarded as *mâyâ* – illusion.

Mîmânsâ (*Sk.*). A school of philosophy; one of the six in India. There are two Mîmânsâ the older and the younger. The first, the "Pârva-Mîmânsâ', was founded by Jamini, and the later or "Uttara Mîmânsâ", by a Vyasa—and is now called the Vedânta school. Sankarâchârya was the most prominent apostle of the latter. The Vedânta school is the oldest of all the six *Darshana* (lit., "demonstrations"), but even to the Pûrva-Mîmânsâ no higher antiquity is allowed than 500 B.C. Orientalists in favour of the absurd idea that all these schools are "due to Greek influence", in order to have them fit their theory would make them of still later date. The *Shad-darshana* (or Six Demonstrations) have all a starting point in common, and maintain that *ex nihilo nihil fit*.

Moksha (*Sk.*). "Liberation." The same as Nirvâna; a post mortem state of rest and bliss of the "Soul-Pilgrim".

Monad (*Gr.*). The Unity, the *one*; but in Occultism it often means the unified triad, Atma-Buddhi-Manas, or the duad, Atma-Buddhi, that immortal part of man which reincarnates in the lower kingdoms, and gradually progresses through them to Man and then to the final goal – Nirvâna.

Monas (*Gr.*). The same as the term *Monad*; "Alone", a unit. In the Pythagorean system the duad emanates from the higher and solitary Monas, which is thus the "First Cause".

Moon. The earth's satellite has figured very largely as an emblem in the religions of antiquity; and most commonly has been represented as Female, but this is not universal, for in the myths of the Teutons and Arabs, as well as in the conception of the Rajpoots of India (see Tod, *Hist.*), and in Tartary the moon was male. Latin authors speak of Luna. and also of Lunus, but with extreme rarity. The Greek name is Selene, the Hebrew Lebanah and also Yarcah. In Egypt the moon was associated with Isis, in Phenicia with Astarte and in Babylon with Ishtar. From certain points of view the ancients regarded the moon also as Androgyne. The astrologers allot an Influence to the moon over the several parts of a man, according to the several Zodiacal signs she traverses; as well as a special influence produced by the house she occupies in a figure.

The division of the Zodiac into the 28 mansions of the moon appears to be older than that into 12 signs: the Copts, Egyptians, Arabs, Persians and Hindoos used the division into 28 parts centuries ago, and the Chinese use it still.

The Hermetists said the moon gave man an astral form, while Theosophy teaches that the Lunar Pitris were the creators of our human bodies and lower principles. (See *Secret Doctrine* 1. 386.) [w.w.w.]

Mukta and **Mukti** (*Sk.*). Liberation from sentient life; one beatified or liberated; a candidate for *Moksha*, freedom from flesh and matter, or life on this earth.

Mûlaprakriti (*Sk.*). The Parabrahmic root, the abstract deific feminine principle—undifferentiated substance. Akâsa. Literally, "the root of Nature" (*Prakriti*) or Matter.

Munis (*Sk.*). Saints, or Sages.

Mysteries. Greek *teletai,* or finishings, celebrations of initiation or the Mysteries. They were observances, generally kept secret from the profane and uninitiated, in which were taught by dramatic representation and other methods, the origin of things, the nature of the human spirit, its relation to the body, and the method of its purification and restoration to higher life. Physical science, medicine, the laws of music, divination, were all taught in the same manner. The Hippocratic oath was but a mystic obligation. Hippocrates was a priest of Asklepios, some of whose writings chanced to become public. But the Asklepiades were initiates of the Æsculapian serpent-worship, as the Bacchantes were of the Dionysia; and both rites were eventually incorporated with the Eleusinia. The Sacred Mysteries were enacted in the ancient Temples by the initiated Hierophants for the benefit and instruction of the candidates. The most solemn and occult Mysteries were certainly those which were performed in Egypt by "the band of secret-keepers", as Mr. Bonwick calls the Hierophants. Maurice describes their nature very graphically in a few lines. Speaking of the Mysteries performed in Philæ (the Nile-island), he says that "it was in these gloomy caverns that the grand and mystic arcana of the goddess (Isis) were unfolded to the adoring aspirant, while the solemn hymn of initiation resounded through the long extent of these stony recesses". The word "mysteries" is derived from the Greek *muô,* "to close the mouth", and every symbol connected with them had, a hidden meaning. As Plato and many other sages of antiquity affirm, the Mysteries were highly religious, moral and beneficent as a school of ethics. The Grecian mysteries, those of Ceres and Bacchus, were only imitations of the Egyptian; and the author of *Egyptian Belief and Modern Thought,* informs us that our own "word *chapel* or *capella* is said to be the *Caph-El* or college of *El,* the Solar divinity". The well-known *Kabiri* are associated with the Mysteries. In short, the Mysteries were in every country a series of dramatic performances, in which the mysteries of cosmogony and nature, in general, were personified by the priests and neophytes, who enacted the part of various gods and goddesses, repeating supposed scenes (allegories) from their respective lives. These were explained in their hidden meaning to the candidates for initiation, and incorporated into philosophical doctrines.

N

Nâga (*Sk.*). Literally "Serpent". The name in the Indian Pantheon of the Serpent or Dragon Spirits, and of the inhabitants of Pâtâla, hell. But as Pâtâla means the *antipodes,* and was the name given to America by the ancients, who knew and visited that continent before Europe had ever heard of it, the term is probably akin to the Mexican Nagals the (now) sorcerers and medicine men. The Nagas are the Burmese *Nats,* serpent-gods, or "dragon demons". In Esotericism, however, and as already stated, this is a nick-name for the "wise men" or adepts in China and Tibet, the "Dragons." are regarded as the titulary deities of the world, and of various spots on the earth, and the word is explained as meaning adepts, yogis, and narjols. The term has simply reference to their great knowledge and wisdom. This is also proven in the ancient Sûtras and Buddha's biographies. The Nâga is ever a wise man, endowed with extraordinary magic powers, in South and Central America as in India, in Chaldea as also in ancient Egypt. In China the "worship" of the Nâgas was widespread, and it has become still more pronounced since Nâgarjuna (the "great Nâga", the "great adept" literally), the fourteenth Buddhist patriarch, visited China. The "Nâgas" are regarded by the Celestials as "the tutelary Spirits or gods of the five regions or the four points of the compass and the centre, as the guardians of the five lakes and four oceans" (**Eitel**). This, traced to its origin and translated esoterically, means that the five continents and their five root-races had always been under the guardianship of "terrestrial deities", i.e., Wise Adepts. The tradition that Nâgas washed Gautama Buddha at his birth, protected him and guarded the relics of his body when dead, points again to the Nâgas being only wise men, Arhats, and no monsters or Dragons. This is also corroborated by the innumerable stories of the conversion of Nâgas to Buddhism. The Nâga of a lake in a forest near Râjagriha and many other "Dragons" were thus converted by Buddha to the good Law.

Nârada (*Sk.*). One of the Seven great Rishis, a Son of Brahmâ This "Progenitor" is one of the most mysterious personages in the Brahmanical sacred symbology. Esoterically Nârada is the Ruler of events during various Karmic cycles, and the personification, in a certain sense, of the great human cycle; a Dhyan Chohan. He plays a great part in Brahmanism, which ascribes to him some of the most occult hymns in the *Rig Veda*, in which sacred work he is described as "of the Kanwa family". He is called Deva-Brahmâ, but as such has a distinct character from the one he assumes on earth – or Pâtâla. Daksha cursed him for his interference with his 5,000 and 10,000 sons, whom he persuaded to remain Yogins and *celibates*, to be reborn time after time on this earth (*Mahâbhârata*). But this is an allegory. He was the inventor of the Vina, a kind of lute, and a great "lawgiver". The story is too long to be given here.

Nârâyana (*Sk.*). The "mover on the Waters" of space: a title of Vishnu, in his aspect of the Holy Spirit, moving on the Waters of Creation. (See *Mânu*, Book II.) In esoteric symbology it stands for the primeval manifestation of the *life-principle*, spreading in infinite Space.

Nâstika (*Sk.*). Atheist, or rather he who does not worship or recognize the gods and idols.

Nephesh (*Heb.*). Breath of life. *Anima, Mens, Vita*, Appetites. This term is used very loosely in the Bible. It generally means *prana* "life"; in the Kabbalah it is the animal passions and the animal Soul. [w.w.w.]. Therefore, as maintained in theosophical teachings, *Nephesh* is the synonym of the Prâna-Kâmic Principle, or the vital animal Soul in man. [H. P. B.]

Nidâna (*Sk.*). The 12 causes of existence, or a chain of causation, "a concatenation of cause and effect in the whole range of existence through 12 links". This is the fundamental dogma of Buddhist thought, "the understanding of which solves the riddle of life, revealing the insanity of existence and preparing the mind for Nirvâna". (Eitel's *Sans. Chin. Dict.*) The 12 links stand thus in their enumeration. (1) Jail, or birth, according to one of the four modes of entering the stream of life and reincarnation – or *Chatur Yoni* (*q.v.*), each mode placing the being born in one of the six *Gâti* (q.v.). (2) *Jarârnarana*, or decrepitude and death, following the maturity of the *Skandhas* (q.v.). (3) *Bhava*, the Karmic agent which leads every new sentient being to be born in this or another mode of existence in the *Trailokya* and Gâti. (4) *Upâdâna*, the creative cause of *Bhava* which thus becomes the cause of *Jati* which is the effect; and this creative cause is the *clinging to life*. (5) Trishnâ, love, whether pure or impure. (6) *Vêdâna*, or sensation; perception by the senses, it is the 5th Skandha. (7) Sparsa, the sense of touch. (8) *Chadâyatana*, the organs of sensation. (9) *Nâmarûpa*, personality, i.e., a form with a name to it, the symbol of the unreality of material phenomenal appearances. (10) *Vijnâna*, the perfect knowledge of every perceptible thing and of all objects in their concatenation and unity. (11) *Samskâra*, action on the plane of illusion. (12) *Avidyâ*, lack of true perception, or ignorance. The Nidânas belonging to the most subtle and abstruse doctrines of the Eastern metaphysical system, it is impossible to go into the subject at any greater length.

Nimitta (*Sk.*). 1. An interior illumination developed by the practice of meditation. 2. The efficient spiritual cause, as contrasted with Upadana, the material cause, in Vedânta philosophy. See also *Pradhâna* in Sankhya philosophy.

Nirguna (*Sk.*). Negative attribute; unbound, or without *Gunas* (attributes), i.e., that which is devoid of all qualities, the opposite of Saguna, that which has attributes (*Secret Doctrine*, II. 95), e.g., Parabrahmam is Nirguna; Brahmâ, Saguna. Nirguna is a term which shows the impersonality of the thing spoken of.

Nirmânakâya (*Sk.*). Something entirely different in esoteric philosophy from the popular meaning attached to it, and from the fancies of the Orientalists. Some call the *Nirmânakâya* body "Nirvana with remains" (Schlagintweit, etc.) on the supposition, probably, that it is a kind of Nirvânic condition during which consciousness and form are retained. Others say that it is one of the *Trikâya* (three bodies), with the "power of assuming any form of appearance in order to propagate Buddhism" (Eitel's idea); again, that "it is the incarnate avatâra of a deity" (*ibid.*), and so on. Occultism, on the other hand, says:that Nirmânakâya, although meaning literally a transformed "body", is a state. The form is that of the adept or yogi who enters, or chooses, that *post mortem* condition in preference to the Dharmakâya or *absolute* Nirvânic state. He does this because the latter *kâya* separates him for ever from the world of form, conferring upon him a state of *selfish* bliss, in which no other living being can participate, the adept being thus precluded from the possibility of helping humanity, or even *devas*. As a Nirmânakâya, however, the man leaves behind him only his physical body, and retains every other "principle" save the Kamic – for he has crushed this out for ever from his nature, during life, and it can never resurrect in his post mortem state. Thus, instead of going into selfish bliss, he chooses a life of self-sacrifice, an existence which ends only with the life-cycle, in order to be enabled to help mankind in an invisible yet most effective manner. (See *The Voice of the Silence*, third treatise, "The Seven Portals".) Thus a Nirmânakâya is not, as popularly believed, the body "in which a Buddha or a Bodhisattva appears on earth", but verily one, who whether a *Chutuktu* or a *Khubilkhan*, an adept or a yogi during life, has since become a member of that invisible Host which ever protects and watches over Humanity within Karmic limits. Mistaken often for a "Spirit", a Deva, God himself, &c., a Nirmânakâya is ever a protecting, compassionate, verily a *guardian* angel, to him who becomes worthy of his help. Whatever objection may be brought forward against this doctrine; however much it is denied, because, forsooth, it has never been hitherto made public in Europe and therefore since it is unknown to Orientalists, it must needs be "a myth of modern invention" – no one will be bold enough to say that this idea of helping suffering mankind at the price of one's own almost interminable self-sacrifice, is not one of the grandest and noblest that was ever evolved from human brain.

Nirupadhi *(Sk.)*. Attributeless; the negation of attributes.

Nirvâna *(Sk.)*. According to the Orientalists, the entire "blowing out", like the flame of a candle, the utter extinction of existence. But in the esoteric explanations it is the state of absolute existence and absolute consciousness, into which the Ego of a man who has reached the highest degree of perfection and holiness during life goes, after the body dies, and occasionally, as in the case of Gautama Buddha and others, during life. (See "Nirvânî".)

Nirvânî (ee) (Sk.). One who has attained Nirvana – an emancipated soul. That Nirvâna means nothing of the kind asserted by Orientalists every scholar who has visited China, India and Japan is well aware. It is "*escape* from misery" but only from that of matter, freedom from *Klêsha*, or *Kâma*, and the complete extinction of animal desires. If we are told that *Abidharma* defines Nirvâna "as a state of absolute annihilation", we concur, adding to the last word the qualification "of everything connected with matter or the physical world", and this simply because the latter (as also all in it) is illusion, *mâyâ*. Sâkyamûni Buddha said in the last moments of his life that "the spiritual body is immortal" (See *Sans. Chin. Dict.*). As Mr. Eitel, the scholarly Sinologist, explains it: "The popular exoteric systems agree in defining Nirvâna *negatively* as a state of absolute exemption from the circle of transmigration; as a state of entire freedom from all forms of existence; to begin with, freedom from all passion and exertion; a state of indifference to all sensibility" and he might have added "death of all compassion for the world of suffering". And this is why the Bodhisattvas who prefer the Nirmânakâya to the Dharmakâya vesture, stand higher in the popular estimation than the Nirvânîs. But the same scholar adds that: "Positively (and esoterically) they define Nirvâna as the highest state of spiritual bliss, as absolute immortality through absorption of the soul (spirit rather) into itself, but *preserving individuality* so that, e.g., Buddhas, after entering Nirvâna, may reappear on earth" – i.e., in the future Manvantara.

Nitya Pralaya (*Sk.*). Lit., "perpetual" Pralaya or dissolution. It is the constant and imperceptible changes undergone by the atoms which last as long as a Mahâmanvantara, a whole age of Brahmâ, which takes fifteen figures to sum up. A stage of chronic change and dissolution, the stages of growth and decay. It is the duration of "Seven Eternities". (See *Secret Doctrine* I. 371, II. 69, 310.) There are four kinds of Pralayas, or states of changelessness. The Naimittika, when Brahmâ slumbers; the Prakritika, a partial Pralaya of anything during Manvantara; Atyantika, when man has identified himself with the One Absolute synonym of Nirvâna; and Nitya, for physical things especially, as a state of profound and dreamless sleep.

Nitya Sarga (*Sk.*). The state of constant creation or evolution, as opposed to *Nitya Pralaya*—the state of perpetual incessant dissolution (or change of atoms) disintegration of molecules, hence change of forms.

Nous (*Gr.*). A Platonic term for the Higher Mind or Soul. It means Spirit as distinct from animal Soul – *psyche*; divine consciousness or mind in man: *Nous* was the designation given to the Supreme deity (third *logos*) by Anaxagoras. Taken from Egypt where it was called *Nout*, it was adopted by the Gnostics for their first conscious Æon which, with the Occultists, is the third *logos*, cosmically, and the third "principle" (from above) or *manas*, in man. (See "Nout".)

Nout (*Gr.*). In the Pantheon of the Egyptians it meant the "One- only-One", because they did not proceed in their popular or exoteric religion higher than the third manifestation which radiates from the *Unknown* and the *Unknowable*, the first unmanifested and the second *logoi* in the esoteric philosophy of every nation. The Nous of Anaxagoras was the *Mahat* of the Hindu Brahmâ, *the first manifested* Deity – "the Mind or Spirit self-potent"; this creative Principle being of course the *primum mobile* of everything in the Universe – its Soul and Ideation. (See "Seven Principles" in man.)

Nyâya (Sk.). One of the six *Darshanas* or schools of Philosophy in India; a system of Hindu logic founded by the Rishi Gautama.

O

Occult Sciences. The science of the secrets of nature – physical and psychic, mental and spiritual; called Hermetic and Esoteric Sciences. In the West, the Kabbalah may be named; in the East, mysticism, magic, and Yoga philosophy, which latter is often referred to by the Chelas in India as the *seventh* "Darshana" (school of philosophy), there being only *six* Darshanas in India known to the world of the profane. These sciences are, and have been for ages, hidden from the vulgar for the very good reason that they would never be appreciated by the selfish educated classes, nor understood by the uneducated; whilst the former might misuse them for their own profit, and thus turn the divine science into *black magic*. It is often brought forward as an accusation against the Esoteric philosophy and the Kabbalah that their literature is full of "a barbarous and meaningless jargon" unintelligible to the ordinary mind. But do not exact Sciences – medicine, physiology, chemistry, and the rest – do the same? Do not official Scientists equally veil their facts and discoveries with a newly coined and most barbarous Græco-Latin terminology? As justly remarked by our late brother, Kenneth Mackenzie – "To juggle thus with words, when the facts are so simple, is the art of the Scientists of the present time, in striking contrast to those of the XVIIth century, who called spades spades, and not 'agricultural implements'." Moreover, whilst their facts would be as simple and as comprehensible if rendered in ordinary language, the facts of Occult Science are of so abstruse a nature, that in most cases no words exist in European languages to express them; in addition to which our "jargon" is a *double* necessity – (a) for the purpose of describing clearly these *facts* to him who is versed in the Occult terminology; and (b) to conceal them from the profane.

Occultist. One who studies the various branches of occult science. The term is used by the French Kabbalists (See Eliphas Lévi's works). Occultism embraces the whole range of psychological, physiological, cosmical, physical, and spiritual phenomena. From the word occultus hidden or secret. It therefore applies to the study of the **Kabbalah**, astrology, alchemy, and all arcane sciences.

Oeaihu, or *Oeaihwu*. The manner of pronunciation depends on the accent. This is an esoteric term for the six in one or the mystic seven. The occult name for the "seven vowelled" ever-present manifestation of the Universal Principle.

Om or Aum (*Sk.*). A mystic syllable, the most solemn of all words in India. It is "an invocation, a benediction, an affirmation and a promise and it is so sacred, as to be indeed *the word at low breath* of occult, *primitive* masonry. No one must be near when the syllable is pronounced for a purpose. This word is usually placed at the beginning of sacred Scriptures, and is prefixed to prayers. It is a compound of three letters a,u,m, which, in the popular belief, are typical of the three Vedas, also of three gods—**A** (Agni) **V** (Varuna) and **M** (Maruts) or Fire, Water and Air. In esoteric philosophy these are the three sacred fires, or the "triple fire"in the Universe and Man, besides many other things. Occultly, this "triple fire" represents the highest *Tetraktys* also, as it is typified by the Agni named Abhimânin and his transformation into his three sons, Pâvana, Pavamâna and Suchi, "who drinks up water", i.e., destroys material desires. This monosyllable is called Udgîtta, and is sacred with both Brahmins and Buddhists.

Omkâra (Sk.). The same as Aum or Om. It is also the name of one of the twelve *lingams,* that was represented by a secret and most sacred shrine at Ujjain—no longer existing, since the time of Buddhism.

Ophiomorphos (*Gr.*). The same, but in its material aspect, as the Ophis-Christos. With the Gnostics the Serpent represented "Wisdom in Eternity".

Ouranos (*Gr.*). The whole expanse of Heaven called the "Waters of Space", the Celestial Ocean, etc. The name very likely comes from the Vedic Varuna, personified as the water god and regarded as the chief Aditya among the seven planetary deities. In Hesiod's Theogony, Ouranos (or Uranus) is the same as Cœlus (Heaven) the oldest of all the gods and the father of the divine Titans.

P

Padma Âsana (*Sk.*). A posture prescribed to and practised by some Yogis for developing concentration.

Padma Kalpa (*Sk.*). The name of the last Kalpa or the preceding Manvantara, which was a year of Brahmâ.

Pancha Kosha (*Sk.*). The five "sheaths". According to Vedantin philosophy, Vijnânamaya Kosha, the fourth sheath, is composed of Buddhi, or is Buddhi. The five sheaths are said to belong to the two higher principles—*Jivâtma* and *Sâkshi,* which represent the *Upathita* and *An-upahita,* divine spirit respectively. The division in the esoteric teaching differs from this, as it divides man's physical-metaphysical aspect into seven principles.

Para (*Sk.*). "Infinite" and "supreme" in philosophy – the final limit.

Parabrahm (*Sk.*). "Beyond Brahmâ", literally. The Supreme Infinite Brahma, "Absolute" – the attributeless, the secondless reality. The impersonal and nameless universal Principle.

Paracelsus. The symbolical name adopted by the greatest Occultist of the middle ages – Philip Bombastes Aureolus Theophrastus von Hohenheim

– born in the canton of Zurich in 1493. He was the cleverest physician of his age, and the most renowned for curing almost any illness by the power of talismans prepared by himself. He never had a friend, but was surrounded by enemies, the most bitter of whom were the Churchmen and their party. That he was accused of being in league with the devil stands to reason, nor is it to be wondered at that finally he was murdered by some unknown foe, at the early age of forty-eight. He died at Salzburg, leaving a number of works behind him, which are to this day greatly valued by the Kabbalists and Occultists. Many of his utterances have proved prophetic. He was a clairvoyant of great powers, one of the most learned and erudite philosophers and mystics, and a distinguished Alchemist. Physics is indebted to him for the discovery of nitrogen gas, or **Azote.**

Paramapadha (*Sk.*). The place where—according to Visishtadwaita Vedantins—bliss is enjoyed by those who reach *Moksha* (Bliss). This "place" is not material but made, says the Catechism of that sect, "of *Suddhasatwa*, the essence of which the body of Iswara", the lord, "is made".

Paramartha (*Sk*) Absolute existence.

Paramâtman (*Sk.*). The Supreme Soul of the Universe.

Paranirvâna (*Sk.*). Absolute *Non-Being*, which is equivalent to absolute *Being* or "Be-ness", the state reached by the human Monad at the end of the great cycle (See *Secret Doctrine* I, 135). The same as *Paraniskpanna*.

Pâtanjala (*Sk.*). The Yoga philosophy; one of the six *Darshanas* or Schools of India.

Patanjali (*Sk.*). The founder of the Yoga philosophy. The date assigned to him by the Orientalists is 200 B.C.; and by the Occultists nearer to 700 than 600 B.C. At any rate he was a contemporary of Pânini.

Personality. In Occultism – which divides man into seven principles, considering him under the three aspects of the *divine*, the *thinking* or the *rational*, and the *animal* man – the lower *quaternary* or the purely astrophysical being; while by *Individuality* is meant the Higher Triad, considered as a Unity. Thus the *Personality* embraces all the characteristics and memories of one physical life, while the *Individuality* is the imperishable *Ego* which re-incarnates and clothes itself in one personality after another.

Phenomenon (*Gr.*). In reality "an appearance", something previously unseen, and puzzling when the cause of it is unknown. Leaving aside various kinds of phenomena, such as cosmic, electrical, chemical, etc., and holding merely to the phenomena of spiritism, let it be remembered that theosophically and esoterically every "miracle" – from the biblical to the theumaturgic – is simply a phenomenon, but that no phenomenon is ever a miracle, *i.e.*, something supernatural or outside of the laws of nature, as all such are impossibilities in nature.

Pitar Devata (*Sk.*). The "Father-Gods", the lunar ancestors of mankind.

Pitaras (*Sk.*). Fathers, Ancestors. The fathers of the human races.

Pitris (*Sk.*). The ancestors, or creators of mankind. They are of seven classes, three of which are incorporeal, *arupa,* and four corporeal. In popular theology they are said to be created from Brahmâ's side. They are variously genealogized, but in esoteric philosophy they are as given in the *Secret Doctrine.* In *Isis Unveiled* it is said of them "It is generally believed that the Hindu term means the spirits of our ancestors, of disembodied people, hence the argument of some Spiritualists that fakirs (and yogis) and other Eastern wonder-workers, are *mediums.* This is in more than one sense erroneous. The Pitris are not the ancestors of the present living men, but those of the human kind, or Adamic races; the spirits of human races, which on the great scale of descending evolution *preceded our races* of men, and they *were physically, as well as spiritually, far superior* to our modern pigmies. In *Mânava Dharma Shâstra* they are called the *Lunar Ancestors.*" The *Secret Doctrine* has now explained that which was cautiously put forward in the earlier Theosophical volumes.

Planetary Spirits. Primarily the rulers or governors of the planets. As our earth has its hierarchy of terrestrial planetary spirits, from the highest to the lowest plane, so has every other heavenly body. In Occultism, however, the term "Planetary Spirit" is generally applied only to the seven highest hierarchies corresponding to the Christian archangels. These have all passed through a stage of evolution corresponding to the humanity of earth on other worlds, in long past cycles. Our earth, being as yet only in its fourth round, is far too young to have produced high planetary spirits. The highest planetary spirit ruling over any globe is in reality the "Personal God" of that planet and far more truly its "over-ruling providence" than the self-contradictory Infinite Personal Deity of modern Churchianity.

Plato. An Initiate into the Mysteries and the greatest Greek philosopher, whose writings are known the world over. He was the pupil of Socrates and the teacher of Aristotle. He flourished over 400 years before our era.

Pragna (*Sk.*) or *Prajna*. A synonym of *Mahat* the Universal Mind. The capacity for perception. (*S. D.,* I. 139) Consciousness.

Prajâpatis (*Sk.*). Progenitors; the givers of life to all on this Earth. They are seven and then ten – corresponding to the seven and ten Kabbalistic Sephiroth; to the Mazdean Amesha-Spentas, &c. Brahmâ the creator, is called Prajâpati as the synthesis of the Lords of Being.

Prakriti (*Sk.*). Nature in general, nature as opposed to Purusha – spiritual nature and Spirit, which together are the "two primeval aspects of the One Unknown Deity". (*Secret Doctrine,* I. 51.)

Pralaya (*Sk.*). A period of obscuration or repose – planetary, cosmic or universal – the opposite of Manvantara (*S. D.,* I. 370.).

Pramantha (*Sk.*). An accessory to producing the sacred fire by friction. The sticks used by Brahmins to kindle fire by friction.

Prâna (*Sk.*). Life-Principle ; the breath of Life.

Pranidhâna (*Sk.*). The fifth observance of the Yogis; ceaseless devotion. (See *Yoga Shâstras,* ii. 32.)

Pratyasarga (*Sk.*). In Sankhya philosophy the "intellectual evolution of the Universe" ; in the *Purânas* the 8th creation.

Prometheus (*Gr.*). The Greek *logos*; he, who by bringing on earth divine fire (intelligence and consciousness) endowed men with reason and mind. Prometheus is the Hellenic type of our Kumâras or *Egos,* those who, by incarnating in men, made of them latent gods instead of animals. The gods (or Elohim) were averse to men becoming "as one of us (*Genesis* iii., 22), and knowing "good and evil". Hence we see these gods in every religious legend punishing man for his desire to know. As the Greek myth has it, for stealing the fire he brought to men from Heaven, Prometheus was chained by the order of Zeus to a crag of the Caucasian Mountains.

Protogonos (*Gr.*). The "first-born"; used of all the manifested gods and of the Sun in our system.

Psyche (*Gr.*). The animal, terrestrial Soul; the lower *Manas.*

Purânas (*Sk.*). Lit., "ancient". A collection of symbolical and allegorical writings – eighteen in number now – supposed to have been composed by Vyâsa, the author of *Mahâbhârata.*

Purusha (*Sk.*). "Man", *heavenly man.* Spirit, the same as Nârâyana in another aspect. "The Spiritual Self."

Pymander (*Gr.*). The "Thought divine". The Egyptian Prometheus and the personified Nous or divine light, which appears to and instructs Hermes Trismegistus, in a hermetic work called "Pymander".

Pythagoras (*Gr.*). The most famous of mystic philosophers, born at Samos, about 586 B.C. He seems to have travelled all over the world, and to have culled his philosophy from the various systems to which he had access. Thus, he studied the esoteric sciences with the *Brachmanes* of India, and astronomy and astrology in Chaldea and Egypt. He is known to this day in the former country under the name of Yavanâchârya ("Ionian teacher"). After returning he settled in Crotona, in Magna Grecia, where he established a college to which very soon resorted all the best intellects of the civilised centres. His father was one Mnesarchus of Samos, and was a man of noble birth and learning. It was Pythagoras. who was the first to teach the heliocentric system, and who was the greatest proficient in geometry of his century. It was he also who created the word "philosopher", composed of two words meaning a "lover of wisdom"—*philo-sophos*. As the greatest mathematician, geometer and astronomer of historical antiquity, and also the highest of the metaphysicians and scholars, Pythagoras has won imperishable fame. He taught reincarnation as it is professed in India and much else of the Secret Wisdom.

Q

Qadmon, Adam, or *Adam Kadmon (Heb.)*. The Heavenly or Celestial Man, the Microcosm *(q.v.)*, He is the manifested Logos; the *third* Logos according to Occultism, or the Paradigm of Humanity.

R

Râga (Sk). One of the five *Kleshas* (afflictions) in Patânjali's Yoga philosophy. In *Sânkhya Kârikâ*, it is the "obstruction" called love and desire in the physical or terrestrial sense. The five *Kleshas* are: *Avidyâ*, or ignorance; *Asmitâ*, selfishness, or "I-am-ness" ; *Râga*, love; *Dwesha*, hatred; and *Abhinivesa*, dread of suffering.

Râjas (*Sk.*). The "quality of foulness" (*i.e.*, differentiation), and activity in the *Purânas.* One of the three *Gunas* or divisions in the correlations of matter and nature, representing form and change.

Rajasâs (*Sk.*). The elder *Agnishwattas* – the Fire-Pitris, "fire" standing as a symbol of enlightenment and intellect.

Râkshasas (*Sk.*). *Lit.*, "raw eaters", and in the popular superstition evil spirits, demons. Esoterically, however, they are the *Gibborim* (giants) of the Bible, the Fourth Race or the Atlanteans. (See *Secret Doctrine*, II., 165.)

Ratnâvabhâsa Kalpa (*Sk.*). The age in which all sexual difference will have ceased to exist, and birth will take place in the *Anupâdaka* mode, as in the second and third Root-races. Esoteric philosophy teaches that it will take place at the end of the sixth and during the seventh and last Root-race in this Round.

Reincarnation. The doctrine of rebirth, believed in by Jesus and the Apostles, as by all men in those days, but denied now by the Christians. All the Egyptian converts to Christianity, Church Fathers and others, believed in this doctrine, as shown by the writings of several. In the still existing symbols, the human-headed bird flying towards a mummy, a body, or "the soul uniting itself with its *sahou* (glorified body of the Ego, and also the *kâmalokic shell*) proves this belief. "The song of the Resurrection" chanted by Isis to recall her dead husband to life, might be translated "Song of Rebirth", as Osiris is collective Humanity. "Oh! Osiris [here follows the name of the Osirified mummy, or the departed], rise again in holy earth (matter), august mummy in the coffin, under thy corporeal substances", was the funeral prayer of the priest over the deceased. "Resurrection" with the Egyptians never meant the resurrection of the mutilated mummy, but of the *Soul* that informed it, the Ego in a new body. The putting on of flesh periodically by the Soul or the Ego, was a universal belief; nor can anything be more consonant with justice and Karmic law.

Rishi Prajâpati (*Sk.*). *Lit.*, "revealers", holy sages in the religious history of Âryavarta. Esoterically the highest of them are the Hierarchies of "Builders" and Architects of the Universe and of living things on earth; they are generally called Dhyan Chohans, Devas and gods.

Rishis (*Sk.*). Adepts; the inspired ones. In Vedic literature the term is employed to denote those persons through whom the various Mantras were revealed.

Rudras (*Sk.*). The mighty ones; the lords of the three upper worlds. One of the classes of the "fallen" or incarnating spirits; they are all born of Brahmâ.

Rûpa (*Sk.*). Body; any form, applied even to the forms of the gods, which are subjective to us.

S

Sabda Brahmam (*Sk.*). "The Unmanifested Logos." The *Vedas*; "Ethereal Vibrations diffused throughout Space ".

Sacred Science. The name given to the *inner* esoteric philosophy, the secrets taught in days of old to the initiated candidates, and divulged during the last and supreme Initiation by the Hierophants.

Sakti (*Sk.*). The active female energy of the gods; in popular Hinduism, their wives and goddesses; in Occultism, the crown of the astral light. Force and the six forces of nature synthesized. Universal Energy.

Sama (*Sk.*). One of the *bhâva pushpas*, or "flowers of sanctity Sama is the fifth, or "resignation". There are eight such flowers, namely: clemency or charity, self-restraint, affection (or love for others), patience, resignation, devotion, meditation and veracity. Sama is also the repression of any mental perturbation,

Sâma Veda (Sk.). *Lit.*, "the Scripture, or *Shâstra*, of peace". One of the four Vedas.

Samâdhâna (Sk.). That state in which a Yogi can no longer diverge from the path of spiritual progress; when everything terrestrial, except the visible body, has ceased to exist for him.

Samâdhi (*Sk.*). A state of ecstatic and complete trance. The term comes from the words *Sam-âdha*, "self-possession ". He who possesses this power is able to exercise an absolute control over all his faculties, physical or mental; it is the highest state of Yoga.

Samâdhindriya (*Sk.*). Lit., "the root of concentration"; the fourth of the five roots called Pancha Indriyâni, which are said in esoteric philosophy to be the agents in producing a highly moral life, leading to sanctity and liberation ; when these are reached, the two *spiritual roots* lying latent in the body (Atmâ and Buddhi) will send out shoots and blossom. *Samâdhindriya* is the organ of ecstatic meditation in Râj-yoga practices.

Samâpatti (*Sk.*). Absolute concentration in Râja-Yoga; the process of development by which perfect indifference (*Sams*) is reached (*apatti*). This state is the last stage of development before the possibility of entering into Samâdhi is reached.

Samskâra (*Sk.*). Lit., from *Sam* and *Krî*, to improve, refine, impress. In Hindu philosophy the term is used to denote the impressions left upon the mind by individual actions or external circumstances, and capable of being developed on any future favourable occasion—even in a future birth. The *Samskâra* denotes, therefore, the germs of propensities and impulses from previous births to be developed in this, or the coming *janmâs* or reincarnations. In Tibet, Samskâra is called Doodyed, and in China is defined as, or at least connected with, action or Karma. It is, strictly speaking, a metaphysical term, which in exoteric philosophies is variously defined; *e.g.*, in Nepaul as illusion, in Tibet as notion, and in Ceylon as discrimination. The true meaning is as given above, and as such is connected with Karma and its working.

Samvriti (*Sk.*). False conception—the origin of illusion.

Samvritisatya (*Sk.*). Truth mixed with false conceptions (Samvriti); the reverse of absolute truth – or *Paramârthasatya*, self-consciousness in absolute truth or reality.

Sanat Kumâra (*Sk.*). The most prominent of the seven Kumâras, the Vaidhâtra the first of which are called Sanaka, Sananda, Sanâtana and Sanat Kumâra; which names are all significant qualifications of the degrees of human intellect.

Sânkhya (*Sk.*). The system of philosophy founded by Kapila Rishi, a system of analytical metaphysics, and one of the six *Darshanas* or schools of philosophy. It discourses on numerical categories and the meaning of the twenty-five *tatwas* (the forces of nature in various degrees). This "atomistic school", as some call it, explains nature by the interaction of twenty-four elements with *purusha* (spirit) modified by the three gunas (qualities), teaching the eternity of *pradhâna* (primordial, homogeneous matter), or the self-transformation of nature and the eternity of the human Egos.

Sânkhya Yoga (*Sk.*). The system of Yoga as set forth by the above school.

Sanskrit (*Sk.*). The classical language of the Brahmans, never known *nor spoken in its true systematized form* (given later *approximately* by Pânini), except by the initiated Brahmans, as it was pre-eminently "a mystery language". It has now degenerated into the so-called Prâkrita.

Saptarshi (*Sk.*). The seven Rishis. As stars they are the constellation of 'the Great Bear, and called as such the *Riksha* and *Chitrasikhandinas,* bright-crested.

Satya Yuga (*Sk.*). The golden age, or the age of truth and purity; the first of the four Yugas, also called Krita Yuga.

Sattva (*Sk.*). Understanding; quiescence in divine knowledge. It follows 'generally the word *Bodhi* when used as a compound word, e.g., "Bodhisattva".

Sattva or *Satwa*, (*Sk.*). Goodness; the same as Sattva, or purity, one of the trigunas or three divisions of nature.

Satya (*Sk.*). Supreme truth.

Satya Loka (*Sk.*). The world of infinite purity and wisdom, the celestial abode of Brahmâ and the gods.

Satya Yuga (*Sk.*). The golden age, or the age of truth and purity; the first of the four Yugas, also called Krita Yuga.

Secret Doctrine. The general name given to the esoteric teachings of antiquity.

Sephira (*Heb.*) An emanation of Deity; the parent and synthesis of the ten Sephiroth when she stands at the head of the Sephirothal Tree; in the Kabbalah, Sephira,or the " Sacred Aged ", is the divine Intelligence (the same as Sophia or Metis), the first emanation from the "Endless" or Ain-Suph.

Sephiroth (*Heb.*). The ten emanations of Deity; the highest is formed by the concentration of the Ain Soph Aur, or the Limitless Light, and each: Sephira produces by emanation another Sephira. The names of the Ten Sephiroth are – 1. Kether – The Crown; 2. Chokmah – Wisdom; 3. Binah – Understanding; 4. Chesed- – Mercy; Geburah – Power; 6. Tiphereth – Beauty; 7. Netzach – Victory; 8. Hod – Splendour; 9. Jesod_Foundation; and 10. Malkuth – The Kingdom.

The conception of Deity embodied in the Ten Sephiroth is a very sublime one, and each Sephira is a picture to the Kabbalist of a group of exalted ideas, titles and attributes, which the name but faintly represents. Each Sephira is called either active or passive, though this attribution may lead to error; passive does not mean a return to negative existence; and the two words only express the relation between individual Sephiroth, and not any absolute quality. [w.w.w.]

Sharîra (Sarîra) *(Sk.)*. Envelope or body.

Siddhas *(Sk.)*. Saints and sages who have become almost divine also a hierarchy of Dhyan Chohans.

Siddhâsana *(Sk.)*. A posture in Hatha-yoga practices.

Siddha-Sena *(Sk.)*. Lit., "the leader of Siddhas"; a title of Kârttikeya, the "mysterious youth" *(kumâra guha)*.

Siddhis *(Sk.)*. Lit., "attributes of perfection"; phenomenal powers acquired through holiness by Yogis.

Sishta *(Sk.)*. The great elect or Sages, left after every minor *Pralaya* (that which is called "obscuration" in Mr. Sinnett's *Esoteric Buddhism*), when the globe goes into its night or rest, to become, on its re-awakening, the seed of the next humanity. Lit. "remnant."

Siva *(Sk.)*. The third person of the Hindu Trinity (the Trimûrti). He is a god of the first order, and in his character of Destroyer higher than Vishnu, the Preserver, as he destroys only to regenerate on a higher plane. He is born as Rudra, the Kumâra, and is the patron of all the Yogis, being called, as such, Mahâdeva the great ascetic, His titles are significant *Trilochana*, "the three-eyed", *Mahâdeva*, "the great god ", *Sankara*, etc., etc., etc.

Skandha or *Skhanda (Sk.)*. Lit., "bundles", or groups of attributes; everything finite, inapplicable to the eternal and the absolute. There are five—esoterically, *seven*—attributes in every human living being, which are known as the *Pancha Shandhas*. These are (1) form, *rûpa*; (2) perception, *vidâna*; (3) consciousness, *sanjnâ*; (4) action, *sanskâra*; (5) knowledge, vidyâna. These unite at the birth of man and constitute his personality. After the maturity of these Skandhas, they begin to separate and weaken, and this is followed by *jarâmarana*, or decrepitude and death.

Son-kha-pa *(Tib.)*. Written also *Tsong-kha-pa*. A famous Tibetan reformer of the fourteenth century, who introduced a purified Buddhism into his country. He was a great Adept, who being unable to witness any longer the desecration of Buddhist philosophy by the false priests who made of it a marketable commodity, put a forcible stop thereto by a timely revolution and the exile of 40,000 sham monks and Lamas from the country. He is regarded as an Avatar of Buddha, and is the founder of the *Gelukpa* (" yellow-cap ") Sect, and of the mystic Brotherhood connected with its chiefs. The "tree of the 10,000 images" *(khoom boom)* has, it is said, sprung from the long hair of this ascetic, who leaving it behind him disappeared for ever from the view of the profane.

Soul. The **yuch**, or *nephesh* of the *Bible*; the vital principle, or the breath of life, which every animal, down to the infusoria, shares with man. In the translated Bible it stands indifferently for *life*, blood and soul. " Let us not kill his *nephesh* ", says the original text: "let us not kill *him* ", translate the Christians (*Genesis* xxxvii. 21), and so on.

Sparsa (*Sk*). The sense of touch.

Spirit. The lack of any mutual agreement between writers in the use of this word has resulted in dire confusion. It is commonly made synonymous with *soul*; and the lexicographers countenance the usage. In Theosophical teachings. the term "Spirit" is applied solely to that which *belongs directly to Universal Consciousness*, and which is its homogeneous and unadulterated emanation. Thus, the higher Mind in Man or his Ego (Manas) is, when linked indissolubly with Buddhi, a spirit; while the term "Soul", human or even animal (the lower Manas acting in animals as instinct), is applied only to Kâma-Manas, and qualified as the living soul. This is *nephesh*, in Hebrew, the "breath of life". Spirit is formless and *immaterial*, being, when individualised, of the highest spiritual substance – *Suddasatwa*, the divine essence, of which the body of the manifesting *highest* Dhyanis are formed. Therefore, the Theosophists reject the appellation " Spirits" for those phantoms which appear in the phenomenal manifestations of the Spiritualists, and call them "shells", and various other names. (See "Sukshma Sarîra".) Spirit, in short, is no entity in the sense of having form ; for, as Buddhist philosophy has it, where there is a form, there is a cause for pain and suffering. But each *individual* spirit – this individuality lasting only throughout the manvantaric life-cycle – may be described as a *centre of consciousness*, a self-sentient and self-conscious centre; a state, not a conditioned individual. This is why there is such a wealth of words in Sanskrit to express the different States of Being, Beings and Entities, each appellation showing the philosophical difference, the plane to which such *unit* belongs, and the degree of its spirituality or materiality. Unfortunately these terms are almost untranslatable into our Western tongues.

Sraddha (*Sk*). Lit., faith, respect, reverence.

Sri Sankarâchârya (*Sk*.). The great religious reformer of India, and teacher of the Vedânta philosophy—the greatest of all such teachers, regarded by the *Adwaitas* (Non-dualists) as an incarnation of Siva and a worker of miracles. He established many *mathams* (monasteries), and founded the most learned sect among Brahmans, called the Smârtava. The legends about him are as numerous as his philosophical writings. At the age of thirty-two he went to Kashmir, and reaching Kedâranâth in the Himalayas, entered a cave alone, whence he never returned. His followers claim that he did not die, but only retired from the world.

Sthûla Sarîram (*Sk*.). In metaphysics, the gross physical body.

Sthûlopadhi (*Sk*.). A "principle" answering to the lower triad in man, i.e., body, astral form, and life, in the Târaka Râja Yoga system, which names only three chief principles in man. *Sthûlopadhi* corresponds to the *jagrata*, or waking conscious *state*.

Sûkshma Sarîra (*Sk.*). The dream-like, illusive body akin to *Mânasarûpa* or "thought-body ". It is the vesture of the gods, or the Dhyânis and the Devas. Written also *Sukshama Sharîra* and called *Sukshmopadhi* by the Târaka Râja Yogis. (*Secret Doctrine*, I.,157)

Sûkshmopadhi (*Sk.*). In Târaka Râja Yoga the "principle" containing both the higher and the lower Manas and Kâma. It corresponds to the *Manomaya Kosha* of the Vedantic classification and to the *Svapna* state. (See "Svapna ".)

Suras (*Sk.*). A general term for gods, the same as devas; the contrary to asuras or "no-gods".

Sûryâvarta (*Sk.*). A degree or stage of Samâdhi.

Sushupti Avasthâ (*Sk.*). Deep sleep; one of the four aspects of Prânava.

Sûtrâtman (*Sk.*). Lit., "the thread of spirit"; the immortal Ego, the Individuality which incarnates in men one life after the other, and upon which are strung, like beads on a string, his countless Personalities. The universal life-supporting air, *Samashti prau*; universal energy.

Svabhâvat (*Sk.*). Explained by the Orientalists as "plastic substance", which is an inadequate definition. Svabhâvat is the world-substance and stuff, or rather that which is behind it – the spirit and essence of substance. The name comes from *Subhâva* and is composed of three words – **su,** good, perfect, fair, handsome; **sva,** self; and **bkâva,** being, or *state of being*. From it all nature proceeds and into it all returns at the end of the life-cycles. In Esotericism it is called "Father-Mother". It is the plastic essence of matter.

Svapna Avasthâ (Sk.). A dreaming state; one of the four aspects of *Prânava*; a Yoga practice.

Svasam Vedanâ (*Sk.*). Lit., "the reflection which analyses itself "; a synonym of Paramârtha.

Svastikâsana (*Sk.*). The second of the four principal postures of the eighty-four prescribed in Hatha Yoga practices.

T

Taijasi (*Sk.*). The radiant, flaming—from *Tejas* "fire"; used sometimes to designate the *Mânasa-rûpa*, the "thought-body", and also the stars.

Tamas (*Sk.*). The quality of darkness, "foulness" and inertia; also of ignorance, as matter is blind. A term used in metaphysical philosophy. It is the lowest of the three *gunas* or fundamental qualities.

Tanha (*Pali*). The thirst for life. Desire to live and clinging to life on this earth. This clinging is that which causes rebirth or reincarnation.

Tanmâtras (*Sk.*). The types or rudiments of the five Elements; the subtile essence of these, devoid of all qualities and identical with the properties of the five basic Elements – earth, water, fire, air and ether; i.e., the *tanmâtras* are, in one of their aspects, smell, taste, touch, sight, and hearing.

Tapas (*Sk.*). "Abstraction", "meditation". "To perform *tapas*" is to sit for *contemplation*. Therefore ascetics are often called Tâpasas.

Târakâ Râja Yoga (*Sk.*). One of the Brahminical Yoga systems for the development of purely spiritual powers and knowledge which lead to Nirvâna.

Tattwa (*Sk.*). Eternally existing " That "; also, the different principles in Nature, in their occult meaning. *Tattwa Samâsa* is a work of Sânkhya philosophy attributed to Kapila himself.

Also the abstract principles of existence or categories, physical and metaphysical. The subtle elements—five exoterically, seven in esoteric philosophy——which are correlative to the five and the seven senses on the physical plane ; the last two senses are as yet latent in man, but will be developed in the two last root-races.

Theosophia (*Gr.*). Wisdom-religion, or "Divine Wisdom". The substratum and basis of all the world-religions and philosophies, taught and practised by a few elect ever since man became a thinking being. In its practical bearing, Theosophy is purely divine ethics; the definitions in dictionaries are pure nonsense, based on religious prejudice and ignorance of the true spirit of the early Rosicrucians and mediæval philosophers who called themselves Theosophists.

Theosophists. A name by which many mystics at various periods of history have called themselves. The Neo-Platonists of Alexandria were Theosophists; the Alchemists and Kabbalists during the mediæval ages were likewise so called, also the Martinists, the Quietists, and other kinds of mystics, whether acting independently or incorporated in a brotherhood or society. All real lovers of divine Wisdom and Truth had, and have, a right to the name, rather than those who, appropriating the qualification, live lives or perform actions opposed to the principles of Theosophy. As described by Brother Kenneth R. Mackenzie, the Theosophists of the past centuries – " entirely speculative, and founding no schools, have still exercised a silent influence upon philosophy; and, no doubt, when the time arrives, many ideas thus silently propounded may yet give new directions to human thought. One of the ways in which these doctrines have obtained not only authority, but power, has been among certain enthusiasts in the higher degrees of Masonry. This power has, however, to a great degree died with the founders, and modern Freemasonry contains few traces of theosophic influence. However accurate and beautiful some of the ideas of Swedenborg, Pernetty, Paschalis, Saint Martin, Marconis, Ragon, and Chastanier may have been, they have but little direct influence on society." This is true of the Theosophists of the last three centuries, but not of the later ones. For the Theosophists of the current century have already visibly impressed themselves on modern literature, and introduced the desire and craving for some philosophy in place of the blind dogmatic faith of yore, among the most intelligent portions of human-kind. Such is the difference between past and modern THEOSOPHY.

Thread Soul. The same as *Sutrâtmâ (q.v.).*

Thumos (*Gr.*). The astral, animal soul; the *Kâmas-Manas; Thumos* means passion, desire and confusion and is so used by Homer. The word is probably derived from the Sanskit *Tamas,* which has the same meaning.

To On (*Gr.*). The "Being", the "Ineffable All" of Plato. He" whom no person has seen except the Son".

Tretâ Yuga (*Sk.*). The second age of the world, a period of 1,296,000 years.

Triad, or *the Three.* The ten Sephiroth are contemplated as a group of three triads: Kether, Chochmah and Binah form the supernal triad; Chesed, Geburah and Tiphereth, the second; and Netzach, Hod and Yesod, the inferior triad. The tenth Sephira, Malkuth, is beyond the three triads. [w.w.w.]

The above is orthodox Western Kabalah. Eastern Occultists recognise but one triad – – the upper one (corresponding to Atmâ-Buddhi and the " Envelope" which reflects their light, the three in one) – and count seven lower Sephiroth, everyone of which stands for a " principle", beginning with the Higher Manas and ending with the Physical Body – of which Malkuth is the representative in the Microcosm and the Earth in the Macrocosm.

Trigunas (*Sk.*). The three divisions of the inherent qualities of differentiated matter—i.e., of pure quiescence (*satva*), of activity and desire (*rajas*), of stagnation and decay (*tamas*) They correspond with Vishnu, Brahmâ, and Shiva. (See " Trimûrti ".)

U

Upâdhi (*Sk.*). Basis; the vehicle, carrier or bearer of something less material than itself: as the human body is the *upâdhi* of its spirit, ether the *upâdhi* of light, etc., etc.; a mould; a defining or limiting substance.

Upanishad (*Sk.*). Translated as "esoteric doctrine ", or interpretation of the *Vedas* by the *Vedânta* methods. The third division of the *Vedas* appended to the *Brâhmanas* and regarded as a portion of *Sruti* or "revealed" word. They are, however, as records, far older than the *Brâhmanas* the exception of the two, still extant, attached to the *Rig -Veda* of the Aitareyins. The term *Upanishad* is explained by the Hindu pundits as "that which destroys ignorance, and thus produces liberation" of the spirit, through the knowledge of the supreme though *hidden* truth; the same, therefore, as that which was hinted at by Jesus, when he is made to say, "And ye shall know the truth, and the truth shall make you free " (*John* viii. 32). It is from these treatises of the *Upanishads*—themselves the echo of the primeval Wisdom-Religion—that the Vedânta system of philosophy has been developed. (See "Vedânta".) Yet old as the *Upanishads* may be, the Orientalists will not assign to the oldest of them more than an antiquity of 600 years B.C. The accepted number of these treatises is 150, though now no more than about twenty are left unadulterated. They treat of very abstruse, metaphysical questions, such as the origin of the Universe; the nature and the essence of the Unmanifested Deity and the manifested gods the connection, primal and ultimate, of spirit and matter; the universality of mind and the nature of the human Soul and Ego.

The *Upanishads* must be far more ancient than the days of Buddhism, as they show no preference for, nor do they uphold, the superiority of the Brahmans as a caste. On the contrary, it is the (now) second caste, the Kshatriya, or warrior class, who are exalted in the oldest of them. As stated by Professor Cowell in Elphinstone's *History of India*——"they breathe a freedom of spirit unknown to any earlier work except the *Rig Veda*. . . The great teachers of the higher knowledge and Brahmans are continually represented as *going to Kshatriya Kings to become their pupils*." The " Kshatriya Kings" were in the olden times, like the King Hierophants of Egypt, the receptacles of the highest divine knowledge and wisdom, the *Elect* and the incarnations of the primordial divine Instructors—the Dhyâni Buddhas or Kumâras. There was a time, æons before the Brahmans became a caste, or even the *Upanishads* were written, when there was on earth but one "lip ", one religion and one science, namely, the speech of the gods, the Wisdom-Religion and Truth. This was before the fair fields of the latter, overrun by nations of many languages, became overgrown with the weeds of intentional deception, and national creeds invented by ambition, cruelty and selfishness, broke the one sacred Truth into thousands of fragments.

Uparati (*Sk*) Absence of outgoing desires; a Yoga state.

V

Vâch (Sk.). To call Vâch "speech" simply, is deficient in clearness. Vâch is the mystic personification of speech, and the female *Logos*, being one with Brahmâ, who created her out of one-half of his body, which he divided into two portions; she is also one with Virâj (called the "female" Virâj) who was created in her by Brahmâ. In one sense Vâch is "speech" by which knowledge was taught to man; in another she is the "mystic, secret speech" which descends upon and enters into the primeval Rishis, as the "tongues of fire" are said to have "sat upon" the apostles. For, she is called "the female creator ", the "mother of the Vedas ", etc., etc. Esoterically, she is the subjective Creative Force which, emanating from the Creative Deity (the subjective Universe, its "privation ", or *ideation*) becomes the manifested "world of speech ", i.e., the *concrete expression of ideation*, hence the "Word" or Logos. Vâch is "the male and female" Adam of the first chapter of *Genesis*, and thus called "Vâch-Virâj" by the sages. (See *Atharva Veda*.) She is also "the celestial Saraswatî produced from the heavens ", a "voice derived from *speechless* Brahmâ" *(Mahâbhârata)*; the goddess of wisdom and eloquence. She is called *Sata-rûpa*, the goddess of *a hundred forms*.

Vâhan(a) *(Sk.)*. A vehicle, the carrier of something immaterial and formless. All the gods and goddesses are, therefore, represented as using vâhanas to manifest themselves, which vehicles are ever symbolical. So, for instance, Vishnu has during Pralayas, *Ânanta* the infinite" (Space), symbolized by the serpent Sesha, and during the Manvantaras – *Garuda* the gigantic half-eagle, half-man, the symbol of the great cycle; Brahma appears as Brahmâ, descending into the planes of manifestations on *Kâlahamsa*, the "swan in time or finite eternity"; Siva (phonet, Shiva) appears as the bull *Nandi*; Osiris as the sacred bull *Apis*; Indra travels on an elephant; Kârttikeya, on a peacock; Kâmadeva on *Makâra*, at other times a parrot; Agni, the universal (and also solar) Fire-god, who is, as all of them are, "a consuming Fire", manifests itself as a ram and a lamb, *Ajâ*, "the unborn"; Varuna, as a fish; etc., etc., while the vehicle of MAN is his body.

Vaikhari Vâch *(Sk.)*. 'That which is uttered; one of the four forms of speech.

Vaisheshika (Sk.). One of the six *Darshanas* or schools of philosophy, founded by Kanâda. It is called the Atomistic School, as it teaches the existence of a universe of atoms of a transient character, an endless number of souls and a fixed number of material principles, by the correlation and interaction of which periodical cosmic evolutions take place without any directing Force, save a kind of mechanical law inherent in the atoms; a very materialistic school.

Vaishnava *(Sk.)*. A follower of any sect recognising and worshipping Vishnu as the one supreme God. The worshippers of Siva are called *Saivas*.

Vaivaswata *(Sk.)*. The name of the Seventh Manu, the forefather of the post-diluvian race, or our own fifth humankind. A reputed son of Sûrya (the Sun), he became, after having been saved in an ark (built by the order of Vishnu) from the Deluge, the father of Ikshwâku, the founder of the solar race of kings. (See "*Sûryavansa*".)

Vâyu *(Sk.)*. Air: the god and sovereign of the air; one of the five states of matter, namely the *gaseous*; one of the five elements, called, as wind, *Vâta*. The *Vishnu Purâna* makes Vâyu King of the Gandharvas. He is the father of Hanumân, in the *Râmâyana*. The trinity of the mystic gods in Kosmos closely related to each other, are " Agni (fire) whose place is on earth; Vâyu (air, or one of the forms of Indra), whose place is in the air ; and Sûrya (the sun) whose place is in the air (*Nirukta.*) In esoteric interpretation, these three cosmic principles, correspond with the three human principles, Kâma, Kâma-Manas and Manas, the sun of the intellect.

Vedânta (*Sk.*). A mystic system of philosophy which has developed from the efforts of generations of sages to interpret the secret meaning of the *Upanishads* (*q.v.*). It is called in the *Shad-Darshanas* (six schools or systems of demonstration), *Uttara Mîmânsâ*, attributed to *Vyâsa*, the compiler of the *Vedas*, who is thus referred to as the founder of the Vedânta. The orthodox Hindus call Vedânta_a term meaning literally the "end of all (Vedic) knowledge " – *Brahmâ-jnâna*, or pure and spiritual knowledge of Brahmâ. Even if we accept the late dates assigned to various Sanskrit schools and treatises by our Orientalists, the Vedânta must be 3,300 years old, as Vyâsa is said to have lived I,400 years B.C. If, as Elphinstone has it in his *History of India*, the *Brahmanas* are the *Talmud* of the Hindus, and the *Vedas* the Mosaic books, then the *Vedânta* may be correctly called the *Kabalah* of India. But how vastly more grand! Sankarâchârya, who was the popularizer of the Vedântic system, and the founder of the *Adwaita* philosophy, is sometimes called the founder of the modern schools of the Vedânta.

Vedas (*Sk.*). The "revelation". the scriptures of the Hindus, from the root *vid*, "to know ", or "divine knowledge". They are the most ancient as well as the most sacred of the Sanskrit works. The *Vedas* , on the date and antiquity of which no two Orientalists can agree, are claimed by the Hindus themselves, whose Brahmans and Pundits ought to know best about their own religious works, to have been first taught orally for thousands of years and then compiled on the shores of Lake Mânasa-Sarovara (phonetically, *Mansarovara*) beyond the Himalayas, in Tibet.

The Vedic writings are all classified in two great divisions, exoteric and esoteric, the former being called *Karma-Kânda*, "division of actions or works ", and the *Jnâna Kânda*, "division of (divine) knowledge", the Upanishads (q.v.) coming under this last classification. Both departments are regarded as *Sruti* or revelation. To each hymn of the *Rig -Veda*, the name of the Seer or Rishi to whom it was revealed is prefixed. It, thus, becomes evident on the authority of these very names (such as Vasishta, Viswâmitra, Nârada, etc.), all of which belong to men born in various manvantaras and even ages, that centuries, and perhaps millenniums, must have elapsed between the dates of their composition.

Vidyâ (*Sk.*). Knowledge, Occult Science.

Vijnânam (Sk.*). The Vedântic name for the principle which dwells in the *Vijnânamaya Kosha* (the sheath of intellect) and corresponds to the faculties of the Higher Manas.

Vishnu (*Sk*.). The second person of the Hindu Trimûrti (trinity), composed of Brahmâ, Vishnu and Siva. From the root **vish**, "to pervade". in the *Rig - Veda*, Vishnu is no high god, but simply a manifestation of the solar energy, described as "striding through the seven regions of the Universe in *three* steps and enveloping all things with the dust (of his beams ".) Whatever may be the six other occult significances of the statement, this is related to the same class of types as the seven and ten Sephiroth, as the *seven* and *three* orifices of the perfect Adam Kadmon, as the seven "principles" and the higher triad in man, etc., etc. Later on this mystic type becomes a great god, the preserver and the renovator, he "of a thousand names – Sahasranâma ".

W

Will. In metaphysics and occult philosophy, Will is that which governs the manifested universes in eternity. *Will* is the one and sole principle of abstract eternal MOTION, or its ensouling essence. " The will", says Van Helmont, "is the first of all powers. . . . The will is the property of all spiritual beings and displays itself in them the more actively the more they are freed from matter." And Paracelsus teaches that "determined will is the beginning of all magical operations. It is because men do not perfectly imagine and believe the result, that the (occult) arts are so uncertain, while they might he perfectly certain." Like all the rest, the Will is *septenary* in its degrees of manifestation. Emanating from the one, eternal, abstract and purely quiescent Will (Âtmâ in Layam), it becomes Buddhi in its Alaya state, descends lower as Mahat (Manas), and runs down the ladder of degrees until the divine Eros becomes, in its lower, animal manifestation, erotic desire. Will as an eternal principle is neither spirit nor substance but everlasting ideation. As well expressed by Schopenhauer in his *Parerga*, " in sober reality there is neither *matter* nor *spirit*. The tendency to gravitation in a stone is as unexplainable as thought in the human brain. . . If matter can—no one knows why——fall to the ground, then it can also—no one knows why—-think. . . . As soon, even in mechanics, as we trespass beyond the purely mathematical, as soon as we reach the inscrutable adhesion, gravitation, and so on, we are faced by phenomena which are to our senses as mysterious as the WILL."

Wisdom. The " very essence of wisdom is contained in the Non- Being ". say the Kabbalists; but they also apply the term to the WORD or Logos, the Demiurge, by which the universe was called into existence. "The one Wisdom is in the Sound ", say the Occultists; the Logos again being meant by Sound, which is the substratum of Âkâsa. Says the *Zohar*, the " Book of Splendour" "It is the Principle of all the Principles, the mysterious Wisdom, the crown of all that which there is of the most High". (*Zohar*, iii., fol. 288, Myers *Qabbalah*.) And it is explained, "Above Kether is the Ayin, or Ens, i.e., Ain, the NOTHING". "It is so named because we do not know, and it is impossible to know, *that which there is* *in that Principle,* because . . . it is above Wisdom itself." (iii., fol. 288.) This shows that the real Kabbalists agree with the Occultists that the essence, or that which is in the principle of Wisdom, is still above that highest Wisdom.

Wisdom Religion. The one religion which underlies all the now-existing creeds. That "faith" which, being primordial, and revealed directly to human kind by their *progenitors* and informing EGOS (though the Church regards them as the "fallen angels"), required no "grace", nor *blind* faith to believe, for it was *knowledge.* (See "Gupta Vidyâ", Hidden Knowledge.) It is on this Wisdom Religion that *Theosophy is based.*

Y

Years of Brahmâ. The whole period of "Brahma's Age" (100 Years). Equals 311,040,000,000,000 years. (See "Yuga ".)

Yoga (*Sk.*). (1) One of the six Darshanas or schools of India; a school of philosophy founded by Patanjali, though the real Yoga doctrine, the one that is said to have helped to prepare the world for the preaching of Buddha, is attributed with good reasons to the more ancient sage Yâjnawalkya, the writer of the *Shatapatha Brâhmana,* of *Yajur Veda,* the *Brihad Âranyaka,* and other famous works. (2) The practice of meditation as a means of leading to spiritual liberation. Psycho-spiritual powers are obtained thereby, and induced ecstatic states lead to the clear and correct perception of the eternal truths, in both the visible and invisible universe.

Yogâchârya (*Sk.*). (1) A mystic school. (2) Lit., a teacher (*âchârya*) of Yoga, one who has mastered the doctrines and practices of ecstatic meditation – the culmination of which are the *Mahâsiddhis.* It is incorrect to confuse this school with the Tantra, or Mahâtantra school founded by Samantabhadra, for there are two Yogâchârya Schools, one esoteric, the other popular. The doctrines of the latter were compiled and glossed by Asamgha in the sixth century of our era, and his mystic tantras and mantras, his formularies, litanies, spells and mudrâ would certainly, if attempted without a Guru, serve rather purposes of sorcery and black magic than real Yoga. Those who undertake to write upon the subject are generally learned missionaries and haters of Eastern philosophy in general. From these no unbiassed views can be expected. Thus when we read in the *Sanskrit -Chinese Dictionary* of Eitel, that the reciting of mantras (which he calls " spells"!) " should he accompanied by music and distortions of the fingers (mudrâ), that a state of mental fixity (*Samâdhi*} might he reached ' – one acquainted, however slightly,. with the real practice of Yoga can only shrug his shoulders. These distortions of the fingers or ,mudrâ are necessary, the author thinks, for the reaching of Samâdhi, "characterized by there being neither thought nor annihilation of thought, and consisting of six-fold bodily (*sic*) and mental happiness (*yogi*) *whence would result endowment with supernatural miracle-*

working power". Theosophists cannot be too much warned against such fantastic and prejudiced explanations.

Yogi (*Sk.*). (1) Not "a state of six-fold bodily and mental happiness as the result, of ecstatic meditation" (Eitel) but a state which, when reached, makes the practitioner thereof absolute master of his six principles", *he now being merged in the seventh*. It gives him full control, owing to his knowledge of SELF and Self, over his bodily, intellectual and mental states, which, unable any longer to interfere with, or act upon, his Higher Ego, leave it free to exist in its original, pure, and divine state. (2) Also the name of the devotee who practises Yoga.

Yuga (*Sk.*). A 1,000th part of a Kalpa. An age of the World of which there are four, and the series of which proceed in succession during the manvantaric cycle. Each Yuga is preceded by a period called in the *Purânas* Sandhyâ, twilight, or transition period, and is followed by another period of like duration called Sandhyânsa, "portion of twilight". Each is equal to one-tenth of the Yuga. The group of four Yugas is first computed by the *divine* years, or "years of the gods" – each such year being equal to 360 years of mortal men. Thus we have, in "divine" years :

AGE	YEARS
Krita or Satya Yuga	4,000
Sandhyâ	400
Sandhyansa	400
	4,800

Tretâ Yuga	3,000
Sandhyâ	300
Sandhyânsa	300
	3,600

Dwâpara Yuga	2,000
Sandhya	200
Sandhyânsa	200
	2,400

Kali Yuga	1,000
Sandhyâ	100
Sandhyânsa	100
	1,200
Total =	**12,000**

This rendered in years of mortals equals:

4800	X	360	=	1,728,000
3600	X	360	=	1,296,000
2400	X	360	=	864,000
1200	X	360	=	432,000
		Total	=	4,320,000

The above is called a Mahâyuga or Manvantara. 2,000 such Mahâyugas, or a period of 8,640,000 years, make a Kalpa the latter being only a "day and a night", or twenty-four hours, of Brahmâ. Thus an "age of Brahmâ", or one hundred of his divine years, must equal 311,040,000,000,000 of our mortal years. The old Mazdeans or Magi (the modern Parsis) had the same calculation, though the Orientalists do not seem to perceive it, for even the Parsi Moheds themselves have forgotten it. But their "Sovereign time of the Long Period" (*Zervan Dareghâ Hvadâta*) lasts 12,000 years, and these are the 12,000 *divine* years of a Mahâyuga as shown above, whereas the *Zervan Akarana* (Limitless Time), mentioned by Zarathustra, is the *Kâla*, out of space and time, of Parabrahm.

INDEX

A

T

U

V

Y

KRISHNA:

This divine discipline, Arjuna, is not to be attained by the man who eateth more than enough or too little, nor by him who hath a habit of sleeping much, nor by him who is given to overwatching. The meditation which destroyeth pain is produced in him who is moderate in eating and in recreation, of moderate exertion in his actions, and regulated in sleeping and waking. When the man, so living, centers his heart in the true Self and is exempt from attachment to all desires, he is said to have attained to Yoga. Of the sage of self-centered heart, at rest and free from attachment to desires, the simile is recorded, 'as a lamp which is sheltered from the wind flickereth not.' When regulated by the practice of yoga and at rest, seeing the self by the self, he is contented; when he becometh acquainted with that boundless bliss which is not connected with objects of the senses, and being where he is not moved from the reality; *having gained which he considereth no other superior to it, and in which, being fixed, he is not moved even by the greatest grief; know that this disconnection from union with pain is distinguished as yoga, spiritual union or devotion, which is to be striven after by a man with faith and steadfastly.

The Bhagavad-Gita, Ch. VI